Frommer's

Cancún, Cozumel & the Yucatán

Here's what the critics say about Frommer's:

"Amazingly easy to use. Very portable, very complete."
—*Booklist*

♦

"The only mainstream guide to list specific prices. The Walter Cronkite of guidebooks—with all that implies."
—*Travel & Leisure*

♦

"Complete, concise, and filled wih useful information."
—*New York Daily News*

♦

"Hotel information is close to encyclopedic."
—*Des Moines Sunday Register*

Gran Oasis

Other Great Guides for Your Trip:

Frommer's Mexico

*Frommer's Portable Puerto Vallarta,
Manzanillo & Guadalajara*

Frommer's Portable Acapulco & Ixtapa/Zihuatanejo

Frommer's Born to Shop Mexico

Frommer's® 99

Cancún, Cozumel & the Yucatán

by David Baird and Lynne Bairstow

MACMILLAN • USA

ABOUT THE AUTHORS

David Baird (chapters 1, 2, 6, and 7) is a writer, editor, and translator based in Austin, Texas. He spent part of his childhood in Morelia, Mexico, and later lived for 2 years among the Mazatec Indians in Oaxaca, while he was doing graduate fieldwork.

Lynne Bairstow (chapters 1, 3, 4, and 5) is a travel writer and Web site developer who has lived in Puerto Vallarta, Mexico, at least part time for the past 7 years. She now lives there year round. In a previous professional life, she was a vice president for Merrill Lynch in Chicago and New York.

They are also the authors of *Frommer's Mexico*.

MACMILLAN TRAVEL

A Simon & Schuster Macmillan Company
1633 Broadway
New York, NY 10019

Find us online at **www.frommers.com**

ISBN 0-02862306-1
ISSN 1064-1416

Editor: Neil E. Schlecht
with thanks to Dan Glover
Production Editor: Lori Cates
Design by Michele Laseau
Digital Cartography by Ortelius Design
Photo Editor: Richard Fox
Maps © copyright by Simon & Schuster, Inc.

SPECIAL SALES

Manufactured in the United States of America

Contents

List of Maps

AN INVITATION TO THE READER

In researching this book, we discovered many wonderful places—resorts, inns, restaurants, shops, and more. We're sure you'll find others. Please tell us about them, so we can share the information with your fellow travelers in upcoming editions. If you were disappointed with a recommendation, we'd love to know that, too. Please write to:

Frommer's Cancún, Cozumel & the Yucatán '99
Macmillan Travel
1633 Broadway
New York, NY 10019

AN ADDITIONAL NOTE

Please be advised that travel information is subject to change at any time—and this is especially true of prices. We therefore suggest that you write or call ahead for confirmation when making your travel plans. The authors, editors, and publisher cannot be held responsible for the experiences of readers while traveling. Your safety is important to us, however, so we encourage you to stay alert and be aware of your surroundings. Keep a close eye on cameras, purses, and wallets, all favorite targets of thieves and pickpockets.

A FEW WORDS ABOUT PRICES

The peso's value continues to fluctuate—at press time it was slightly more than 8 pesos to the dollar. Prices in this book (which are always given in U.S. dollars) have been converted to U.S. dollars at 8 pesos to the dollar. Most hotels in Mexico—with the exception of places that receive little foreign tourism—quote prices in U.S. dollars. Thus, currency fluctuations are unlikely to affect the prices charged by most hotels.

Mexico has a **Value-Added Tax** of 15% (Impuesto de Valor Agregado, or IVA, pronounced "ee-bah") on most everything, including restaurant meals, bus tickets, and souvenirs. (Exceptions are Cancún, Cozumel, and Los Cabos, where the IVA is 10%; as ports of entry, they receive a special 5% break on taxes.) Hotels charge the usual 15% IVA, plus a locally administered bed tax of 2% (in many but not all areas), for a total of 17%. In Cancún, Los Cabos, and Cozumel, hotels charge the 10% IVA plus 2% room tax. IVA will not necessarily be included in the prices quoted by hotels and restaurants. You may find that upper-end properties (three stars and above) quote prices without IVA included, while lesser-price hotels include IVA in their quotes. Always ask to see a printed price sheet, and always ask if the tax is included.

WHAT THE SYMBOLS MEAN

✪ Frommer's Favorites

Our favorite places and experiences—outstanding for quality, value, or both.

The following abbreviations are used for credit cards:

AE	American Express	EURO	Eurocard
CB	Carte Blanche	JCB	Japan Credit Bank
DC	Diners Club	MC	MasterCard
DISC	Discover	V	Visa
ER	enRoute		

FIND FROMMER'S ONLINE

Arthur Frommer's Outspoken Encyclopedia of Travel (www.frommers.com) offers more than 6,000 pages of up-to-the-minute travel information—including the latest bargains and candid, personal articles updated daily by Arthur Frommer himself. No other Web site offers such comprehensive and timely coverage of the world of travel.

The Best of Cancún, Cozumel & the Yucatán

The Yucatán Peninsula, its tremendous variety making it a magnet for every kind of traveler, welcomes more visitors than any other part of Mexico. The Yucatán offers an unequaled mix of sophisticated resorts, ancient Maya culture, lovely beaches, and adrenaline-inducing adventures. Between the two of us, we've logged thousands of miles crisscrossing the peninsula, and these are our personal favorites: the best places to go, the best restaurants, the best hotels, and must-see, one-of-a-kind experiences.

1 The Best Beach Vacations

- **Cancún:** Essentially one long ribbon of white sand bordering aquamarine water, Cancún is Mexico's ultimate beach vacation. Pick this as your beach vacation if you want tropical drinks brought to you while you lounge in the sand, or if a day at the beach is primarily meant for catching up on sleep lost the night before—before going out to do it again! The most tranquil waters and beaches on Cancún Island are those at the northern tip, facing the Bahía de Mujeres. See chapter 4.
- **Isla Mujeres:** If laid-back is what you're after, this idyllic island offers peaceful, small-town beach life at its best. Most accommodations are smaller, inexpensive inns—with a couple of unique, luxurious places tossed in. Bike around the island to explore rocky coves and sandy beaches, or focus your tanning efforts on the wide beachfront of Playa Norte. Here you'll find calm waters and palapa restaurants, where you can have fresh-caught fish for lunch. You're also close to great diving (in the cave of the sleeping sharks), snorkeling just offshore, and the Isla Contoy National Park, which features great birdlife and its own dramatic, uninhabited beach. In addition, you're only a ferry ride away from all the action in Cancún! See chapter 5.
- **Playa del Carmen:** This is our absolute favorite Mexican beach vacation for 1999. Stylish and hip, Playa del Carmen offers the incredibly beautiful beaches that this coast is known for, as well as an eclectic assortment of inns, B&Bs, and cabañas. Activity centers on the small but excellent selection of restaurants, clubs, sidewalk cafes, and funky shops that run the length of pedestrians-only avenida 5. You're also close to all the major attractions of the coast, including Tulum, cenote diving, and

Cozumel Island (just 45 minutes away by ferry). Enjoy it while it's a manageable size. See chapter 5.

- **Xcalak:** For many, the best beach vacation gets them far from "civilization." If living out fantasies of Robinson Crusoe is your ambition, the entire coastal area between Majahual and Xcalak is ideal for isolated beach getaways. Sportfishing and diving the Chinchorro reef just offshore are excellent ways to pass the days. Accommodations are rustic, but then, that's what you're looking for, right? Spirited adventurers can check out more details in chapter 5.

2 The Best Cultural Experiences

- **Streets and Park Entertainment** (Mérida): Few cities have so vibrant a street scene as Mérida. Throughout the week there are music and dance performances in plazas about the city—but on Sundays, Mérida really gets going. Streets are closed off, food stalls spring up everywhere, and you can enjoy a book fair, flea market, comedy acts, band concerts, and dance groups. At night the main plaza is the place to be: People dance in the street in front of the town hall to mambos and rumbas. See chapter 6.
- **Exploring the Inland Yucatán Peninsula:** Travelers who venture only to the peninsula's resorts and cities will miss the tidy inland villages, where women wear colorful embroidered dresses and life seems to proceed as though the modern world (except for highways) didn't exist. Also not to be missed is the adventure of seeing newly uncovered ruins deep in jungle settings. See chapter 6.
- **San Cristóbal de las Casas:** The city of San Cristóbal is a living museum, with 16th-century colonial architecture and pre-Hispanic native influences. The highland Maya live in surrounding villages and arrive daily in town wearing colorful and unique handmade clothing. The outlying villages are a unique window into another world, which gives visitors a glimpse of traditional Indian dress, religious customs, churches, and ceremonies. See chapter 7.
- **Regional Cuisine:** A trip to the Yucatán allows for a culinary tour of some of Mexico's finest foods. Don't miss specialties like *pollo* or *cochinita pibil* (chicken or pork in a savory achiote sauce); great seafood dishes; the many styles of tamal found throughout Chiapas and the Yucatán; and Caribbean-influenced Tabasco foods such as fried bananas, black beans, and yucca root.

3 The Best Archaeological Sites

- **Tulum:** Some dismiss Tulum as less important than others in the Yucatán Peninsula, but this seaside Maya fortress is still inspiring. The sight of its crumbling stone walls are a stark contrast to the clear turquoise ocean just beyond. See chapter 5.
- **Uxmal:** No matter how many times you see Uxmal, the splendor of its stone carvings is awe-inspiring. A stone rattlesnake undulates across the facade of the Nunnery complex, and 103 masks of Chaac—the rain god—project from the Governor's Palace. See chapter 6.
- **Chichén-Itzá:** Stand beside the giant serpent head at the foot of El Castillo pyramid and marvel at the architects and astronomers who positioned the building so precisely that shadow and sunlight form a serpent's body slithering from peak to the earth at each equinox (March 21 and September 21). See chapter 6.

- **Palenque:** The ancient builders of these structures now in ruin carved histories in stone that scholars have only now been able to decipher. Imagine the magnificent ceremony in A.D. 683 when King Pacal was buried below ground in a secret pyramidal tomb—unspoiled until its discovery in 1952. See chapter 7.

4 The Best Active Vacations

- **Scuba Diving in Cozumel:** The reefs off the island of Cozumel are among the world's premier diving destinations, renowned for their deep walls covered with coral and sponges, teeming with life. Underwater caves and canyons also form part of this intricate reef system. Most hotels in Cozumel offer special dive packages. And, while there are three recompression chambers on the island (just in case), beach diving and snorkeling make Cozumel's reefs accessible to everyone. See chapter 5.
- **Sportfishing:** Billfishing for graceful marlin and sailfish is notable offshore in Cozumel and Playa del Carmen—though you might hook any number of edible fish in these waters. Serious sportsmen should try their hand at fly-fishing for bone, permit, and snook in the saltwater flats and lagoons of Ascension Bay, near Punta Allen, south of Tulum. You can stay at the Cuzan Guest House (☎ **983/ 4-0358**). See chapter 5.
- **Cenote diving on the Yucatán mainland:** Dive into the clear depths of the Yucatán's cenotes (sinkholes or natural wells) for an interesting twist on underwater exploration. The Maya considered the cenotes sacred; indeed, their vivid colors are otherworldly. Most are located between Playa del Carmen and Tulum, and shops in these areas regularly run trips for experienced divers. See chapter 5.
- **An Excursion to Bonampak, Yaxchilán, and the Usumacinta River:** Bonampak and Yaxchilán—two remote, jungle-surrounded Maya sites along the Usumacinta River—can be reached by air (landing in a four-seater plane on a jungle airstrip), or by adding rafting and hiking to air travel. The experience could well be the highlight of any trip. See chapter 7.
- **Birding:** The Yucatán Peninsula, Tabasco, and Chiapas are an ornithological paradise, with hundreds of species awaiting the birder's gaze and list.

5 The Best Places to Get Away from It All

A handful of places in the Yucatán are perfect escapes—for a moment, a day, a week, or more of sublime tranquillity. Some of these, while not posh, rate high on romance and ambience.

- **Isla Mujeres:** If there's one island in Mexico that encourages relaxation, it's Isla Mujeres. Though there are plenty of hotels and restaurants, they're as laid-back as are their patrons. Here, life moves along in pure vacation mode. Visitors mainly stretch out and doze beneath shady palms or languidly stroll about. See chapter 5.
- **The Yucatán's Costa Turquesa:** Away from the busy resort of Cancún, a string of quiet getaways, including Capitán Lafitte, Paamul, Xcalacoco, and a portion of Xpuha, offer tranquillity at low prices on beautiful beaches. See chapter 5.
- **The Yucatán's Punta Allen Peninsula:** South of the Tulum ruins, a handful of beachside budget inns offers some of the most peaceful getaways in the country. Life here among the birds and coconut palms seems never to have been anything but leisurely. See chapter 5.

- **Lago Bacalar's Rancho Encantado Cottage Resort** (☎ 800/505-MAYA in the U.S.): The attractive *casitas* are the place to unwind at this resort, where hammocks stretch between trees. The hotel is on the shores of placid Lake Bacalar, south of Cancún near Chetumal, and there's nothing around for miles. But if you want adventure, you can head a kayak out on the lake; follow a birding trail; or take an excursion to Belize and the intriguing, but obscure, nearby Maya ruins on the Río Bec ruin route. See chapter 5.
- **Villas Delfines** (Isla Holbox; ☎ 98/84-8606 in Cancún): This small, immaculate compound was made for people who want comfort, good food, and deserted-island privacy. Stay in a raised palapa on a white-sand beach with no phone, no TV, no roads, and only a small village nearby—the anti-Cancún. See chapter 6.

6 The Best Museums

- **Museo de la Isla de Cozumel** (Cozumel): More than something to do on a rainy day, this well-done museum is worth a visit anytime. It unveils the island's past in an informative way not found anywhere else. There's a good bookstore on the first floor and a rooftop restaurant overlooking the Malecón and Caribbean. See chapter 5.
- **Museo de la Cultura Maya** (Chetumal): This new museum featuring Maya archaeology, architecture, history, and mythology is one of the best in the country. It has interactive exhibits and a glass floor that allows visitors to walk above replicas of Maya sites. See chapter 5.
- **Museo Regional de Antropología** (Mérida): Housed in the Palacio Cantón, one of the most beautiful 19th-century mansions in the city, this museum showcases area archaeology and anthropological studies in handsome exhibits. See chapter 6.
- **Museo Olmeca de la Venta** (Villahermosa): The Olmec, considered Mexico's mother culture, are the subject of this park/museum, which features the magnificent stone remains that were removed from the La Venta site not far away. Stroll through a jungle setting where tropical birds alight, and savor these relics of the mysterious Olmec. See chapter 7.
- **Museo Regional de Antropología Carlos Pellicer Camara** (Villahermosa): This anthropology museum addresses Mexican history, in the form of objects found at archaeological sites, with particular emphasis on the pre-Hispanic peoples of the Gulf Coast region. See chapter 7.

7 The Best Shopping

Some tips on bargaining: Although haggling over prices in markets is expected and part of the fun, don't try to browbeat the vendor or bad-mouth the goods. Vendors won't bargain with people they consider disrespectful unless they are desperate to make a sale. Be insistent but friendly.

- **Resort wear in Cancún:** Resort clothing—especially if you can find a sale—can be a bargain here. And the selection may be wider than you have available at home. Mall after mall on the island contains trendy boutiques specializing in locally crafted and imported clothing. See chapter 4.
- **5th Avenue, Playa del Carmen:** Once Playa del Carmen was considered a shopping wasteland. All that has changed, and today, the pedestrian-only avenida 5 is lined with small boutiques selling batik clothing and fabric, Guatemalan

textiles, Mexican dance masks, premium tequilas, Cuban cigars, and decorative pottery from Mexico's best pottery villages. See chapter 5.

- **Mérida:** It's *the* marketplace for the Yucatán, the best place to buy hammocks, guayaberas, Panama hats, and Yucatecan *huipils.* See chapter 6.
- **San Cristóbal de las Casas:** Deep in the heart of the Maya highlands, San Cristóbal has shops, open plazas, and markets that feature the distinctive waist-loomed wool and cotton textiles of the region, as well as leather shoes, handsomely crude pottery, genre dolls, and Guatemalan textiles. Highland Maya Indians sell direct to tourists from their armloads of textiles, dolls, and handmade miniature likenesses of Subcomandante Marcos—complete with ski masks. See chapter 7.

8 The Hottest Nightlife

While much of the Yucatán's nightlife expectedly is found in Cancún, that resort city isn't the only place to have a good time after dark. Along the Yucatán's Caribbean coast, nightlife is dominated by beachside dance floors with live bands, and extended "happy hours" in seaside bars. Cancún has the greatest variety and most sophisticated nightlife. From live music in hotel lobby bars to the hippest techno dance clubs, there's a multitude of options. Here are some favorite hot spots.

- **Mango Tango, La Boom, Carlos 'n Charlie's, Planet Hollywood, and Dady Rock Bar and Grill:** These Cancún bars all offer good food, hot bands, and great dance floors. **Azucar Bar Caribeño** is a top spot for live Caribbean rhythms in Cancún. See chapter 4.
- **The Lobby Lounge:** Located in Cancún's luxurious Ritz-Carlton Hotel, this is by far the most elegant evening spot on the island. The romantic live music and over 120 premium tequilas (plus tastings) allow you to savor the spirit of Mexico. See chapter 4.
- **Forum by the Sea:** One place that has it all: This new seaside entertainment center in Cancún has a dazzling array of dance clubs, sports bars, fast food, and fine dining, with shops open late as well. You'll find plenty of familiar names here, including the Hard Rock Cafe and Rainforest Cafe. See chapter 4.
- **Ciudad Maya** (Mérida; ☎ **99/24-3313**): An outdoor club built on a grand scale with multistory replicas of Maya temples, a dance troupe of scantily clad Cubans, music by a rumba band, comedy, magic, acrobatics—everything but elephants. See chapter 6.

9 The Most Luxurious Hotels

Cancún, Cozumel, and the Yucatán Peninsula offer a long list of special places where the service is as polished as the quality of the establishment. Below are a few that should be on your short list of accommodations where you can indulge yourself.

- **Caesar Park Beach & Golf Resort** (Cancún; ☎ **800/228-3000** in the U.S.): The 18-hole golf course is just out the front door, the swank pool is out the side door, and the Caribbean is steps away. It's so self-contained (three restaurants, tennis, golf, and a fully equipped gym) that some visitors (especially golfers) never feel the need to venture beyond the grounds. See chapter 4.
- **Fiesta Americana Coral Beach** (Cancún; ☎ **800/343-7821** in the U.S.): Lavish use of imported marble and plenty of rich wood accents lead the way to luxurious rooms with views of the Bahía de Mujeres. Sports facilities, a prime

location near the Convention Center, and one of the best beaches in the city are the draws here. See chapter 4.

- **Ritz-Carlton Cancún** (Cancún; ☎ 800/241-3333 in the U.S.): Thick carpets, sparkling glass and brass, and rich mahogany surround guests at this hotel, which clearly sets the standard for luxury in Cancún. The service is impeccable, leaving guests with an overall sense of pampered relaxation. See chapter 4.
- **Puerto Isla Mujeres Resort & Yacht Club** (Isla Mujeres; ☎ 800/960-ISLA in the U.S.): Spacious villas face the Laguna Macax, where yachts glide up and anchor. Those who immerse themselves in the tranquillity and luxury of this 30-room enclave pass the word on to others, who dock for days or weeks on end. See chapter 5.
- **Presidente Inter-Continental Cozumel** (Cozumel; ☎ 800/327-0200 in the U.S.): Surrounded by shady palms, this hotel also has the best beach on the island, located right in front of Paraíso Reef. Favorite rooms are the deluxe beachfront rooms with spacious patios and direct access to the beach—you can even order romantic in-room dining on these patios, complete with a trio to serenade you! See chapter 5.

10 The Best Budget Inns

Some inns stand out for their combination of hospitality and simple-but-colorful surroundings. These are places guests return to again and again.

- **Hotel Safari Inn** (Cozumel; ☎ 987/2-0101): The comforts here are simple—a clean, basic room, a comfortable bed, good reading lights, powerful air-conditioning, and a great location. The inn is above the Aqua Safari dive shop (one of the top shops on the island) across from the dive shop's pier—you can book dives and a room at the same time. It's 3 blocks from the plaza and in the heart of the shopping district. What more do you need in Cozumel? See chapter 5.
- **Villa Catarina Rooms & Cabañas** (Playa del Carmen; ☎ 987/3-0970): These stylishly rustic rooms are nestled into a garden of tall palms, flowering trees, and singing birds. Just a block to the wide beach and tranquil Caribbean, it's also a short walk to the action of avenida 5. See chapter 5.
- **Hotel Mucuy** (Mérida; ☎ 99/28-5193): Alfredo and Ofelia Comin, owners of perhaps the most hospitable budget hotel on the peninsula, strive to make guests feel at home with cheery, clean rooms; comfortable outdoor tables and chairs; a communal refrigerator in the lobby; and laundry facilities. See chapter 6.

11 The Best Unique Inns

- **La Casa de los Sueños** (Isla Mujeres; ☎ 800/551-2558): Energizing colors and a tranquil ambience will help put life back into perspective at this upscale B&B. The sculpted architecture frames pools that look out over Garrafon Reef to Cancún across the bay. This nonsmoking property encourages healthful rejuvenation. See chapter 5.
- **Hotel Jungla Caribe** (Playa del Carmen; ☎ 987/3-0650): In a town filled with exceptional inns, this one's a standout. The eclectic decor combines neo-classical details with a decidedly tropical touch. The 26 rooms and suites surround a stylish courtyard restaurant and pool. With an entrance on happening avenida 5, and a block from the beach, you couldn't be better located. See chapter 5.

- **Cuzan Guest House** (Punta Allen Peninsula; ☎ **983/4-0358**): Getting to the isolated lobster-fishing village of Punta Allen is half the adventure. Then you can retreat to one of the thatched-roof cottages, swing in a hammock, dine on lobster and stone crabs, and absolutely forget there's an outside world. There are no phones, televisions, or newspapers, and "town" is 35 miles away. Nature trips and fly-fishing are readily arranged. See chapter 5.
- **Casa Mexilio Guest House** (Mérida; ☎ **800/538-6802** in the U.S.): Here, an imaginative arrangement of rooms around a courtyard features a pool surrounded by a riot of tropical vegetation. The rooms are divided among different levels for the sake of privacy, and connected by stairs and catwalks. Breakfast here provides an extra incentive for getting out of bed. See chapter 6.
- **Casa Na-Bolom** (San Cristóbal de las Casas; ☎ **967/8-1418**): This unique house-museum is terrific for anthropology buffs. Built as a seminary in 1891, it was transformed into the headquarters of two anthropologists. The 12 guest rooms, named for surrounding villages, are decorated with local objects and textiles; all rooms have fireplaces and private baths, and breakfast is included. See chapter 7.
- **El Jacarandal** (San Cristóbal de las Casas; ☎ **967/8-1065**): There are just four rooms here, and it isn't cheap, but a stay at this essentially private home—which includes all meals, drinks, and activities—is lodging as high-concept art. You can choose one of the horses from the stable and go on a morning ride, or take a guided trip to the Indian villages, the Huitepec cloud forest, and nearby Maya ruins. Meals are outstanding. See chapter 7.

12 The Best Restaurants

Best doesn't necessarily mean most luxurious. Although some of those listed below are fancy affairs, others are simple places to get fine, authentic Yucatecan cuisine.

- **Restaurant Los Almendros** (with locations in Cancún, ☎ **98/87-1332**; Mérida, ☎ **99/28-5459**; and Ticul, ☎ **997/2-0021**): This family-owned restaurant chain features Yucatecan specialties. Its much-copied poc chuc, a grilled pork dish, was created at the original restaurant in Ticul some years ago. This is the place locals go when they want to eat Yucatecan. See chapters 4 and 6.
- **Club Grill** (Cancún; ☎ **98/85-0808**): The international cuisine served at this Ritz-Carlton restaurant is as excellent and elegant as the sumptuous setting. Soft, quiet, and utterly refined, dining here is a memorable experience. Also, there's a dance floor with oh-so-slow romantic music. See chapter 4.
- **La Dolce Vita** (Cancún; ☎ **98/84-1384**): Once you've discovered this Italian restaurant, you'll keep coming back, tempted by blissfully flavorful dishes such as green tagliolini with lobster medallions, linguine with clams or seafood, and fresh salmon with cream sauce. See chapter 4.
- **Zacil-Ha** (Isla Mujeres; ☎ **987/7-0279**): With its sandy floor beneath thatched palapas and palms, it's hard to beat this relaxed and casual place for island atmosphere and well-prepared food—terrific pasta with garlic, shrimp in tequila sauce, fajitas, and delicious mole enchiladas. And great nachos. See chapter 5.
- **Lobster House (Cabaña del Pescador)** (Cozumel; ☎ **987/2-4132**): If you want an ideally seasoned, succulent lobster dinner, this is the place. If you want anything else, you're out of luck—lobster dinner, expertly prepared, is all that's served here. When you achieve perfection, why bother with anything else? See chapter 5.

- **Prima** (Cozumel; ☎ **987/2-4242**): The Italian food here is fresh, fresh, fresh—from the hydroponically grown vegetables to the pasta and garlic bread. And it's all prepared after you walk in, most of it by owner Albert Domínguez, who concocts an unforgettable shrimp fettuccine with pesto, crab ravioli with cream sauce, and crispy house salad in a chilled bowl. See chapter 5.
- **Media Luna** (Playa del Carmen; no phone): The inviting atmosphere of this sidewalk cafe on avenida 5 is enough to lure you in to dine. The expertly executed and innovative menu, together with great prices, makes it one of the top choices along the entire Caribbean coast. See chapter 5.
- **La Pigua** (Campeche; ☎ **981/1-3365**): Campeche's regional food is seafood, and nowhere else will you find seafood like this. Mexican caviar, coconut-battered shrimp, and chiles stuffed with shark are just a few of the unique specialties. Thinking about La Pigua's pompano in a fine herb green sauce makes us want to start checking flight schedules. See chapter 6.
- **El Pórtico del Peregrino** (Mérida; ☎ **99/28-6163**): There are few things so delightful as an evening spent dining at this elegant and unpretentious setting. The menu offers a varied assortment of national and international dishes with an underlying Mediterranean influence. Main courses are nourishing but not heavy, while the salads, soups, and vegetable dishes recommend themselves. See chapter 6.
- **Virrey de Mendoza** (Mérida; ☎ **99/25-3082**): If you're in Mérida and feel like splurging for a night, this is the place. It specializes in highly refined versions of Mexico's most elaborate dishes. The Yucatecan specialties are superb—especially the seafood. The setting, lighting, and background music are first-rate. See chapter 6.
- **Madre Tierra** (San Cristóbal de las Casas; ☎ **967/8-4297**): No sooner do we arrive in San Cristóbal than we head to this restaurant for the filling and wonderfully prepared *comida corrida*. It comes with soup; a choice of three entrees, such as pork in adobo sauce, barbecued ribs, perhaps chicken curry, or poblano chile; fruit-flavored purified water; and dessert—all in a cozy setting with classical music playing in the background. See chapter 7.

Getting to Know the Yucatán

first visited the Yucatán many years ago. At the time, I was attempting to keep my small business afloat, an effort that absorbed every waking minute of my life. My brother suggested I set everything down for a week and take a vacation; he suggested Mexico's oft-visited Yucatán Peninsula. I was reluctant, but I ended up falling in love with the place, and my trip there was the best vacation I could have imagined. The Caribbean is what it is—turquoise-blue waters and perfect temperatures—and hardly needs me to praise it. The Yucatán being part of Mexico, the food is a lot better than much of what you get on many islands, and the people are every bit as warm and friendly. On subsequent trips I headed inland to check out the famed pyramids—they didn't disappoint—and I got an unexpected bonus in discovering Mérida, a terrific town from which the visitor can embark on a variety of exciting excursions. In all my explorations of the Yucatán, I haven't been bored yet.

On the Caribbean side of the Yucatán is Mexico's most famous and most sought-after megaresort, **Cancún;** the island of **Cozumel,** where Mexico's superlative diving is enjoyed offshore; **Isla Mujeres,** Mexico's best laid-back island vacation destination; and the **Costa Turquesa,** south of Cancún, with its hidden beachfront inns and splendid beaches. Farther south on the Costa Turquesa are the ruins of **Tulum,** while inland the peninsula's Maya ruins include **Chichén-Itzá, Uxmal, Cobá, Becán, Dzinbanché,** and **Kohunlich.**

Add to these highlights the possibilities offered by the neighboring states of Chiapas and Tabasco—neither part of the Yucatán itself, but within striking distance—and you have a wide range of settings and activities. The premier destinations in Tabasco and Chiapas, southwest of the Yucatán Peninsula, are the **Museo Olmeca de la Venta,** the majestic Maya ruins of **Palenque,** and the mountain city of **San Cristóbal de las Casas,** which is surrounded by villages of living Maya. We have included these two states with the Yucatán because together they compose Mexico's so-called **Maya Route,** which includes all the territory of the present-day Maya, as well as the archaeological monuments left behind by their ancestors in what is now Mexico.

1 The Land & Its People

Although Mexico is part of North America, its culture is dramatically different from that of its neighbors to the north. It has often

Mexico

UNITED STATES

iedras Negras

Nuevo Laredo

5D

nterrey
EVO
DN

85

Matamoros

180

TAMAULIPAS

Ciudad Victoria

Ciudad Mante

Tampico

SAN LUIS
POTOSÍ

Miguel
Allende

UERÉTARO

Tuxpan

Poza Rica

erétaro

HIDALGO

180

Pachuca

Mexico City

Jalapa

uca

TLAXCALA

Tlaxcala

ernavaca

Puebla

Veracruz

MORELOS PUEBLA

Orizaba

xco

95

Tehuacán VERACRUZ

Catemaco

JERRERO

190D

175

Coatzacoalcos

Chilpancingo

Oaxaca

186

apulco

200

OAXACA

Puerto Escondido

Salina
Cruz

Puerto
Ángel

Huatulco

*Gulf of
Tehuantepec*

200

Tapachula

Gulf of Mexico

Río Lagartos

Isla
Mujeres

Progreso

Valladolid

Cancún

Celestún

Mérida

180

YUCATÁN

Playa del
Carmen

Cozumel

Campeche

QUINTANA
ROO

Punta
Allen

*Bay of
Campeche*

CAMPECHE

Bacalar

261

Escárcega

Xcalak

Chetumal

Peninsula

TABASCO

Villahermosa

186

Caribbean Sea

Tuxtla
Gutierrez

San Cristóbal de las Casas

BELIZE

CHIAPAS

Comitán

GUATEMALA

HONDURAS

EL
SALVADOR

11

been observed by American and English travelers that life in Mexico obeys slower rhythms: Mexicans have a different conception of time. This is true, and yet few of these observers go on to explain more than superficially what the consequences of this are for the visitor to Mexico. This is a shame, because an imperfect comprehension of this difference causes a good deal of misunderstanding between the tourist and the native Mexican.

SOCIAL MORES   Americans, in addition to many Canadians and Northern Europeans, tend to do things at a faster pace and skip some of the niceties of social interaction. One of the most important pieces of advice I can give the traveler is always to give a proper greeting when addressing Mexicans; don't try to abbreviate social intercourse. When walking into a store, many Americans simply smile at a clerk and launch right into a question or demand. The smile, in effect, replaces the greeting. In Mexico, it doesn't work that way. Smiles, when there is no context, can be ambiguous; they can convey amusement, smugness, superiority, etc.

On several occasions, I have been asked by Mexican acquaintances why Americans grin all the time. I didn't know what to make of the question the first time I heard it; it was only gradually that I began to appreciate what was at issue. Mexican culture places a higher value on proper social form than on saving time. For Mexicans, civil society requires individuals to show that they recognize and treat people as fellow persons and not simply as a means to their ends. A Mexican must at least say "*¡ Buenos Dias!*" (or its equivalent) even to total strangers—a show of proper respect. And when an individual meets a group of people he or she will greet each member of the group by shaking hands, kissing, or whatever is proper for the occasion. This can take a while, depending on the size of the party. We might consider such behavior obtrusive and presumptuous; for us, the polite thing would be to keep our interruption to a minimum, and give a general greeting to all.

Mexicans, like most people, will consciously or subconsciously make quick judgments about someone they meet. Most divide the world into well-raised and cultured (*bien educado*), on the one hand, and poorly raised (*mal educado*) on the other. Unfortunately, many visitors are reluctant to try out their Spanish, preferring to keep exchanges to a minimum. Don't do this. To be categorized as a foreigner isn't a big deal. What's important in Mexico is to be categorized as one of the cultured foreigners and not one of the barbarians. This makes it easier to get the attention of waiters, hotel desk clerks, and people on the street.

TODAY'S MAYA CULTURE & PEOPLES   As with lowlanders elsewhere in Mexico, Yucatecans are exceedingly warm and friendly and show little reserve. It's quite easy to enter into conversation with them. In the peninsula's interior, you might find people who are unexpectedly reticent; most likely these are Maya Indians who aren't comfortable speaking Spanish. But you'll meet Maya individuals all over the Yucatán; many work at hotels and restaurants in Cancún and can switch easily among Spanish, English, and Yukatek, the local Mayan language. More than 350,000 Maya living in the Yucatán's three states speak Yukatek Mayan, and most, especially men, speak Spanish, too.

Most Indian women remain in the villages, going about their lives, seemingly oblivious to the peninsula's fame as a premier resort destination. Their day-to-day cultural and belief system holds many elements that can be traced to pre-Hispanic times. You see them walking about in their embroidered cotton shifts, and though their Spanish may not be perfect, they're happy to get you going in the right direction.

Impressions

. . . we both learned that the Maya are not just a people of the past. Today, they live in their millions in Mexico, Guatemala, Belize and western Honduras, still speaking one of the 35 Mayan languages as their native tongue. They continue to cultivate their fields and commune with their living world in spite of the fact that they are encapsulated within a larger modern civilization whose vision of reality is often alien to their own.
—Linda Schele and David Freidel, *A Forest of Kings,* 1990

Completely different are the estimated 1 million **Tabascan** and **Chiapan Maya,** who speak four different Mayan languages with dozens of dialects. The Maya groups around San Cristóbal de las Casas generally choose not to embrace outside cultures, preferring to live in small mountain hamlets and meeting only for ceremonies and market days. Their forest- and cloud-draped high mountain homeland in Chiapas is cold—in contrast to the heat predominant in the lowland regions of Tabasco and the Yucatán Peninsula. They, too, live much as their ancestors did, but with beliefs distinct from their peninsular relatives.

THE YUCATÁN'S GEOGRAPHY   The Yucatán is physically interesting and varied. It's edged by the dull aquamarine Gulf of Mexico on the west and north, and the clear cerulean blue Caribbean Sea on the east. The Yucatán covers almost 84,000 square miles, with nearly 1,000 miles of shoreline. Most terrain is porous limestone, with thin soil supporting a primarily low, scrubby jungle. There are almost no surface rivers; instead, rainwater filters through the limestone into underground rivers. Natural wells called *cenotes,* or collapsed caves, dot the region.

The only sense of height comes from the curvaceous terrain rising from the western shores of Campeche inland to the border with Yucatán state. This rise, called the Puuc Hills, is the Maya "Alps"—though they are a mere 980 feet high. Locally, the hills are known as the Sierra de Ticul or Sierra Alta. The highways undulate a bit as you go inland, and south of Ticul there's a rise in the highway that provides a marvelous view of the "valley" and the misty Puuc hills lining the horizon.

AGRICULTURE & COMMERCE   Crumbling haciendas surrounded by fields of henequen punctuate the peninsular landscape. Henequen, a member of the agave family from which hemp is made, was the king crop in the Yucatán in the 19th century, and the industry is still going strong, with rope, packing material, shoes, and purses manufactured from the spiny plant. Besides henequen, other crops in the mostly agricultural peninsula are corn, coconuts, oranges, mangos, and bananas. In Tabasco and Chiapas, coffee, chocolate, and oil are commercially exploited, but the indigenous people raise some of their own vegetables as well as corn for food and fodder, tend sheep for their wool, and barter for life's other necessities.

NATURAL LIFE & PROTECTED AREAS   Enormous strides have been made to protect the Yucatán's abundant natural life in the last decade. The nature reserves have not been significantly opened to tourism and may never be; the idea is to protect them, and money is lacking to staff and patrol opened areas. But wildlife, especially birds, is easy to see in or outside a reserve, once you get away from developed areas.

The Yucatán Peninsula

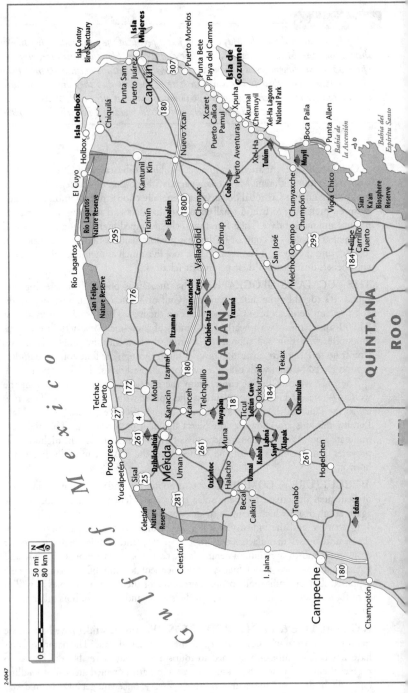

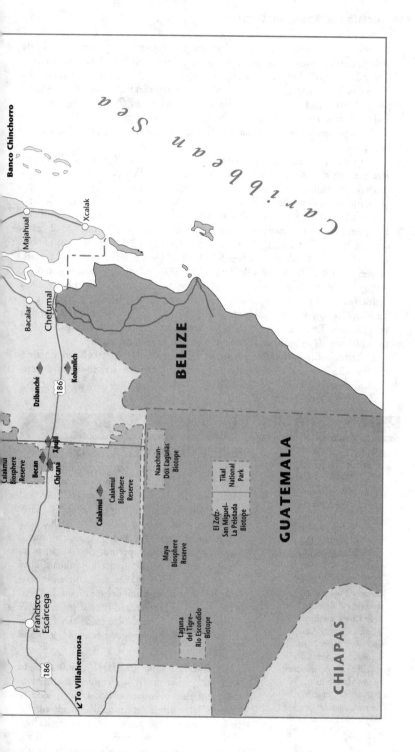

Banco Chinchorro

Caribbean Sea

Majahual

Xcalak

Bacalar

Chetumal

Dzibanché

Kohunlich

186

Calakmul
Biosphere
Reserve

Xpujil

Becan

Chicaná

Calakmul

Calakmul
Biosphere
Reserve

Naachtun-
Dos Lagunas
Biotope

BELIZE

Tikal
National
Park

El Zotz-
San Miguel-
La Palotada
Biotope

GUATEMALA

Francisco
Escárcega

Maya
Biosphere
Reserve

Laguna
del Tigre-
Río Escondido
Biotope

186

To Villahermosa

CHIAPAS

15

Yucatán state's nature reserves include the 118,000-acre **Río Lagartos Wildlife Refuge** north of Mérida, where North America's largest flock of flamingos nests; the **Celestún Wildlife Refuge,** covering more than 14,000 acres, which exists for the protection of flamingos and other tropical birds and plant life; and, adjacent to it, the 123,398-acre **El Palmar Wildlife Refuge,** important for its springs, cenotes, and black mangroves, established in 1990 on the upper Yucatán coast. The state also has incorporated nature trails into the archaeological site of **Dzibilchaltún,** north of Mérida.

In 1989, Campeche state set aside 178,699 acres in the **Calakmul Biosphere Reserve** that it shares with the country of Guatemala. The area includes the state's ruins of Calakmul, as well as significant plants, animals, and birdlife.

Quintana Roo's protected areas are some of the region's most beautiful, wild, and important. In 1986 the state ambitiously set aside the 1.3 million-acre **Sian Ka'an Biosphere Reserve,** conserving a significant part of the coast in the face of development south of Tulum. **Isla Contoy,** also in Quintana Roo, off the coast of both Isla Mujeres and Cancún, is a beautiful island refuge for hundreds of bird species, turtles, and other plants and wildlife. And in 1990 the 150-acre **Jardín Botánico,** south of Puerto Morelos, was opened to the public; along with the Botanical Garden at Cozumel's Chancanaab Lagoon, it gives visitors an excellent idea of the Yucatán's lengthy shoreline, since four of Mexico's eight marine turtle species nest on Quintana Roo's shores—loggerhead, green, hawksbill, and leatherback. More than 600 species of birds, reptiles, and mammals have been counted.

El Triunfo Biosphere Reserve, near the Lagunas de Montebello in Chiapas, preserves 25,000 acres of the rain-forest habitat of the rare and endangered quetzal bird.

2 A Look at the Past

Dateline

- **10,000–2,300 B.C.** Pre-Historic period: Cultivation of chiles, corn, beans, avocado, amaranth, and pumpkin. Mortars and pestles in use. Stone bowls and jars, obsidian knives, and open-weave basketry developed.
- **1500–300** Pre-Classic period: Olmec culture spreads and develops over Gulf Coast, southern Mexico, Central America, and lower Mexican Pacific Coast and is eventually linked to the development of the Maya culture.
- **1000–900** Olmec San Lorenzo center is destroyed; they begin anew at La Venta.

continues

PRE-HISPANIC CIVILIZATIONS

The earliest "Mexicans" were Stone Age hunter-gatherers coming from the north, descendants of a race that had crossed the Bering Strait and reached North America before 12,000 B.C. They arrived in what is now Mexico by 10,000 B.C. Sometime between 5200 and 1500 B.C., in what is known as the **Archaic period,** they began practicing agriculture and domesticating animals. They wove baskets; grew corn, beans, squash, and tomatoes; and kept turkeys and dogs for food. By 2400 B.C., the art of pottery had been discovered. We find evidence of "artists" who made clay figurines for use as votive offerings or household gods and goddesses.

THE PRECLASSIC PERIOD (1500 B.C. to A.D. 300) Eventually, agriculture improved to the point that it could provide enough food to support large communities and enough surplus to free some of the population from agricultural work. A civilization emerged that we call the **Olmec**—an enigmatic people who settled the lower Gulf Coast in what is now Tabasco and Ver-acruz. Anthropologists regard them as the mother culture of Mesoamerica, since they established a pattern for later civilizations in a wide area stretching from northern Mexico into Central America. The Olmec developed the basic calendar used throughout the region, established the pre-dominance of a 52-year cycle—and used it to schedule the construction of pyramids—estab-lished principles of urban layout and architecture, and originated the cult of the jaguar and the sacredness of jade. They may also have bequeathed the sacred ritual of "the ball game"—a universal element of Mesoamerican culture.

The Olmec also left behind colossal stone heads—one habit that seems to have died out in later cultures. We still don't know what purposes these heads served, but they were immense pro-jects; the basalt stone from which they were sculpted was mined miles inland and transported to the Olmec cities on the coast, probably by river rafts. The heads share a rounded, baby-faced look, marked by the peculiar "jaguar mouth"—a high-arched lip that is an identifying mark of Olmec sculpture.

All of the heads wear what looks like a helmet; those with open eyes are slightly cross-eyed. This style of sculpture has been found at the later Maya site **Chacan Bacan,** a newly uncovered ruin in the Río Bec region in southern Yucatán, where a pyramid was recently unearthed revealing a facade covered with the classic look of the Olmec heads.

The Maya civilization began developing in the late Preclassic, around 500 B.C. Our under-standing of this period is only sketchy, but Olmec influences are apparent everywhere. Somewhere along the way the Maya perfected the Olmec cal-endar and developed their ornate system of hiero-glyphic writing and their early architecture. Two other civilizations also began their rise to promi-nence around this time: the people of Teotihuacán, just north of present-day Mexico City, and the Zapotec of Monte Albán in the valley of Oaxaca.

THE CLASSIC PERIOD (A.D. 300 to 900)
The flourishing of these three civilizations marks the boundaries of this period, the heyday of Pre-Columbian Mesoamerican artistic and cultural achievements. These include the pyramids and palaces in Teotihuacán; the ceremonial center of Monte Albán; and the stelae and temples of Palen-que, Bonampak, and the Tikal site in Guatemala.

- **600** La Venta Olmec cultural zenith. Zapotec culture emerges near Monte Albán Oaxaca.
- **500–100** The Zapotec flourish and invent the Calendar Round, which is later used near the end of the Olmec period and later by Maya. Olmec culture disintegrates. Teotihuacán settlement is started in central Mexico.
- **A.D. 100** Building begins on Sun and Moon pyramids at Teotihuacán; Palenque dynasty emerges in Yucatán.
- **300–900** Classic period begins: Xochicalco estab-lished where pyramids bearing Maya-like figures are eventually built; Maya civilization develops in Yucatán and Chiapas.
- **500–650** Teotihuacán culture from central Mexico exerts strong influence in the Maya world, including inter-marrying with the Maya.
- **683** Maya Lord Pacal is buried in an elaborate tomb below the Palace of the Inscriptions at Palenque.
- **650–800** Teotihuacán burns and is deserted. Cacaxtla, in central Mexico, is at its zenith with brilliantly colored murals of Maya warriors splashed across its walls.
- **750** Zapotecs conquer the Valley of Oaxaca and invent first Mesoamerican writing system.
- **800** Bonampak battle/victory mural painted.
- **900** Postclassic period begins: Toltec culture emerges at Tula and spreads to Chichén-Itzá on the Yucatán Peninsula by 978.
- **909** A small monument at Toniná (near San Cristóbal de las Casas) has this as the last Long Count date

continues

discovered so far, symbolizing the end of the Classic Maya era.

- **1156–1230** Tula, the Toltec capital, is abandoned.
- **1290** Zapotec decline, and Mixtec emerge at Monte Albán; Mitla becomes refuge of Zapotecs.
- **1325–45** Aztec capital Tenochtitlán founded; Aztecs begin to dominate Mexico, but not Chiapas or the Yucatán Peninsula.
- **1443** Calkaní founded after destruction of Mayapán.
- **1511** Santo Domingo–bound Spanish sailors sailing from the Darien Gap near Panama are shipwrecked off the coast of what is today Quintana Roo, and two passengers survive. One survivor is a clergyman, Jerónimo de Aguilar, who learns to speak Yukatek Mayan and later becomes Cortés's translator. The other, Gonzalo Guerrero, adopts the Maya culture, marries a Maya woman, and has a family. Guerrero eventually leads Maya in battle against Spaniards.
- **1516** Gold found on Cozumel in aborted Spanish expedition of Yucatán Peninsula arouses interest of Spanish governor in Cuba, who sends Juan de Grijalva on an expedition, followed by another, led by Hernán Cortés.
- **1517** Cortés arrives in Cozumel and rescues Aguilar, but Gonzalo Guerrero prefers to remain with his family and adopted culture.
- **1518** Spaniards first visited what is today Campeche.
- **1519** Conquest of Mexico begins: Hernán Cortés and

continues

Beyond their achievements in art and architecture, the Maya made significant discoveries in science, including the use of the zero in mathematics and a complex calendar with which the priests could predict eclipses and the movements of the stars for centuries to come.

The Maya were warlike, raiding their neighbors to acquire slaves and land and to take captives for their many blood rituals. Recent studies, notably *Blood of Kings* (Braziller, 1986) by Linda Schele and Mary Ellen Miller, have debunked the long-held theory that the Maya were a peaceful people. Scholars continue to decipher the Maya hieroglyphs, murals, and relief carvings to reveal a Maya world based on the belief that blood sacrifice was necessary for dynastic survival. Through sacrifice the Maya nourished their gods and ancestors, and they honored royal births, deaths, marriages, and accessions in a calendar full of sacred meanings. Numerous carvings and murals show that members of the ruling class ritualistically mutilated themselves to draw sacrificial blood.

The inhabitants of **Teotihuacán** (100 B.C. to A.D. 700—near present-day Mexico City) built a city that at its zenith is thought to have had 100,000 or more inhabitants covering 9 square miles. It was an extremely well-organized city, built on a grid with streams channeled to follow the city's plan. Different social classes such as artisans and merchants were assigned to specific neighborhoods. At its height, Teotihuacán was the greatest cultural center in Mexico, with tremendous influence as far as Guatemala and the Yucatán Peninsula. The ceremonial center is so large that it was thought by the Aztecs to have been built by gods. Its feathered serpent, later known as **Quetzalcoatl**, became part of the pantheon of many succeeding cultures. The ruling classes were industrious, literate and cosmopolitan; their trading posts extended into the Maya and Zapotec heartlands. The beautiful sculpture and ceramics of Teotihuacán display a highly stylized and refined aesthetic whose influences can be seen clearly in objects of Maya and Zapotec origin. Around the 7th century, the city was abandoned for unknown reasons. Who these people were and where they went remains a mystery.

Further south, the **Zapotecs,** influenced by the Olmecs, raised an impressive culture in the region of Oaxaca. Their two principal cities were **Monte**

Albán, inhabited by an elite of merchants and artisans, and Mitla, reserved for the high priests.

THE POSTCLASSIC PERIOD (A.D. 900–1521)

Warfare becomes a more conspicuous activity of the civilizations that flourished in this period. Social development was impressive, but not as cosmopolitan as the Maya, Teotihuacán, and Zapotec societies. In central Mexico, a people known as the Toltecs established their capital at Tula in the 10th century. They were originally one of the barbarous hordes of Indians that periodically migrated from the north. At some stage in their development, the Toltec were influenced by remnants of Teotihuacán culture and adopted the feathered serpent Quetzalcoatl as their god, but they also revered a god known as Tezcatlipoca or "smoking mirror," who later became god of the Aztec. The Toltecs maintained a large military class divided into orders symbolized by animals. At its zenith, Tula may have had 40,000 people, and it spread its influence across Mesoamerica. By the 13th century, however, the Toltec had exhausted themselves, probably in civil wars and in battles with the invaders from the north.

Of those northern tribes, the Aztecs were the most warlike. At first they occupied themselves as mercenaries for the established cities in the valley of Mexico—one of which allotted to them an unwanted marshy piece of land in the middle of Lake Texcoco for their settlement. This eventually grew into the island city of Tenochtitlán. Through aggressive diplomacy and military measures, the Aztec soon conquered all of central Mexico and extended their rule east to the Gulf Coast and south to the valley of Oaxaca.

After the Classic period, the Maya migrated from their historic homelands in Guatemala and Chiapas into the lowlands of the Yucatán (roughly the modern states of Yucatán and Campeche), where they spent the centuries, from A.D. 900 to 1500, trying to recover their former greatness.

During this period, the cities near the Yucatán's low western Puuc hills were built. The region's architecture, called Puuc style, is characterized by elaborate exterior stonework appearing above door frames and extending to the roofline. Examples of this architecture, such as the Codz Poop at Kabah and the palaces at Sayil and Labná, are beautiful and quite impressive.

- troops arrive near present-day Veracruz.
- 1521 Conquest is complete after Aztec defeat at Tlaltelolco in 1521.
- 1521–1524 Cortés organizes Spanish empire in Mexico and begins building Mexico City on the ruins of Tenochtitlán.
- 1524 First Franciscan friars arrive from Spain.
- 1524–1535 Cortés removed from leadership. Spanish King sends officials, judges, and finally an *audiencia* to govern.
- 1526 Francisco Montejo permitted by King of Spain to colonize the Yucatán.
- 1530 Territory of Tabasco conquered by Francisco Montejo.
- 1535–1821 Viceregal period: Mexico governed by 61 viceroys appointed by King of Spain. Landed aristocracy, a small elite class owning huge portions of land (haciendas) emerges. Yucatán is led by a governor who reports to the king rather than to viceroys.
- 1540 Campeche, Mérida, and Valladolid are founded.
- 1542 Mérida established as capital of Yucatán Peninsula.
- 1546 Maya rebel and take control of peninsula.
- 1559 French and Spanish pirates attack Campeche.
- 1562 Friar Diego de Landa destroys 5,000 Maya religious stone figures and burns 27 hieroglyphic-painted manuscripts at Maní, Yucatán. Widespread torture and death are meted out to Maya believed to secretly practice pre-Hispanic beliefs.

continues

- **1563–1566** Diego de Landa forced to return to Spain to answer for his actions. In defense of himself he writes his now-famous and invaluable *Yucatán Before and After the Conquest,* which was published 298 years later.
- **1579** Diego de Landa dies in the Yucatán.
- **1739** What became known as the *Dresden Codex,* a lost Maya calendar text, is purchased in Vienna by the Royal Library of Dresden, where it languishes for more than a century.
- **1767** Jesuits expelled from New Spain.
- **1810–1821** War of Independence: Miguel Hidalgo starts movement for Mexico's independence from Spain, but is executed within a year; leadership and goals change during the war years, but a compromise between monarchy and a republic is outlined by Augustín de Iturbide.
- **1821** Independence from Spain achieved. The Spanish governor of Yucatán resigns and the Yucatán Peninsula becomes an independent country.
- **1822** First Empire: Iturbide ascends throne as Emperor of Mexico.
- **1823** The Yucatán Peninsula decides to become part of Mexico.
- **1824** Iturbide is expelled, returns, and is executed by firing squad.
- **1824–1855** Federal Republic period: Guadalupe Victoria is elected first president of Mexico in 1824; he is followed by 26 presidents and interim presidents, among them José López de Santa Anna.
- **1828** Slavery abolished.

continues

The Yucatán was profoundly affected by strong influences from central Mexico; the great city of **Chichén-Itzá** is clearly a melding of Toltec and Maya styles, but the nature of this Toltec influence is a subject of great debate. Most prominent are the depictions of a feathered serpent, Kukulcan. In central Mexico there is an intriguing story told in mythographic shorthand of a civil war in Tula between the followers of Tezcatlipoca and those of Quetzalcoatl, the plumed serpent. The followers of Quetzalcoatl lost and fled to the Gulf Coast from whence they sailed east toward the morning star, vowing to return. Did they arrive in the Yucatán and become involved in the building of Chichén-Itzá? In the language of myth, the head priest would naturally have been identified with the god Quetzalcoatl, so when read literally, it was the god, not the priests, who would return one day. This myth became, in the hands of the Spanish, a powerful weapon of conquest.

Some theories claim that a distantly related branch of the Maya people, called the **Putun Maya,** came from the borders of the Yucatán Peninsula between mainland Mexico and the Classic Maya lands in Péten and Chiapas. They spoke the Mayan language poorly and used many Nahuatl (Aztec) words.

When the Putun Maya left their ships and moved inland, they became known as the **Itzáes** and settled in what eventually became known as Chichén-Itzá (Well of the Itzá). They brought with them years of experience in trading with distant cultures, which could explain the Toltec influence at Chichén-Itzá.

Uxmal was inhabited during this same period (around A.D. 1000), by the tribe known as the **Tutul Xiú,** who came from the region of Oaxaca and Tabasco. Some scholars think that the Xiú took the city from earlier builders, since archaeological evidence shows that the region around Uxmal was inhabited as early as 800 B.C.

The three great Maya centers of Chichén-Itzá, Mayapán, and Uxmal lived in peace under a confederation: The Itzá ruled in Chichén-Itzá, the Cocom tribe in Mayapán, and the Xiú in Uxmal. Authorities don't agree on the exact year, but sometime during the 12th century A.D. the people of Mayapán overthrew the confederation, sacked Chichén-Itzá, conquered Uxmal, and captured the leaders of the Itzá and the Xiú. Held in Mayapán, the Itzá and the Xiú princes reigned over but did not rule their former cities. Mayapán remained the seat of the confederation for over 200 years.

The Xiú took their revenge in 1441 when they marched from Uxmal on Mayapán, capturing and destroying the city, and killing the Cocom rulers. They founded a new city at Mani. Battles and skirmishes continued to plague the Maya territory until conquered by the Spanish conquistadores.

THE CONQUEST

In 1517, the first Spaniards to arrive in what is today known as Mexico skirmished with Maya Indians off the coast of the Yucatán Peninsula. One of these fledgling expeditions ended in shipwreck, leaving several Spaniards stranded as prisoners of the Maya. The Spanish sent out another expedition, under the command of **Hernán Cortés,** which landed on Cozumel in February 1519. Cortés inquired about the gold and riches of the interior, and the coastal Maya were happy to describe the wealth and splendor of the Aztec empire in central Mexico. Cortés promptly decided to disobey all orders of his superior, the governor of Cuba, and sailed to the mainland where he rescued the Spaniard Jerónimo de Aguilar, one of the shipwrecked Spaniards. Farther down the coast he received as a gift a slave woman known as Malintzin, who became Cortés's interpreter in his dealings with Moctezuma. Soon he disembarked in what is now Veracruz, and then burned his boats for the encouragement of his men. From here he headed for the interior with his small force of 550 men.

Cortés arrived when the Aztec empire was at the height of its wealth and power. **Moctezuma** ruled over the central and southern highlands and extracted tribute from lowland peoples. His greatest temples were literally plated with gold and encrusted with the blood of sacrificial captives. Moctezuma himself was a fool, a mystic, and something of a coward. Despite his wealth and military power, he dithered in his capital at Tenochtitlán sending messengers with gifts and suggestions that Cortés leave while Cortés blustered and negotiated his way into the highlands, always cloaking his real intentions. Moctezuma, terrified by the military tactics and technology of the Spaniard, convinced himself that Cortés was in fact the god Quetzalcoatl making his long-awaited return. By the time the Spaniards arrived in the Aztec capital, Cortés had gained some ascendancy

- **1829** Dresden Codex is faithfully reproduced in watercolor, and a few copies are published.
- **1836** Santa Anna defeats Texans at Battle of the Alamo, at San Antonio, Texas, but is later defeated and captured at the Battle of San Jacinto outside Houston, Texas.
- **1838** France invades Mexico at Veracruz.
- **1839–1841** Americans John L. Stephens and Frederick Catherwood whack their way to Yucatecan ruins in two journeys that were to become the talk of the literary world.
- **1841–1843** Stephens publishes his three volumes of *Incidents of Travel,* illustrated by Catherwood, which stimulate interest in the Yucatán.
- **1845** United States annexes Texas.
- **1846–48** War with the United States: For $15 million, Mexico relinquishes half of its national territory to the United States in Treaty of Guadalupe Hidalgo.
- **1847–1866** War of the Castes: Degrading segregationist policies by Yucatán leaders against the Maya cause revolt, upheaval, and decimation of half the Maya population. Strife lasts well into 20th century. Exportation of henequen (agave plant) products, such as hemp for rope, and chicle (for gum) bring Yucatán into the world economy.
- **1855–72** Reform Years: Includes a 3-year war in Mexico, pitting cities against villages and rich against poor in search for ideology, stability, and political leadership. Benito Juárez is president in fact and in exile

continues

off and on between Reform Wars and during reign of Emperor Maximilian. Juárez nationalizes church property and declares separation of church and state.

- 1858 Campeche and Yucatán become territories.
- 1862 England, Spain, and France send troops to Mexico to demand debt payment, and all except France withdraw.
- 1862 Diego de Landa's 1566 account of *Yucatán Before and After the Conquest* is discovered in the Royal Academy of History in Madrid.
- 1863 Campeche gains statehood.
- 1864–67 Second Empire: French Emperor Napoleon Bonaparte III sends Maximilian of Hapsburg to be Emperor of Mexico.
- 1867 Juárez orders execution of Maximilian at Querétaro and resumes presidency in Mexico City until his death in 1872.
- 1872–84 Post-Reform period: Only four presidents hold office, but country is nearly bankrupt.
- 1876–1911 Porfiriato: Porfirio Díaz is president/dictator of Mexico for 35 years, leads country to modernization at the expense of human rights. Díaz opponents, including Yaqui Indians from Northern Mexico, are exiled to the Yucatán Peninsula to suffer and die as slaves.
- 1902 Quintana Roo becomes Mexican territory.
- 1911–17 Mexican Revolution: Franciso Madero drafts revolutionary plan. Díaz resigns. Leaders jockey for power during period of great violence, national upheaval, and tremendous loss of life.

continues

over the lesser Indian states that were resentful tributaries to the Aztec. In November of 1519, Cortés confronted Moctezuma and took him hostage in an effort to leverage from him control of the Empire.

In the middle of Cortés's dangerous game of manipulation, another Spanish expedition arrived with orders to end Cortés's authority over the mission. The Spaniard hastened to meet the rival's force and persuade them to join his own. In the meantime, the Aztecs chased the garrison out of Tenochtitlán, and either they or the Spaniards killed Moctezuma. For the next year and a half, Cortés planned and executed the siege of Tenochtitlán with the help of rival Indians and a decimating epidemic of smallpox, to which the Indians had no resistance. In the end, the Aztec capital fell, and when it did, it lay all of central Mexico at the feet of the conquistadores.

The Spanish conquest started out as a pirate expedition by Cortés and his men, unauthorized by the Spanish crown or its governor in Cuba. The Spanish King legitimized Cortés following his victory over the Aztecs and ordered the forcible Christianization of this new colony, to be called **New Spain.** Guatemala and Honduras were explored and conquered, and by 1540 the territory of New Spain included Spanish possessions from Vancouver to Panama. In the 2 centuries that followed, Franciscan and Augustinian friars converted millions of Indians to Christianity, and the Spanish lords built up huge feudal estates on which the Indian farmers were little more than serfs. The silver and gold that Cortés looted made Spain the richest country in Europe.

The conquest of the Yucatán Peninsula occurred after Cortés had subjugated the highlands. In 1526, the King of Spain granted permission to **Francisco Montejo** to conquer the Yucatán Peninsula—and the Maya fought desperately up to their decisive defeat 20 years later. The Maya never quite accepted the rule of Europeans; when their opportunity to rebel came in the 1840s, a civil war broke out that allowed them to gain control of most of the peninsula. This is known as the **Caste War.** The Maya eventually lost, but the southern and eastern half of the peninsula remained a virtual no-man's-land (to outsiders); the Maya resided almost untouched by the outside world until coastal development began in the late 1960s. (See also the box "Centuries of

Conflict: Spanish & Maya in the Yucatán" in chapter 6).

THE COLONIAL PERIOD

Hernán Cortés set about building a new city and the the seat of government of New Spain upon the ruins of the old Aztec capital. For indigenous peoples (besides the Tlaxcaltecans, Cortés's Indian allies), heavy tributes once paid to the Aztecs were now rendered in forced labor to the Spanish. In many cases they were made to provide the materials for the building of New Spain as well. Diseases carried by the Spaniards, against which the Indian populations had no natural immunity, wiped out most of the native population.

Over 3 centuries of the Colonial period, 61 viceroys appointed by the king of Spain governed Mexico. From the beginning, more Spaniards arrived as overseers, merchants, craftsmen, architects, and silversmiths, and eventually African slaves were brought in as well. Spain became rich from New World gold and silver, chiseled out by backbreaking Indian labor. The colonial elite built lavish homes both in Mexico City and in the countryside. They filled their homes with ornate furniture, had many servants, and adorned themselves in velvets, satins, and jewels imported from abroad. A new class system developed. Those born in Spain considered themselves superior to the *criollos* (Spaniards born in Mexico). Those of other races and the *castas* (mixtures of Spanish and Indian, Spanish and Negro, or Indian and Negro) occupied the bottom rung of society.

It took great cunning to stay a step ahead of the avaricious Crown, which demanded increasingly higher taxes and contributions from its fabled foreign conquests. Still, wealthy colonists prospered grandly enough to develop an extravagant society.

However, discontent with the mother country simmered for years over social and political hot points, taxes, the royal bureaucracy, Spanish-born citizens' advantages over Mexican-born subjects, and restrictions on commerce with Spain and other countries. Dissatisfaction with Spain found an opportune moment in 1808 when Napoleon invaded Spain and crowned his brother Joseph king in place of Charles IV. To many in Mexico, allegiance to France was out of the question; Mexico, discontent with the mother country, reached the level of revolt.

- **1913** President Madero assassinated.
- **1914, 1916** United States invades Mexico.
- **1915** Payo Obispo becomes capital of territory of Quintana Roo.
- **1917–1940** Reconstruction: Present constitution of Mexico signed; land and education reforms are initiated, and labor unions strengthened; Mexico expels U.S. oil companies and nationalizes all natural resources and railroads. Pancho Villa, Zapata, and presidents Obregón and Carranza are assassinated.
- **1931** Citizens of Yucatán Peninsula protest division of Quintana Roo territory between the states of Yucatán and Campeche.
- **1935** Quintana Roo is restored to territorial status.
- **1940** Mexico enters period of political stability and makes tremendous economic progress and improvement in the quality of life, although problems of corruption, inflation, national health, and unresolved land and agricultural issues continue.
- **1946** Locals living in the jungle show Giles Healy the magnificent Maya murals at Bonampak, which he reports to the world.
- **1950** The first train links Campeche with Coatzacoalcos.
- **1952** Dr. Yuri Valentinovich Knorosov, a Russian scholar who had never seen a Maya ruin, publishes the modern-day key to deciphering Maya hieroglyphics; it is not fully accepted for at least 20 years. Mexican archaeologist Alberto Ruz Lhuller uncovers King Pacal's tomb in the Temple of the Inscriptions at Palenque—one of the

continues

greatest discoveries of the
Maya world.

- **1974** Quintana Roo
achieves statehood, and
Cancún opens to tourism.
- **1982** President Echeverría
nationalizes the country's
banks.
- **1988** Mexico enters the
General Agreement on Trade
and Tariffs (GATT).
- **1991** Mexico, Canada, and
the United States begin Free
Trade Agreement negotia-
tions. Mexico begins massive
push to excavate "new"
Maya sites and re-excavate
and conserve others.
- **1992** Sale of *ejido* land
(peasant communal prop-
erty) to private citizens is
allowed. Mexico and the
Vatican establish diplomatic
relations after an interruption of 100 years.
- **1993** Mexico deregulates
hotel and restaurant prices;
New Peso currency begins
circulation.
- **1994** Mexico, Canada, and
the United States sign the
North American Free Trade
Agreement (NAFTA). An
Indian uprising in Chiapas
sparks protests countrywide
over government policies
concerning land distribu-
tion, bank loans, health,
education, and voting and
human rights. In an unre-
lated incident, PRI candidate Luis Donaldo Colossio
is assassinated 5 months
before the election; replacement candidate Ernesto
Zedillo Ponce de Leon is
elected and inaugurated as
president in December.
Within weeks, the peso is
devalued, throwing the
nation into turmoil.
- **1995** The peso loses half
its value within the first
3 months of the year. The
government raises prices on

continues

INDEPENDENCE

The rebellion began in 1810, when a priest, **Father Miguel Hidalgo** gave the *grito,* a cry for indepen-dence, from his church in the town of Dolores, Guanajuato. The uprising soon became a full-fledged revolution, as Hidalgo and Ignacio Allende gathered an "army" of citizens and threatened Mexico City. Although ultimately Hidalgo was executed, he is honored as "the Father of Mexican Independence." Another priest, José María Morelos kept the revolt alive with several successful campaigns through 1815, when he, too, was cap-tured and executed.

Rebel prospects for independence were rather dim until the Spanish King who replaced Joseph Bonaparte decided to make social reforms in the colonies, which convinced the conservative powers in Mexico that they didn't need Spain after all. With their tacit approval, Agustín de Iturbide, then commander of royalist forces, declared Mexico independent and himself emperor. It was not long, however, before internal dissension brought about the fall of the emperor, and Mexico was proclaimed a republic.

In 1821 the Spanish governor of Yucatán resigned, and Yucatán, too, became an indepen-dent country. Though Yucatecans made an uneasy union with Mexico 2 years later, this brief period of sovereignty is testimony to the Yucatecan spirit of independence. That same spirit was revived in 1840 when Yucatán seceded from Mexico.

The young Mexican republic was inflamed by political instability and ran through a dizzying suc-cession of presidents and dictators as struggles between federalists and centralists, and conserva-tives and liberals divided the country and con-sumed its energy. Moreover, there was a disastrous war with the U.S. in which Mexico lost half its ter-ritory. A central figure was **Antonio López de Santa Anna,** who assumed the leadership of his country no fewer than 11 times and was flexible enough in those volatile times to portray himself variously as a liberal, a conservative, a federalist, or a centralist. He probably holds the record for fre-quency of exile; by 1855 he was finally left without a political comeback and remained the rest of his days in Venezuela.

Political instability persisted, and the conserva-tive forces, with some encouragement from Napoleon III, lit upon the bright idea of inviting in a Hapsburg (as if that strategy had ever worked for Spain). They found a willing Hapsburg in Archduke Maximilian of Austria, who, being at the time unemployed in ruling anyone, accepted the position of Mexican emperor with the support of French troops. The first French forces—a modern, well-equipped army—were defeated by the rag-tag Mexican forces in a battle near Puebla (now celebrated annually as **Cinco de Mayo**). The second attempt was more successful, and Ferdinand Maximilian Joseph of Hapsburg became emperor for 3 years of civil war in which the French were finally induced to abandon the emperor's cause. **Maximilian** was captured and executed by a firing squad near Querétaro in 1867. His adversary and successor (as president of Mexico) was **Benito Juárez,** a Zapotec Indian lawyer and one of the great heroes of Mexican history. Juárez did his best to unify and strengthen his country before dying of a heart attack in 1872; his effect on Mexico's future was profound, and his plans and visions bore fruit for decades.

THE PORFIRIATO & THE REVOLUTION

A few years after Juárez's death, one of his generals, **Porfirio Díaz,** assumed power in a coup and ruled Mexico from 1877 to 1911, a period now called the "Porfiriato." He stayed in power through brutal repression of the opposition and by courting the favor of the powerful nations of the time. Generous in his dealings with foreign investors, who were grateful in return, Díaz became, in the eyes of most Mexicans, the archetypal *entreguista* (one who sells out his country for private gain). With foreign investment came the concentration of great wealth in few hands. Social conditions worsened.

In 1910, Francisco Madero called for an armed rebellion that became the **Mexican Revolutión** ("La Revolución" in Mexico; the revolution against Spain is called the "Guerra de Independencia"). Díaz was sent into exile; while in London, he became a celebrity at the age of 81, when he jumped into the Thames to save a drowning boy. Díaz is buried in Paris. Madero became President but was promptly betrayed and executed by a heavy straight out of the Hollywood school of villains—the despicable **Victoriano Huerta.** Those who had answered Madero's call responded again—the great peasant hero **Emiliano Zapata** in the south and the seemingly invincible **Pancho Villa** in the central north with Álvaro Obregón

oil and utilities. Interest on debt soars to 140 percent; businesses begin to fail; un-employment rises. The Chia-pan rebels threaten another rebellion, which is quickly quashed by the government. Former President Carlos Salinas de Gortari, with the devaluation having left his reputation for economic leadership in a shambles, leaves Mexico for the United States. Salinas's brother is accused of plotting the assassination of their brother-in-law, the head of the PRI. The United States extends Mexico $40 billion in loans to stabilize the economy following the peso crisis.

- **1996** Effects of the devaluation continue as in 1995, but many businesses without debt expand and prosper. Mexico begins repaying the loan from the United States extended in 1995; the wife of the president's brother is arrested attempting to remove millions of dollars from a Swiss bank—drug ties are alleged; former Presi-dent Salinas's whereabouts unknown, though he speaks out occasionally; the Chiapan crisis remains unsettled, but some progress has been made.
- **1997** Mexico continues early repayment of its debt to the United States; Mexico's economy shows signs of improving, but the people struggle under effects of inflation, low pay, and lack of jobs. The Chiapas issue flares up again when 45 villagers are massacred in Acteal. The fourth Chiapanecan governor in 4 years is forced to resign, and the government makes arrests.

continues

❷ Did You Know?

- Four Maya books (or partial books) survived the 16th-century Maya book burning, but none is in Mexico today.
- The mingling of the blood of Spain with that of Mexico began with the marriage of Gonzalo Guerrero, a Spaniard shipwrecked off the coast of Yucatán in 1511, to a Maya woman with whom he fathered at least three sons. He refused to leave his family and join Cortés. A statue of Guerrero, commemorating the beginning of a new race, stands in Puerto Morelos, south of Cancún.
- The Celustún estuary, on the Yucatán Gulf Coast, is home to the largest flock of flamingos in North America.
- Cacao beans, grown in Tabasco and Chiapas, were Aztec currency.
- Cancún opened to tourism in 1974 with one hotel.
- In 1841, the Texas Navy was hired to protect the Yucatán Peninsula from invasion by Mexico.
- The Maya predicted that the earth's destruction will occur in the year A.D. 2012.
- During the 300 years that Mexico belonged to Spain, no Spanish king ever visited the country.
- Mexico's Indian population was approximately 30 million in 1519. By 1550, it was down to only 3 million, largely because of the spread of diseases brought by the Spaniards.
- Half the population of Mexico is under the age of 16.
- Cortés prevented his troops from returning to Cuba by sinking all of his ships.

■ **1998** Cuauhtemoc Cárdenas becomes the first opposition candidate to become mayor of Mexico City, the second most powerful office in the country.

and Venustiano Carranza flanking him. They eventually put Huerta to flight and began hashing out a new constitution.

For the next few years, the revolutionaries Carranza, Obregón, and Villa fought among themselves; Zapata did not seek national power, though he fought tenaciously for land for peasants. He was betrayed and assassinated by Carranza, who at that time was President. Obregón finally consolidated power and executed Carranza, but was assassinated when he ried to break one of the tenets of the revolution—no reelection. His protégé, Plutarco Elias Calles, learned the lesson and installed one puppet president after another until **Lázaro Cárdenas** severed the puppeteer's strings and banished him to exile.

Until Cárdenas's election in 1934, the eventual outcome of the revolution remained in doubt. There had been some land redistribution, but other measures took a back seat to political expediency. Cárdenas changed all that. He implemented a massive redistribution of land and nationalized the oil industry. He instituted many reforms and gave shape to the ruling political party (now the **Partido Revolucionario Institucional,** or PRI) by bringing under its banner a broad representation of Mexican society and establishing the mechanisms for consensus building. Cárdenas is practically canonized by most Mexicans.

MODERN MEXICO

The presidents who followed are more noted for graft than leadership. The party's base narrowed when many of the reform-minded elements were marginalized. Progress, a lot of it in the form of large development projects, became the PRI's main basis for legitimacy. In 1968, the government violently repressed a democratic student movement at a massacre in Tlatelolco, a section of Mexico City. Though the PRI maintained its grip on power, it lost all semblance of being a progressive party. In 1985 there was a devastating **earthquake in Mexico City** that brought down many of the Government's new, supposedly earthquake-proof buildings, thus exposing shoddy construction and the widespread government corruption that fostered it. There was heavy criticism, too, for how it handled the relief efforts. In 1994, a political/military **uprising in Chiapas** brought Mexico's great social problems to the world's attention. A new political force, the Zapatista National Liberation Army (EZLN), has skillfully publicized the plight of the peasant in today's Mexico. The government was forced into negotiations with the EZLN, a position that can bring it little if any political capital. Its tactics have been to make some easy concessions and to stall on other demands.

In recent years, opposition political parties have grown in power and legitimacy. Facing enormous pressure and scrutiny from national and international organizations, and widespread public discontent, the PRI has had to concede electoral defeats for state governors and congresspersons. But the power structure within the party is inflexible; the party cannot adapt to changing situations and is in an internal crisis of its own, manifested in the several political assassinations that have occurred in the last few years. For the first time ever, the PRI has had to concede the loss of the mayoralty of Mexico City, the second most powerful position in the country. The new opposition mayor is Cuauhtémoc Cárdenas, son of the PRI's brightest star, Lázaro. What will happen now is anyone's guess.

3 Art & Architecture 101

Mexico's artistic and architectural legacy reaches back more than 3,000 years. Until the conquest of Mexico in A.D. 1521, art, architecture, politics, and religion in Mexico were inextricably intertwined and remained so through the colonial period.

PRE-HISPANIC FORMS

Mexico's **pyramids** are truncated platforms, not true pyramids, and come in many different shapes. Many sites have circular buildings, such as El Caracol at Chichén-Itzá, usually called the observatory and dedicated to the god of the wind. El Castillo at Chichén-Itzá has 365 steps—one for every day of the year. The Temple of the Magicians at Uxmal has beautifully rounded and sloping sides. Evidence of building one pyramidal structure on top of another, a widely accepted practice, has been found throughout Mesoamerica.

The Temple of the Inscriptions at Palenque is one of the few pyramids in Mesoamerica with a pyramid built specifically to conceal an underground tomb, although tombs have been found in many other pyramids. Cobá has the longest road (*sacbe*), stretching 62 miles. Numerous sites in Mesoamerica had ballcourts. In Mexico the longest is at Chichén-Itzá—nearly the length of a football field.

Architects of many Toltec, Aztec, and Teotihuacán edifices used a sloping panel (*talud*) alternating with a vertical panel (*tablero*). Elements of this style occasionally show up in the Yucatán. Dzinbanché, a newly excavated site near Lago Bacalar in southern Quintana Roo state, has at least one temple with this characteristic. The true arch was unknown in Mesoamerica, so the Maya made use of the corbeled arch; they would stack stones so that each successive stone was cantilevered out a little farther than the one below it until the two sides met at the top, forming the shape of an inverted V.

The Olmec, considered the parent culture in Mexico, built pyramids of earth. Little remains to tell us what their buildings looked like. The Olmec, however, left an enormous sculptural legacy from small, intricately carved pieces of jade to 40-ton carved basalt rock heads.

Throughout Mexico, pyramids were embellished with carved stone or mural art for religious and historic reasons rather than the purpose of pure adornment. **Hieroglyphs,** picture symbols etched on stone or painted on walls or pottery, functioned as the written language of the ancient peoples, particularly the Maya. By deciphering the glyphs, scholars allow the ancients to speak again, giving us specific names to attach to rulers and their families, and demystifying the great dynastic histories of the Maya. For more on this, be sure to read *A Forest of Kings* (1990) by Linda Schele and David Freidel and *Blood of Kings* (1986) by Linda Schele and Mary Ellen Miller. Good hieroglyphic examples can be seen in the site museum at Palenque.

Carving important historic figures on freestanding stone slabs, or **stelae,** was a common Maya commemorative device. Several are in place at Cobá, Calakmul has the most, and good examples are in the Museum of Anthropology in Mexico City and the Carlos Pellicer Museum in Villahermosa. **Pottery** played an important role, and different indigenous groups are distinguished by their use of color and style in pottery. The Maya were known for pottery painted with scenes from daily and historic life.

Pre-Hispanic cultures left a number of fantastic painted **murals,** some of which are remarkably preserved, such as those at Bonampak and Cacaxtla. Amazing stone murals or mosaics using thousands of pieces of fitted stone to form figures of warriors, snakes, or geometric designs decorate the pyramid facades at Uxmal and Chichén-Itzá.

SPANISH INFLUENCE

With the arrival of the Spaniards, a new form of architecture came to Mexico (the next 300 years are known as the Viceregal period, when Spain's appointed viceroys ruled Mexico). Many sites that were occupied by indigenous groups at the time of the conquest were razed, and in their place appeared Catholic churches, public buildings, and palaces for conquerors and the king's bureaucrats. In the Yucatán, existing churches at Izamal, Calkani, Santa Elena, and Muná rest atop former pyramidal structures. Indian artisans, who formerly worked on pyramidal structures, were recruited to give life to the new buildings, often guided by drawings of European buildings. Frequently left on their own, the indigenous artisans sometimes implanted traditional symbolism in the new buildings: a plaster angel swaddled in feathers, reminiscent of the god Quetzalcoatl; or the face of an ancient god surrounded by corn leaves. They used pre-Hispanic calendar counts—the 13 steps to heaven or the nine levels of the underworld—to determine how many florets to carve around the church doorway.

To convert the native populations, New World Spanish priests and architects altered their normal ways of teaching and building. Often before the church was built, an open-air atrium was first constructed so that large numbers of parishioners could be accommodated for services. *Posas* (shelters) at the four corners of church-yards were another architectural technique unique to Mexico, again for the purpose

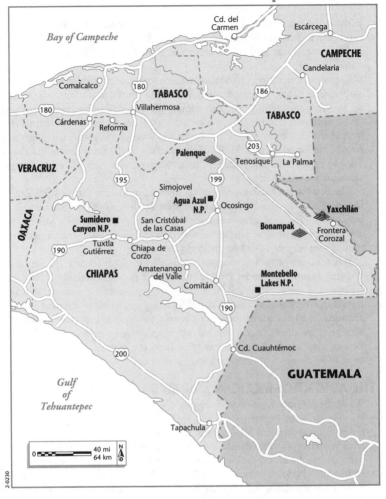

of accommodating crowds during holy sacraments. Because of the language barrier between the Spanish and the natives, church adornment became more explicit. Biblical tales came to life in frescoes splashed across church walls. Christian symbolism in stone supplanted that of pre-Hispanic ideas as the natives tried to make sense of it all. Baroque became even more baroque in Mexico and was dubbed *churrigueresque,* for the Spanish architect José Benito Churriguera (1665–1725) who originated the style. Exuberant and complicated, it combines Gothic, baroque, and plateresque elements.

Almost every village in the Yucatán Peninsula has the hulking remains of enormous fortress-like **missions, monasteries, convents,** and **parish churches.** Many were built in the 16th century following the early arrival of Franciscan friars (the Franciscans were for a long time the only order allowed into the Yucatán to Christianize the natives). Highlights include the Mission of San Bernardino de Sisal in Valladolid; the fine altarpiece at Teabo; the folk-art retablo at Calkani; the large church and convent at Mani with its unique retablos (altarpieces) and limestone crucifix; the facade, altar, and central retablo of the church at Oxkutzcab; the 16-bell belfry at Ytholin; the baroque facade and altarpiece at Maxcanu; the cathedral at Mérida; the vast atrium and church at Izamal; and the baroque retablo and murals at Tabi.

Concurrent with the building of religious structures, **public buildings** took shape, modeled after those in European capitals. Colorful locally made tile was used to decorate public walls and church domes. The hacienda architecture sprang up in the countryside, resulting in massive, thick-walled, fortresslike structures built around a central patio. Remains of haciendas, some of them still operating, can be seen in almost all parts of Mexico and especially in the north-central part of the Yucatán Peninsula, where great henequen haciendas were built to process the spiny agave for a world market.

The **San Carlos Academy of Art** was founded in Mexico City in 1785. Though the emphasis was on a Europeanized Mexico, by the end of the 19th century, the subject matter of easel artists was becoming Mexican: Still lifes with Mexican fruit and pottery and Mexican landscapes with cacti and volcanoes appeared, as did portraits whose subjects wore Mexican regional clothing.

When Porfirio Díaz became president in the late 19th century, the nation's art and architecture experienced another infusion of European sensibility. Díaz idolized Europe, and during this time he lavished on the country a number of striking European-style public buildings, including many opera houses still used today. He provided European scholarships to promising young artists who later returned to Mexico to produce Mexican subject paintings using techniques learned abroad. Because the Yucatán Peninsula was so far from the heart of Mexico, it developed more of an affinity with European and Cuban cultures than it did with Mexico.

THE ADVENT OF MEXICAN MURALISM

While the Mexican Revolution, following the resignation and exile of Díaz, ripped the country apart between 1911 and 1917, the result was the birth of a Mexico claimed and appreciated by Mexicans. In 1923 Minister of Education José Vasconcelos was charged with educating the illiterate masses. As one means of reaching many people, he started the muralist movement when he invited **Diego Rivera** and several other budding artists to paint Mexican history on the walls of the Ministry of Education building and the National Preparatory School in Mexico City. From then on, the "big three" muralists—**David Siquieros, José Clemente Orozco,** and Rivera—as well as others depicted Mexico's history on the walls of public buildings throughout the country for all to see and interpret. The years that followed eventually brought about a return to easel art, an exploration of Mexico's culture, and a new generation of artists and architects who were free to invent and draw upon subjects and styles from around the world. The new **Museo de Arte Contemporáneo Atenco de Yucatán** (MACAY) in Mérida is one place to see regional artists and visiting exhibitions from Mexico and the world.

4 Religion, Myth & Folklore

Mexico is predominantly Roman Catholic, a religion introduced by the Spaniards during the Conquest of Mexico. Despite its preponderance, the Catholic faith in many places in Mexico (Chiapas and Oaxaca, for example) has pre-Hispanic overtones. One need only visit the *curandero* section of a Mexican market (where one can purchase copal—an incense agreeable to the gods; rustic beeswax candles, a traditional offering; the native species of tobacco used from the earliest times to ward off evil; etc.), or attend a village festivity featuring pre-Hispanic dancers, to understand that supernatural beliefs often run parallel to Christian ones.

PRE-HISPANIC MYTHOLOGY

Mexico's complicated mythological heritage from pre-Hispanic religion is full of images derived from nature—the wind, jaguars, eagles, snakes, flowers, and more— all intertwined with elaborate mythological stories to explain the universe, climate, seasons, and geography. Most groups believed in an underworld (not a hell), usually containing nine levels, and a heaven of 13 levels—which is why the numbers 9 and 13 are so mythologically significant. The solar calendar count of 365 days and the ceremonial calendar of 260 days are numerically significant. **How one died** determined one's resting place after death: in the underworld (*Xibalba* to the Maya), in heaven, or at one of the four cardinal points. For example, men who died in battle or women who died in childbirth went straight to the sun. Everyone else first had to make a journey through the underworld.

One of the richest sources of mythological tales is the *Book of Popol Vuh,* a Maya bible of sorts, recorded after the Conquest. The *Chilam Balam,* another such book, existed in hieroglyphic form at the Conquest and was recorded using the Spanish alphabet to transliterate Maya words that could be understood by the Spaniards. The *Chilam Balam* differs from the *Popol Vuh* in that it is the collected histories of many Maya communities.

GODS & GODESSES

Each of the ancient cultures had its set of gods and goddesses, and while the names might not have crossed cultures, their characteristics or purposes often did. Chaac, the hook-nosed rain god of the Maya, was Tlaloc, the squat rain god of the Aztecs; Quetzalcoatl, the plumed-serpent god/man of the Toltecs, became Kukulkán of the Maya. The tales of the powers and creation of these deities make up Mexico's rich mythology. Sorting out the pre-Hispanic pantheon and mythological beliefs in ancient Mexico can become an all-consuming study (the Maya alone had 166 deities), so below is a list of some of the most important gods:

Chaac: Maya rain god.

Ehécatl: Wind god whose temple is usually round; another aspect of Quetzalcoatl.

Itzamná: Maya god above all, who invented corn, cacao, and writing and reading.

Ixchel: Maya goddess of water, weaving, and childbirth.

Kinich Ahau: Maya sun god.

Kukulkán: Quetzalcoatl's name in the Yucatán.

Ometeotl: God/goddess, all-powerful creator of the universe, ruler of heaven, earth, and the underworld.

Quetzalcoatl: A mortal who took on legendary characteristics as a god (or vice versa). When he left Tula in shame after a night of succumbing to temptations, he promised to return. He reappeared in the Yucatán. He is also symbolized as Venus, the moving star, and Ehécatl, the wind god. Quetzalcoatl is credited with giving the Maya cacao (chocolate) and teaching them how to grow it, harvest it, roast it, and turn it into a drink with ceremonial and magical properties.

Tlaloc: Aztec rain god.

5 Food & Drink

Authentic Mexican food differs quite dramatically from versions and derivatives of it served in the U.S. For many travelers, then, Mexico will be new and exciting culinary territory. Even grizzled veterans will find much that is new to them when they visit different parts of the country because each region as its own specialties. The differences from mainstream Mexican cooking in the Yucatán, Tabasco, and Chiapas are even more pronounced than in other regions.

Some general rules apply. Mexican food usually isn't pepper-hot when it arrives at the table (though many dishes must have a certain amount of piquancy, and some home cooking can be very spicy, depending on a family's or chef's tastes). Generally, the picante flavor is added with chiles and sauces after the food is served; you'll never see a table in Mexico without one or both of these condiments. Mexicans don't drown their cooking in cheese and sour cream, à la Tex-Mex, and they use a greater variety of ingredients than most people believe. But the basis of Mexican food is simple—tortillas, beans, chiles, squash and tomatoes—the same as it was centuries ago, before the arrival of the Europeans.

THE BASICS

TORTILLAS Traditional tortillas are made from corn that's been soaked and cooked in water and lime, then ground into *masa* (a grainy dough), patted and pressed into thin cakes and cooked on a hot griddle known as a *comal*. In many households the tortilla takes the place of fork and spoon; Mexicans merely tear them into wedge-shaped pieces, which they use to scoop up their food. Restaurants often serve bread rather than tortillas because it's easier, but you can always ask for tortillas. A more recent invention from northern Mexico is the flour tortilla, which is seen less frequently in the rest of Mexico.

ENCHILADAS The tortilla is the basis of several Mexican dishes, but the most famous of these is the enchilada. The original name for this dish would have been tortilla enchilada, which simply means a tortilla dipped in a chile sauce. In like manner, there's the *entomatada* (tortilla dipped in a tomato sauce) and the *enfrijolada* (in a bean sauce). The enchilada began as a very simple dish. A tortilla is dipped in chile sauce (usually with ancho chile) and then into very hot oil, then quickly folded or rolled on a plate and sprinkled with chopped onions and a little *queso cotija* (crumbly white cheese). You can get this basic enchilada in food stands across the country. I love them, and if you come across them in your travels, give them a try. In restaurants you get the more elaborate enchilada, with different fillings of cheese, chicken, or pork, or even seafood, and sometimes prepared as a casserole. These are often a restaurant's best dish.

TACOS—Another food based on the tortilla is the famous taco. A taco is anything folded or rolled into a tortilla, and sometimes a double tortilla. The tortilla can be served either soft or fried. *Flautas* and *quesadillas* (except in Mexico City where they are something quite different) are species of tacos. For Mexicans, the taco is the quintessential fast food, and the taco stand (*taquería*)—a ubiquitous sight—is a great place to get a cheap, good, and filling meal. See the section below, "Eating Out—Restaurants, *Taquerías* & Tipping," for information on *taquerías*.

FRIJOLES An invisible "bean line" divides Mexico: It starts at the Gulf Coast in the southern part of the state of Tamaulipas and moves inland through the eastern quarter of San Luis Potosí and most of the state of Hidalgo, then straight through

Mexico City and Morelos and into Guerrero, where it curves slightly westward to the Pacific. To the north and west of this line the pink bean known as the *flor de mayo* is the staple food; to the south and east the standard is the black bean. The Yucatán, Chiapas, and Tabasco of course adhere to the black bean standard. (Curiously enough, this line also roughly determines whether a taco will come with one or two tortillas; to the north and west you get two tortillas, to the south and east, only one.)

In private households, beans are served at least once a day, and among the working class and peasantry with every meal if the family can afford it. Mexicans almost always prepare beans with a minimum of condiments, usually just a little onion and garlic and perhaps a pinch of herbs. They want their beans to serve as a quiet contrast to the other heavily spiced foods in a meal. Sometimes they are served at the end of a meal with a little Mexican-style sour cream.

Mexicans often fry leftover beans and serve them on the side as *frijoles refritos*. "Refritos" is usually translated as refried, but this is a misnomer—the beans are fried only once. The prefix "re" actually means well, and what Mexicans mean is well-fried.

TAMALES   You make a tamal by mixing corn masa with a little lard, adding one of several fillings—meats flavored with chiles (or no filling at all)—then wrapping it in a corn shuck or banana leaf and steaming it. Every region in Mexico has its own traditional way of making tamales. In some places a single tamal can be big enough to feed a family, while in others they are only 3 inches long and an inch thick.

CHILES   There are many kinds of chiles, and Mexicans call each of them by one name when they're fresh and another when they're dried. Some are blazing hot with only a mild flavor; some are mild but have a rich, complex flavor. They can be pickled, smoked, stuffed, stewed, chopped, and used in an endless variety of dishes.

FOR CARNIVORES & VEGETARIANS

MEAT   The most common meats used in Mexican cooking are chicken, pork, and turkey (except in northern Mexico, where they have always had large cattle ranches). Traditional dishes such as chiles rellenos, tamales, and enchiladas rarely have beef in them. It used to be that you could get only tough and stringy beef—usually made palatable by cutting it very thin and tenderizing it heavily—but in the last several years, the quality of beef has improved. Cattle raising has become a big business in the Yucatán and in parts of Chiapas, Tabasco, and Veracruz. Mexican ranchers have developed good beef cattle well-adapted to the tropical climate. Beef is becoming increasingly popular in restaurants, and the quality has improved so much that some Americans insist that it is better than what they get at steak houses in the U.S. The filet mignon is a good bet (and a good buy) in Mexico, but the most popular cut of meat is *arrachera*, which is actually skirt steak—a very tough cut of meat known as the *faja*, which is used to make fajitas in the American Southwest. But unlike gringo fajitas, arrachera isn't marinated or tenderized, and it's usually served by itself with no fixings. Ten years ago you never saw this on a menu; now you see it everywhere. Many Mexicans believe it to have more taste than filet (an assertion I don't find to be true), and some have told me that it is leaner and better for the circulatory system. Regardless, in a land of such rich and varied cooking, it is bound to disappoint the traveler.

VEGGIES   It is not at all hard for vegetarians to eat well in Mexico. First of all, there are vegetarian restaurants in every city and large town, as well as health food stores (*tiendas naturistas*) and juice bars specializing in blended fruit drinks. Mexican cooking has many vegetarian dishes, including different kinds of enchiladas, tacos, chiles rellenos, and crêpes using ingredients like cheese, chiles, squash, mushrooms, and huitlacoche or corn fungus.

Yucatecan cooking is the most distinct of the many kinds of regional cooking, probably because it was influenced by the Maya and Caribbean cultural traditions. Yucatecans are great fans of achiote (or annatto, a red seed pod from a tree that grows in the Caribbean area), which is the basic ingredient for perhaps its most famous dish, *cochinita pibil* (pork wrapped in banana leaves, pit-baked, and served with a pibil sauce of achiote, sour orange, and spices). And good seafood is readily available. Many of the most common Mexican dishes are given a different twist here and may be known by a completely different name. But waiters are happy to explain what's what, and with a couple of meals under your belt, you'll feel like a native.

MEALS

MORNING   The morning meal, known as *el desayuno,* can be something very light, such as coffee and sweet bread, or something more substantial: eggs cooked in a Mexican fashion, beans, tortillas, bread, fruit, and juice. It can be eaten early or late and is always a sure bet in Mexico. The variety and sweetness of the fruits is remarkable, and you can't go wrong with Mexican egg dishes.

MIDAFTERNOON   The main meal of the day, known as *la comida,* is eaten between 2 and 4pm. Stores and businesses close, and most people will go home to eat and perhaps take a short afternoon siesta before going about their business. The first course is the *sopa*, which can be either soup (*caldo*) or rice (*sopa de arroz*) or both; then comes the main course, which ideally would be a meat or fish dish prepared in some kind of sauce and probably served with beans, followed by dessert.

EVENING   Between 8 and 10pm, most Mexicans will have a light meal called *la cena.* If eaten at home, it will be something like a sandwich or bread and jam or perhaps a couple of tacos made from some of the day's leftovers. At restaurants, the most common thing to eat is *antojitos* (literally, "little cravings"), a general label for light fare. Antojitos include tostadas, tamales, tacos, and simple enchiladas, and are big hits with travelers. Large restaurants will offer complete meals as well. In the Yucatán, antojitos include *papadzules* (a species of enchilada filled with hard-boiled egg), *sincronizadas* (small tostadas), and *panuchos* (fried tortillas filled with bean paste and topped with cochinita pibil and marinated onions).

EATING OUT—RESTAURANTS, *TAQUERÍAS* & TIPPING

First of all, I feel compelled to debunk the prevailing myth that the cheapest place to eat in Mexico is in the market. Actually, this is almost never the case. You can usually find better food at a better price without going more than 2 blocks out of your way. Why? Food stalls in the marketplace pay high rents; they have a near-captive clientele of market vendors and truckers; and they get a lot of business from many Mexicans for whom eating in the market is a traditional way of confirming their culture.

On the other side of the spectrum, avoid eating at those inviting sidewalk restaurants that you see beneath the stone archways that border the main plazas. These places usually cater to tourists and don't need to count on getting any return business. But they are great for getting a coffee or beer and watching the world turn.

In most nonresort towns, there are always one or two restaurants (sometimes it's a coffee shop) that are social centers for a large group of established patrons. These establishments over time become virtual institutions, and change comes very slowly to them. The food is usually good standard fare, cooked as it was 20 years ago; the decor is simple. The patrons have known each other and the staff for years, and the *charla* (banter), gestures, and greetings are friendly, open, and unaffected. If you're curious about Mexican culture, these places are great fun to eat in and observe the goings-on.

In your trip you're going to see many **taco joints** (*taquerías*). These are generally small places with a counter or a few tables set around the cooking area; you get to see exactly how they make their tacos before deciding whether to order. Most tacos come with a little chopped onion and cilantro, but not with tomato and lettuce. Find one that seems popular with the locals and where the cook performs with brio (a good sign of pride in the product). Sometimes there will be a woman making the tortillas right there (or working the masa into *gorditas, sopes,* or *panuchos* if these are also served). You will never see men doing this—this is perhaps the strictest gender division in Mexican society. Men do all other cooking and kitchen tasks, and work with already-made tortillas, but will never be found working masa.

For the main meal of the day, many restaurants offer a multicourse blue-plate special called *comida corrida* or *menu del día.* This is the most inexpensive way to get a full dinner. In Mexico, you need to ask for your check; if you're in a hurry to get somewhere, ask for the check when your food arrives; otherwise it can be slow in coming.

Tips are about the same as in the U.S. You'll find a 15% **value-added tax** on restaurant meals, which shows up on the bill as "IVA." This is a boon to arithmetic-challenged tippers, saving them from undue exertion.

To summon the waiter, wave or raise your hand, but don't motion with your index finger, which is a demeaning gesture that may even cause the waiter to ignore you. Or if it's the check you want, you can motion to the waiter from across the room using the universal pretend-like-you're-writing gesture.

Most restaurants do not have **nonsmoking sections;** when they do, we mention it in the reviews. But Mexico's wonderful climate makes for many open-air restaurants, usually set inside a courtyard of a colonial house, or in rooms with tall ceilings and plenty of open windows.

DRINKS

All over Mexico you'll find shops selling **juices** and **smoothies** from several kinds of tropical fruit. They're excellent and refreshing; while traveling I take full advantage of them. You'll also come across *aguas frescas*—water flavored with hibiscus, melon, tamarind, or lime. Soft drinks come in more flavors than in any other country I know. Pepsi and Coca-Cola taste the way they did in the U.S. years ago, before the makers started adding corn syrup. The coffee is generally good, and **hot chocolate** is a traditional drink, as is *atole*—a hot, corn-based beverage that can be sweet or bitter.

Of course, Mexico has a proud and lucrative **beer** brewing tradition. A less-known brewed beverage is pulque, a pre-Hispanic drink: the fermented juice of a few species of maguey or agave. Mostly you find it for sale in *pulquerías* in central Mexico. It is an acquired taste, and not every gringo acquires it. **Mezcal** and **tequila** also come from the agave. Tequila is a variety of mezcal produced from the *a. tequilana* species of agave in and around the area of Tequila, in the state of Jalisco. Mezcal comes from various parts of Mexico and from different varieties of agave. The distilling process is usually much less sophisticated than that of tequila, and, with its stronger smell and taste, mezcal is much more easily detected on the drinker's breath. In some places like Oaxaca it comes with a worm in the bottle; you are supposed to eat the worm after polishing off the mezcal. But for those teetotalers out there who are interested in just the worm, I have good news—you can find these worms for sale in Mexican markets when in season. *¡Salud!*

6 Recommended Books & Recordings

BOOKS
HISTORY

By the time Cortés arrived in Mexico, the indigenous people were already masters of literature, recording their poems and histories by painting in fanfold books (*códices*) made of deerskin and bark paper or by carving on stone. To record history, gifted students were taught the art of bookmaking, drawing, painting, reading, and writing—abilities the general public didn't possess. A contemporary book that tells the story of the Indians' "painted books" is *The Mexican Codices and Their Extraordinary History* (Ediciones Lara, 1985), by María Sten.

The ancient Maya produced two important epic works, the *Book of Popol Vuh* and the *Chilam Balam*. Dennis Tedlock produced the most authoritative translation of the *Popul Vuh* (Simon & Schuster, 1985). Anthropologist Michael D. Coe said, "The *Popul Vuh* is generally considered to be the greatest single work of Native American literature." Unfortunately, other than the *Popul Vuh* and the *Chilam Balam*, there are only four surviving códices (or portions of them) because, after the Conquest, the Spaniards deliberately destroyed native books. However, several Catholic priests, among them Bernardo de Sahugun and Diego de Landa (who was one of the book destroyers), encouraged the Indians to record their customs and history. These records are among the best documentation of life before the Conquest.

During the Conquest, Cortés wrote his now-famous five letters to King Charles V, which gave us the first printed Conquest literature, but the most important record is that of Bernal Díaz de Castillo. Enraged by an inaccurate account of the Conquest written by a flattering friend of Cortés, 40 years after the conquest, Bernal Díaz de Castillo, one of the conquerors, wrote his lively and very readable version of the event, *True History of the Conquest of Mexico;* it's regarded as the most accurate.

In an attempt to defend himself for burning 27 Maya hieroglyphic rolls in 1562, Friar Diego de Landa collected contemporary Maya customs, beliefs, and history and wrote *Relación de las Cosas de Yucatán* (today entitled *Yucatán Before and After the Conquest*, Dover Press, 1978). It was first published in 1566 and remains the most significant record of its kind.

A Short History of Mexico (Doubleday, 1962), by J. Patrick McHenry, is a concise historical account. A remarkably readable and thorough college textbook is *The Course of Mexican History* (Oxford University Press, 1995), by Michael C. Meyer and William L. Sherman. *Sons of the Shaking Earth* (University of Chicago Press, 1959), by Eric Wolf, is an excellent introduction to Mexican history and culture. *Ancient Mexico: An Overview* (University of New Mexico Press, 1985), by Jaime Litvak, is a short, very readable history of pre-Hispanic Mexico. *The Hummingbird and the Hawk* (Columbus, 1967), by R. C. Padden is a well-written account of the Conquest of Mexico.

The Wind That Swept Mexico (University of Texas Press, 1971), by Anita Brenner, is a classic illustrated account of the Mexican Revolution. *Barbarous Mexico*, by

John Kenneth Turner (University of Texas Press, 1984), was written in the early 1900s as a shocking exposé of the atrocities of the Porfirio Díaz presidency, which included enslaving Yaqui Indians from Sonora in camps in the Yucatán and Oaxaca. *The Lost World of Quintana Roo,* by Michel Peissel (E.P. Dutton, 1963), is the thrilling account of a young man's journey on foot in search of undiscovered ruins along the Yucatán's almost uninhabited Caribbean coast in the late 1950s.

Passionate Pilgrim, by Antoinette May (Paragon House, 1993), is the fascinating biography of Alma Reed, an American journalist and amateur archaeologist whose life spanned the exciting 1920s to 1960s. Her journalistic assignments included early archaeological digs at Chichén-Itzá, Uxmal, and Palenque; breaking the story to *The New York Times* of archaeologist Edward Thompson's role in removing the contents of the sacred cenote at Chichén-Itzá to the Peabody Museum at Harvard; and serving as a columnist for the *Mexico City News.* She also had a love affair with Felipe Carrillo Puerto, the governor of Yucatán, who commissioned the famous Mexican song, "La Peregrina" in her honor. She later championed the career of Mexican muralist José Clemente Orozco at her art gallery in New York.

CULTURE

Mexican and Central American Mythology (Peter Bedrick Books, 1983), by Irene Nicholson, is a concise illustrated book that simplifies the subject.

Though not focused on life in the Yucatán or Chiapas and Tabasco—where thinking, culture, and customs developed apart from the rest of Mexico—several books, nevertheless, are good background reading on Mexico in general. A good, but controversial, all-around introduction to contemporary Mexico and its people is *Distant Neighbors: A Portrait of the Mexicans* (Random House, 1984), by Alan Riding. In a more personal vein is Patrick Oster's *The Mexicans: A Personal Portrait of the Mexican People* (Harper & Row, 1989), a reporter's insightful account of ordinary Mexican people. A novel with valuable insights into the Mexican character is *The Labyrinth of Solitude* (Grove Press, 1985), by Octavio Paz.

Anyone going to San Cristóbal de las Casas should first read *Living Maya* (Harry N. Abrams, 1987), by Walter F. Morris, with excellent photographs by Jeffrey J. Foxx. The book is all about the Maya living today in the state of Chiapas. Peter Canby's *Heart of the Sky: Travels Among the Maya* (Kodansha International, 1994) takes readers on a rare and rugged journey as he seeks to understand the real issues facing the Maya of Mexico and Guatemala today.

The best single source of information on Mexican music, dance, and mythology is Frances Toor's *A Treasury of Mexican Folkways* (Crown, 1967).

ART, ARCHAEOLOGY & ARCHITECTURE

Travelers heading for the Yucatán should consider reading amateur archaeologist John L. Stephens's wonderfully entertaining accounts of travel in that region in the 19th century. His book, *Incidents of Travel in Central America, Chiapas and Yucatán,* and also his account of his second trip, *Incidents of Travel in Yucatán,* have been reprinted by Dover Publications. The series also includes Friar Diego de Landa's *Yucatán Before and After the Conquest.*

The Maya (Thames and Hudson, 1993), by Michael D. Coe, is extremely helpful in relating to the different Maya periods. *A Forest of Kings: The Untold Story of the Ancient Maya* (William Morrow, 1990), by Linda Schele and David Freidel, uses the written history of Maya hieroglyphs to tell the incredible dynastic history of selected Maya sites. You'll never view the sky the same way after reading *Maya Cosmos: Three Thousand Years on the Shaman's Path* (William Morrow, 1993) by

David Freidel, Linda Schele, and Joy Parker, whose personal insights and scholarly work take us along a very readable path into the amazing sky-centered world of the Maya. *The Blood of Kings: Dynasty and Ritual in Maya Art* (George Braziller, Inc., 1986), by Linda Schele and Mary Ellen Miller, is a pioneer work that unlocks the bloody history of the Maya.

In *Breaking the Maya Code* (Thames & Hudson, 1992) readers follow Michael D. Coe on the fascinating, circuitous 100-year journey through reading the mysterious written texts left by the Maya in partially remaining books, pottery, murals, and carved in stone. Another must-read, and a real page-turner, it's a modern-day mystery complete with a cast of real-life characters. *Maya History*, by Tatiana Proskouriakoff (University of Texas Press, 1993), is the last work of one of the most revered Maya scholars. Linda Schele, a contemporary Maya scholar, calls Proskouriakoff "the person who was to our field as Darwin was to biology." Her contributions included numerous drawings of now-ruined Maya temples and glyphs, of which there are over 300 in this book.

Try a used bookstore for *Digging in Mexico*, by Ann Axtell Morris (Doubleday, Doran, 1931). The book is as interesting for its photographs of Chichén-Itzá before and during the excavations as it is for the author's lively and revealing anecdotes. Morris was a young writer and the artist wife of Earl Morris, director of excavations at Chichén-Itzá during the Carnegie Institution's work there in the 1920s.

In *Maya Missions*, authors Richard and Rosalind Perry (Espadana Press, 1988) reveal the mysteries of the Yucatán Peninsula's many centuries-old colonial-era missions with inviting detail. *An Archaeological Guide to Mexico's Yucatán Peninsula,* by Joyce Kelly (University of Oklahoma, 1993), is a companion to *Maya Missions* that covers the other side of the peninsula's architecture; it is the most comprehensive guide to Maya ruins. Carrying these two books with you will enrich your visit many times over.

Mexico: Splendors of Thirty Centuries (Metropolitan Museum of Art, 1990), the catalog of the 1991 traveling exhibition, is a wonderful resource on Mexico's art from 1500 B.C. through the 1950s. Another superb catalog, *Images of Mexico: The Contribution of Mexico to 20th Century Art* (Dallas Museum of Art, 1987), is a fabulously illustrated and detailed account of Mexican art gathered from collections around the world. *Art and Time in Mexico: From the Conquest to the Revolution* (Harper & Row, 1985), by Elizabeth Wilder Weismann, illustrated with 351 photographs, covers Mexican religious, public, and private architecture with excellent photos and text. *Casa Mexicana* (Stewart, Tabori & Chang, 1989), by Tim Street-Porter, takes readers through the interiors of some of Mexico's finest homes-turned-museums, public buildings, and private homes. *Mexican Interiors* (Architectural Book Publishing Co., 1962), by Verna Cook Shipway and Warren Shipway, uses black-and-white photographs to highlight architectural details from homes all over Mexico.

FOLK ART

Chloë Sayer's *Costumes of Mexico* (University of Texas Press, 1985) is a beautifully illustrated and written work. *Mexican Masks* (University of Texas Press, 1980), by Donald Cordry, based on the author's collection and travels, remains the definitive work on the subject. *Cordry's Mexican Indian Costumes* (University of Texas Press, 1968) is another classic. Carlos Espejel wrote both *Mexican Folk Ceramics* and *Mexican Folk Crafts* (Editorial Blume, 1975 and 1978), two comprehensive books that explore crafts state by state. *Folk Treasures of Mexico* (Harry N. Abrams, 1990), by Marion Oettinger, curator of folk art and Latin American art at the San Antonio

Museum of Art, is the fascinating illustrated story behind the 3,000-piece Mexican folk-art collection amassed by Nelson Rockefeller over a 50-year period, as well as much information about individual folk artists.

NATURE

A Naturalist's Mexico (Texas A&M University Press, 1992), by Roland H. Wauer, is a fabulous guide to birding in Mexico. *A Hiker's Guide to Mexico's Natural History* (Mountaineers, 1995), by Jim Conrad, covers Mexican flora and fauna and tells how to find the easy-to-reach as well as out-of-the-way spots he describes. *Peterson Field Guides: Mexican Birds* (Houghton-Mifflin, 1973), by Roger Tory Peterson and Edward L. Chalif, is an excellent guide to the country's birds. *Birds of the Yucatán* (*Amigos de Sian Ka'an*) by Barbara MacKinnon has color illustrations and descriptions of 100 birds found primarily in the Yucatán Peninsula. *A Guide to Mexican Mammals and Reptiles* (Minutiae Mexicana), by Normal Pelham Wright and Dr. Bernardo Villa Ramírez, is a small but useful guide to some of the country's wildlife.

RECORDINGS

Mexicans take their music very seriously. Notice the tapes for sale almost everywhere, ceaseless music in the streets, and the bus drivers with collections of tapes to entertain passengers. For the collector, choices range from contemporary rock to revolutionary ballads, ranchero, salsa, and romantic trios.

Marimba music is heard often in the Yucatán as well as in Tabasco and Chiapas. Peña Ríos makes excellent marimba recordings. Though marimba musicians seldom ask for requests, some typical renditions would include "Huapango de Moncayo" and "El Bolero de Ravel."

Mariachi music is played and sold all over Mexico. Among the top recording artists is Mariachi Vargas. No mariachi performance is complete without "Guadalajara," "Las Mañanitas," and "Jarabe Tapatió."

Other music from the Yucatán includes the recordings by the Trio Los Soberanos and Dueto Yucalpetén. Typical Yucatecan songs are "Las Golondrinas Yucatecas," "Peregrina," "Ella," "El Pájaro Azul," and "Ojos Tristes." Heartthrob soloists from years past include Pedro Vargas, Pedro Infante, Hector Cabrera, Lucho Gatica, Pepe Jara, and Alberto Vázquez.

For trio music from elsewhere, some of the best are by Los Tres Diamantes and Los Tres Reyes. If you're requesting songs of a trio, good ones to ask for are "Sin Ti," "Usted," "Amor de la Calle," and "Cielito Lindo." Traditional ranchero songs to request, which can be sung by soloists or trios, are "Tú Solo Tú," "No Volveré," and "Adios Mi Chaparita."

3

Planning a Trip to the Yucatán

A little advance planning can make the difference between a good trip and a great trip. When should you go? What's the best way to get there? How much should you plan on spending? What festivals or special events will be taking place during your visit? We'll answer these and other questions for you in this chapter.

1 Visitor Information, Entry Requirements & Money

SOURCES OF INFORMATION

The **Mexico Hotline** (☎ 800/44-MEXICO) is a good source for very general informational brochures on the country and for answers to the most commonly asked questions. If you have a fax, Mexico's Ministry of Tourism also offers **FaxMeMexico** (☎ 541/385-9282). Call, give them your fax number, and select from a variety of topics from accommodations (the service lists 400 hotels) to shopping, dining, sports, sightseeing, festivals, and nightlife. They'll then fax you the materials you're interested in.

More information (15,000 pages worth, they say) about Mexico is available on the Mexico Ministry of Tourism's Web site: **www.mexico-travel.com**.

The **U.S. State Department** (☎ 202/647-5225 for travel information and Overseas Citizens Services) offers a **Consular Information Sheet** on Mexico, with a compilation of safety, medical, driving, and general travel information gleaned from reports by official U.S. State Department offices in Mexico. You can also request the Consular Information Sheet (☎ 202/647-2000) by fax. The State Department is also on the Internet; check out **www.travel.state.gov/mexico.html** for the Consular Information Sheet on Mexico; **www.travel.state.gov/travel_warnings.html** for other Consular Information Sheets and travel warnings; and **www.travel.state.gov/tips_mexico.html** for the State Department's "Tips for Travelers to Mexico."

The **Centers for Disease Control hot line** (☎ 404/332-4559), is another source for medical information affecting travelers to Mexico and elsewhere. The center's Web site, **www.cdc.gov/**, provides lengthy information on health issues for specific countries.

MEXICAN GOVERNMENT TOURIST OFFICES Mexico's foreign tourist offices (**MGTO**) throughout the world—with the exception of those in the United States and Canada—were closed effective January 1997. Those operating in North America include the following:

United States: Chicago, IL (☎ 312/606-9252); Houston, TX (☎ 713/629-1611); Los Angeles, CA (☎ 310/203-8191); Miami, FL (☎ 305/443-9160); New York, NY (☎ 212/421-6655); and the Mexican Embassy Tourism Delegate, 1911 Pennsylvania Ave., Washington, DC 20005 (☎ 202/728-1750). At publication time, the MGTO offices were being combined with Mexican Consulate offices in the same cities, but this was still up for confirmation. The telephone numbers should still be operational, but if not, check with your nearest Mexican Consulate.

Canada: 1 Place Ville-Marie, Suite 1526, Montréal, PQ H3B 2B5 (☎ 514/871-1052); 2 Bloor St. W., Suite 1801, Toronto, ON M4W 3E2 (☎ 416/925-2753); 999 W. Hastings, Suite 1610, Vancouver, BC V6C 2W2 (☎ 604/669-2845).

STATE TOURISM DEVELOPMENT OFFICES   Two Mexican states have tourism and trade development offices in the United States: Guerrero State Convention and Visitors Bureau, 5075 Westheimer, Suite 980 West, Houston, TX 77056 (☎ 713/339-1880; fax 713/339-1615); and Casa Nuevo León State Promotion Office, 100 W. Houston St., Suite 1400, San Antonio, TX 78205 (☎ 210/225-0732; fax 210/225-0736).

OTHER SOURCES   The following newsletters may be of interest to readers: *Mexican Meanderings,* P.O. Box 33057, Austin, TX 78764, aimed at readers who travel to off-the-beaten-track destinations by car, bus, or train (six to eight pages, published six times annually, subscription $18); *Travel Mexico,* Apdo. Postal 6-1007, 06600 Mexico, D.F., from the publishers of the *Traveler's Guide to Mexico*—the book frequently found in hotel rooms in Mexico—covers a variety of topics from archaeology news to hotel packages, new resorts and hotels, and the economy (six times annually, subscription $18).

For other newsletters, see "For Seniors" under "Tips for Travelers with Special Needs," below.

ENTRY REQUIREMENTS

DOCUMENTS   All travelers to Mexico are required to present **proof of citizenship,** such as an original birth certificate with a raised seal, a valid passport, state-issued driver's license or official ID, or naturalization papers. Those using a birth certificate should also have a current photo identification such as a driver's license. Those whose last name on the birth certificate is different from their current name (women using a married name, for example) should also bring a photo identification card *and* legal proof of the name change such as the *original* marriage license or certificate. This proof of citizenship may also be requested when you want to reenter either the United States or Mexico. Note that photocopies are *not* acceptable.

You must also carry a **Mexican Tourist Permit,** which is issued free of charge by Mexican border officials after proof of citizenship is accepted. The tourist permit is more important than a passport in Mexico, so guard it carefully. If you lose it, you may not be permitted to leave the country until you can replace it—a bureaucratic hassle that takes several days to a week at least. (If you do lose your tourist permit, get a police report from local authorities indicating that your documents were stolen; having one *might* lessen the hassle of exiting the country without all your identification.)

A tourist permit can be issued for up to 180 days, and although your stay south of the border may be shorter than that, you should ask for the maximum time, just in case. Sometimes officials don't ask—they just stamp a time limit, so be sure to say "6 months" (or at least twice as long as you intend to stay). If you should decide to extend your stay, you won't have to go through the hassle of renewing your papers.

Note that children under age 18 traveling without parents or with only one parent must have a notarized letter from the absent parent or parents authorizing the travel.

Lost Documents   To replace a **lost passport,** contact your embassy or nearest consular agent (see "Fast Facts: Mexico," below). You must establish a record of your citizenship and also fill out a form requesting another Mexican Tourist Permit (assuming it, too, was lost). Without the **tourist permit,** you can't leave the country, and without an affidavit affirming your passport request and citizenship, you may have problems at Customs when you get home. So it's important to clear everything up *before* trying to leave. Mexican Customs may, however, accept the police report of the loss of the Tourist Permit and allow you to leave.

CUSTOMS ALLOWANCES   When you enter Mexico, customs officials will be tolerant as long as you have no illegal drugs or firearms. You're allowed to bring in two cartons of cigarettes, or 50 cigars, plus a kilogram (2.2 pounds) of smoking tobacco; the liquor allowance is two 1-liter bottles of anything, wine or hard liquor; you are also allowed 12 rolls of film. A laptop computer, camera equipment, and sporting equipment (golf clubs, scuba gear, a bicycle) that could feasibly be used during your stay are also allowed. The underlying guideline is that they will disallow anything that appears as if you will be attempting to resell it in Mexico.

When you reenter the **United States,** federal law allows you to bring in up to $400 in purchases duty free every 30 days. The first $1,000 over the $400 allowance is taxed at 10%. You may bring in a carton (200) of cigarettes or 50 cigars or 2 kilograms (4.4 pounds) of smoking tobacco, plus 1 liter of an alcoholic beverage (wine, beer, or spirits).

Canadian citizens are allowed $20 in purchases after a 24-hour absence from the country or $100 after a stay of 48 hours or more.

British travelers returning from outside the EU are allowed to bring in £145 worth of goods, in addition to the following: up to 200 cigarettes, 50 cigars or 250 grams of tobacco; 2 liters of wine; 1 liter of liqueur greater than 22% alcohol by volume; and 60cc/ml of perfume. If any item worth more than the limit of £145 is brought in, payment must be made on the full value, not just on the amount above £145.

Citizens of New Zealand are allowed to return with a combined value of up to NZ$700 in goods, duty free.

Going Through Customs   Mexican Customs inspection has been streamlined. At most points of entry, tourists are requested to punch a button in front of what looks like a traffic signal, which alternates on touch between red and green signals. Green light and you go through without inspection; red light and your luggage or car may be inspected briefly or thoroughly. If you have an unusual amount of luggage or an oversized piece, you may be subject to inspection despite the traffic signal routine.

MONEY
CASH/CURRENCY   The currency in Mexico is the Mexican **peso.** Paper currency comes in denominations of 10, 20, 50, 100, 200, and 500 pesos. Coins come in denominations of 1, 2, 5, and 10 pesos and 20 and 50 **centavos** (100 centavos equal 1 peso). The current exchange rate for the U.S. dollar is around 8 pesos; at that rate, an item that costs 10 pesos would be equivalent to $1.25 U.S.

Centavos will appear on restaurant bills and credit cards, but are paid differently depending on whether you pay in cash or by credit card. On restaurant bills that you pay in cash, for example, centavos will be rounded up or down to the nearest 5 centavos. Credit-card bills, however, will show the exact amount (not rounded), and will be billed in pesos, then later converted into dollars by the bank issuing the credit card. Generally you receive the favorable bank rate when paying by credit card.

Getting **change** continues to be a problem in Mexico. Small-denomination bills and coins are hard to come by, so start collecting them early in your trip and continue as you travel. Shopkeepers everywhere seem always to be out of change and small bills; that's doubly true in a market.

Note: The **universal currency sign ($)** is used to indicate pesos in Mexico. The use of this symbol in this book, however, denotes U.S. currency.

Many establishments dealing with tourists, especially in coastal resort areas, quote prices in dollars. To avoid confusion, they use the abbreviations "Dlls." for dollars and "M.N." (*moneda nacional,* or national currency) for pesos. All dollar equivalencies in this book were assuming an exchange rate of 8 pesos per dollar.

Every effort has been made to provide the most accurate and up-to-date information in this guide, but price changes are inevitable. Hotel prices especially will most likely change by April 1999.

EXCHANGING MONEY   The rate of exchange fluctuates a tiny bit daily, so you probably are better off not exchanging too much of your currency at once. Don't forget, however, to have enough pesos to carry you over a weekend or Mexican holiday, when banks are closed. In general, avoid carrying the U.S. $100 bill, the bill most commonly counterfeited in Mexico, and therefore the most difficult to exchange, especially in smaller towns. Since small bills and coins in pesos are hard to come by in Mexico, the U.S. $1 bill is very useful for tipping.

The bottom line on exchanging money of all kinds: It pays to ask first and shop around. Banks pay the top rates. Exchange houses (*casas de cambio*) are generally more convenient than banks since they have more locations and longer hours; the rate of exchange may be the same as a bank or slightly lower. *Note:* Before leaving a bank or exchange-house window, always count your change in front of the teller before the next client steps up.

Large airports have currency-exchange counters that often stay open whenever flights are arriving or departing. Though convenient, these generally do not offer the most favorable rates.

A hotel's exchange desk almost always pays less favorable rates than banks.

BANKS & ATMS   Banks in Mexico are going through a rapid advancement in services. New hours tend to be from 9am until 5 or 6pm, with many open for at least a half-day on Saturdays, and some even offering limited hours on Sundays. The exchange of dollars, which used to be limited until noon, can now be accommodated anytime during business hours. Some, but not all, banks charge a service fee of about 1% to exchange traveler's checks. However, most purchases can be paid for directly with traveler's checks at the stated exchange rate of the establishment. Personal checks may be cashed, but not without weeks of delay—a bank will wait for your check to clear before giving you your money.

Travelers to Mexico can also access money from **automated teller machines (ATMs),** now available in most major cities and resort areas in Mexico. Universal bank cards (such as the Cirrus and PLUS systems) can be used, and this is a convenient way to withdraw money from your bank and avoid carrying too much with you at any time. A service fee generally is charged by your bank for each transaction. Most machines offer Spanish/English menus and dispense pesos. For Cirrus locations abroad, call ☎ **800/424-7787,** or check out MasterCard's Web site (www.mastercard.com). For PLUS usage abroad, visit Visa's Web site (www.visa.com).

TRAVELER'S CHECKS   Traveler's checks are readily accepted nearly everywhere, but they can be difficult to cash on a weekend or holiday or in an out-of-the-way place. Their best value is in replacement in case of theft. Frequently in Mexico, a bank or establishment will pay more for traveler's checks than for cash dollars.

CREDIT CARDS   You'll be able to charge most hotel, restaurant, and store purchases, as well as almost all airline tickets, on your credit card. You can get cash advances of several hundred dollars on your card, but there may be a wait of 20 minutes to 2 hours. You can't charge gasoline purchases in Mexico. Visa ("Bancomer" in Mexico), MasterCard ("Carnet" in Mexico), and American Express are the most accepted cards.

CRIME, BRIBES & SCAMS

The areas covered by this book are not prone to extensive bribes, scams, robberies or other malevolent crimes. However, you may encounter difficulties: with Customs officials at the Mérida airport, Mérida taxi drivers, and police officers on the outskirts of Mérida; along the lonely highway from Villahermosa through Escarcega to Xpuhil; with traffic police in Chetumal; as well as the occasional car contents thief in Cancún. Generally speaking, there's no need to be overly guarded as you travel in the Yucatán. More than likely, anything lost will be returned to you. A good rule of thumb is that you can generally trust people whom you approach for help or directions, but you should be wary of anyone who approaches you offering the same. The more insistent someone is, the more cautious you should be.

If you find yourself hit up for a **bribe**—called *mordidas* (bites), sometimes masquerading as a tip (*propina*)—here's how to deal with it.

Extortion exists everywhere in the world, but in Mexico, as in other developing countries, the amounts are smaller and collected more often. The country is rapidly changing, and offering a bribe today, especially to a police officer, can be considered an insult, and can land you in deeper trouble.

If you believe a bribe is being requested, here are a few tips on dealing with the situation. Even if you speak Spanish, don't utter a word of it to Mexican officials. You'll appear innocent, all the while understanding every word.

When you are crossing the border, officials are supposed to stamp your passport or birth certificate and perhaps lightly inspect your luggage, then wave you on through. If the man who inspects your car (if you're driving) asks for a tip, you can ignore this request, but understand that the official may suddenly decide that a complete search of your belongings is in order.

If faced with a situation where you feel you are being asked for a *propina,* how much should you offer? Usually $3 to $5 or the equivalent in pesos will do the trick. There's a number to **report irregularities with Customs officials** (☎ **01-800-0-0148** in Mexico). Your call will go to the office of the Comptroller and Administrative Development Secretariat (SECODAM); however, be forewarned that most personnel do not speak English. Be sure you have some basic information—such as the name of the person who requested a bribe or acted in a rude manner, as well as the place, time, and day of the event.

Whatever you do, avoid impoliteness; under no circumstances should you insult a Latin American official. Mexico is ruled by extreme politeness, even in the face of adversity. In Mexico, gringos have a reputation for being loud and demanding. By adopting the local custom of excessive courtesy, you'll have greater success in negotiations of any kind. Stand your ground, but do it politely.

As you travel in Mexico, you may encounter several types of **scams,** which are typical throughout the world. One involves some sort of a **distraction** or feigned commotion. While your attention is diverted, a pickpocket makes a grab for your wallet. In another common scam, an **unaccompanied child** pretends to be lost and frightened and takes your hand for safety. Meanwhile the child, or an accomplice, manages to plunder your pockets. A third involves **confusing currency.** A shoeshine boy, street musician, guide, or other individual might offer you a service for a price that seems reasonable—in pesos. When it comes time to pay, they tell you the price is in dollars, not pesos, and become very hostile if payment is not made. Be very clear on the price and currency when services are involved.

2 When to Go

THE SEASONS   **High season**—from just before Christmas through Easter Sunday—is certainly the best time to be in the Yucatán if you're here for calm, warm weather; snorkeling, diving, and fishing (the calmer weather means clearer and more predictable seas); or to visit the ruins that dot the interior of the peninsula. Book well in advance if you're planning to be in Cancún around the holidays.

Low season in Mexico runs from Easter Sunday through approximately December 20, and airlines often offer discounted airfares. Many of these fares are unadvertised, especially during the slowest months mentioned above (mid-summer), and again in January, when the Christmas travelers have dispersed and hotel and airline occupancies are low.

Low season yields even greater discounts in hotel rates than airfares—prices are 20% or more lower than during high season. There's often a lull after New Year's in Cancún and Cozumel—prices can fall to somewhere between high- and low-season norms.

In most of Mexico, July and August are very slow months, but there are some exceptions. Mexicans and Europeans take vacations in those months, and some hotels in Isla Mujeres and Playa del Carmen raise their prices then.

Generally speaking, Mexico's **dry season** runs from November through April, with the **rainy season** stretching from May through October. It isn't a problem if you're staying close to the beaches, but for those bent on road-tripping to Chichén-Itzá, Uxmal, or other sites, temperatures and humidity in the interior can be downright stifling from May through July. Later in the rainy season the frequency of **tropical storms** and **hurricanes** increases; such storms, of course, can put a crimp in your vacation. But they can also cool off temperatures, making ruins climbing a real joy, accompanied by cool air and a slight wind. I especially like November for Yucatán travels.

Villahermosa is sultry and humid all the time. San Cristóbal de las Casas, at an elevation of 7,100 feet, is much cooler than the lowlands, and downright cold in winter.

FESTIVALS & SPECIAL EVENTS   You may also wish to plan a trip around a **festival.** In **Mérida,** Carnaval—the 3 days before Ash Wednesday—is the main festival; **San Cristóbal de las Casas** is known for its Carnaval as well as Days of the Dead (November 1 and 2); the December 12 celebration of Día de la Virgen de Guadalupe; Easter week when there are processions; the Fería de Primavera (the week after Easter); and the Fiesta de San Cristóbal (July 17 to 25). An especially memorable event is **spring equinox at Chichén-Itzá.** On the first day of spring, the Temple of Kukulcan—Chichén-Itzá's main pyramid—aligns with the sun and the shadow of the plumed serpent moves slowly from the top of the building down. When the shadow reaches the bottom, the body joins the carved stone snake's head at the base of the pyramid. According to ancient legend, at the moment that the serpent is whole, the earth is fertilized to assure a bountiful growing season. Visitors come from around the world for the spectacle, so advance arrangements are advisable. The shadow can be seen from March 19 to 23, and the show repeats itself during the fall equinox, September 21 to 22.

YUCATÁN CALENDAR OF EVENTS

January
- **New Year's Day (Año Nuevo).** National holiday. Parades, religious observances, parties, and fireworks welcome in the new year everywhere. In traditional indigenous communities, new tribal leaders are inaugurated with colorful ceremonies rooted in the pre-Hispanic past. January 1.
- **Three Kings Day.** Commemorates the Three Kings' bringing of gifts to the Christ Child. On this day, the Three Kings "bring" gifts to children. Friends and families gather to share the *Rosca de Reyes,* a special cake. Inside the cake there is a small doll representing the Christ Child; whoever receives the doll in his piece must host a tamales and atole party the next month. January 6.

February
- **Candlemas.** Music, dances, processions, food, and other festivities lead up to a blessing of seed and candles in a tradition that mixes pre-Hispanic and European traditions marking the end of winter. All those who attended the Three Kings Celebration reunite to share atole and tamales at a party hosted by the recipient of the doll found in the Rosca. February 2.
- ✪ **Carnaval.** Carnaval takes place the 3 days preceding Ash Wednesday and the beginning of Lent. It is celebrated with special reverence in the cities of Chamula and Cozumel; the celebration resembles New Orleans's Mardi Gras, with a festive atmosphere and parades. In Chamula, however, the event harks back to pre-Hispanic times with ritualistic running on flaming branches. In some towns there will be no special celebration, while in others there will be a few parades. Transportation and hotels are packed, so it's best to make reservations 6 months in advance and arrive a couple of days ahead of the beginning of celebrations. February 17 to 25.
- **Ash Wednesday.** The start of Lent and time of abstinence. It's a day of reverence nationwide, but some towns honor it with folk dancing and fairs. The date varies from year to year.

March
- **Spring Equinox.** Chichén-Itzá. On the first day of spring, the Temple of Kukulcan—Chichén-Itzá's main pyramid—aligns with the sun and the shadow of the plumed serpent moves slowly from the top of the building down. When the shadow reaches the bottom, the body joins the carved stone snake's head at the base of the pyramid. According to ancient legend, at the moment that the serpent is whole, the earth is fertilized to assure a bountiful growing season. Visitors come from around the world for the spectacle, so advance arrangements are advisable. March 21. (The shadow can be seen from March 19 to 23.)
- ✪ **Holy Week.** Celebrates the last week in the life of Christ from Palm Sunday through Easter Sunday with somber religious processions almost nightly, spoofing of Judas,

and reenactments of specific biblical events, plus food and craft fairs. Businesses close during this traditional week of Mexican national vacations.

If you plan on traveling to or around Mexico during Holy Week, make your reservations early. Airline seats on flights into and out of the country will be reserved months in advance. Buses to these towns or to almost anywhere in Mexico will be full, so try arriving on the Wednesday or Thursday before Good Friday. Easter Sunday is quiet. March or April (dates vary).

May

- **Labor Day.** Nationwide. Workers' parades countrywide, and everything closes. May 1.
- **Holy Cross Day** (Día de la Santa Cruz). Workers place a cross on top of unfinished buildings and celebrate with food, bands, folk dancing, and fireworks around the work site. May 3.
- **Cinco de Mayo.** Puebla and nationwide. A national holiday that celebrates the defeat of the French at the Battle of Puebla. May 5.
- **Feast of San Isidro.** The patron saint of farmers is honored with a blessing of seeds and work animals. May 15.
- **Cancún Jazz Festival.** Under new management. For dates call ☎ 800/44-MEXICO. TBA.

June

- **Navy Day.** Celebrated by all port cities. Boat parades, fishing tournaments, and sailing competitions. June 1.
- ✪ **Corpus Christi.** Celebrated nationwide. Honors the Body of Christ (the Eucharist) with religious processions, masses, and food. Festivities include performances of *voladores* (flying pole dancers) beside the church and at the ruins of El Tajín. *Mulitas* (mules) handmade from dried corn husks and painted, often with a corn-husk rider, and sometimes accompanied by pairs of corn-husk dolls, are traditionally sold there on that day. Dates vary (66 days after Easter).
- **St. Peter and St. Paul's Day** (Día de San Pedro). Nationwide. Celebrated wherever St. Peter is the patron saint and honors anyone named Pedro or Peter. June 29.

August

- ✪ **Assumption of the Virgin Mary.** Celebrated throughout the country with special masses and in some places with processions. August 20 to 22.

September

- **Independence Day.** Celebrates Mexico's independence from Spain. A day of parades, picnics, and family reunions throughout the country. At 11pm on September 15, the president of Mexico gives the famous independence *grito* (shout) from the National Palace in Mexico City. At least half a million people are crowded into the Zócalo, and the rest of the country watches the event on TV. The enormous military parade on September 16 starts at the Zócalo and ends at the Independence Monument on Reforma. Tall buildings downtown are draped in the national colors—red, green, and white—and the Zócalo is ablaze with lights; it's popular to drive downtown at night to see the lights. The schedule of events is exactly the same in every village, town, and city across Mexico. September 15 to 16.
- **Fall Equinox, Chichén-Itzá.** The same shadow play that occurs during the spring equinox repeats itself for the fall equinox. September 21 to 22.

October

- **Feast of San Francisco de Asis.** Those named Frances, Francis, or Francisco, as well as towns whose patron saint is Francisco, celebrate with barbecue parties, regional dancing, and religious observances. October 4.
- **Día de la Raza** ("Ethnicity Day," or Columbus Day). Commemorates the fusion of the Spanish and Mexican peoples. October 12.

November

☼ **Day of the Dead.** What's commonly called the Day of the Dead is actually 2 days, All Saints' Day—honoring saints and deceased children—and All Souls' Day, honoring deceased adults. Relatives gather at cemeteries countrywide, carrying candles and food, often spending the night beside graves of loved ones. Weeks before, bakers begin producing bread formed in the shape of mummies or round loaves decorated with bread "bones." Decorated sugar skulls emblazoned with glittery names are sold everywhere. Many days ahead, homes and churches erect special altars laden with Day of the Dead bread, fruit, flowers, candles, and favorite foods and photographs of saints and of the deceased. On the 2 nights, children dress in costumes and masks, often carrying mock coffins and pumpkin lanterns, into which they expect money will be dropped, through the streets. November 1 to 2.

- **Revolution Day.** Commemorates the start of the Mexican Revolution in 1910 with parades, speeches, rodeos, and patriotic events. November 20.

December

☼ **Feast of the Virgin of Guadalupe.** Throughout the country the patroness of Mexico is honored with religious processions, street fairs, dancing, fireworks, and masses. It is one of Mexico's most moving and beautiful displays of traditional culture. The Virgin of Guadalupe appeared to a young man, Juan Diego, in December 1531 on a hill near Mexico City. He convinced the bishop that he had seen the apparition by revealing his cloak, upon which the Virgin was emblazoned. It's customary for children to dress up as Juan Diego, wearing mustaches and red bandannas. One of the most famous and elaborate celebrations takes place at the Basílica of Guadalupe, north of Mexico City, where the Virgin appeared. But every village celebrates this day, often with processions of children carrying banners of the Virgin and with *charreadas* (rodeos), bicycle races, dancing, and fireworks. December 12.

- **Christmas Posadas.** On each of the 12 nights before Christmas, it's customary to reenact the Holy Family's search for an inn, with door-to-door candlelit processions in cities and villages nationwide. These are also hosted by most businesses and community organizations, taking the place of the northern tradition of a Christmas Party. December 15 to 24.
- **Christmas.** Mexicans extend this celebration and leave their jobs often beginning 2 weeks before Christmas all the way through New Year's. Many businesses close, and resorts and hotels fill up. On December 23 there are significant celebrations.
- **New Year's Eve.** As in the rest of the world, New Year's Eve in Mexico is celebrated with parties, fireworks, and plenty of noise. December 31.

3 Active Vacations in the Yucatán

Mexico has numerous **golf** courses, especially in the resort areas; there are excellent ones in Cancún and Playa del Carmen.

Visitors can enjoy **tennis, racquetball, squash, water-skiing, surfing, bicy-cling, horseback riding,** and **scuba diving.** Scuba diving especially is excellent off the Yucatán's Caribbean coast. The island of Cozumel is considered to be one of the top five dive spots in the world.

TOUR OPERATORS

Mexico is catching up with other countries in **ecological adventure and wilder-ness travel.** There's a new association in Mexico of eco- and adventure tour operators—AMTAVE (Asociación Mexicana de Turismo de Aventura y Ecoturismo, A.C.). It publishes an annual catalog of participating firms and their offerings, all of which must meet certain criteria for security, quality and training of the guides, as well as for sustainability of natural and cultural environments. For more information, contact them (in Mexico City) ☎ **5/255-4400;** ask for Augustín Arroyo. Most of the national parks and nature reserves are understaffed or unstaffed.

The following companies offer a variety of off-the-beaten-path travel experiences:

Apertours, ℅ Dietz Productions, calle Tonalá 27, San Cristóbal de las Casas, Chiapas (☎ 800/303-4983; ☎ and fax **967/8-5727;** www.mexonline.com/aper.1. htm; e-mail apertour@sancristobal.podernet.com.mx;) is led by photographer and San Cristóbal resident Craig Dietz, who offers photography classes for no more than three people at a time. Classes are outdoors, in the villages, and many are scheduled to coincide with special festivals in San Cristóbal.

ATC Tours and Travel, calle 5 de Febrero no. 15, 29200 San Cristóbal de las Casas, Chiapas (☎ **967/8-2550;** fax 967/8-3145), a Mexico-based tour operator with an excellent reputation, offers specialist-led trips primarily in southern Mexico. In addition to trips to the ruins of Palenque and Yaxchilán (extending into Belize and Guatemala by river, plane, and bus if desired), ATC also offers horseback tours and day trips to the ruins of Toniná around San Cristóbal de las Casas, Chiapas; birding in the rain forests of Chiapas and Guatemala (including in the El Triunfo Reserve of Chiapas, where you can see the rare quetzal bird and orchids); hikes out to the shops and homes of native textile artists of the Chiapas highlands; and walks from the Lagos de Montebello in the Montes Azules Biosphere Reserve, with camping and canoeing.

Ecoturismo Yucatán, calle 3 no. 235, Col. Pensiones, 97219 Mérida, Yuc. (☎ **99/20-2772;** fax 99/25-9047), offers a variety of tours including those focused on wildlife (especially birding) and ruins, among them the Río Bec ruin route.

Far Flung Adventures, P.O. Box 377, Terlingua, TX 79852 (☎ **800/359-4138** or 915/371-2489), takes clients on specialist-led Mexico river trips, including the Río Usumacinta, which runs between Mexico and Guatemala, combining rafting and camping at archaeological sites.

Far Horizons, P.O. Box 91900, Albuquerque, NM 87199-1900 (☎ **800/552-4575** or 505/343-9400; e-mail: journey@farhorizon.com; Web site: www.farhorizon.com), offers an extensive list of exploration-type tours led by degreed specialists. Among the offerings are a drawing class in the Yucatán and lengthy trips that include the ruins of Río Bec, Dzibanché, Chicanń, Kohunlich, and Palenque.

Mexico Sportsman, 202 Milam Building, San Antonio, TX 78205 (☎ and fax **210/494-9916**) is sportfishing central for anyone interested in advance arrange-ments for fishing in Cancún and Cozumel. The company offers complete informa-tion from the cost (nothing hidden) to the length of a fishing trip, kind of boat, line and tackle used, and whether or not bait, drinks, and lunch are included. Prices are as good as you'll get on-site in Mexico.

Trek America, P.O. Box 189, Rockaway, NJ 07866 (☎ **800/221-0596** or 201/983-1144; fax 201/983-8551) organizes lengthy, active trips that combine trekking, hiking, van transportation, and camping in the Yucatán Peninsula and Chiapas as well as other places in Mexico.

Victor Emanuel Tours, P.O. Box 33008, Austin, TX 78764 (☎ **800/328-VENT** or 512/328-5221), is an established leader in birding and natural-history tours.

Wildland Adventures, 3516 NE 155th, Seattle, WA 98155 (☎ **800/345-4453**), offers an interesting mix of nature- and history-oriented tours in Mexico. They include the Belize–Yucatán Adventure, using Rancho Encantado on Lake Bacalar as a base for forays into the Río Bec ruin route and Lamanai in nearby Belize.

DIVING PACKAGES

In Cozumel, you may be able to save money by purchasing diving packages, which include the price of the hotel and a given number of dives. Many divers, however, save more money by staying in a cheaper hotel than a package calls for and booking dives directly with a diving concession. This method may be particularly practical in the fall, when stormy seas often preclude diving, and you therefore won't have to pay for unused dives.

4 Health, Safety & Insurance

STAYING HEALTHY

COMMON AILMENTS   Elevation Sickness is another problem travelers experience; San Cristóbal de las Casas is at an elevation of 7,100 feet, as are a number of other central Mexican cities. At high elevations, it takes about 10 days to acquire the extra red blood corpuscles you need to adjust to the scarcity of oxygen. Symptoms include shortness of breath, fatigue, headache, insomnia, and even nausea.

Take it easy for the first few days after you arrive at a high elevation. Drink extra fluids but avoid alcohol. If you have heart or lung problems, talk to your doctor before going above 8,000 feet.

Mosquitoes and gnats are prevalent along the coast and in the Yucatán lowlands. Insect repellent (*repelente contra insectos*) is a must, and it's not always available in Mexico. If you'll be in these areas, and are prone to bites, bring a repellent along that contains the active ingredient DEET. Avon's "Skin So Soft" also works extremely well. If you're sensitive to bites, pick up some antihistamine cream from a drugstore at home.

Most readers won't ever see a scorpion (*alacrán*). But if you're stung, go immediately to a doctor.

MORE SERIOUS DISEASES   You shouldn't be overly concerned about tropical diseases if you stay on the normal tourist routes and don't eat street food. However, both dengue fever and cholera have appeared in Mexico in recent years. Talk to your doctor, or a medical specialist in tropical diseases, about any precautions you should

Over-the-Counter Drigs in Mexico

Antibiotics and other drugs that you'd need a prescription to buy in the States are sold over-the-counter in Mexican pharmacies (*farmacias*). Mexican pharmacies also have common over-the-counter sinus and allergy remedies, although perhaps not the broad selection we're accustomed to finding easily.

Turista on the Toilet: What to Do if You Get Sick

It's called "traveler's diarrhea" or *turista*, the Spanish word for "tourist": the persistent diarrhea, often accompanied by fever, nausea, and vomiting, that used to attack many travelers to Mexico. Some in the U.S. call this "Montezuma's Revenge," but you won't hear it referred to this way in Mexico. Widespread improvements in infrastructure, sanitation, and education have practically eliminated this ailment, especially in well-developed resort areas. Most travelers make a habit of drinking only bottled water, which also helps to protect against unfamiliar bacteria. In resort areas, and generally throughout Mexico, only purified ice is used. Doctors say it's not caused by just one "bug," but by a combination of consuming different food and water, upsetting your schedule, being overtired, and experiencing the stresses of travel. A good high-potency (or "therapeutic") vitamin supplement, and even extra vitamin C, is a help; yogurt is good for healthy digestion. If you do happen to come down with this ailment, nothing beats Pepto Bismol, readily available in Mexico.

How to Prevent It: The U.S. Public Health Service recommends the following measures for preventing traveler's diarrhea:

• *Drink only purified water.* This means tea, coffee, and other beverages made with boiled water; canned or bottled carbonated beverages and water; beer; and wine. Most restaurants with a large tourist clientele use only purified water and ice.

• *Choose food carefully.* In general, avoid salads, uncooked vegetables, and unpasteurized milk or milk products (including cheese). However, salads in a first-class restaurant, or one serving a lot of tourists, are generally safe to eat. Choose food that is freshly cooked and still hot. Peelable fruit is ideal. Don't eat undercooked meat, fish, or shellfish.

In addition, something so simple as clean hands can go a long way toward preventing *turista*.

Since **dehydration** can quickly become life-threatening, the Public Health Service advises that you be especially careful to replace fluids and electrolytes (potassium, sodium, and the like) during a bout of diarrhea. Do this by drinking Pedialyte, a rehydration solution available at most Mexican pharmacies, or glasses of natural fruit juice (high in potassium) with a pinch of salt added, or you can also try a glass of boiled pure water with a quarter teaspoon of sodium bicarbonate (baking soda) added.

take. You can also get medical bulletins from the U.S. State Department and the Centers for Disease Control (see "Sources of Information," above). You can protect yourself by taking some simple precautions. Watch what you eat and drink; don't swim in stagnant water (ponds, slow-moving rivers, or wells); and avoid mosquito bites by covering up, using repellent, and sleeping under mosquito netting. The most dangerous areas seem to be on Mexico's west coast, away from the big resorts (which are relatively safe).

EMERGENCY EVACUATION   For extreme medical emergencies there's a service from the United States that will fly people to American hospitals: **Air-Evac,** a 24-hour air ambulance (☎ **800/854-2569,** or call collect 510/293-5968). You can also contact the service in Guadalajara (☎ **01-800/305-9400,** 3/616-9616, or 3/615-2471).

SAFETY

I have lived and traveled in Mexico for over 8 years, have never had any serious trouble, and rarely feel suspicious of anyone or any situation. You will probably feel physically safer in most Mexican cities and villages than in any comparable place at home.

Crime, especially petty robbery, is becoming more of a problem in Mexico than it used to be. Be smart and careful: Take all the normal precautions you'd take to deter pickpockets and muggers traveling in any large American city. Use hotel security boxes or in-room safes for your passport and other valuables.

See "Sources of Information" at the beginning of this chapter for how to contact the **U.S. State Department** for their latest advisories. At press time their crime cautions included warnings about bold highway holdups in the Yucatecan state of **Campeche** (including robbery of buses on Highway 186 heading east from Escarcega, and between Escarcega and Candalaria), and **nighttime bus travel,** especially long-distance overnight buses. They urge travelers to contact them for security information before traveling to **Chiapas.**

While these dangers are to be taken seriously, I urge you not to let them deter you from traveling in Mexico. Mexico is a wonderful country, and your good experiences with its people and culture will far outweigh any negative incidents.

INSURANCE

HEALTH/ACCIDENT/LOSS   Even the most careful of us can still experience a traveler's nightmare: You discover you've lost your wallet, your passport, your airline ticket, or your tourist permit. Always keep a photocopy of these documents in your luggage—it makes replacing them easier. To be reimbursed for insured items once you return, you'll need to report the loss to the Mexican police and get a written report. If you don't speak Spanish, take along someone who does. If you lose official documents, you'll need to contact both Mexican and U.S. officials in Mexico before you leave the country.

Health Care Abroad, Wallach and Co. Inc., 107 W. Federal St. (P.O. Box 480), Middleburg, VA 22117 (☎ **800/237-6615** or 540/687-3166), and **World Access,** 6600 W. Broad St., Richmond, VA 23230 (☎ **800/628-4908** or 804/285-3300), offer medical and accident insurance as well as coverage for luggage loss and trip cancellation. Always read the fine print on the policy to be sure that you're getting the coverage you want.

5 Tips for Travelers with Special Needs

FOR FAMILIES   Children are considered the national treasure of Mexico, and Mexicans will warmly welcome and cater to your children. Hotels can often arrange for a baby-sitter. Some hotels in the moderate-to-luxury range have small playgrounds and pools for children and hire caretakers with special activity programs during the day. Few budget hotels offer these amenities.

Before leaving, you should check with your doctor to get advice on medications to take along. Disposable diapers cost about the same in Mexico but are of poorer quality. You can get Huggies Supreme and Pampers identical to the ones sold in the U.S., but at a higher price. Gerber's baby foods are sold in many stores. Dry cereals, powdered formulas, baby bottles, and purified water are all easily available in mid-size and large cities.

Cribs, however, may present a problem. Only the largest and most luxurious hotels provide cribs. However, rollaway beds to accommodate children staying in the room with parents are often available. Child seats or high chairs at restaurants are common, and most restaurants will go out of their way to accommodate the comfort of your child.

FOR PEOPLE WITH DISABILITIES   Mexico may seem like one giant obstacle course to travelers in wheelchairs or on crutches. At airports, you may encounter steep stairs before finding a well-hidden elevator or escalator—if one exists. Airlines will often arrange wheelchair assistance for passengers to the baggage area. Porters are generally available to help with luggage at airports and large bus stations, once you've cleared baggage claim.

In addition, escalators (there aren't many in the country) are often out of operation. Few rest rooms are equipped for disabled travelers, or when one is available, access to it may be via a narrow passage that won't accommodate a wheelchair or someone on crutches. Many deluxe hotels (the most expensive) now have rooms with baths for people with disabilities. Those traveling on a budget should stick with one-story hotels or those with elevators. Even so, there will probably still be obstacles somewhere. Stairs without handrails abound in Mexico. Generally speaking, no matter where you are, someone will lend a hand, although you may have to ask for it.

Few airports offer the luxury of boarding an airplane from the waiting room. You either descend stairs to a bus that ferries you to the waiting plane that's boarded by climbing stairs, or you walk across the airport tarmac to your plane and ascend the stairs. Deplaning presents the same problem in reverse.

FOR GAY & LESBIAN TRAVELERS   Mexico is a conservative country, with deeply rooted Catholic religious traditions. As such, public displays of same-sex affection are rare and still considered shocking, for men especially. Women in Mexico frequently walk hand in hand; anything more would cross the bounds of acceptability here. However, gay and lesbian travelers are generally treated with respect and should not experience any harassment, assuming the appropriate respect is given to local culture and customs.

The International Gay and Lesbian Association (☎ **506/234-2411**) can provide helpful information and additional tips.

FOR SENIORS   Mexico is a popular country for retirees. For decades, North Americans have been living indefinitely in Mexico by returning to the border and recrossing with a new tourist permit every 6 months.

The following newsletter is written for prospective retirees: *AIM,* Apdo. Postal 31–70, 45050 Guadalajara, Jal., Mexico, is a well-written, candid, and very informative newsletter on retirement in Mexico. Subscriptions cost $18 to the United States and $21 to Canada. Back issues are three for $5.

FOR SINGLES   Mexico may be an old favorite for romantic honeymoons, but it's also a great place to travel on your own without really being or feeling alone. Although offering an identical room rate regardless of single or double occupancy is slowly becoming a trend in the Yucatán, most of the inexpensive and moderately priced hotels mentioned in this book still offer singles at lower rates.

Mexicans are very friendly, and it's easy to meet other foreigners. Isla Mujeres, Playa del Carmen, Celestún, Cancún, Palenque, and San Cristóbal are great places to go to on your own.

For Women   As a female traveling alone, I can tell you firsthand that I feel safer traveling in Mexico than in the United States. Mexicans are very warm and welcoming people, and I'm not afraid to be friendly wherever I go. But I use the same commonsense precautions I use traveling anywhere else in the world and am alert to what's going on around me.

If taxi drivers or others with whom you don't want to become friendly ask about your marital status, family, etc., my advice is to make up a set of answers (regardless of the truth): "I'm married, traveling with friends, and I have three children." Saying you are single and traveling alone may send out the wrong message about availability. Movies and television shows exported from the U.S. have created an image of sexually aggressive North American women. If bothered by someone, don't try to be polite—just leave or head into a public place.

If you don't like the idea of traveling alone, then try **Travel Companion Exchange,** P.O. Box 833, Amityville, NY 11701 (☎ **800/392-1256** or 516/454-0880; fax 516/454-0170), which brings prospective travelers together. Members complete a profile, then place an anonymous listing of their travel interests in the newsletter. Prospective traveling companions then make contact through the exchange. Membership costs $99 for 6 months or $159 for a year.

FOR STUDENTS   Because higher education is still considered more of a luxury than a birthright in Mexico, a formal network of student discounts and programs does not exist in this country. Also, most students within the country travel with their families, rather than with other students—thus student discount cards are not commonly recognized here.

For those wishing to study in Mexico, however, there are a number of university-affiliated and independent programs geared for intensive Spanish-language study. Frequently, these will also assist with accommodations, usually living with a local family in their home. One such program is **KABAH Travel and Education Tourism,** based in Guadalajara, which offers study and travel programs throughout the country. It can be contacted by fax: **800/596-4768.** More information is available at KABAH's Web site, mexplaza.com.mx/kabah/.

The **Council on International Educational Exchange (CIEE),** 205 E. 42nd St., New York, NY 10017 (☎ 212/661-1414 or 212/661-1450), can assist students interested in a working vacation in Mexico. CIEE also issues official student identity cards and has offices across the United States.

6 Getting There

BY PLANE

The airline situation in Mexico is changing rapidly, with many new regional carriers offering scheduled service to areas previously not served. In addition to regularly scheduled service, charter service direct from U.S. cities to resorts is making Mexico more accessible.

THE MAJOR INTERNATIONAL AIRLINES   The main airlines operating direct or nonstop flights from the United States to Cancún, Cozumel, and Mérida include **Aero California** (☎ 800/237-6225), **Aeromexico** (☎ 800/237-6639), **Air France** (☎ 800/237-2747), **American** (☎ 800/443-7300), **Continental** (☎ 800/231-0856), **Lacsa** (☎ 800/225-2272), **Mexicana** (☎ 800/531-7921), **Northwest** (☎ 800/225-2525), **United** (☎ 800/241-6522), and **US Airways** (☎ 800/428-4322).

CHARTERS   Charter service is growing, especially during winter months, and usually is sold as a package combination of air and hotel. Charter airlines, however, may sell air packages only, without hotel. Check your local paper for seasonal charters.

Well-known **tour companies** operating charters include **Club America Vacations, Apple Vacations, FunJet, GoGo Vacations,** and **Friendly Holidays.** You can make arrangements with these companies through your travel agent.

CyberDeals for Net Surfers

A great way to find the cheapest fare is by using the Internet to do your searching for you. There are too many companies to mention them all, but a few of the better-respected ones are **Travelocity** (**www.travelocity.com**), **Microsoft Expedia** (**www.expedia.com**), and **Yahoo's Flifo Global** (**travel.yahoo.com/travel**). Each has its own little quirks—Travelocity, for example, requires you to register—but all provide variations of the same service. Just enter the dates you want to fly and the cities you want to visit, and the computer looks for the lowest fares. The Yahoo site has a feature called "Fare Beater," which will check flights on other airlines or at different times or dates in hopes of finding an even cheaper fare. Expedia's site will e-mail you the best airfare deal once a week if you so choose. Travelocity uses the SABRE computer reservations system that most travel agents use, and has a "Last Minute Deals" database that advertises really cheap fares for those who can get away at a moment's notice.

Great last-minute deals are also available directly from the airlines themselves through a free e-mail service called **E-savers.** Each week, the airline sends you a list of discounted flights, usually leaving the upcoming Friday or Saturday, and returning the following Monday or Tuesday. You can sign up for all the major airlines at once by logging on to **Epicurious Travel** (**travel.epicurious.com/travel/c_planning/02_airfares/email/signup.html**), or go to each individual airline's Web site.

- **American Airlines:** www.americanair.com
- **Continental Airlines:** www.flycontinental.com
- **Northwest Airlines:** www.nwa.com
- **US Airways:** www.usairways.com
- **Aeromexico**: www.aeromexico.com
- **Mexicana:** www.mexicana.com
- **America West:** www.americawest.com
- **Alaska Airlines:** www.alaskaair.com

One caveat: Charter airfares and those offered through wholesalers (like Apple Vacations, FunJet, etc.) are generally not included in these online services, meaning you still may want to check with a travel agent to ensure you have the best all-around package price.

Excursion and package tours proliferate, especially in the off-season. Package tours offer some of the best values to the coastal resorts, especially during high season—from December until after Easter. Off-season packages can be real bargains. Packages are usually per person, and single travelers pay a supplement. In the high season a package may be the only way of getting to certain places in Mexico because wholesalers have optioned a large portion of the airline seats. A good travel agent will be able to give you all the latest schedules, details, and prices.

All-inclusive hotels are becoming more prevalent, even in the major resort destinations in Mexico. Since all meals, beverages, sports, and entertainment are included in the price of your stay, these are a great way of pre-planning your budget. Some charter packages will further combine airfare with an all-inclusive property, thus providing a "fixed-price" value vacation package. See also "Tips on Package Deals," later in this chapter.

BY CAR

Driving is certainly not the cheapest way to get to Mexico, but it is the best way to see the country. Even so, you may think twice about taking your own car south of the border once you've pondered the many bureaucratic requirements that affect foreign drivers here. One option would be to rent a car, for touring around a specific region, once you arrive in Mexico. Rental cars in Mexico are now generally new, clean, and very well-maintained. Although pricier than in the U.S., discounts are often available for rentals of a week or longer, especially when arrangements are made in advance, from the U.S. (See "Car Rentals," below, for more details).

If, after reading the section that follows, you have any additional questions or you want to confirm the current rules, call your nearest Mexican consulate, Mexican Government Tourist Office, AAA, or Sanborn's (☎ **800/395-8482**). To check on road conditions or to get help with any travel emergency while in Mexico, call ☎ **01800/903-9200** or 5/250-0151. Both offices are staffed by English-speaking operators.

In addition, check with the **U.S. State Department** (see "Sources of Information" at the beginning of this chapter) for their warnings about dangerous driving areas.

CAR DOCUMENTS   To drive your car into Mexico, you'll need a **temporary car importation permit,** which is granted after you complete a long and strictly required list of documents (see below). The permit can be obtained either through Banco del Ejército (*Banjercito*) officials, who have a desk, booth, or office at the Mexican Customs (*Aduana*) building after you cross the border into Mexico. Or you can obtain the permit before you travel through Sanborn's Insurance or the American Automobile Association (AAA), each of which maintains border offices in Texas, New Mexico, Arizona, and California. These companies may charge a fee for this service, but it will be worth it to avoid the uncertain prospect of traveling all the way to the border without proper documents for crossing. However, even if you go through Sanborn's or AAA, your credentials *may* be reviewed again by Mexican officials at the border; you must take them all with you since they are still subject to questions of validity.

The following requirements for border crossing were accurate at press time:

- A valid driver's license, issued outside of Mexico.
- Current, original car registration and a copy of the original car title. If the registration or title is in more than one name and not all the named people are traveling with you, then a notarized letter from the absent person(s) authorizing use of the vehicle for the trip is required; have it ready just in case. The car registration and your credit card (see below) must be in the same name.
- *A valid international major credit card.* Using only your credit card, you are required to pay a $12 car-importation fee. The credit card must be in the same name as the car registration.

    Note: If you don't have a major credit card, you won't have to pay the $12 importation fee, but you will be required to post a cash bond based on the value of the car. The rules and procedures are complicated (and expensive), so contact AAA or Sanborn's for details.
- *A signed declaration promising to return to your country of origin with the vehicle.* This form is provided by AAA or Sanborn's before you go or by Banjercito officials at the border. There's no charge. The form does not stipulate that you return through the same border entry you came through on your way south.

If you receive your documentation at the border (rather than through Sanborn's or AAA), Mexican border officials will make two copies of everything and charge you for the copies.

Important reminder: Someone else may drive the car, but the person (or relative of the person) whose name appears on the car importation permit must *always* be in the car at the same time. (If stopped by police, a nonregistered family member driver, driving without the registered driver, must be prepared to prove familial relationship to the registered driver—no joke.) Violation of this rule makes the car subject to impoundment and the driver to imprisonment and/or a fine. You can only drive a car with foreign license plates if you have an international (non-Mexican) driver's license.

MEXICAN AUTO INSURANCE   Auto insurance is not legally required in Mexico. U.S. insurance is invalid in Mexico; to be insured in Mexico, you must purchase Mexican insurance. Anyone involved in an accident who has no insurance is automatically sent to jail and his or her car impounded until all claims are settled. This is true even if you just drive across the border to spend the day, and it may be true even if you're injured.

Car insurance can be purchased through **Sanborn's Mexico Insurance,** P.O. Box 310, Dept. FR, 2009 S. 10th, McAllen, TX 78505-0310 (☎ **210/686-0711;** fax 210/686-0732 in Texas or 800/222-0158 elsewhere in the U.S.). The company has offices at all of the border crossings in the United States. Its policies cost the same as the competition's do, but you get legal coverage (attorney and bail bonds if needed) and a detailed mile-by-mile guide for your proposed route. Most of Sanborn's border offices are open Monday through Friday, and a few are staffed on Saturday and Sunday. You can purchase your auto liability and collision coverage by phone in advance and have it waiting at a 24-hour location if you are crossing when the office is closed. The annual insurance includes a type of evacuation assistance in case of emergency, and emergency evacuation insurance for shorter policies is available for a small daily fee. The company also offers a medical policy.

AAA auto club also sells insurance.

All agencies selling Mexican insurance will show you a full table of current rates and recommend the coverage they think is adequate. The policies are written along lines similar to those north of the border, with the following exception: The contents of your vehicle aren't covered. It's no longer necessary to overestimate the

Required Car Documents

You must carry your temporary car importation permit, tourist permit (see "Entry Requirements," above), and, if you purchased it, your proof of Mexican car insurance (see above) in the car at all times. The temporary car importation permit papers will be issued for 6 months and the tourist permit is usually issued for 180 days, but they might stamp it for half that, or even 30 days, so state your preference *before* the official stamps your papers. It's a good idea also to overestimate the time you'll spend in Mexico, so that if something unforeseen happens and you have to (or want to) stay longer, you'll have avoided the long hassle of getting your papers renewed. Whatever you do, don't overstay either permit. Doing so invites heavy fines and/or confiscation of your vehicle, which will not be returned. Remember also that 6 months does not necessarily work out to be 180 days; be sure that you return before whichever expiration date comes first.

amount of time you plan to be in Mexico (for insurance purposes) because it's now possible to get your policy term lengthened by fax from the insurer. However, if you are staying longer than 62 days, it's more economical to buy a nonrefundable annual policy. For example, Sanborn's Insurance quotes that a car (registered to an individual, not a business) with a value of $10,000 can be insured for $141.32 for 2 weeks or $75.60 for 1 week. If you join Sanborn's Amigo Club (the $40 membership includes hotel discounts, emergency air ambulance, legal assistance, towing, and a newsletter), you can get an annual policy for a car valued at $10,000 for the reduced rate of $624.70. Be sure the policy you buy will pay for repairs in both the United States and Mexico and will pay out in dollars, not pesos.

PREPARING YOUR CAR　　Check the condition of your car thoroughly before you cross the border. Parts for all car types may not be available in Mexico, but service generally is quite good and relatively inexpensive. Mexican mechanics are known for being able to fix anything. Carry a spare radiator hose and belts for the engine fan and air-conditioner. Be sure your car is in tune to handle Mexican gasoline.

Don't forget a flashlight and a tire gauge—Mexican filling stations generally have air to fill tires but no gauge to check the pressure. Not that many Mexican cars comply, but Mexican law requires that every car have **seat belts** and a **fire extinguisher.**

CROSSING THE BORDER WITH YOUR CAR　　After you cross the border into Mexico from the United States and you've stopped to get your tourist card and car permit, somewhere between 12 and 16 miles down the road you'll come to a Mexican Customs post. In the past, all motorists had to stop and present travel documents and possibly have their cars inspected. Now there is a new system under which some motorists are stopped at random for inspection. All car papers are examined, however, so you must stop. If the light is green, go on through; if it's red, stop for inspection. In the Baja Peninsula the procedures may differ slightly—first you get your tourist permit, then farther down the road you may or may not be stopped for the car inspection.

RETURNING TO THE UNITED STATES WITH YOUR CAR　　The car papers you obtained when you entered Mexico *must* be returned when you cross back with your car or at some point within the time limit of 180 days. (You can cross as many times as you wish within the 180 days.) If the documents aren't returned, heavy fines are imposed ($250 for each 15 days late), and your car may be impounded and confiscated or you may be jailed if you return to Mexico. You can only return the car documents to a Banjercito official on duty at the Mexican Customs (*Aduana*) building *before* you cross back into the United States. Some border cities have Banjercito officials on duty 24 hours a day, but others do not; some also do not have Sunday hours. On the U.S. side, Customs agents may or may not inspect your car from stem to stern.

The driver of the car may leave the country without the car, but it complicates the paperwork a bit. If it's undrivable, you can leave it at a mechanic's shop if you get a letter to that effect from the mechanic and present it to the nearest Secretaria de Hacienda y Credito Público (a treasury department official) for further documentation, which you then present to a Banjercito official upon leaving the country. Then you must return personally to retrieve the car. If the driver of the car has to leave the country without the car due to an emergency, the car must be put under Customs seal at the airport, and the driver's tourist permit must be stamped to that effect. There may be storage fees. If the car is wrecked or stolen, your Mexican insurance adjuster will provide the necessary paperwork for presentation to Hacienda officials. Basically, your car will carry the same status as you do. If you receive an extension on your tourist permit, your car will also. If you apply for and receive a more permanent status (FM2 or FM3) your car will be subject to those terms as well.

BY SHIP

Numerous cruise lines serve the Mexican Caribbean. Possible trips might run from Miami to the Caribbean (which often includes stops in Cancún, Playa del Carmen, and Cozumel).

If you don't mind making last-minute arrangements, several cruise-tour specialists arrange substantial discounts on unsold cabins. One such company is **The Cruise Line, Inc.,** 4770 Biscayne Blvd., Penthouse 1–3, Miami FL 33137 (☎ **800/777-0707,** 305/327-3021, or 305/576-0036).

BY BUS

Greyhound-Trailways (or its affiliates) offers service from around the United States to the Mexican border, where passengers disembark, cross the border, and buy a ticket for travel into the interior of Mexico. At many border crossings there are scheduled buses from the U.S. bus station to the Mexican bus station.

7 Getting Around

An important note: If your travel schedule depends on an important connection, say a plane trip between points, or a ferry or bus connection, use the telephone numbers in this book or other information resources mentioned here to find out whether the connection you are depending on is still available. Although we've done our best to provide accurate information, transportation schedules can and do change.

BY PLANE

To fly from point to point within Mexico, you'll rely on Mexican airlines. Mexico has two large privately owned national carriers: **Mexicana** (☎ **800/531-7921**) and **Aeroméxico** (☎ **800/237-6639**), in addition to several up-and-coming regional carriers. Mexicana and Aeroméxico both offer extensive connections to the United States as well as within Mexico.

Several of the new regional carriers are operated by or can be booked through Mexicana or Aeroméxico. Regional carriers are **Aerocancún** (see Mexicana) and **Aerocaribe** (see Mexicana). The regional carriers are expensive, but they go to difficult-to-reach places. In each applicable section of this book, I've mentioned regional carriers with all pertinent telephone numbers.

Because major airlines can book some regional carriers, read your ticket carefully to see if your connecting flight is on one of these smaller carriers; they may leave from a different airport or check in at a different counter.

AIRPORT TAXES   Mexico charges an airport tax on all departures. Passengers leaving the country on an international departure pay $12—in dollars or the peso equivalent. It has become a common practice to include this departure tax in your ticket price, but double check to make sure so you're not caught by surprise at the airport upon leaving. Taxes on each domestic departure you make within Mexico cost around $8, unless you're on a connecting flight and have already paid at the start of the flight; you shouldn't be charged again if you have to change planes for a connecting flight. These taxes are usually included in the price of your ticket.

RECONFIRMING FLIGHTS Although airlines in Mexico say it's not necessary to reconfirm a flight, it's still a good practice. To avoid getting bumped on popular, possibly overbooked flights, check in for an international flight the required hour and a half in advance of travel.

BY CAR

Most Mexican roads are not up to U.S. standards of smoothness, hardness, width of curve, grade of hill, or safety marking. Driving at night is dangerous—the roads aren't good enough and are rarely lit; the trucks, carts, pedestrians, and bicycles usually have no lights; and you can hit potholes, animals, rocks, dead ends, or bridges out with no warning.

The "spirited" style of Mexican driving sometimes requires super vision and reflexes. Be prepared for new procedures, as when a truck driver flips on his left-turn signal when there's not a crossroad for miles. He's probably telling you the road's clear ahead for you to pass—after all, he's in a better position to see than you are. Another custom that's very important to respect is how to make a left turn. Never turn left by stopping in the middle of a highway with your left signal on. Instead, pull off the highway onto the right shoulder, wait for traffic to clear, then proceed across the road.

GASOLINE There's one government-owned brand of gas and one gasoline station name throughout the country—**Pemex** (Petroleras Mexicanas). There are three types of gas in Mexico: *nova,* an 82-octane leaded gas; *magna sin,* an 87-octane unleaded gas (slowly disappearing from the market); and the newer *premium* 92-octane. Magna sin costs around $1.15 a gallon; premium costs slightly more, nova slightly less. In Mexico, fuel and oil are sold by the liter, which is slightly more than a quart (40 liters equals about 10½ gallons). Nova is readily available, magna is now everywhere, and premium is available in most areas of Mexico, along major highways, and in the larger cities. Plan ahead; fill up every chance you get, and keep your tank topped off. *Important note:* No credit cards are accepted for gas purchases. Stations are generally full-service with attendants. Children will usually be available to clean your windshield for a tip.

DRIVING RULES If you park illegally or commit some other infraction and are not around to discuss it, police are authorized to remove your license plates (*placas*). You must then pay a fine at the police station to get them back.

Be attentive to road signs. A drawing of a row of little bumps means there are speed bumps (*topes*) across the road. Slow down when coming to a village whether you see the *topes* sign or not.

Mexican roads are never as well marked as you'd like. Whenever you see a highway route sign, take note and make sure you're on the right road. Don't count on plenty of notice of where to turn, even on major interchanges; more often than not, the directional sign appears without prior notice exactly at the spot where you need to make a decision. Common road signs include these:

Camino en Reparación	Road Repairs
Conserve Su Derecha	Keep Right
Cuidado con el Ganado, el Tren	Watch Out for Cattle, Trains
Curva Peligrosa	Dangerous Curve
Derrumbes	Falling Rocks

Deslave	Caved-in Roadbed
Despacio	Slow
Desviación	Detour
Disminuya Su Velocidad	Slow Down
Entronque	Highway Junction
Escuela	School (Zone)
Grava Suelta	Loose Gravel
Hombres Trabajando	Men Working
No Hay Paso	Road Closed
Peligro	Danger
Puente Angosto	Narrow Bridge
Raya Continua	Continuous (Solid) White Line
Tramo en Reparación	Road under Construction
Un Solo Carril	One-Lane Road
Zone Escolar	School Zone

TOLL ROADS   Mexico charges among the highest tolls in the world to use its network of new toll roads. As a result, they are comparatively little used. Generally speaking, using the toll road between Cancún and Mérida will cut your travel time from 5 hours to 4. The old road, on which no tolls are charged, is generally in good condition and offers the most scenic route through villages; traffic is generally light.

MAPS   Guia Roji, AAA, and International Travel Map Productions have good maps of Mexico. In Mexico, maps are sold at large drugstores like Sanborn's, at bookstores, and in hotel gift shops.

BREAKDOWNS   Your best guide to repair shops is the Yellow Pages. For specific makes and shops that repair cars, look under "Automoviles y Camiones: Talleres de Reparación y Servicio"; auto-parts stores are listed under "Refacciones y Accesorios para Automóviles." To find a mechanic on the road, look for a sign that says "taller mecánico."

If your car breaks down on the road, help might already be on the way. Radio-equipped green repair trucks operated by uniformed English-speaking officers patrol the major highways during daylight hours to aid motorists in trouble. These **"Green Angels"** will perform minor repairs and adjustments for free, but you pay for parts and materials.

MINOR ACCIDENTS   When possible, many Mexicans drive away from minor accidents to avoid hassles with police. If the police arrive while the involved persons are still at the scene, everyone may be locked in jail until blame is assessed. In any case, you have to settle up immediately, which may take days of red tape. Foreigners who don't speak fluent Spanish are at a distinct disadvantage when trying to explain their side of the event. Three steps may help the foreigner who doesn't wish to do as the Mexicans do: If you're in your own car, notify your Mexican insurance company, whose job it is to intervene on your behalf. If you're in a rental car, notify the rental company immediately and ask how to contact the nearest adjuster. (You did buy insurance with the rental, right?) Finally, if all else fails, ask to contact the nearest Green Angel, who may be able to explain to officials that you are covered by insurance.

See also "Mexican Auto Insurance" in "By Car," above.

PARKING   When you park your car on the street, lock it up and leave nothing within view inside (day or night). Guarded parking lots, especially at night, are preferable to avoid vandalism and break-ins. When pay lots are not available, small boys usually offer to watch your car for you—tip them well on your return.

Money-Saving Tip

Take advantage of Avis's *prepay* offer. You prepay the daily rental by credit card before you go and receive a considerable discount. Under this plan, you pay tax and insurance in Mexico.

CAR RENTALS Car-rental rules change often in Mexico. The best prices are obtained by reserving your car in the United States a week or more in advance of travel. Cancún, Mérida, Villahermosa, and now Playa del Carmen have international companies such as **Avis** (☎ **800/331-1212** in the U.S., 800/TRY-AVIS in Canada), **Hertz** (☎ **800/654-3131** in the U.S. and Canada), and **National** (☎ **800/CAR-RENT** in the U.S. and Canada), plus many local companies. You'll find rental desks at airports, all major hotels, and many travel agencies. Renting a car during a major holiday may prove difficult. To avoid being stranded without a vehicle, if possible plan your arrival a day or two before the anticipated rush of travelers.

Cars are easy to rent if you have a major charge or credit card, are 25 or over, and have a valid driver's license and passport with you. Without a credit card you must leave a cash deposit, usually a big one. Rent-here/leave-there arrangements are usually simple to make but more costly.

Costs Car-rental costs are high in Mexico, because cars are more expensive to purchase and maintain here. The condition of rental cars has improved greatly over the years, however, and clean, comfortable, new cars are the norm. When I checked recently, the basic cost of a 1-day rental of a Volkswagen Beetle, with unlimited mileage (but before 15% tax and $15 daily insurance) was $44 in Cancún and $27 in Mérida. Renting by the week gets you a lower daily rate.

It makes a difference where you rent, for how long, and when. If you have a choice of renting in Mérida and driving to Cancún, you might save more money than if you rent in Cancún. Mileage-added rates can run up the bill considerably, so avoid those. Car-rental companies will write up a credit-card charge in U.S. dollars or in pesos at the end of the trip, but you must leave a signed credit-card voucher when you rent the car.

Rental Confirmation Make your reservation directly with the car-rental company in your home country. Write down your confirmation number and request that a copy of the confirmation, which states the agreed-upon price, be mailed to you so you can present it when you pick up your car in Mexico. If you're dealing with a U.S. company, the confirmation must be honored, even if the company has to upgrade you to another class of car. Don't allow them to send you to another agency or try to charge you more than the price on the confirmation.

Deductibles Be careful; these can vary greatly in Mexico. Some are as high as $2,500, which comes out of your pocket immediately in case of car damage. Hertz's deductible is $1,000 on a VW Beetle; Avis's is $500 for the same car.

Insurance Insurance is offered in two parts: **Collision and damage** insurance covers your car and other cars if the accident is your fault, and **personal accident** insurance covers you and anyone in your car.

Car Rental Insurance Many credit-card companies offer their cardholders free rental-car insurance. I wouldn't rely on this insurance in Mexico for several reasons. First, if you buy the insurance offered by the rental company and your car is vandalized or stolen, you will only have to pay the deductible. If you don't have the rental company's insurance, you'll have to pay for everything, including the full value of the car if it is unrepairable—a determination made only by the car-rental company. While your credit-card company may eventually reimburse you, you will have to pay in the meantime.

Read the fine print on the back of your rental agreement and note that insurance may be invalid if you have an accident while driving on an unpaved road.

Damage Always inspect your car carefully and note every damaged or missing item, no matter how minute, on your rental agreement, or you may be charged.

Trouble Number It's advisable to carefully note both the rental company's trouble number, as well as the direct number of the agency where you rented the car.

BY TAXI

Most airports and bus stations in large cities have *colectivo* (minibuses or minivans) or fixed-rate taxis to town. The colectivo is always the least expensive way to go. Buy a special colectivo ticket from a booth that's usually located near the exit door or main airport concourse. The taxi ticket booth is also close to the colectivo, but the price may be more than double that of a colectivo.

Taxis in the area covered by this book aren't metered, so you must agree on a price before you get in. Taxi prices to the most common destinations are usually posted inside the front door of most hotels. Use these prices as guides to taxi costs, since taxi drivers are notorious for bargaining high. Mérida taxi drivers are the most difficult to deal with since some like to confuse visitors by quoting in dollars when the passenger thinks the price is in pesos.

For longer trips, or excursions to nearby sites, taxis can generally be hired for around $10 to $15 per hour, or for a negotiated daily rate. Even drops to different destinations, say between Cancún and Playa del Carmen, can be arranged. A negotiated one-way price is usually much less than the cost of a rental car for a day, and service is much faster than traveling by bus. For anyone who is uncomfortable driving in Mexico, this is a convenient, comfortable route. An added bonus is that you have a Spanish-speaking person with you in case you run into any car or road trouble. Many taxi drivers speak at least some English. Your hotel can assist you with the arrangements.

BY BUS

Bus service in the Yucatán Peninsula is beginning to catch up to the high standard seen elsewhere in Mexico. Buses are frequent, readily accessible, and can get you to almost anywhere you want to go. Buses are an excellent way to get around, and they're often the only way to get from large cities to other nearby cities and small villages.

Dozens of Mexican companies operate large, air-conditioned, Greyhound-type buses between most cities. Travel classes are generally labeled first, second, and deluxe; the latter is referred to by a variety of names—*plus, de lujo, ejecutivo, primera plus,* and so on. The deluxe buses often have fewer seats than regular buses, show video movies en route, are air-conditioned, and have few stops; some have complimentary refreshments. Many run *express* (without stops) from origin to the final destination. They are well worth the few dollars more you'll pay than you would for first-class buses. First-class buses may get there as fast as a deluxe bus, but without

---

Traveler's Tip

There's little English spoken at bus stations, so come prepared with your destination written down, then double-check the departure.

A Safety Precaution

The U.S. State Department notes that bandits target long-distance buses traveling at night, but there have also been daylight robberies as well. The State Department particularly warns about hijackings on **Highway 186** between Escárcega and Xpujil in the southern Yucatán Peninsula. (See "Sources of Information," above, for contact information, and "Safety," above, for specific areas of caution.)

the comfort; they may also have many stops—you'll have to ask. Second-class buses have many stops and often cost only slightly less than first-class or deluxe buses. In rural areas, buses are often of the school-bus variety, with lots of local color.

Whenever possible, it's best to buy your reserved-seat ticket, often via a computerized system, a day in advance on many long-distance routes and especially before holidays. Schedules are fairly dependable, so be on time. Current information must be obtained from local bus stations.

See the appendix for a list of helpful bus terms in Spanish.

8 Tips on Accommodations

Here are some tips on getting the most for your money when it comes to accommodations.

Note: All hotels listed in this book have private bathrooms, unless otherwise noted. Fewer and fewer hotels in Mexico have rooms without private bathrooms. The few bathless rooms listed in this book are somewhat cheaper, but not necessarily by very much, than those with bathrooms.

• Rooms with air-conditioning are almost always more expensive than those with only fans. Rooms with a view of the street may be more expensive (not to mention noisier) than those with windows opening onto an airshaft. Water views cost more than garden or street views at the same resort. A room with a balcony or patio, however, may cost the same as one without.

• Hotels a block or two from the beach may cost 50% less than those right on the sand. Similarly, hotels on the main square are often slightly higher priced than hotels a block or two away.

• Some hotels, especially inexpensive and moderately priced hotels, offer single-room rates that are cheaper than the double-room rates. Ask about single rooms if you are traveling alone. Many hotels, however, charge the same rate for singles and doubles. For more on single rooms, see "For Singles," under "Tips for Travelers with Special Needs," above.

• If you ask a desk clerk to price a room, the quote he gives you may not be for the cheapest room available. If that's what you want, then ask to see a cheaper room by saying: *"Quiero ver un cuarto más barato, por favor."* It can't hurt.

• By law, hotel rates should be posted within view of the reception desk, but they rarely are. If a hotel's quoted rate seems too high, ask to see their official rate sheet and ask about discounts (*discuentos*) and promotional rates (*tarifas promocionales*). Walk away if the price seems too high.

Additionally, budget quality hotels may charge you 10% to 15% more if you want a receipt. It isn't wise to pay a desk clerk for a room without getting a receipt for your payment—for example, readers have reported paying an evening clerk on check-in, only to discover upon checkout that the day clerk has no record of the transaction. As an alternative, I've asked the clerk to write, sign, and date an informal receipt in my notebook.

- If you're traveling in the off-season (and not during a Mexican holiday), it is not necessary to make reservations at an inexpensive or moderately priced hotel. Arrive at your destination early in the day and target your choice of hotel. This will save you the price of a long-distance call to reserve a room and the uncertainty of not knowing whether your reservation deposit has been received. Mexican hotels often do not respond to reservation requests made by mail, even though they may honor such requests on arrival—you just never know.

- If you arrive in a city without a hotel reservation, call a hotel from the public telephone/fax office in most bus stations and airports. For only the cost of a local call, you'll be assured of a room when you arrive. In addition, you will not incur hefty taxi fares while you shop for a hotel. If you don't speak Spanish and if the person at the telephone office isn't busy, ask him or her to make the call for you.

- Most hotels allow children under age 12 to stay for free in their parents' room. Many hotels will accommodate kids with a roll-away bed. When making your reservation, always verify that the hotel has this service, and note the name of the person with whom you spoke.

- Although Mexican campsites are not of the same quality as those in the United States, a few beach destinations south of Cancún have designated camping areas; you'll find rustic campgrounds at Playa del Carmen, Punta Bete, Xcacel, Xpuha, and the Punta Allen Peninsula; there's a fine trailer park on the beach at Paamul and hookups available on the Xcalak/Majahual Peninsula.

- Finally, some destinations *do* have cheaper places to stay than those written up for this book. But we purposely have not listed rock-bottom hotels in this guide because of frequent reports of thefts at such places—especially of cameras and money from backpackers. While nothing can guarantee complete security, we have chosen hotels that feel safe.

9 Tips on Package Deals

Say the words "package tour" and many people automatically feel as though they're being forced to choose: your money or your lifestyle. This isn't necessarily the case. Most Mexican packages let you have both your independence *and* your in-the-black bank account balance. Package tours are not the same thing as escorted tours. They are simply a way of buying your airfare, accommodations, and other pieces of your trip (usually airport transfers, and sometimes meals and activities) at the same time.

For popular destinations like Mexico they're often the smart way to go, because they can save you a ton of money. In many cases, a package that includes airfare, hotel, and transportation to and from the airport will cost you less than just the hotel alone if you booked it yourself. That's because packages are sold in bulk to tour operators, who resell them to the public.

You can buy a package at any time of the year, but the best deals usually coincide with low season—May through early December—when room rates and airfares plunge. But packages vary widely. Some offer a better class of hotels than others. Some offer the same hotels for lower prices. Some offer flights on scheduled airlines while others book charters. In some packages, your choices of accommodations and travel days may be limited. Each destination usually has some packagers that are better than the rest because they buy in even bigger bulk. Not only can that mean better prices, but it can also mean more choices—a packager that just dabbles in Mexico may only have a half-dozen or so hotels for you to chose from, while a packager that focuses much of its energy on south-of-the-border vacations may have dozens of hotels for you to choose from, with a good selection in every price range.

PACKAGE TOUR WARNINGS

- **Read the fine print.** Make sure you know *exactly* what's included in the price you're being quoted, and what's not.
- **Don't compare Mayas and Aztecs.** When you're looking over different packagers, compare the deals that they're offering on similar properties. Most packagers can offer bigger savings on some hotels than others.
- **Know what you're getting yourself into—and if you can get yourself out of it.** Before you commit to a package, make sure you know how much flexibility you have.
- **Use your best judgment.** Stay away from fly-by-nights and shady packagers. Go with a reputable firm with a proven track record. This is where your travel agent can come in handy.

WHERE TO BROWSE

- For one-stop shopping on the Web, go to **www.vacationpackager.com**, an extensive search engine that'll link you up with more than 30 packagers offering Mexican beach vacations—and even let you custom design your own package.
- Check out **www.2travel.com** and find a page with links to a number of the big-name Mexico packagers, including several of the ones listed here.

PACKAGERS PACKIN' A PUNCH

- **Aeromexico Vacations** (☎ 800/245-8585; **www.aeromexico.com**). Year-round packages for Cancún, Cozumel, and Ixtapa/Zihuatanejo. Aeromexico has a large selection of resorts in these destinations (39 in Cancún, 11 in Cozumel, and 12 in Ixtapa/Zihuatanejo) in a variety of price ranges. The best deals are from Houston, Dallas, San Diego, Los Angeles, Miami, and New York, in that order. Aeromexico's **Sun-Brero** packages give you 3 nights in Mexico City and your choice of 4 nights in Cancún or Ixtapa/Zihuatanejo, plus a half-day city tour of Mexico's major city. You get to choose the hotel category—standard, superior, or deluxe—but have no options within those parameters.
- **American Airlines Vacations** (☎ 800/321-2121; **www.americanair.com**). American has seasonal packages to Acapulco and year-round deals for Cancún and Cozumel. You don't have to fly with American if you can get a better deal on another airline; land-only packages include hotel, airport transfers, and hotel room tax. American's hubs to Mexico are Dallas/Fort Worth, Chicago, and Miami, so you're likely to get the best prices—and the most direct flights—if you live near those cities.
- **Apple Vacations** (☎ 800/365-2775). Apple offers inclusive packages to all the beach resorts, and has the largest choice of hotels: 48 in Cancún, 17 in Cozumel, and 13 in Ixtapa. Scheduled carriers booked for the air portion include American, United, Mexicana, Delta, TWA, American, US Airways, Reno Air, Alaska Airlines, AeroCalifornia, and Aeromexico. Apple perks include

baggage handling and the services of an Apple representative at the major hotels.

- **Continental Vacations** (☎ 800/634-5555; www.flycontinental.com). With Continental, you've got to buy air from the carrier if you want to book a room. The airline has year-round packages available to Cancún, Cozumel, and Ixtapa, and the best deals are from Houston, Newark, and Cleveland.

- **Friendly Holidays** (☎ 800/344-5687; www.2travel.com/friendly/mexico. html). This major player in the Mexico field is based in upstate New York, but also has offices in California and Houston, so they've got their bases covered. They offer trips to all the resorts. Although they don't have the largest variety of hotels from which to choose, the ones they work with are high quality. In addition, their Web site is very user-friendly, listing both a starting price for 3 nights' hotel room and a figure for air add-ons, so at least you have a rough idea of what your trip is likely to cost you.

- **Funjet Vacations** (bookable through travel agents or on-line at www.funjet. com). One of the largest vacation packagers in the U.S., Funjet has packages to Cancún, Cozumel, and Ixtapa. You can choose a charter or fly on American, Continental, Delta, Aeromexico, US Airways, Alaska Airlines, TWA, or United.

GOING WITH THE AIRLINES

Alaska Airlines Vacations (☎ 800-396-4371; www.alaskair.com) sells packages in high season to Ixtapa/Zihuatanejo. Alaska flies direct to Mexico from Los Angeles, San Diego, San Jose, San Francisco, Seattle, Vancouver, Anchorage, and Fairbanks.

Delta Vacations (☎ 800/872-7786; www.delta-air.com) has year-round packages to Cancún, Cozumel, and Ixtapa Zihuantanejo. Atlanta is the hub, so expect the best prices from there.

Mexicana Vacations (or MexSeaSun Vacations) (☎ 800/531-9321; www. mexicana.com) offers getaways to all the resorts except Manzanillo, buttressed by Mexicana's daily direct flights from Los Angeles to Cancún and Ixtapa/Zihuatanejo.

TWA Vacations (☎ 800/438-2929; www.twa.com) runs year-round packages to Cancún.

US Airways Vacations (☎ 800/455-0123; www.usairways.com) features Cancún in its year-round Mexico packages, departing from most major U.S. cities.

REGIONAL PACKAGERS

From the East Coast: Liberty Travel (lots of offices but no central number) frequently runs Mexico specials. Here the best bet is to check the ads in your Sunday travel section or go to a Liberty rep near you.

From the West Coast: Sunquest Holidays (☎ 800/357-2400, or 888/888-5028 for departures within 14 days) is one of the largest packagers for Mexico on the West Coast, arranging regular charters to Cancún and Cozumel from L.A., paired with a large selection of hotels.

From the Southwest: Town and Country (bookable through travel agents) packages regular deals to Ixtapa, Cancún, and Cozumel with America West from the airline's Phoenix and Las Vegas gateways.

RESORTS

The biggest hotel chains and resorts also sell packages. The Mexican-owned Fiesta Americana/Fiesta Inns, for example, run **Fiesta Break** deals that include airfare from New York, Los Angeles, Dallas, or Houston, airport transfers, optional meal plans, and more. Call ☎ 800-9BREAK for details.

FAST FACTS: Mexico

Abbreviations   Dept. (apartments); Apdo. (post office box); av. (avenida; avenue); c/ (calle; street); calz. (calzada; boulevard). "C" on faucets stands for *caliente* (hot), and "F" stands for *fría* (cold). PB (*planta baja*) means ground floor.

Business Hours   In general, businesses in larger cities are open between 9am and 7pm; in smaller towns many close between 2 and 4pm. Most are closed on Sunday. Bank hours are Monday through Friday from 9 or 9:30am to 5 or 6pm. Increasingly, banks are offering Saturday hours for at least a half–day.

Camera/Film   Film costs about the same as in the United States. Tourists wishing to use a video or still camera at any archaeological site in Mexico and at many museums operated by the Instituto de Antropología e Historia (INAH) may be required to pay $4 per video camera and/or still camera in their possession at each site or museum visited. Such fees are noted in the listings for specific sites and museums. Also, use of a tripod at any archaeological site in Mexico requires a permit from INAH. It's courteous to ask permission before photographing anyone. In some areas, such as around San Cristóbal de las Casas, there are other restrictions on photographing people and villages. Such restrictions are noted in specific cities, towns, and sites.

Customs   See "Visitor Information, Entry Requirements & Money," earlier in this chapter.

Doctors/Dentists   Every embassy and consulate is prepared to recommend local doctors and dentists with good training and modern equipment; some of the doctors and dentists even speak English. See the list of embassies and consulates under "Embassies/Consulates," below. Hotels with a large foreign clientele are often prepared to recommend English-speaking doctors. Almost all first-class hotels in Mexico have a doctor on call.

Drug Laws   To be blunt, don't use or possess illegal drugs in Mexico. Mexican officials have no tolerance for drug users, and jail is their solution, with very little hope of getting out until the sentence (usually a long one) is completed or heavy fines or bribes are paid. Remember—in Mexico the legal system assumes you are guilty until proven innocent. (*Important note:* It isn't uncommon to be befriended by a fellow user, only to be turned in by that "friend"—he's collected a bounty for turning you in.) Bring prescription drugs in their original containers. If possible, pack a copy of the original prescription with the generic name of the drug.

I don't need to go into detail about the penalties for illegal drug possession upon return to the United States. Customs officials are also on the lookout for diet drugs sold in Mexico, possession of which could also land you in a U.S. jail because they are illegal here. If you buy antibiotics over the counter (which you can do in Mexico)—say, for a sinus infection—and still have some left, you probably won't be hassled by U.S. Customs.

Drugstores   Drugstores (*farmacias*) will sell you just about anything you want, with a prescription or without one. Most drugstores are open Monday through Saturday from 8am to 8pm. There are generally one or two 24–hour pharmacies now located in the major resort areas. If you are in a smaller town and need to buy medicines after normal hours, ask for the *farmacia de turno;* pharmacies take turns staying open during off-hours.

Electricity   The electrical system in Mexico is 110 volts AC (60 cycles), as in the United States and Canada. However, in reality it may cycle more slowly and overheat your appliances. To compensate, select a medium or low speed for hair dryers. Many older hotels still have electrical outlets for flat two-prong plugs; you'll need an adapter for using any modern electrical apparatus that has an enlarged end on one prong or that has three prongs. Many first-class and deluxe hotels have the three-holed outlets (*trifacicos* in Spanish). Those that don't may have loan adapters, but to be sure, it's always better to carry your own.

Embassies/Consulates   They provide valuable lists of doctors and lawyers, as well as regulations concerning marriages in Mexico. Contrary to popular belief, your embassy cannot get you out of a Mexican jail, provide postal or banking services, or fly you home when you run out of money. Consular officers can provide you with advice on most matters and problems, however. Most countries have a representative embassy in Mexico City, and many have consular offices or representatives in the provinces.

The Embassy of **Australia** in Mexico City is at Jaime Balmes 11, Plaza Polanco, Torre B (☎ 5/395-9988 or 5/566-3053); it's open Monday through Friday from 8am to 1pm.

The Embassy of **Canada** in Mexico City is at Schiller 529, in Polanco (☎ 5/254-3288); it's open Monday through Friday from 9am to 1pm and 2 to 5pm (at other times the name of a duty officer is posted on the embassy door). In Acapulco, the Canadian consulate is in the Hotel Club del Sol, Costera Miguel Alemán, at the corner of Reyes Católicos (☎ 74/85-6621); it's open Monday through Friday from 8am to 3pm.

The Embassy of **New Zealand** in Mexico City is at Homero 229, 8th floor (☎ 5/540-7780); it's open Monday through Thursday from 9am to 2pm and 3 to 5pm and Friday from 9am to 2pm.

The Embassy of the **United Kingdom** in Mexico City is in Bosques de las Lomas (☎ 5/596-6333); it's open Monday through Friday from 9am to 2pm.

Irish and **South African** citizens must go to the British Consulate.

The Embassy of the **United States** in Mexico City is next to the Hotel María Isabel Sheraton at Paseo de la Reforma 305, at the corner of Río Danubio (☎ 5/557-2238 or 5/209-9100). There are U.S. Consulates General in Ciudad Juárez, López Mateos 924-N (☎ 16/13-4048); Guadalajara, Progreso 175 (☎ 3/825-2998); Monterrey, av. Constitución 411 Poniente (☎ 83/45-2120); and Tijuana, Tapachula 96 (☎ 66/81-7400). In addition, consular agencies are in Acapulco (☎ 74/84-0300 or 74/69-0556); Cabo San Lucas (☎ 114/3-3566); Cancún (☎ 98/83-0272); Hermosillo (☎ 621/7-2375); Matamoros (☎ 88/12-4402); Mazatlán (☎ 69/13-4444, ext. 285); Mérida (☎ 99/25-5011); Nuevo Laredo (☎ 871/4-0512); Oaxaca (☎ 951/4-3054); Puerto Vallarta (☎ 322/2-0069); San Luis Potosí (☎ 481/2-1528); and San Miguel de Allende (☎ 465/2-2357 or 465/2-0068).

Emergencies   The 24-hour Tourist Help Line in Mexico City is ☎ 5/250-0151.

Legal Aid   International Legal Defense Counsel, 111 S. 15th St., 24th Floor, Packard Building, Philadelphia, PA 19102 (☎ 215/977-9982), is a law firm specializing in legal difficulties of Americans abroad. See also "Embassies/Consulates" and "Emergencies," above.

Newspapers/Magazines   Two English-language newspapers, *The News* and *The Mexico City Times,* are published in Mexico City, distributed nationally and carry world news and commentaries, plus a calendar of the day's events, including concerts, art shows, and plays. Newspaper kiosks in larger Mexican cities will carry a selection of English-language magazines.

Pets   Taking a pet into Mexico is easy, but requires a little preplanning. Each country has a different treaty agreement concerning this matter. For travelers coming from the U.S. and Canada, your pet needs to be checked for health within 30 days of arrival into Mexico. Most veterinarians in major cities have the appropriate paperwork—an official Health Certificate, to be presented to Mexican Customs officials, which they will give you at the time of their checkup, which also ensures the pet is up to date on its vaccinations. When you and your pet return from Mexico, the same type of paperwork will be required by U.S. Customs officials. If your stay extends beyond the 30-day time frame of your U.S.-issued certificate, you'll need to get an updated Certificate of Health issued by a veterinarian in Mexico that also states the condition of your pet, and the status of its vaccinations. I have traveled in and out of Mexico many times with my pet, and have never had a problem or delay. You will also need to reserve space in advance if you are flying. Airlines charge an extra fee for transporting your pet, and have a limit as to the number of live animals that can be on any one flight. Generally one or two small pets (which can fit under the seat in front of you) will be allowed on board, subject to prior reservation. To be certain of any last-minute changes in requirements, consult the Mexican Government Tourist Office nearest you (see "Visitor Information, Entry Requirements & Money," earlier in this chapter).

Police   Police in general in Mexico are more suspect than trustworthy; however, you'll find many who are quite honest and helpful with directions, even going so far as to lead you where you want to go.

Rest Rooms   The best bet in Mexico is to use rest rooms in restaurants and hotel public areas. Public facilities, usually near the central market, vary in cleanliness and usually have an attendant who charges a few pesos for toilet use and a few squares of toilet paper. No matter where you are, even if there's enough water pressure to carry away paper in the toilet, there'll be a wastebasket for paper disposal.

Taxes   There's a 12% to 17% IVA tax on goods and services in the areas covered in this book, and it may or may not be included in the posted price. This tax is 12% in Cancún, Cozumel, and Isla Mujeres and 17% elsewhere.

Telephone/Fax   Generally within a city, you will be dialing a five- or six-digit number. **To call long distance (abbreviated *lada*) within Mexico,** you'll need to dial the national long-distance code **01** prior to dialing a two- or three-digit area code. In total, Mexico's telephone numbers are eight digits in length. Mexico's area codes (*claves*) are usually listed in the front of telephone directories. Area codes are listed before all phone numbers in this book.

International long-distance calls to the United States or Canada are accessed by dialing **001,** then the area code and seven-digit number. For other international dialing codes, dial the operator, at **04.**

If you seem to be having a problem using the phone this way, see if the area codes and city exchanges have been changed. Mexico is going through a rapid upgrading of its telephone infrastructure, so this is a possibility. Mexico does not have recordings to inform you of changes or new numbers. Many **fax numbers** are also regular telephone numbers; you have to ask whoever answers your call for the fax tone ("*tono de fax, por favor*").

Most **public pay phones** in the country have been upgraded and converted to Ladatel phones, many of which are both coin- and card-operated, but a growing number that are only card-operated. This is by far the least expensive way to make an international long-distance call. Dialing from your hotel may be more convenient, but the surcharges can exceed 200% of the price of the call. Instructions on the phones tell you how to use them, but basically you simply insert the card, dial your number, and start talking. A digital display will advise you of the balance remaining on the card. When your time limit for local calls is about to end (about 3 minutes), you'll hear three odd-sounding beeps, and then you'll be cut off unless you deposit more coins. Ladatel cards come in denominations of 20, 50, and 100 pesos and can be purchased at most pharmacies, liquor stores, and mini-markets. In airports and other public places there are frequently Ladatel card machines.

Another option is the *caseta de larga distancia* (long-distance telephone office), found all over Mexico. Most bus stations and airports now have specially staffed rooms exclusively for making long-distance calls and sending faxes. Often they are efficient and inexpensive, providing the client with a computer printout of the time and charges. In other places, often pharmacies, the clerk will place the call for you, then you step into a private booth to take the call. Whether it's a special long-distance office or a pharmacy, there's usually a service charge of around $3.50 to make the call, which you pay in addition to any call costs if you didn't call collect.

For **long-distance calls** you can access an English-speaking AT&T operator by pushing the star button twice and then 09. If that fails, try dialing 09 for an international operator. To call the United States or Canada, tell the operator that you want a collect call (*una llamada por cobrar*) or station-to-station (*teléfono a teléfono*) or person-to-person (*persona a persona*). Collect calls are the least expensive of all, but sometimes caseta offices won't make them, so you'll have to pay on the spot.

To place a phone call to Mexico from your home country, dial the international service (011), Mexico's country code (52), then the Mexican area code (for Cancún, for example, that would be 98), then the local number.

Better hotels, which have more sophisticated tracking equipment, may charge for each local call made from your room. Budget or moderately priced hotels often don't charge, since they can't keep track. To avoid check-out shock, it's best to ask in advance if you'll be charged for local calls. These cost between 50¢ and $1 per call. In addition, if you make a long-distance call from your hotel room, there is usually a hefty service charge added to the cost of the call.

Water Most hotels have decanters or bottles of purified water in the rooms, and the better hotels have either purified water from regular taps or special taps marked *agua purificada*. In the resort areas, especially in the Yucatán, hoteliers are beginning to charge for in-room bottled water. Virtually any hotel, restaurant, or bar will bring you purified water if you specifically request it, but you'll usually be charged for it. Bottled purified water is sold widely at drugstores and grocery stores.

4 Cancún

Can over 2,000,000 people a year be wrong? The sheer number of annual travelers to Cancún underscores the magnetic appeal of this resort on Mexico's eastern coast.

Cancún is home to an impressive array of hotels set alongside translucent turquoise water and blinding white sand—all bordered by mangrove jungles. It is the peak of Caribbean splendor, with the added lure of ancient cultures evident in all directions. As the showcase of Mexico to the world, Cancún is the unrivaled favorite place for travelers to this country—Mexico's calling card of breathtaking natural beauty and the depth of its thousand-year-old history.

But Cancún is also a modern megaresort. Even a traveler feeling apprehensive about visiting foreign soil will feel completely at home and at ease here. English is spoken, dollars are accepted, roads are well paved, and lawns are manicured. Malls are the mode for shopping and dining, and you would swear some hotels are larger than a small town. Travelers feel comfortable in Cancún. You do not need to spend a day getting your bearings, as you immediately see familiar names for dining, shopping, nightclubbing, and sleeping.

You may have heard that in 1974, a Mexican government computer analyst picked Cancún for tourism development for its ideal mix of elements to attract travelers—he was right on. It's actually an island, a 14-mile-long sliver of land connected to the Mexican mainland by two bridges and separated from it by an expansive lagoon. (Cancún means "golden snake" in the Mayan language.)

In addition to attractions of its own, Cancún is a convenient distance from the traditional, less expensive resorts of **Isla Mujeres, Playa del Carmen,** and **Cozumel.** The **Maya ruins** at Tulum, Chichén-Itzá, and Cobá are within driving distance.

You will run out of vacation days before you run out of things to do in Cancún. Snorkeling, JetSkiing, jungle tours, and visits to ancient Maya ruins or modern ecological theme parks are among the most popular diversions. There are a dozen malls with name-brand and duty-free (better-than-U.S.-priced European goods) shops, plus over 350 restaurants and nightclubs. More than 20,000 hotel rooms in the area offer something for every taste and every budget.

Cancún's luxury hotels have pools so spectacular you may find it tempting to remain poolside, but don't. Put aside some time to simply gaze into the water the color of a dream and wriggle your toes in the powdery-fine, absolutely white sand. This is, after all, Cancún's calling card.

1 Orientation

GETTING THERE

BY PLANE   Several airlines connect Cancún with other Mexican and Central American cities. **Aeromexico** (☎ 800/237-6639 in the U.S., 98/84-1186 in Cancún, or 91/800-90999 toll-free within Mexico) offers direct service from Atlanta, Houston, Miami, New Orleans, and New York; plus connecting service via Mexico City from Dallas, Los Angeles, and San Diego. **Mexicana** (☎ 800/531-7921 from the U.S.; 98/86-0123 or 98/86-0124 in Cancún; 91/800-36654 toll-free within Mexico) flies in from Chicago, Denver, Guadalajara, Los Angeles, San Antonio, San Francisco, and San Jose via Mexico City; with nonstop service from Miami and New York. Regional carriers **Aerocozumel** (☎ 98/84-2000; affiliated with Mexicana) fly from Cozumel, Havana, Mexico City, and other points within Mexico. The regional airline **Aviateca** (☎ 98/84-3938) flies from Cancún to Mérida, Villahermosa, Tuxtla Gutiérrez, Guatemala City, and Flores (near Tikal). **Taesa** (☎ 98/87-4314) has flights from Tijuana, Chetumal, Mérida, and other cities within Mexico.

You'll want to confirm departure times for flights back to the States. Here are the Cancún airport numbers of the major international carriers: **American** (☎ 98/84-0129), **Continental** (☎ 98/86-0006), **Northwest** (☎ 98/86-0044 or 98/86-0046).

Most major **rental-car firms** have outlets at the airport, so if you're renting a car, consider picking it up and dropping it off at the airport to save on airport-transportation costs. Another way to save money is to arrange for the rental before you leave your home country. If you rent on the spot after arrival, the daily cost of a rental car will be around $65 to $75 for a VW Beetle. Major rental services include **Avis** (☎ 800/331-1212 from the U.S., or 98/86-0238); **Budget** (☎ 800/527-0700 from the U.S., or 98/84-5011); **Dollar** (☎ 98/86-0159); **National** (☎ 800/328-4567 from the U.S., or 98/86-4493); and **Hertz** (☎ 98/84-4692). The hotel zone is about a 15-minute drive from the airport along wide, well-paved roads.

Rates for a **taxi** run around $20 to $25, depending on your destination. Special **vans** (colectivos) run from Cancún's international airport into town. Tickets are purchased as you exit the building and cost about $8. There's expensive minibus transportation from the airport to the Puerto Juárez passenger ferry that takes you to Isla Mujeres. The least expensive way to get to the ferry is to take the colectivo to the bus station in downtown Cancún and from there bargain for a taxi.

There is no colectivo service returning to the airport from Ciudad Cancún or the Zona Hotelera, so you'll have to hire a taxi. Ask at your hotel what the fare should be.

BY CAR   From Merida or Campeche, take Highway 180 east to Cancún. This is mostly a winding, two-lane road, which branches off into the express toll road 180D between Izamal and Nuevo Xcan. Nuevo Xcan is approximately 26 miles from Cancún. Mérida is about 52 miles, and it takes about 3½ hours to drive between the two cities.

BY BUS   Cancún's bus terminal (☎ 98/84-4804 or 98/84-4352) is in downtown Ciudad Cancún at the intersection of avenidas Tulum and Uxmal. All out-of-town buses arrive here. Buses run to Playa del Carmen, Tulum, Chichén-Itzá, and other nearby beach and archaeological zones, as well as to other points within Mexico. Green-line buses offer packages (*paquetes*) to popular nearby destinations. The package to Chichén-Itzá departs at 9am and includes the round-trip air-conditioned bus ride, with video, for the 3-hour trip, entry to the ruins, 2 hours at the ruins, lunch, a brief stop for shopping, and a visit to a cenote. The tour returns to Cancún by 5pm. The trip to Xcaret (which is much cheaper than the same trip offered at the Xcaret terminal office) includes round-trip transportation and entry to the park; the tours depart daily at 9 and 10am and return at 5pm. Package trips to Cozumel depart at 8, 9, and 10am (returning at 5pm) and include round-trip, air-conditioned bus transportation to and from Playa del Carmen and the ferry ticket to and from Cozumel.

VISITOR INFORMATION

The State Tourism Office (☎ 98/84-8073) is centrally located downtown on the east side of avenida Tulum 26 next to Banco Inverlat, immediately left of the Ayuntamiento Benito Juárez building between avenidas Cobá and Uxmal. It's open daily from 9am to 9pm. A second tourist information office, the **Fondo Mixto of Cancún** (☎ 98/84-3238 or 98/84-3438), is located on avenida Cobá at avenida Tulum, next to Pizza Rolandi, and is open Monday to Friday from 9am to 9pm. Hotels and their rates are listed at each office, as are ferry schedules.

Pick up free copies of the monthly *Cancún Tips* booklet and a seasonal tabloid of the same name. Both are useful and have fine maps. The publications are owned by the same people who own the Captain's Cove restaurants, a couple of sightseeing boats, and time-share hotels, so the information (though good) is not completely unbiased.

CITY LAYOUT

There are two Cancúns: **Isla Cancún** (Cancún Island) and **Ciudad Cancún** (Cancún City). The latter, on the mainland, has restaurants, shops, and less expensive hotels, as well as all the other establishments that make life function—pharmacies, dentists, automotive shops, banks, travel and airline agencies, car-rental firms—all within an area about 9 blocks square. The city's main thoroughfare is **avenida Tulum.** Heading south, avenida Tulum becomes the highway to the airport and to Tulum and Chetumal on farther south; heading north, it intersects the highway to Mérida and the road to Puerto Juárez and the Isla Mujeres ferries.

The famed **Zona Hotelera** (alternately called the **Zona Turística**) stretches out along Isla Cancún, a sandy strip 14 miles long, shaped like a "7." It's now joined by bridges to the mainland at the north and south ends. Avenida Cobá from Cancún City becomes Paseo Kukulkán, the island's main traffic artery. Cancún's international airport is just inland from the south end of the island.

FINDING AN ADDRESS The street-numbering system is left over from Cancún's early days. Addresses are still given by the number of the building lot and by the *manzana* (block) or *supermanzana* (group of city blocks). The city is still relatively small, and the downtown section can easily be covered on foot.

On the island, addresses are given by kilometer number on Paseo Kukulkán or by reference to some well-known location.

2 Getting Around

BY TAXI Taxi prices in Cancún are clearly set by zone, although keeping track of what's in which zone can take some doing. Within the downtown area, the cost is

Downtown Cancún

ACCOMMODATIONS:
Hotel Antillano **3**
Hotel Hacienda Cancún **13**
Hotel Parador **6**
Mexhotel Centro **9**

DINING:
100% Natural **11**
Pastelería Italiana **10**
La Habichuela **8**
Périco's **10**
Pizza Rolandi **2**
Restaurant Curva **12**
Restaurant El Pescador **5**
Restaurant Rosa Mexicano **4**
Restaurant Santa María **7**
Stefano's **1**

about $1; within any other zone, about $2 per cab ride (not per person). Between zones runs around $3, and if you cross two zones, that'll cost $3.50. Settle on a price in advance, or check at your hotel where destinations and prices are generally posted. Trips to the airport from most zones cost $8. Taxis can also be rented by the hour for about $10 per hour for travel around the city and hotel zone.

BY BUS   In town, almost everything is within walking distance. Ruta 1 and Ruta 2 (*Hoteles*) city buses travel frequently from the mainland to the beaches along avenida Tulum (the main street) and all the way to Punta Nizuc at the far end of the Zona Hotelera on Isla Cancún. Ruta 8 buses go to Puerto Juárez/Punta Sam for ferries to Isla Mujeres. They stop on the east side of avenida Tulum. Both of these city buses operate between 6am and midnight daily. Beware of private buses along the same route; they charge far more than the public ones. The public buses have the fare amount painted on the front; at publication the fare was 2.5 pesos (30¢).

BY MOPED   Mopeds are a dangerous way to cruise around through the very congested traffic. Rentals start at $25 for a day. A credit-card voucher is required as security for the moped. You should receive a crash helmet (it's the law) and instructions on how to lock the wheels when you park. Read the fine print on the back of the rental agreement regarding liability for repairs or replacement in case of accident, theft, or vandalism.

FAST FACTS: Cancún

American Express   The local office is at av. Tulum 208 and Agua (☎ **98/ 84-1999** or 98/84-5441), open Monday to Friday from 9am to 2pm and 4 to 6pm and Saturday from 9am to 1pm. It's 1 block past the Plaza México.

Area Code   The telephone area code is **98.**

Climate   It's hot but not overwhelmingly humid. The rainy season is May to October. August to October is the hurricane season, which brings erratic weather. November to February can be cloudy, windy, somewhat rainy, and even cool, so a sweater is handy, as is rain protection.

Consulates   The **U.S.** Consular Agent is in the Plaza Caracol Two, third level, no. 320–323, km 8.5 blv. Kukulkán (☎ **98/83-0272**). The office is open Monday to Friday from 9am to 2pm and 3 to 6pm. The **Canadian** Consulate is in the Plaza Mexico 312 (☎ **98/84-3716**). The office is open Monday to Friday from 10am to 2pm. The U.K. has a consular office in Cancún (☎ **98/85-1166,** ext. 462; fax 98/85-1225). Irish, Australian, and New Zealand citizens should be referred to their embassies in Mexico City.

Crime   Car break-ins are just about the only crime, and they happen frequently, especially around the shopping centers in the Zona Hotelera. VW Beetles and Golfs are frequent targets.

Currency Exchange   Most banks are downtown along avenida Tulum and are usually open Monday to Friday from 9:30am to 5pm, and many now have automated tellers for after-hours cash withdrawals. In the hotel zone you'll find banks in the Plaza Kukulkán and next to the convention center. There are also many *casas de cambio* (exchange houses). Downtown merchants are eager to change cash dollars, but island stores don't offer good exchange rates. Avoid changing money at the airport as you arrive, especially at the first exchange booth you see—its rates are less favorable than any in town or others farther inside the airport concourse.

Drugstores   Next to the Hotel Caribe Internacional, **Farmacia Canto,** av. Yax-chilán 36 at Sunyaxchen (☎ **98/84-9330**), is open 24 hours. American Express, MasterCard, and Visa are accepted.

Emergencies   To report an emergency dial ☎ **06,** which is supposed to be similar to 911 in the United States. For first aid, the **Cruz Roja** (Red Cross; ☎ **98/84-1616**) is open 24 hours on avenida Yaxchilán between avenidas Xcaret and Labná, next to the Telemex building. **Total Assist,** a small nine-room emergency hospital with English-speaking doctors at Claveles 5, SM22, at av. Tulum (☎ **98/84-1058** or 98/84-1092), is open 24 hours. American Express, Master-Card, and Visa are accepted. Desk staff may have limited English. *Urgencias* means "Emergencies."

Luggage Storage/Lockers   Hotels will generally tag and store excess luggage while you travel elsewhere.

Newspapers/Magazines   For English-language newspapers and books, go to **Fama** on avenida Tulum between Tulipanes and Claveles (☎ **98/84-6586**), open daily from 8am to 10pm. American Express, MasterCard, and Visa are accepted.

Police   To reach the **police** (Seguridad Pública), dial ☎ **98/84-1913** or 98/84-2342. The ***Procuraduria del Consumidor*** (consumer protection agency) is opposite the Social Security Hospital at av. Cobá 10 (☎ **98/84-2634** or 98/84-2701).

Post Office   The **main post office** is at the intersection of avenidas Sunyaxchen and Xel-Ha (☎ **98/84-1418**). It's open Monday to Friday from 8am to 7pm and Saturday from 9am to 1pm.

Safety   There is very little crime in Cancún. People in general are safe late at night in touristed areas; just use ordinary common sense. As at any other beach resort, don't take money or valuables to the beach. See "Crime," above.

Swimming on the Caribbean side presents a danger from undertow. See "The Beaches" in "Beaches & Water Sports," below, for flag warnings.

Seasons   Technically, high season is December 15 to Easter; low season is May to November, when prices are reduced 10% to 30%. Some hotels are starting to charge high-season rates between July and September when travel is high for Mexican national, European, and school-holiday visitors. There's a short low season in January just after the Christmas–New Year's holiday.

Telephones   The phone system for Cancún changed in 1992. The area code is now **98** (it was 988). All local numbers now have six digits instead of five; all numbers begin with 8. If a number is written 988/4-1234, when in Cancún you must dial 84-1234.

3 Where to Stay

Island hotels are stacked along the beach like dominoes, with almost all offering clean, modern facilities available from numerous chains. Extravagance is the byword in the more recently built hotels, many of which are awash in a sea of marble and glass. Some hotels, however, while exclusive, effect a more relaxed attitude. The water is placid on the upper end of the island facing Bahía de Mujeres, while beaches lining the long side of the island facing the Caribbean are subject to choppier water and crashing waves on windy days (for more information on swimming safety, see "Beaches & Water Sports," later in this chapter). Be aware that the

Important Note on Hotel Prices

Cancún's hotels, even in budget and moderately priced hotels, generally set their rates in dollars, so they are immune to any swings in the peso. Travel agents and wholesalers always have air/hotel packages available, with Sunday papers often advertising inventory-clearing packages. There are also several all-inclusive properties in Cancún that allow you to have a fixed-cost vacation, if this is desirable. Note that the price quoted to you when you call a hotel's reservation number from the United States may not include Cancún's 12% tax. Prices can vary considerably at different times of the year, so it pays to consult a travel agent or shop around.

farther you go south on the island, the longer it takes (20 to 30 minutes in traffic) to get back to the "action spots," which are primarily between the Plaza Flamingo and Punta Cancún on the island and along avenida Tulum on the mainland. On Cancún island, almost all major hotel chains are represented, so this list can be viewed as a representative summary, with a select number of notable places to stay. Ciudad Cancún offers independently owned, smaller, and less expensive stays. Prices are lower during the off-season (from April to November).

The hotel listings in this chapter begin on Cancún Island and finish in Cancún City, where bargain lodgings are available.

Parking is available at all island hotels.

CANCÚN ISLAND
VERY EXPENSIVE

✪ **Caesar Park Beach & Golf Resort.** Km 17 Paseo Kukulkán, Retorno Lacandones, 77500 Cancún, Q. Roo. ☎ **800/228-3000** in the U.S., or 98/81-8000. Fax 98/81-8080. 427 units. A/C MINIBAR TV TEL. High-season standard rooms $275–$350 double; Royal Beach Club $300–$485 double; suites $375–$500. Low-season standard rooms $200–$300 double; Royal Beach Club $290–$370 double; suites $350–$550. AE, DC, MC, V.

A true resort in every sense of the word, the Caesar Park, which is affiliated with the Westin chain and is a member of the Leading Hotels of the World, opened in 1994 on 250 acres of prime Cancún beachfront property with two restaurants, seven interconnected pools, an 18-hole, par-72 golf course across the street, and a location that gives every room a sea view. Like the sprawling resort, rooms are grandly spacious and immaculately decorated in an austere Japanese style. Marble floors and bathrooms throughout are softened with area rugs and pastel furnishings. All rooms have sea views, and some have both sea and lagoon views. Other amenities in each luxurious room include robes, house shoes, hair dryers, and safety deposit boxes. Suites have coffeemakers. Royal Beach Club guests enjoy nightly cocktails and each Tuesday a manager's cocktail party on the patio. The elegant Royal Beach Club rooms are set off from the main hotel in two- and three-story buildings (no elevators) and have their own check-in and concierge service.

Dining: Spices Restaurant serves the cuisines of Mexico, Argentina, and Italy, while **Serenita** offers selections from Japanese and seafood cuisine.

Amenities: 18-hole, par-72 golf course; seven interconnected swimming pools with a swim-up bar; two whirlpools; two lighted tennis courts; water sport center; large fully equipped gym with daily aerobics; massage; beauty salon; and sauna. A Kids Club is part of the gym program. Greens fee is $75 for 18 holes for guests and $100 for nonguests; carts cost $22. Laundry and room service, ice machine on each floor, concierge, tour desk, beauty salon, gift shop and boutiques, golf clinic, car rental.

Isla Cancún (Zona Hotelera)

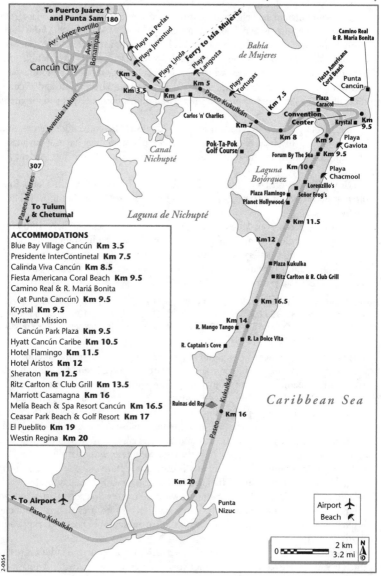

ACCOMMODATIONS
Blue Bay Village Cancún **Km 3.5**
Presidente InterContinetal **Km 7.5**
Calinda Viva Cancún **Km 8.5**
Fiesta Americana Coral Beach **Km 9.5**
Camino Real & R. Mariá Bonita
 (at Punta Cancún) **Km 9.5**
Krystal **Km 9.5**
Miramar Mission
 Cancún Park Plaza **Km 9.5**
Hyatt Cancún Caribe **Km 10.5**
Hotel Flamingo **Km 11.5**
Hotel Aristos **Km 12**
Sheraton **Km 12.5**
Ritz Carlton & Club Grill **Km 13.5**
Marriott Casamagna **Km 16**
Melía Beach & Spa Resort Cancún **Km 16.5**
Ceasar Park Beach & Golf Resort **Km 17**
El Pueblito **Km 19**
Westin Regina **Km 20**

✪ **Fiesta Americana Coral Beach.** Km 9.5 Paseo Kukulkán, 77500 Cancún, Q. Roo.
☎ **800/343-7821** in the U.S., or 98/83-2900. Fax 98/83-3173. 602 units. A/C MINI-
BAR TV TEL. High season $405 double. Low season $260 double. AE, DC, MC, V.

This sophisticated, spectacular hotel, which opened in 1991, has a lot to recommend it: perfect location; gracious service; grand public areas; a full range of water
sports, beach activities, and indoor tennis. It's enormous in a Mexican way and
grandly European in its lavish public halls and lobby. It's embellished with elegant
dark green granite from France, deep red granite from South Africa, black and green

marble from Guatemala, beige marble from Mexico, a canopy of stained glass from Guadalajara, and hardwood floors from Texas. The elegance seeps into the guest rooms, which are decorated with more marble, area rugs, and tasteful Mexican decorations. All rooms have balconies facing the ocean. Master suites have double vanities, dressing room, bathrobes, whirlpool baths, and large terraces; all rooms have hair dryers. Two concierge floors feature daily continental breakfast and evening cocktails, and a 24-hour reception-cashier. Two junior suites are equipped for guests with disabilities.

The hotel's great Punta Cancún location (opposite the convention center, and within walking distance of shopping centers and restaurants) has the advantage of facing the beach to the north, meaning the surf is calm and just perfect for swimming.

Dining/Diversions: The five-star **La Jolla** serves Mexican fare; the **Coral Reef** offers seafood and international cuisine; and there's a casual pool dining area. There are five bars.

Amenities: A 660-foot-long free-form swimming pool; swim-up bars; 1,000 feet of beach; three indoor tennis courts with stadium seating; gymnasium with weights, sauna, and massage; water-sport rentals on the beach; business center; tennis pro shop; fashion and spa boutiques; and beauty and barber shops. Laundry and room service, travel agency, car rental, and massage.

Hotel Meliá Cancún Beach & Spa Resort. Km 16.5 Paseo Kukulkán, 77500 Cancún, Q. Roo. ☎ **800/336-3542** in the U.S., or 98/85-1114. Fax 98/85-1085. 450 units. A/C MINIBAR TV TEL. High season $300–$340 double; $400–$550 suite. Low season $210 double; $370 suite. AE, DC, MC, V.

The impressive entrance to this grand hotel is an eight-storied circular interior with a jungle of plants set against a fountain. The marble-and-teakwood backdrop is decorated with majolica pottery from Guanajuato and lacquer chests from Olinalá, Guerrero. This is another of Cancún's hotels that could easily become an island—everything is here, even a pampering spa and a golf course. The spacious rooms, all with sitting areas and balconies, are appropriately stylish and feature in-room security boxes, hair dryers, and purified tap water. There are four rooms on the first floor especially equipped with extra-wide bathrooms for guests with disabilities.

Dining/Diversions: Five restaurants feature foods from Italy, Mexico, and the United States with the casual **Cafe Quetzal** featuring a daily breakfast buffet. Poolside dining is available at two restaurants, with the **Caribe Spa** serving special low-calorie menus. The **La Cascada** Mexican restaurant also features a popular Sunday brunch. Five bars serve guests all day, with the **Turquesa** (lobby) bar featuring Latin rhythms starting at 8pm.

Amenities: Three pools; beach; 18-hole, par-54 golf course on the property; three lighted tennis courts; Ping-Pong; volleyball; complete spa with gymnasium, massage, sauna, whirlpool, facials, seaweed and mud therapy, body scrubs, aerobic and aquatic classes, weights, hydromassage showers, and dressing room; and beauty and barber shop. During high season or times of high hotel occupancy, there's a full daily list of activities for children posted in the lobby. Laundry and room service, travel agency, shops, car rental, and baby cribs and baby-sitters.

✪ **Ritz-Carlton Cancún.** Retorno del Rey, off km 13.5 Paseo Kukulkán, 77500 Cancún, Q. Roo. ☎ **800/241-3333** or 98/85-0808. Fax 98/85-1015. 369 units. A/C MINIBAR TV TEL. High season $329–$369 double; $425–$4,000 suite. Low season $220–$250 double; $275–$3,200 suite. AE, MC, V. Free guarded parking.

On 7½ acres, the nine-story Ritz-Carlton has set the standard for excellence in

Cancún and in Mexico. It is easily the island's most elegant hotel and a member of Leading Hotels of the World. The hotel has won countless recognitions and accolades for its impeccable service and stunning decor of stained glass, marble, and lush carpets. Fresh flowers are found throughout the property.

The spacious guest rooms are as sumptuous as the public areas. Each room has safety-deposit boxes, electronic locks, and twice-daily maid service. Suites are large, and some have a private dressing area, two TVs, balconies, and 1½ bathrooms. In all rooms, marble bathrooms have telephones, separate tubs and showers, lighted makeup mirror, scales, robes, and hair dryers. Floors 8 and 9 are for Ritz-Carlton Club members and offer guests special amenities, including five mini-meals a day. The hotel fronts a 1,200-foot white-sand beach, and all rooms overlook the ocean, pool and tropical gardens. Special packages for golfing, spa, and weekend getaways are worth exploring.

Dining/Diversions: Of the five exceedingly stylish restaurants, **Club Grill,** a fashionable English pub, is one of the best restaurants in the city (See "Where to Dine," below), offering grilled specialties, nightly entertainment, and a dance floor. The **Caribe Bar and Grill** is open for snacks during pool hours. The **Lobby Lounge** opens at 5pm daily offering tea and later live music between 7:30 and 11pm. This bar was the original home of proper tequila tastings, and features one of the world's most extensive menus of fine tequilas, plus Cuban cigars.

Amenities: On the beach, deluxe cabanas for two with thickly cushioned lounges are available, just in front of the two connecting swimming pools (heated during the winter months) with Jacuzzi. For play, there are three lighted tennis courts and a fully equipped gym with Universal weight training and cardiovascular equipment, personal trainers, steam, sauna, and massage service. A Ritz Kids program offers supervised activities for children. Rounding out the offerings are a pharmacy/gift shop, exclusive shopping arcade, and beauty and barber shops. Laundry and dry cleaning, 24-hour room service, travel agency, and concierge also available.

EXPENSIVE

✪ **Camino Real Cancún.** Av. Kukulkán, 77500 Punta Cancún (Apdo. Postal 14), Cancún, Q. Roo. ☎ **800/722-6466** in the U.S., or 98/83-0100. Fax 98/83-1730. 381 units. A/C MINIBAR TV TEL. High season $265–$415 double; $1,600 suite; Camino Real Club $220–$305 double. Low season $185–$305 double; $1,320 suite; Camino Real Club $200 double. AE, DC, MC, V. Daily fee for guarded parking adjacent to hotel.

On 4 acres right at the tip of Punta Cancún, the Camino Real is among the island's most appealing places to stay. The rooms are elegantly outfitted with pink breccia-marble floors, tropical high-backed raffia easy chairs, and drapes and spreads in soft pastel colors. Some rooms in the new 18-story Camino Real Club have elegant Mexican decor, while standard rooms in this section are much like rooms in the rest of the resort. Master suites have expansive views, large dining tables with four chairs, and hot tubs on the balconies. Camino Real Club guests receive a complimentary full breakfast daily in the Beach Club lobby, as well as complimentary cocktails and snacks there each evening. Lower-priced rooms have lagoon views.

Dining/Diversions: Three restaurants include a seafood specialties restaurant; indoor casual dining with flame-broiled meat; and an elegant evening-only restaurant featuring Mexican cuisine. There's a children's menu at the more casual restaurants, an Italian night on Wednesdays, and a Mexican Grill Party on Fridays. The lobby bar features Mexican music nightly from 5:30 to 7:30pm, and the seaview **Azúcar Disco** swings into action Monday to Saturday at 9:30pm.

Amenities: Freshwater pool; private saltwater lagoon with sea turtles and tropical fish; private beach; sailing pier; water-sports center. There are also three lighted tennis courts, beach volleyball, boutiques, gift shops, barber and beauty shops, and a state-of-the-art fitness center with steambath. Laundry and room service, travel agency, car rental, in-room safety boxes, baby-sitting (with advance notice), medical service, 24–hour room service, and massages.

Hyatt Cancún Caribe. Km 10.5 Paseo Kukulkán, 77500 Cancún, Q. Roo. ☎ **800/ 233-1234** in the U.S., or 98/83-0044. Fax 98/83-1514. 230 units. A/C MINIBAR TV TEL. High season $260 double; Regency room $350. Low season $180 double; Regency room $215. AE, DC, MC, V.

The elegant Hyatt Caribe is south of Punta Cancún where there's another Hyatt: the Regency. Because of its dramatic crescent shape, all units face the sparkling Caribbean and have terraces on which to enjoy the view. Regency rooms, set off by themselves, have their own pool and such in-room amenities as lighted makeup mirrors, scales, hairdryers, robes, and security boxes. Regency guests also receive a complimentary continental breakfast, evening drinks, and crudités. Thirty new Premier beachfront suites have just been added.

Dining/Diversions: Blue Bayou serves Cajun and Creole food, **Cocay Cafe** features buffets and contemporary cuisine. **Le Jazz Club** has live music nightly.

Amenities: Swimming pool, beach, 3 tennis courts, beauty shop, pharmacy, and boutiques. Room and laundry service, travel agency, free valet parking, safety deposit boxes, and car rental.

Krystal Cancún. Km 7.5 Paseo Kukulkán, 77500 Cancún, Q. Roo. ☎ **800/231-9860** in the U.S., or 98/83-1133. Fax 98/83-1790. 322 units. A/C MINIBAR TV TEL. High season $210–$450 double. Low season $140–$170 double. AE, DC, MC, V.

The Krystal Cancún lies on Punta Cancún along with the Camino Real and the Hyatt Regency, near the convention center, shops, restaurants, and clubs. The Krystal uses lots of cool marble in its decor. The guest rooms, in two buildings, have an option of bed configurations, with drapes and spreads in earthy tones, and water views. The hotel's tap water is purified, and there are ice machines on every floor. The presidential suites have Jacuzzis. Club Krystal rooms come with in-room safety boxes, complimentary continental breakfast, and evening canapés and drinks; guests in those rooms also have access to the Club Lounge, a rooftop sun lounge with a whirlpool and concierge service.

Dining/Diversions: Among the hotel's four restaurants are two that have gained countrywide recognition for fine cuisine—**Bogart's,** a chic dining room with a Moroccan "Casablanca" theme, and the luxurious **Hacienda El Mortero,** a replica of a colonial hacienda featuring Mexican cuisine. The hotel also hosts theme nights throughout the week. In the evening there's live entertainment in the lobby bar. **Christine's,** one of the most popular discos in town, is open nightly.

Amenities: Swimming pool complex overlooking the Caribbean and a beach with fairly safe swimming; pharmacy; barber and beauty shop; boutiques and a silver shop; two tennis courts with an on-duty tennis pro; a racquetball court; a dive shop; and a fitness club with whirlpool, sauna, and massage facilities. Laundry, room service, travel agency, and car and moped rental.

Marriott Casamagna. Km 20 Paseo Kukulkán, 77500 Cancún, Q. Roo. ☎ **800/228-9290** in the U.S., or 98/81-2000. Fax 98/81-2071. 443 units. A/C MINIBAR TV TEL. High season $225–$270 double; $350–$695 suite. Low season $135–$165 double; $300–$550 suite. Ask about available packages. AE, CB, DC, MC, V.

Luxury is this hotel's hallmark. Entering through a half-circle of Roman columns, you pass through a long, domed foyer to a wide, lavishly marbled 44-foot-high lobby filled with plants. The lobby expands in three directions with wide, Mexican cantera-stone arches branching off outdoors, where columns vanish into shallow pools like Roman baths. Guest rooms have contemporary furnishings, tiled floors, and ceiling fans; most have balconies. All suites occupy corners and have enormous terraces, ocean views, and TVs in both the living room and the bedroom. All rooms have been remodeled.

Dining/Diversions: The hotel has four restaurants: La Capilla overlooks the pool and ocean and features an international menu; Las Islas serves light snacks and beverages poolside; the Bahía Club offers the same fare, only served on the beach; and the recently remodeled Mikado offers Japanese and Thai cuisine. The lobby bar features nightly mariachi music.

Amenities: Beach; swimming pool; two lighted tennis courts; health club with saunas, whirlpool, aerobics, and juice bar; and beauty and barber shop. Massage and facials available. Laundry and room service, travel agency, and car rental.

Presidente Inter-Continental Cancún. Km 7.5 Paseo Kukulkán, 77500 Cancún, Q. Roo. ☎ **800/327-0200** in the U.S., or 98/83-0200. Fax 98/83-2515. 298 units. A/C TV TEL. High season $215–$485 double. Low season $155–$450 double. AE, MC, V.

On the island's best beach facing the placid Bahía de Mujeres, the Presidente's location is tops. Cool and spacious, the Presidente sports a post-modern design with lavish marble and wicker accents and a strong use of color. Guests have a choice of two double beds or one king bed. All rooms have private balconies, tastefully simple unfinished pine furniture, and in-room safes. Sixteen rooms on the first floor have patios with outdoor whirlpool tubs. The club floors offer robes, magnified makeup mirrors, complimentary continental breakfast, evening drinks and canapés, 1 hour free use of tennis court, complimentary use of fitness club, and use of a private key-activated elevator. Two rooms are available for guests with disabilities, and two floors are reserved for nonsmokers. The expansive pool has a pyramid-shaped waterfall, and is surrounded by cushioned lounge chairs. Coming from Cancún City, you'll reach the Presidente on the left side of the street before you get to Punta Cancún—it's behind the golf course and next to million-dollar homes.

Dining: The fine-dining **Mediterraneo** restaurant features foods from France, Greece, Italy, Spain, and Morocco. **El Caribeño,** a three-level palapa restaurant by the beach and pool, serves all meals. **Frutas y Flores** is a family-style coffee shop.

Amenities: Two landscaped swimming pools with a waterfall; whirlpools; fitness center; a great beach fronting Bahía de Mujeres; lighted tennis courts; water-sports equipment; and marina. Laundry and room service, travel agency, car rental.

Sheraton Resort and Towers. Km 12.5 Paseo Kukulkán, 77500 Cancún, Q. Roo. ☎ **800/325-3535** in the U.S., or 98/83-1988. Fax 98/83-1660. 471 units. A/C MINIBAR TV TEL. High season $380–$405 double. Low season $215–$225 double. Ask about summer "Temptation" packages. AE, DC, MC, V. Free parking.

A six-story pyramid-shaped building and a seven-story building are set on their own vast stretch of beach. The impressive lobby has large expanses of green tiles and a dramatic stainless-steel sculpture of birds in flight. Emerald lawns extend in every direction from the main buildings, and a small reconstructed Maya ruin crowns a craggy limestone hillock. Rooms and suites are luxurious, with views of the Caribbean (to the east) or of the lagoon (to the west). In the wedge-shaped tower section, all units have in-room security boxes, and guests enjoy the services of a personal butler who attends to a variety of tasks from shoe shining to snack service. All rooms in this section were just remodeled in 1998. There's a nonsmoking floor, and rooms are available for guests with disabilities.

Dining/Diversions: Four restaurants offer everything from grilled food by the beach to lavish breakfast buffets to Italian feasts to Mexican food. There are four bars, including the lobby bar where there's live music from noon to midnight.

Amenities: Two swimming pools; four lighted tennis courts with tennis pro on duty; beach; fitness center with sauna and steam bath; hammock garden, basketball court, minigolf; aerobics; children's playground; table games; pharmacy; beauty and barber shop; business center; flower shop; and boutiques. Laundry and room service, travel agency, car rental, massage, and baby-sitting.

Westin Regina Cancún. Km 20 Paseo Kukulkán, 77500 Cancún, Q. Roo. ☎ **800/ 228-3000** in the U.S., or 98/85-0086. Fax 98/85-0779. 385 units. A/C MINIBAR TV TEL. High season $245–$300 double. Low season $180–$220. AE, MC, V.

The strikingly austere but grand and beautiful architecture, immediately impressive with its elegant use of stone and marble, is the stamp of leading Latin American architect Ricardo Legorreta. The hotel is divided into two sections, the main hotel and the more exclusive six-story hot-pink tower section. Standard rooms are unusually large and beautifully furnished in cool, contemporary furniture. Those on the sixth floor have balconies, and first-floor rooms have terraces. Rooms in the tower all have ocean or lagoon views, oodles of marble, furniture with Olinalá lacquer accents, Berber carpet area rugs, oak tables and chairs, and marble terraces with lounge chairs. Bear in mind that this hotel is a 15- to 20-minute ride from the "action" strip that lies between the Plaza Flamingo and Punta Cancún. Buses stop in front, and taxis are readily available.

Dining: Two restaurants—**Arrecifes** for elegant dining and **El Palmar** for casual—plus two bars keep guests satisfied.

Amenities: Five swimming pools; three whirlpools; beach; two lighted tennis courts; gymnasium with Stairmaster, bicycle, weights, aerobics, sauna, steam, and massage; pharmacy/gifts; boutiques; beauty and barber shop. Laundry and room service, baby-sitting, concierge, travel agency, car rental, purified tap water, and ice machine on each floor.

MODERATE

Blue Bay Village Cancún. Km 3.5 Paseo Kukulkán, 77500 Cancún, Q. Roo. ☎ **800/BLUE-BAY** in the U.S., or 98/83-1725. Fax 98/83-1724. 220 units. A/C TV TEL. High season $280 double; low season $180 double. All-inclusive. AE, DC, MC, V.

Blue Bay Village Cancún is a spirited yet relaxing all-inclusive resort for adults only. Surrounded by acres of tropical gardens, it's ideally located at the northern end of the hotel zone close to the major shopping plazas, restaurants and nightlife, and where the waters are calm for swimming. Rooms are comfortable, clean, and modern, and guests can choose from two sections: the central building features 72 rooms decorated in rustic wood, the main lobby, administrative offices, restaurants and Tequila Sunrise bar. The remaining nine buildings offer guests 148 rooms, featuring traditional Mexican decor with laguna, garden, and ocean views available. Nonsmoking rooms and wheelchair-accessible rooms are available upon request. All rooms feature satellite TV, private bathroom with shower, and safety deposit boxes. Blue Bay allows guests to use the amenities and facilities at its sister resort, the Blue Bay Club and Marina, located just outside of Ciudad Cancún, near the ferry to Isla Mujeres. There's a free bus and boat shuttle service provided between both Blue Bay Resorts.

Keeping guests active is the obvious objective here, with two swimming pools, four Jacuzzis, windsurfing, kayaks, catamarans, boogie boards, complimentary snorkeling and scuba lessons in the swimming pool, a marina, an exercise room with daily aerobics classes, tennis court, bicycles, and a game room with pool and Ping-Pong tables.

All meals and drinks are included with the room price, served at one of four restaurants. Among them, **El Embarcadero** is an oceanview restaurant serving buffet-styled international cuisine. **La Largata** features natural, healthful breakfasts and a "snack bar" menu during the day, then an à la carte Italian menu for dinner. The four bars include a video bar and disco. In addition, there are theme-night dinners, nightly shows, and live entertainment in the outdoor theater with capacity for 150 guests.

Calinda Viva Cancún. Km 8.5 Paseo Kukulkán, 77500 Cancún, Q. Roo. ☎ **800/221-2222** in the U.S., or 98/83-0800. Fax 98/83-2087. 210 units. A/C TV TEL. High season $145–$185 double. Low season $135 double. AE, MC, V.

From the street, this hotel looks like a blockhouse, but on the ocean side you'll find a small but pretty patio garden and Cancún's best beach for safe swimming. Its location is ideal, close to all the shops and restaurants clustered near Punta Cancún and the convention center. You have a choice of rooms with either lagoon or ocean view. The rooms are large and undistinguished in decor, but comfortable with marble floors and either two double beds or a king-size bed. Facilities include one swimming pool for adults and one for children, two lighted tennis courts, water-sports equipment rental, and a marina. The main restaurant is open for all meals. Two others, both beside the pool, serve drinks and light meals. They're joined by three bars.

Flamingo Cancún. Km 11.5 Paseo Kukulkán, 77500 Cancún, Q. Roo. ☎ **98/83-1544.** Fax 98/83-1029. 220 units. A/C TV TEL. High season $160 double. Low season $118 double. AE, MC, V. Free unguarded parking across the street in the Plaza Flamingo.

The Flamingo seems to have been inspired by the dramatic, slope-sided architecture of the Camino Real, but the Flamingo is considerably smaller. The clean, comfortable, and modern guest rooms form a courtyard facing the swimming pool. A colorful open-air restaurant faces the pool, where guests lounge with a view of the Caribbean. The Flamingo is in the heart of the island hotel district, opposite the Flamingo Shopping Center and close to other hotels, shopping centers, and restaurants. A restaurant and snack bar are both open daily, and a lobby bar and pool bar offer libations.

Miramar Misión Cancún Park Plaza. Km 9.5 Paseo Kukulkán, 77500 Cancún, Q. Roo. ☎ **800/215-1333** in the U.S., or 98/83-1755. Fax 98/83-1136. 300 units. A/C MINIBAR TV TEL. $145 double. AE, DC, MC, V.

Each of the ingeniously designed rooms has partial views of the lagoon and ocean. Public spaces throughout the hotel have lots of dark wood, cream-beige stucco, red tile, and pastel accents. The big swimming pool is next to the beach. Rooms are on the small side but comfortable, with bamboo furniture offset by pastel-colored cushions and bedspreads; bathrooms have polished limestone vanities. In-room amenities include hair dryers and safe-deposit boxes.

Three restaurants serve cuisine of Mexico and the United States. There's live music nightly in the lobby bar, and a bar by the pool serves guests during pool hours. A nightclub also has live music for dancing from 9pm to 4am Tuesday to Sunday.

INEXPENSIVE

El Pueblito. Km 19.5 Paseo Kukulkán, 77500 Cancún, Q. Roo. ☎ **98/85-0422** or 98/85-0797. Fax 98/85-0422. 239 units. A/C TV TEL. High season $155. Low season $95–$130. AE, MC, V.

Dwarfed by its ostentatious neighbors, El Pueblito nevertheless has several three-story buildings (no elevators) terraced in a V-shape down a gentle hillside toward the sea. A meandering swimming pool with waterfalls runs between the two series of buildings. Rooms have just been repainted and restyled with modern rattan furnishings, travertine marble floors, and large bathrooms. Many have balconies facing the pool or sea. Three restaurants and two bars are on the grounds. Minigolf and a water style make this an ideal place for families with children. The hotel is located toward the southern end of the island past the Caesar Park Resort.

Hotel Aristos. Km 12 Paseo Kukulkán (Apdo. Postal 450), 77500 Cancún, Q. Roo. ☎ **800/527-4786** in the U.S., or 98/83-0011. 244 rms. A/C TV TEL. High season $100–$130 double. Low season $85 double. All-inclusive option for 3 meals and drinks, add $36 daily. AE, MC, V. Free parking; unguarded.

This was one of the island's first hotels. Rooms are neat and cool, with red-tile floors, small balconies, and yellow Formica furniture. All rooms face either the Caribbean or the paseo and lagoon; the best views (with no noise from the paseo) face the Caribbean side. The hotel has one restaurant and several bars and offers room and laundry service, a travel agency, and baby-sitting service. The central pool overlooks the ocean with a wide stretch of beach one level below the pool and lobby. You'll also find a marina with water-sports equipment and two lighted tennis courts. Beware of spring break here, when the hotel blares loud music poolside all day.

CANCÚN CITY
MODERATE

✪ Mexhotel Centro. Yaxchilán 31, SM 22, 77500 Cancún, Q. Roo. ☎ **98/84-3078.** Fax 888/594-6835 in the U.S., or 98/84-3478. 80 units. A/C TV TEL. High season $80 double. Low season $60 double. AE, MC, V.

The nicest hotel in Ciudad Cancún, the Mexhotel Centro has the warmth and style of a small hacienda when entering from the back; on the street side, it's been incorporated into a small shopping mall. The three stories of rooms (with elevator) front a lovely palm-shaded pool area with comfortable tables and chairs and restaurant. Standard rooms are extra clean, with muted decor, two double beds framed with wrought iron headboards, large tile bathrooms with separate sink, desks, and overbed reading lights. Although prices may seem high for the location, beach and pool facilities at its sister resort in the hotel zone make it a great bargain. The hotel is between Jazmines and Gladiolas catercorner from **Perico's.**

INEXPENSIVE

Hotel Antillano. Claveles 1 at the corner of Tulum, 77500 Cancún, Q. Roo. ☎ **98/84-1532.** Fax 98/84-1878. 48 units. A/C TV TEL. High season $60 double. Low season $40 double. MC, V.

A quiet and very clean choice, close to the Ciudad Cancún bus terminal. Rooms overlook either avenida Tulum, the side streets, or the interior lawn and pool, with the latter being the most desirable since they are quieter. Each room has nicely coordinated furnishings, one or two double beds, a sink area separate from the bath, red-tile floors, and a small TV. There's a small bar to one side of the reception area and a travel agency in the lobby. The hotel offers guests use of its beach club on the island. Baby-sitting can be arranged. To find it from Tulum, walk west on Claveles a half block; it's opposite the **Restaurant Rosa Mexicana.** Parking is on the street.

Hotel Hacienda Cancún. Sunyaxchen 39–40, 77500 Cancún, Q. Roo. ☎ **98/84-3672.** Fax 98/84-1208. 40 units. A/C MINIBAR TV TEL. $35 double. AE, MC, V.

This extremely pleasing little hotel is another great value. The facade has been remodeled to look like a hacienda, and all rooms were refurbished in 1997. The guest rooms are clean and plainly furnished but very comfortable, and all have two double beds and windows (but no views). There's a nice small pool and cafe under a shaded palapa in the back. The hotel is also a member of the Imperial Las Perlas beach club in the Zona Hotelera. To find it from avenida Yaxchilán, turn west on Sunyaxchen; it's on your right next to the Hotel Caribe International, opposite 100% Natural. Parking is on the street.

Hotel Parador. Tulum 26, 77500 Cancún, Q. Roo. ☎ **98/84-1043** or 98/84-1310. Fax 98/84-9712. 66 units. A/C TV TEL. High season $45 double. Low season $35 double. Ask about promotional rates. MC, V.

One of the most popular downtown hotels, the three-story Parador is conveniently located. Guest rooms are arranged around two long, narrow garden courtyards leading back to a pool (with separate children's pool) and grassy sunning area. The rooms are modern, each with two double beds, a shower, and cable TV. Help yourself to bottled drinking water in the hall. There's a restaurant/bar, and it's next to **Pop's** restaurant, almost at the corner of Uxmal. Street parking is limited.

4 Where to Dine

The restaurant scene in Cancún is dominated by the known names of U.S.-based franchise chains—which really need no introduction. These include Hard Rock Cafe, Planet Hollywood, All Star Cafe, Rainforest Cafe, Tony Roma's, TGI Friday's, Ruth's Chris Steak House, and the gamut of fast-food burger places. The restaurants listed here are either locally owned, one-of-a-kind restaurants, or exceptional selections at area hotels.

CANCÚN ISLAND
VERY EXPENSIVE

Captain's Cove. Km 15 Paseo Kukulkán. ☎ **98/85-0016.** Breakfast buffet $6.95; main courses $16–$20. AE, V, MC. Daily 7am–11pm. INTERNATIONAL.

Though it sits almost at the end of Paseo Kukulkán, far from everything, the Captain's Cove continues to pack customers into its several dining levels. Diners face big open windows overlooking the lagoon and Royal Yacht Club Marina. During breakfast there's an all-you-can-eat buffet. Main courses of steak and seafood are the norm at lunch and dinner, and there's a menu catering especially to children. For dessert there are flaming coffees, crêpes, and Key lime pie. The restaurant is on the lagoon side opposite the Omni Hotel.

✪ **Club Grill.** Ritz-Carlton Cancún, km 13.5 Paseo Kukulkán. ☎ **98/85-0808.** Reservations required. Main courses $30–$50. AE, DC, MC, V. Tue–Sun 6–11pm. INTERNATIONAL.

Cancún's most elegant and stylish restaurant is also its best. Even rival restaurateurs give it an envious thumbs up. The gracious service starts as you enter the anteroom with its comfortable couches and chairs and selection of fine tequilas and Cuban cigars. It continues into the candlelit dining room with padded side chairs and tables shimmering with silver and crystal. Under the trained eye of chef de cuisine John Patrick Gray, elegant plates of peppered scallops, truffles, and potatoes in tequila sauce, or grilled lamb, or mixed grill arrive without feeling rushed after the appetizer. The restaurant has both smoking and nonsmoking sections (a rarity in Mexico). A band plays romantic music for dancing from 8pm on. This is the place for that truly special night out. Dress code enforced. Gentlemen must wear long pants; no sandals for ladies or tennis shoes for gentlemen.

✪ **María Bonita.** Hotel Camino Real, Punta Cancún. ☎ **98/83-0100**, ext. 8060 or 8061. Main courses $10–$25. AE, DC, MC, V. Daily 6:30–11:30pm. REGIONAL/MEXICAN/NOU-VELLE MEXICAN.

Enjoy Mexico at its very best—its music, food, and atmosphere—in an stylish setting that captures the essence of Mexico with every bite and glance. Overlooking the water, the interior is divided by cuisine—La Cantina Jalisco includes an open colorful Mexican kitchen (with pots and pans on the wall) and tequila bar (with more than 50 different tequilas); the Salon Michoacán in the center features food from that state's cuisine; and the Patio Oaxaca is on the lower level. The menu includes foods from these three states, as well as the best of Mexico's other cuisines, as excellently prepared as you'll find them anywhere, with a few international dishes thrown in for variety. While you dine, you'll be serenaded by duets, marimba music, jarocho, and the ever-enchanting mariachis. The different peppers used in sauces and preparation are explained on the front of the menu, and each dish is marked for its heat quotient (from zero chiles to two chiles). A nice starter is the Mitlan salad, which has Oaxaca cheese slices (the state is known for its excellent cheese) dribbled with a little olive oil and a coriander dressing. The stuffed chile "La Doña"—a poblano pepper (mildly hot) filled with lobster and huitlacoche, in a cream sauce—comes as either an appetizer or a main course and is wonderful. The restaurant is to the left of the entrance of the hotel and is entered from the street.

EXPENSIVE

✪ **La Dolce Vita.** Km 14.6 Paseo Kukulkán. ☎ **98/84-1384** or 98/85-0150. Reservations required for dinner. Main courses $10–$21. MC, V. Daily 12pm–midnight. ITALIAN.

Prepare to dine on some of the best Italian food in Mexico. Now at its new location on the lagoon, and opposite the Marriott Casamagna, the casually elegant La Dolce Vita is even more pleasant and popular than its old garden location downtown. Appetizers include pâté of quail liver and carpaccio in vinaigrette, or watercress salad. You can order such pastas as green tagliolini with lobster medallions, linguine with clams or seafood, or rigatoni Mexican style (with chorizo, mushrooms, and chives), as an appetizer for half price or as a main course for full price. Other main courses include veal with morels, fresh salmon with cream sauce, scampi, and various fish.

La Fisheria. Plaza Caracol, 2nd floor. ☎ **98/83-1395.** Main courses $6.50–$21. AE, MC, V. Daily 11am–11:30pm. SEAFOOD.

Patrons find a lot to choose from at this restaurant overlooking bulevar Kukulkán and the lagoon. The expansive menu offers shark fingers with a jalapeño dip, grouper fillet stuffed with seafood in a lobster sauce, Acapulco-style ceviche (in a tomato sauce), New England clam chowder, steamed mussels, grilled red snapper with pasta—you get the idea. The menu changes daily, but there's always *tikin xik,* that great Yucatecan grilled fish marinated in achiote sauce. And for those not inclined toward seafood, a wood-burning oven pizza might do, or one of the grilled chicken or beef dishes.

✪ **Lorenzillo's.** Km 10.5 Paseo Kukulkán. ☎ **98/83-1254.** Main courses $8–$50. AE, MC, V. Daily 10am–11:30pm. SEAFOOD.

Live lobster is the overwhelming favorite here, and selecting your "dinner" out of the giant lobster tank is part of the appeal. Lorenzillo's sits on the lagoon under a giant palapa roof. A dock leads down to the main dining area, and when that's packed (which is often), a wharf-side bar handles the overflow. In addition to lobster—which comes grilled, steamed, or stuffed—good bets are the shrimp stuffed with cheese and wrapped in bacon, the Admiral's filet—coated in toasted almonds and a light mustard sauce—or the seafood-stuffed squid. Desserts include the tempting Martinique, Belgian chocolate with hazelnuts, almonds, and pecans, served with vanilla ice cream.

Mango Tango. Km 14.2 Paseo Kukulkán, opposite the Ritz-Carlton. ☎ **98/85-0303.** Main courses $6–$16; dinner show $25–$35. AE, MC, V. Daily 2pm–2am. INTERNATIONAL.

Mango Tango's made a name for itself with its floor shows (see "Cancún After Dark," below), but its kitchen is deserving of attention as well. Try the peel-your-own shrimp, Argentine-style grilled meat with chimichuri sauce, and other grilled specialties. The Mango Tango Salad has shrimp, chicken, avocado, red onion, tomato, and mushrooms on mango slices. Entrees includes Mango Tango rice with seafood and fried bananas. The Creole gumbo comes with lobster, shrimp, and squid.

Savio's. Plaza Caracol. ☎ **98/83-2085.** Main courses $8.25–$20. AE, MC, V. Daily 10am–midnight. ITALIAN.

Savio's, in stylish black and white with tile floors and green marble–topped tables, is on two levels, and faces Paseo Kukulkán through two stories of awning-shaded windows. Its bar is always crowded with patrons sipping everything from cappuccino to imported beer. Repeat diners look forward to large fresh salads and richly flavored, subtly herbed Italian dishes. The ravioli stuffed with ricotta and spinach is served in a delicious tomato sauce.

CANCÚN CITY
EXPENSIVE

La Habichuela. Margaritas 25. ☎ **98/84-3158.** Reservations recommended in high season. Main courses $8–$30. AE, DC, MC, V. Daily 1pm–midnight. GOURMET SEAFOOD/BEEF/MEXICAN.

In a garden setting with tables covered in pink-and-white linens and soft music playing in the background, this restaurant is ideal for a romantic evening. For an all-out culinary adventure, try *habichuela* (string bean) soup; shrimp in any number of sauces including Jamaican tamarindo, tequila, and a ginger and mushroom combination; and the Maya coffee with xtabentun (a strong, sweet, anise-based liquor). The grilled seafood and steaks are excellent as well, but this is a good place to try a Mexican specialty such as enchiladas suizas or tampiqueña-style (thinly sliced, marinated, and grilled) beef. For something totally new, try the Cocobichuela, which is lobster and shrimp in a curry sauce served in a coconut shell and topped with fruit.

MODERATE

100% Natural. Av. Sunyaxchen 6. ☎ **98/84-3617.** Breakfast $2.25–$3.25; spaghetti $5; fruit or vegetable shakes $2.50; sandwiches and Mexican plates $3–$6. MC, V. Daily 7am–11pm. SEMIVEGETARIAN.

Of all the 100% Natural branches around Mexico, this has one of the most appealing settings, with white rattan tables on a white tile floor and large dining areas on the street or interior patio. It's the best spot in town for great mixed-fruit shakes and salads. Full meals include large portions of chicken or fish, spaghetti, or soup and sandwiches. Dine on the pretty patio in back to avoid the roar of traffic out in front. The restaurant is near the corner of avenidas Yaxchilán and Sunyax-chen opposite the Hotel Caribe Internacional. Three other locations are in the Zona Hotelera at Plaza Terramar (☎ **98/83-1180**); Forum by the Sea (☎ **98/83-4478**); and Plaza Kukulkán (☎ **98/85-2904**).

✪ **Périco's.** Yaxchilán 61. ☎ **98/84-3152.** Main courses $9–$20. Daily 1pm–1am. AE, MC, V. MEXICAN/SEAFOOD/STEAKS.

Périco's has colorful murals that almost dance off the walls, a bar area overhung with baskets and saddles for bar stools, colorfully bedecked leather tables and chairs, and accommodating waiters; it's always booming and festive. The extensive menu offers well-prepared steak, seafood, and traditional Mexican dishes for moderate rates (except lobster). This is a place not only to eat and drink but to let loose and join in the fun, so don't be surprised if everybody drops their forks and dons huge Mexican sombreros to bob and snake in a conga dance around the dining room. It's fun whether or not you join in. There's marimba music from 7:30 to 10:30pm, and mariachis from 10:30pm to midnight. This is a popular spot, so expect a crowd.

✪ **Restaurant El Pescador.** Tulipanes 28, off Av. Tulum. ☎ **98/84-2673.** Fax 98/84-3639 or 98/85-0505. Main courses $9–$35; Mexican plates $5–$9. AE, MC, V. Daily 11am–11pm. SEAFOOD.

There's often a line at this restaurant, which serves well-prepared fresh seafood in its street-side patio and upstairs venue overlooking Tulipanes. Feast on shrimp cocktail, conch, octopus, Creole-style shrimp (camarones à la criolla), charcoal-broiled lobster, and stone crabs. Zarzuela is a combination seafood plate cooked in white wine and garlic. There's a Mexican specialty menu as well. Another branch, **La Mesa del Pescador,** is in the Plaza Kukulkán on Cancún Island and is open the same hours, but is more expensive.

✪ **Restaurant Los Almendros.** Av. Bonampak and Sayil. ☎ **98/87-1332.** Main courses $4–$6. AE, MC, V. Daily 11am–10pm. YUCATECAN.

To steep yourself in Yucatecan cuisine, head directly to this large, colorful, and air-conditioned restaurant. Many readers have written to say they ate here almost exclusively, since the food and service are good and the illustrated menu, with color pictures of dishes, makes ordering easy. Some of the regional specialties include lime soup, *poc chuc* (a marinated, barbecue-style pork), chicken or *pork pibil* (a sweet and spicy, shredded meat), and such appetizers as panuchos Yucatecos. The combinado Yucateco is a sampler of four typically Yucatecan main courses: chicken, poc chuc, sausage, and *escabeche* (onions marinated in vinegar and sour orange). A second location opened in 1994 on Cancún Island on Paseo Kukulkán across from the convention center. The downtown location is opposite the bullring.

Restaurant Rosa Mexicana. Claveles 4. ☎ **98/84-6313.** Reservations recommended for parties of 6 or more. Main courses $6–$12; lobster $20. AE, MC, V. Daily 5–11pm. MEXICAN HAUTE.

This beautiful little place has candlelit tables and a plant-filled patio in back, and it's almost always packed. Colorful paper banners and piñatas hang from the ceiling, efficient waiters wear bow ties and cummerbunds color-themed to the Mexican flag, and a trio plays romantic Mexican music nightly. The menu features "refined" Mexican specialties. Try the pollo almendro, which is chicken covered in a cream sauce sprinkled with ground almonds, or the pork baked in a banana leaf with a sauce of oranges, lime, chile ancho, and garlic. The steak tampiqueño is a huge platter that comes with guacamole salad, quesadillas, beans, salad, and rice.

INEXPENSIVE

Pizza Rolandi. Cobá 12. ☎ **98/84-4047.** Pasta $5–$8; pizza and main courses $4–$9. AE, V, MC. Daily 12:30pm–midnight. ITALIAN.

At this shaded outdoor patio restaurant you can choose from almost two dozen different wood-oven pizzas and a full selection of spaghetti, calzones, and Italian-style chicken and beef and desserts. There's a full bar list as well. There's another Pizza Rolandi in Isla Mujeres at 110 av. Hidalgo (☎ **98/704-30**) with the same food and prices. Open Monday to Sunday 11am to 11pm.

✪ **Restaurant Curva.** Av. Yaxchilán at Sunyaxchen. No phone. Breakfast $1.75–$2.50; comida corrida $2.50–$3. No credit cards. Mon–Sat 9am–5pm. MEXICAN.

It's worth the wait for a seat at one of the six tables in this tiny and spotless storefront cafe. You'll join young office workers and students for an inexpensive home-style lunch. The daily comida includes soup, rice, beans, and meat. There's usually a choice of main courses, such as beef tips, pozole, pollo adobado, and pollo frito. Lingering is not appreciated during lunchtime.

Restaurante Santa María. Azucenas at Parque Palapas. ☎ **98/84-3158.** Main courses $3.50–$9; tacos 75¢–$5. No credit cards. Daily 5pm–10pm. MEXICAN.

The open-air Santa María restaurant is a clean, gaily decked-out place to sample authentic Mexican food. It's cool and breezy with patio dining that's open on two sides and is furnished with leather tables and chairs covered in multicolored cloths. A bowl of frijoles de olla and an order of beefsteak tacos will fill you up for a low price. You may want to try the tortilla soup or enchiladas, or go for one of the grilled U.S.-cut steaks, or an order of fajitas, ribs, or grilled seafood, all of which arrive with a baked potato.

Stefano's. Bonampak 177. ☎ **98/87-9964.** Main courses $4–$6; pizza $4.75–$6.75. AE, MC, V. Wed–Mon 2pm–midnight. ITALIAN/PIZZA/PASTA.

Tourists are beginning to find Stefano's, which serves Italian food with a few Mexican accents. On the menu you'll find a huitlacoche and shrimp pizza, rigatoni in tequila sauce, and seafood with chile peppers, nestled proudly alongside the Stefano special pizza, made with fresh tomato, cheese, and pesto, and calzones stuffed with spinach, mozzarella, and tomato sauce. For dessert, the ricotta strudel is something out of the ordinary, or else try the tiramisú. There are lots of different coffees and mixed drinks, as well. New decor and ambience; also a new wine list.

COFFEE & PASTRIES

Pasteleria Italiana. Av. Yaxchilán 67, SM 25, near Sunyaxchen. ☎ **98/84-0796.** Pastries $1.75–$2.25; ice cream $2; coffee $1–$2. AE. Mon–Sat 9am–11pm, Sun 1–9pm. COFFEE/PASTRIES/ICE CREAM.

More like a casual neighborhood coffeehouse than a place aimed at tourists, this shady little respite has been doing business here since 1977. You'll spot it by the white awning that covers the small outdoor, plant-filled table area. Inside are refrigerated cases of tarts and scrumptious-looking cakes, ready to be carried away in their entirety or by the piece. The coffeehouse is in the same block as Perico's, between Maraño and Chiabal.

5 Beaches & Water Sports

THE BEACHES   The best stretches of beach are dominated by the big hotels. All of Mexico's beaches are public property, so you can use the beach of any hotel by walking through the lobby. Be especially careful on beaches fronting the open Caribbean, where the undertow is quite strong. By contrast, the waters of Bahía de Mujeres at the north end of the island are usually calm. Get to know Cancún's water-safety pennant system, and make sure to check the flag at any beach or hotel before entering the water. Here's how it goes:

White	Excellent
Green	Normal conditions (safe)
Yellow	Changeable, uncertain (use caution)
Black or red	Unsafe; use the swimming pool instead!

In the Caribbean, storms can arrive and conditions can change from safe to unsafe in a matter of minutes, so be alert: If you see dark clouds heading your way, make your way to shore and wait until the storm passes.

Playa Tortuga (Turtle Beach), Playa Langosta, Playa Linda, and Playa Las Perlas are some of the public beaches. At most beaches besides swimming, you can rent a sailboard and take lessons, ride a parasail, or partake in a variety of watersports. There's a small but beautiful portion of public beach on Playa Caracol, by the Xcaret Terminal. Both of these face the calm waters of Bahía de Mujeres and for that reason are preferable to those facing the Caribbean.

WATER SPORTS   Many beachside hotels offer water-sports concessions that include rental of rubber rafts, kayaks, and snorkeling equipment. On the calm Nichupte Lagoon are outlets for renting **sailboats, water jets, Windsurfers,** and **water skis.** Prices vary and are often negotiable, so check around.

For windsurfing, go to the Playa Tortuga public beach, where there's a **Wind-surfing School** (☎ 98/84-2023) with equipment for rent.

DEEP-SEA FISHING   You can arrange a day of **deep-sea fishing** at one of the numerous piers or travel agencies for around $200–$360 for 4 hours, $420 for 6 hours, and $520 for 8 hours for up to four people. Marinas will sometimes assist in putting a group together. Charters include a captain, a first mate, bait, gear, and beverages. Rates are lower if you depart from Isla Mujeres, or from Cozumel Island.

SNORKELING AND SCUBA   Known for its shallow reefs, dazzling color, and diversity of life, Cancún is one of the best places in the world for beginning **scuba diving.** Punta Nizuc, the northern tip of the Great Meso American Reef (Gran Ari-cife Mayan) begins in Cancún. This is the largest reef in the Western Hemisphere, and one of the largest in the world. In addition to the sealife present along this reef system, several sunken boats add a variety of dive options. Inland, a series of caverns and wellsprings, known as cenotes, are fascinating venues for the more experienced diver. Drift diving is the norm here, with popular dives going to the reefs at **El Garrafón** and **the Cave of the Sleeping Sharks.**

Resort courses, offered in a variety of hotels, teach the basics of diving—enough to make shallow dives and slowly ease your way into this underwater world of unimaginable beauty. Scuba trips run around $60 for two-tank dives at nearby reefs, $100 and up for locations farther out. **Scuba Cancún,** km 5 Paseo Kukulkán, on the lagoon side (☎ **98/83-1011;** fax 98/84-2336; open 8:30am to 10pm, phone reservations also available in the evenings from 7:30 to 10:30pm using the fax line), offers a 4-hour resort course for $88. Full certification takes 4 to 5 days and costs around $325. The largest operator is **Aquaworld** (☎ **98/85-2288** or 98/83-3007, located across from the Meliá Cancún at km 15.2 Paseo Kukulkán), offering resort courses and diving from their manmade anchored dive platform, **Paradise Island.** Their **Sub See Explorer** provides non-divers with a look at life beneath the sea. **Scuba Cancún** also offers diving trips to 20 nearby reefs, including Cuevones at 30 feet and the open ocean at 30 to 60 feet (offered in good weather only). The average dive is around 35 feet. One-tank dives cost $45, and two-tank dives cost $60. Discounts apply if you bring your own equipment. Dives usually start around 9am and return by 2:15pm. Snorkeling trips cost $25 and leave every afternoon after 2pm for shallow reefs about a 20-minute boat ride away.

Besides **snorkeling** at **Garrafón National Park** (see "Boating Excursions," below), travel agencies offer an all-day excursion to the natural wildlife habitat of **Isla Contoy,** which usually includes time for snorkeling. This island, located an hour and a half past Isla Mujeres, is a major nesting area for birds, and is a treat for true nature lovers. Only two boats hold permits for excursions there, departing at 9am and returning by 5pm. The price of $60 includes drinks and snorkeling equipment.

6 Excursions & Organized Tours

Cancún's beaches beckon visitors here to the lucid waters, for pure relaxation. But they also invite play, in a lively variety of ways. The options for exploring beyond your beach chair are many. To start, I highly recommend **Perfect Host,** km 20 Paseo Kukulkán, in the Hotel Westin Regina (☎ **98/87-5537,** fax 98/87-5541). The company has investigated every provider of tour services in the region and offers unbiased advice, tailored to your expectations. With so many offering similar tour routes, they can help you match the service and price to the level of organization and amenities you're looking for. The most popular, according to manager Andrés Brakke, are the routes south to **Tulum** and **Xel-Ha** or **Xcaret;** the route west to the ruins of **Chichén-Itzá,** a boat cruise over to the nearby **Isla Mujeres,** and the **Jungle Cruise** (by wave runners), exploring Cancún's lagoon and reefs.

Day trips are the most popular way to explore the seaside ruins of Tulum and the ecological theme parks of Xcaret and Xel-Ha, and are detailed below. Besides these, see also "Road Trips from Cancún," at the end of the chapter, for suggestions on getting to the ruins of Chichén-Itzá, Cobá, El Eden—a 500,000-acre private biological reserve northwest of Cancún—and the 2-million-acre Sian Ka'an Biosphere Reserve south of Cancún and Tulum. Each can be explored as a day trip, or seen in a more extended stay.

The popular **Jungle Cruise** is offered by several companies, and takes you by JetSki or waverunner through Cancún's lagoon and mangrove estuaries out into the Caribbean sea and a shallow reef. The excursion runs about 2½ hours driving your own boat, and is priced from $35 to $40, with snorkeling and beverages included. Some of the motorized mini-boats seat one person behind the other; others seat you side-by-side.

Xcaret has become almost a reason in itself to visit Cancún. An ecological theme park, it's as close to Disneyland as is found in Mexico, with myriad attractions in one location, most participatory. Promoters claim this was an ancient Maya city, and whether truth or fiction, it's like a mini-city today, complete with ruins of its own, plus museums, galleries, aviaries, restaurants, shops, and an amphitheater for regular performances. Most visitors, however, come for the range of outdoor activities that include snorkeling in a natural aquarium, swimming with dolphins ($80 extra charge, first-come basis, no reservations), floating through a river dotted with underground caverns and natural cenotes, horseback riding, botanical hiking trails, and its own beautiful beach. Located on a peninsula 45 miles (about an hour) south of Cancún, the park can be entered on your own, but the favored way is through one of the many tours that travel here daily. Xcaret's own colorfully converted buses depart each day at 9am and 10am from the bus terminal in front of Plaza Caracol. Children under 5 are admitted free. You can reach the Xcaret offices at ☎ **98/ 83-3144** or 98/83-3143. Day tours ($50), departing at 8am and returning at 6pm, include transportation in a deluxe air-conditioned bus, guide, and entrance fee. Xcaret Day & Night ($60) returns at 9:30pm.

Another popular day excursion combines a visit to the ruins at **Tulum** with the ecological water park **Xel-Ha.** Ancient Tulum is the only Maya ruin by the sea. It is a stunning site, poised on a rocky hill overlooking the transparent, turquoise Caribbean sea. Not the largest or most important of the Maya ruins in this area, it is still memorable due to its location and the intriguing carvings and reliefs that decorate the well-preserved structures. The site dates back to between the 12th and 16th centuries A.D, in the Postclassic period. "Tulum" means fence, trench, or wall, and is the name given to this site due to the wall surrounding it on three sides. Its ancient name is believed to have been **Záma,** a derivative of the Mayan word for morning, associated with the dawn. Sunrise at Tulum is dramatic. The wall is believed to have been constructed after the original buildings to protect the interior religious altars from a growing number of invaders. It is considered to have been principally a place of worship, with members of upper classes later taking residence there due to its protective wall. Between the two most dramatic structures—the Castle and the Temple of the Wind—lies Tulum cove. A small inlet with a beach of fine, white sand, it was a point of departure for Maya trading vessels in ancient times. Today, it's a playground for tourists. Entrance to the site without a tour is $2; use of video camera requires a $4 permit.

Xel-Ha (☎ 98/84-9412) is a natural water park that covers 10 acres. A series of crystal-clear lagoons, coves, and inlets, filled with tropical fish, lead to the Caribbean ocean. Visitors float through the waters or enjoy the beach, along with shops, restaurants, and other attractions. For non-snorkelers, platforms have been constructed that allow decent sealife viewing. Snorkeling and hiking are added activities. It opens daily at 8:30am. Admission only is $15 and includes use of inner tubes, life vest, and shuttle train to the river. Parking is free. Excursions combining Xel-Ha with a stop at Tulum depart at 8am, return at 6pm, and include deluxe transportation, guide, and admission fees for a price of $49.

Day tours to **Chichén-Itzá** cost $52, including transportation, admission, guide, and buffet lunch. The special "Sound & Light" tour, which includes the evening light show, and buffet dinner costs $70, returning at 11pm. See also, "Road Trips from Cancún" at the end of the chapter, for more details on getting to these ruins.

BOATING EXCURSIONS   The island of **Isla Mujeres,** just 10 miles offshore, is one of the most pleasant day trips from Cancún. At one end is **El Garrafón National Underwater Park,** which is excellent for snorkeling. And at the other end is the captivating village with small shops, restaurants, and hotels, and **Playa Norte,** the island's best beach. (See chapter 5 for more on Isla Mujeres.) If you're looking for relaxation and can spare the time, Isla Mujeres is worth several days.

There are four ways to get there: by frequent **public ferry** from Puerto Juárez, which takes between 20 and 45 minutes; by a **shuttle boat** from Playa Linda or Playa Tortuga (an hour ride) but with irregular service; by the **Watertaxi** (also with limited service), next to the Xcaret Terminal; and by one of the daylong **pleasure boat trips,** most of which leave from the Playa Linda pier. The cost of the public ferry from Puerto Juárez is the least expensive, and a very convenient way to travel there.

The inexpensive Puerto Juárez **public ferries** are just a few miles from downtown Cancún. From Cancún City, take the Ruta 8 bus on avenida Tulum to Puerto Juárez; the ferry docks in downtown Isla Mujeres by all the shops, restaurants, hotels, and Norte beach. You'll need a taxi to go to Garrafón Park at the other end of the island. You can stay as long as you like on the island (even overnight) and return by ferry, but be sure to ask about the time of the last returning ferry—don't depend on the posted hours. (For more details and a shuttle schedule, see chapter 5.)

Pleasure boat cruises to Isla Mujeres are a favorite pastime here. Modern motor yachts, catamarans, trimarans, and even old-time sloops—more than 25 boats a day—take swimmers, sunners, snorkelers, and shoppers out into the translucent waters. Some tours include a snorkeling stop at Garrafón, lunch on the beach, and a short time for shopping in downtown Isla Mujeres. Most leave at 9:30 or 10am, last about 5 or 6 hours, and include continental breakfast, lunch, and rental of snorkel gear. Others, particularly the sunset and night cruises, go to beaches away from town for pseudo-pirate shows and include a lobster dinner or Mexican buffet. If you want to actually see Isla Mujeres, go on a morning cruise, or go on your own using the public ferry at Puerto Juárez mentioned above. Prices for the day cruises run around $45 per person.

Other excursions go to the **reefs** in glass-bottom boats, so you can have a near-scuba-diving experience and see many colorful fish. However, the reefs are a distance from shore and impossible to reach on windy days with choppy seas. They've also suffered from overuse, and their condition is far from pristine. The glass-bottomed **Nautibus** ($25 adults, $12.40 children; ☎ 98/83-3552 or 98/83-2119; AE, V, MC) has been around for years. The morning and afternoon trips in a glass-bottom boat from the Playa Pier to the Chitale coral reef to see colorful fish take about 1 hour and 20 minutes, with around 50 minutes of it consumed going to and from the reef. The **Atlantis Submarine** takes you even closer to the subaquatic action. Departures are variable, depending on weather conditions. Prices range from $44 to $65, depending on the length of the trip. Still other boat excursions visit **Isla Contoy**, a **national bird sanctuary** that's well worth the time. If you are planning to spend time in Isla Mujeres, the Contoy trip is easier and more pleasurable to take from there.

The operators and names of boats offering excursions change often. To find out what's available when you're there, check with a local travel agent or hotel tour desk, for they should have a wide range of options. You can also go to the Playa Linda Pier either a day ahead or the day of your intended outing and buy your own ticket for trips on the Nautibus or to Isla Mujeres. If you go on the day of your trip, arrive at the pier around 8:45am since most boats leave by 9 or 9:30am.

7 Outdoor Activities & Other Attractions

OUTDOOR ACTIVITIES

DOLPHIN SWIMS   On Isla Mujeres, you have the opportunity to swim with dolphins at **Dolphin Discovery** (☎ 98/83-0779). Each session is 1 hour, with an educational introduction followed by 30 minutes of swim time. Price is $119, with transportation to Isla Mujeres an additional $15. Advanced reservations are required, as capacity is limited each day.

GOLF & TENNIS   The 18-hole **Club de Golf Cancún** (☎ 98/83-0871), also known as the Pok-Ta-Pok Club, was designed by Robert Trent Jones Sr. and is located on the northern leg of the island. Greens fees run $100 per 18 holes, with clubs renting for $18 and a caddy $20 per bag. The club is open daily, and American Express, MasterCard, and Visa are accepted. It also has tennis courts available for play. The Melía Cancún offers an 18-hole, par-54 executive course, and the Caesar Park Cancún also has its own championship 18-hole, par-72 course designed around the Ruinas el Rey. It's open 6am to 6pm.

HORSEBACK RIDING   Rancho Loma Bonita (☎ **98/87-5465** or 87-5423) is Cancún's most popular option for horseback riding. Five-hour packages are available that include 2 hours of riding to caves, cenotes, lagoons, Maya ruins, and along the Caribbean coast, plus Donkey Polo game and some time for relaxing on the beach. Located about 30 minutes south, the price of $45 includes transportation to the ranch, riding, soft drinks and lunch, plus guide and insurance.

IN-LINE SKATING   You can rent in-line skates outside Plaza Las Glorias Hotel and in front of Plaza Caracol, where the valet parking is located. The jogging track that runs parallel to avenida Kukulkán along the Hotel Zone is well-maintained and safe.

OTHER ATTRACTIONS

RUINAS EL REY   Cancún has its own **Maya ruins.** It's a small site and not impressive compared to ruins at Tulum, Cobá, or Chichén-Itzá. The Maya fishermen built this small ceremonial center and settlement very early in the history of Maya culture. It was then abandoned, to be resettled later near the end of the Postclassic period, not long before the arrival of the conquistadors. The platforms of numerous small temples are visible amid the banana plants, papayas, and wildflowers. A new golf course has been built around the ruins, but there is a separate entrance for sightseers. You'll find the ruins about 13 miles from town, at the southern reaches of the Zona Hotelera, almost to Punta Nizuc. Look for the Caesar Park hotel on the left (east), then the ruins on the right (west). Admission is $4.50 (free on Sundays and holidays); the hours are daily from 8am to 5pm.

A MUSEUM   To the right side of the entrance to the Cancún Convention Center is the **Museo Arqueológico de Cancún,** a small but interesting museum with relics from archaeological sites around the state. Admission is $1.75 (free on Sundays and holidays); the hours are Tuesday to Saturday from 9am to 7pm, Sunday from 10am to 5pm.

BULLFIGHTS   Cancún has a small bullring (☎ **98/84-8372**) near the northern (town) end of Paseo Kukulkán opposite the Restaurant Los Almendros. Bullfights are held every Wednesday at 3:30pm during the winter tourist season. There are usually four bulls, and the spectacle begins with a folkloric dance exhibition, followed by a performance of the Charros. Travel agencies in Cancún sell tickets: $32 for adults and children over 11.

8 Shopping

Cancún is known throughout Mexico as having the most diverse array of shops that cater to a large number of international tourists. Where tourists arriving from the U.S. may find apparel more expensive in Cancún, the selection is much broader than in other Mexican resorts. There are numerous duty-free shops that offer excellent value on European goods.

Handcrafts and other artisanía works are more limited and more expensive in Cancún than in other regions of Mexico, but they are available here. There are several **open-air crafts markets** easily visible on avenida Tulum in Cancún City and near the convention center in the hotel zone. One of the biggest is **Coral Negro,** located at km 9.5 av. Kukulkán (☎ **98/83-0758**), open daily from 7am.

The main venue for shopping in Cancún is the **mall,** not quite as grand as its U.S. counterpart, but coming close to the experience. All of Cancún's malls are air-conditioned, sleek, and sophisticated, with most located on avenida Kukulkán between km 7 and km 12—Plaza Lagunas, Costa Brava, La Mansión, Mayfair, Plaza Terramar, Plaza Caracol, Plaza Flamingo, Plaza Kukulkán, and the newest, Forum by the Sea. Everything from fine crystal and silver to designer clothing and decorative objects can be found with numerous restaurants and clubs interspersed. Stores are generally open daily from 10am to 8 or 10pm. Stores in malls near the convention center generally stay open all day, but some—especially in malls farther out—close between 2 and 4pm. Here's a brief rundown on the malls and some of the shops each contains.

Inside the **Plaza Kukulkán** (☎ **98/85-2200**), you'll find a branch of Banco Serfin, OK Maguey Cantina Grill, a movie theater with U.S. movies, Tikal, a shop with Guatemalan textile clothing, several crafts stores, a liquor store, a bathing suit specialty store, a record and tape outlet, all leather goods including shoes and sandals, and another shop specializing in silver from Taxco. In the food court are a number of U.S. franchise restaurants including Ruth's Chris Steakhouse, plus one featuring specialty coffee. For entertainment, it has a bowling alley, Q-Zar laser game pavilion, and video game arcade. There's indoor parking for 1,000 cars.

Planet Hollywood anchors the **Plaza Flamingo,** but inside you'll also pass branches of Bancrecer, Denny's, Subway sandwiches, and La Casa del Habana for Cuban cigars.

The longstanding **Plaza Caracol** holds Cartier jewelry, Aca Joe, Guess, Señor Frog clothing, Waterford crystal, Samsonite luggage, Thomas Moore Travel, Gucci, Fuji film, Mr. Papa's, and La Fisheria restaurant.

Mayfair Plaza/Centro Comercio Mayfair is the oldest, with an open-bricked center that's lively with people sitting in open-air restaurants and bars such as Tequila Sunrise, Fat Tuesday, El Mexicano (a dinner show restaurant), Pizza Hut, and several stores selling silver, leather, and crafts.

The newest and largest of the malls is the entertainment-oriented **Forum by the Sea,** km 9 Paseo Kukulkán (☎ **98/83-4425**). Shops include Tommy Hilfiger and Aca Joe, but most people come here for the food and fun, choosing from Hard Rock Cafe, Rainforest Cafe, Santa Fe Beer Factory, and an extensive food court. Open 10am to midnight; with bars open later.

9 Cancún After Dark

One of Cancún's principal draws is its active nightlife. The two hottest centers of action are the **Centro Comercio Mayfair** and the new **Forum by the Sea,** both on the island near Punta Cancún. Hotels also compete with happy hour entertainment and special drink prices to entice visitors and guests from other resorts—lobby bar hopping at sunset is one great way to plan next year's vacation.

THE CLUB & MUSIC SCENE   Clubbing in Cancún, still called discoing here, is a favorite part of the vacation experience, and can go on each night until the sun rises over that incredibly blue sea. Several of the big hotels have nightclubs, usually a disco, or entertain in their lobby bars with live music. At discos, expect to pay a cover charge of $10 to $20 per person, and $5 to $8 for a drink. Some of the higher-priced discos include open bar or live entertainment.

Numerous restaurants, such as **Carlos 'n' Charlie's, Planet Hollywood, Hard Rock Cafe, All Star Cafe, Señor Frog's, TGI Friday's,** and **Iguana Wana** double as nighttime party spots; the first four offer wildish fun at a fraction of the prices of more costly discos.

The most refined and upscale of all Cancún's nightly gathering spots is the **Lobby Lounge** at the **Ritz-Carlton Cancún** (☎ **98/85-0808**), with live dance music and a list of over 120 premium tequilas.

Azúcar Bar Caribeño (☎ **98/83-0441**), adjacent to the Hotel Camino Real, offers spicy tropical dancing of the salsa, meringue, and bolero kind, with bands from Cuba, Jamaica, and the Dominican Republic; it's open Monday to Saturday from 9:30pm to 4am.

La Boom, km 3.5 bulevar Kukulkán (☎ **98/83-1152**), has two sections: On one side is a video bar, and on the other is a bilevel disco with cranking music. Both sides offer air-conditioning. Each night special client-getting attractions are offered, such as no cover, free bar, ladies' night, or bikini night. It's popular with people in their early twenties. It's open nightly from 8pm to 6am. A sound-and-light show begins at 11:30pm in the disco.

Carlos 'n' Charlie's, km 4.5 Paseo Kukulkán (☎ **98/83-0846**), is a reliable place to find both good food and packed frat house–level entertainment in the evenings. There's a dance floor to go along with the live music that starts nightly around 9pm. A cover charge kicks in if you're not planning to eat. It's open daily from noon to 2am.

With taped music, **Carlos O'Brian's,** av. Tulum 107, SM 22 (☎ **98/84-1659**), is only slightly tamer then other Carlos Anderson restaurants/night spots in town (Señor Frog and Carlos 'n' Charlie's are two others). It's open daily from 11am to 12:30am.

Christine's, at the Hotel Krystal on the island (☎ **98/83-1793**), is where disco lives. Although the music is more hip and alternative, the laser light shows, infused oxygen, and large video screens take you back to the glitz style of high disco. The dress code is no shorts or jeans. It opens at 9:30pm nightly.

Dady'O, km 9.5 Paseo Kukulkán (☎ **98/83-3333**), is another rave—highly favored, with frequent long lines. It opens nightly at 9:30pm.

Dady Rock Bar and Grill, km 9.5 Paseo Kukulkán (☎ **98/83-1626**), the offspring of Dady'O, opens early (7pm) and goes as long as any other night spot, offering a new twist on entertainment with a combination of live bands and DJ-orchestrated music, along with an open bar, full meals, a buffet, and dancing.

Hard Rock Cafe, in Plaza Lagunas Mall and Forum by the Sea (☎ **98/83-3269** or 98/83-2024), entertains with a live band at 10:30pm every night except Wednesday. Other hours you'll get your share of lively recorded music to munch by—the menu combines the most popular foods from American and Mexican cultures. It's open daily from 11am to 2am.

Planet Hollywood, Flamingo Shopping Center, km 11 Paseo Kukulkán (☎ **98/85-3044**), is the trendy brainchild of Sylvester Stallone, Bruce Willis, and Arnold Schwarzenegger. It's both a restaurant and nighttime music/dance spot with megadecibel live music. It's open daily from 11am to 2am.

THE PERFORMING ARTS   Nightly performances of the **Ballet Folklórico de Cancún** (☎ **98/83-0199,** ext. 193 and 194), are held at the Cancún Convention Center. Tickets are sold between 8am and 9pm at a booth just as you enter the convention center. You can go for dinner and the show. Dinner-show guests pay around

$48, and arrive at 6:30pm for drinks, followed by dinner at 7pm and the show at 8pm. The price includes an open bar, dinner, show, tax, and tip. Several hotels host **Mexican fiesta nights,** including a buffet dinner and a folkloric dance show; admission, including dinner, ranges from $35 to $50. A Ballet Folklórico appears Monday to Saturday nights in a 1¼-hour show at the Continental Villas Plaza (☎ **98/85-1444,** ext. 5690). The Hyatt Regency Cancún (☎ **98/83-1234**) has a dinner, folkloric show, and mariachi fiesta Tuesday to Sunday nights during the high season, as does the Camino Real (☎ **98/83-1200**). In the Costa Blanca shopping center, **El Mexicano** restaurant (☎ **98/84-4207**) hosts a tropical dinner show every night as well as live music for dancing. The entertainment alternates each night with mariachis entertaining off-and-on from 7 to 11pm and a folkloric show from 8 to 9:30pm.

You can also get in the party mood at **Mango Tango,** km 14 Paseo Kukulkán (☎ **98/85-0303**), a lagoon-side restaurant/dinner show establishment. Diners can choose from two levels, one nearer the music and the other overlooking it all. Music is loud and varied. The 1-hour-and-20-minute dinner show begins at 8pm nightly and costs $25 to $35. At 9:30pm live reggae music begins, and there's no cover. If you want to enjoy the show without a meal, just order a drink and be seated at an upper-level table. It's opposite the Jack Tar Village.

For something that mingles tourists with the locals, head for the downtown **Parque de las Palapas** (the main park) for *Noches Caribeños,* where live tropical music is provided at no charge for anyone who wants to listen and dance. Performances begin at 7:30pm on Fridays.

SPORTS WAGERING   This form of entertainment seems to be sweeping Mexico's resorts. TV screens mounted around the room of **LF Caliente** (☎ **98/ 83-3704**), at the Fiesta Americana Hotel, show all the action in racetrack, football, soccer, and so on in a bar/lounge setting.

10 Road Trips from Cancún

Outside of Cancún lie the many wonders of the Yucatán Peninsula; you'll find the details in chapters 5 and 6. Cancún can be a perfect base for day or overnight trips or the starting point for a longer exploration. Any travel agency or hotel tour desk in Cancún can book these tours, or you can elect to do them on your own via local bus or rental car. The Maya ruins to the south at **Tulum** or **Cobá** should be your first goal, then perhaps the *caleta* (cove) of **Xel-Ha** or the day trip to **Xcaret.** If you're going south, consider staying a night or two on the island of **Cozumel** or at one of the budget resorts on the **Tulum coast** or **Punta Allen,** south of the Tulum ruins. **Isla Mujeres** is an easy day trip off mainland Cancún (see chapter 5).

About 80 miles south of Cancún begins the **Sian Ka'an Biosphere Reserve,** a 1.3 million–acre area set aside in 1986 to preserve a region of tropical forests, savannas, mangroves, canals, lagoons, bays, cenotes, and coral reefs, all of which are home to hundreds of birds and land and marine animals (see chapter 5 for details). The Friends of Sian Ka'an, a nonprofit group based in Cancún, offers biologist-escorted day trips (weather permitting) from the **Cabañas Ana y José** just south of the Tulum ruins. Trips take place on Monday, Tuesday, Friday, and Saturday for $50 per person using their vehicle or $40 per person if you drive yourself. The price includes chips and soft drinks, round-trip van transportation to the reserve from the Cabañas, a guided boat/birding trip through one of the reserve's lagoons, and use of binoculars. Tours can accommodate up to 19 people. Trips start from the Cabañas at 9:30am and return there around 2:30pm. For reservations, contact Amigos de Sian Ka'an, Cobá 5, Plaza America (☎ **98/84-9583;** fax 98/87-3080) in Cancún. Office hours are 9am to 3pm and 6 to 8pm.

Although I don't recommend it, by driving fast or catching the right buses, you can go inland to **Chichén-Itzá,** explore the ruins, and return in a day, but it's much better to spend at least 2 days seeing Chichén-Itzá, Mérida, and Uxmal. See chapter 6 for transportation details and further information on these destinations.

Reserva Ecológica El Eden, established in 1990, is a privately owned 500,000-acre reserve dedicated to research for biological conservation in Mexico. Only 30 miles northwest of Cancún, it takes around 2 hours to reach the center of this reserve deep in the jungle. It's intended as an overnight (or more) excursion for people who want to know more about the biological diversity of the peninsula. Within the reserve, or near to it, are found marine grasslands, mangrove swamps, rain forests, savannas, wetlands, and sand dunes, as well as evidence of archaeological sites and at least 205 different species of birds, plus orchids, bromeliads, and cacti. Among the local animals are spider monkey, jaguar, cougar, deer, and ocelot. The "ecoscientific" tours offered include naturalist-led bird watching, animal tracking, star gazing, spotlight surveys for nocturnal wildlife, and exploration of cenotes and Maya ruins. Comfortable, basic accommodations are provided. Tours include transportation from Cancún, 1 or 2 nights accommodation at La Savanna Research Station, meals, nightly cocktail, guided nature walks, and tours. The tours cost $235 to $315 depending on the length of stay, with a fee of $90 per extra night. Contact Reserva El Eden, Apdo. Postal 770, 77500 Cancún, Q. Roo (☎ and fax **98/80-5032;** e-mail: mlazcano@Cancun.rce.com.mx; **maya.ucr.edu/pril/el_eden/ Front.html**).

Isla Mujeres, Cozumel & the Caribbean Coast

5

A Mexican friend of mine reminded me that the Mayas never settled in Cancún. "The original inhabitants always choose the best places to live," he reasoned, pointing to neighboring Cozumel, Tulum, Isla Mujeres, and other sites along the Yucatán coastline. Each of these holds remnants of ancient settlements in addition to many modern attractions.

In fact, those who shun the highly stylized, rather Americanized ways of Cancún will find that these and other stops in the Yucatán offer abundant natural pleasures, authentic experiences, and a relaxed charm. They're so close to the easy air access of Cancún, yet miles away in mood and matter.

The **Quintana Roo** coast, dubbed the Costa Turquesa (Turquoise Coast) or the Tulum Corridor as far as Tulum, stretches south from Cancún all the way to Chetumal. It's 230 miles of powdery white-sand beaches, scrubby jungle, and crystal-clear lagoons full of coral and colorful fish. Along this coastline—and the islands off the peninsula—are a few places worthy of being designated "resorts," as well as a handful of inexpensive hideaways. Some treasured spots on both the Punta Allen Peninsula and the Majahual Peninsula also merit travelers' attention. This whole coastal region is rapidly evolving, and it offers more and more options for a wider range of travelers.

Many travelers become acquainted with these areas through an initial stay in Cancún, and day trips that take them sailing over to Isla Mujeres, venturing down the Caribbean coast to Tulum, or exploring the reefs off Cozumel. Their next trip often becomes a closer concentration of one or more of these smaller towns.

Points west of Cancún, such as Chichén-Itzá and Mérida, are detailed in chapter 6.

EXPLORING MEXICO'S CARIBBEAN

ISLA MUJERES   A day trip to Isla Mujeres on a party boat is one of the most popular excursions from Cancún. This fish-shaped island is located just 8 miles northeast of Cancún. It's a quick boat ride away, allowing ample time to get a taste of the peaceful pace of life here. But to fully explore the small village of shops and cafes, relax at the broad, tranquil Playa Norte, or snorkel or dive El Garrafón Reef (a national underwater park), more time is needed. Overnight accommodations range from rustic to offbeat chic on this small island where relaxation rules.

On the Road in the Yucatán

Here's a few things to keep in mind if you're planning to hit the road and explore the Yucatán.

Exchanging money is easiest in Cancún, Isla Mujeres, Playa del Carmen, and Cozumel, with many smaller resorts along the coast operating on a cash-only basis. And though Isla Mujeres and Cozumel are breezy enough to keep them at bay, everywhere else on this coast **mosquitoes** are numerous, so bring plenty of mosquito repellent that has DEET as the main ingredient.

The best way to see the Yucatán is **by car.** It's one of the most pleasant parts of the country for a driving vacation. The jungle- and beach-lined roads, while narrow, straight, and without shoulders, are generally in good condition and have little traffic. The section with the most traffic—the stretch from Cancún to Puerto Morelos—has just been widened to four lanes, with a shoulder.

The four-lane toll road between Cancún and Mérida is complete. Costing around $20 one way, it cuts the trip from 5 to around 4 hours. The old two-lane free road is still in fine shape and passes through numerous villages with many speed-control bumps (*topes*)—this route is much more interesting. New directional signs seem to lead motorists to the toll road (*cuota*) and don't mention the free road (*libre*), so if you want to use it, ask locals for directions.

Traffic can become quite heavy on certain stretches from Cancún to Tulum, and drivers go too fast. A stalled or stopped car is hard to see, and there are no shoulders for pulling off the roadway. Follow these precautions for a safe journey: Never turn left while on the highway (it's against Mexican law anyway). Always go to the next road on the right and turn around and come back to the turnoff you want. Occasionally, a specially constructed right-hand turnoff, such as at Xcaret and Playa del Carmen, allows motorists to pull off to the right in order to cross the road when traffic has passed. There have been many accidents and fatalities on this road, so use caution. After Tulum, traffic is much lighter.

Be aware of the **long distances** in the Yucatán. Mérida, for instance, is 400 miles from Villahermosa, 125 miles from Campeche, and 200 miles from Cancún.

Note: Gas stations are found in all major towns, but they're only open from around 8am to around 7pm in smaller villages. If you're planning to rent a car to travel the area, see "Car Rentals" in chapter 3, "Planning a Trip to the Yucatán."

Passenger ferries go to Isla Mujeres from Puerto Juárez near Cancún, and car ferries leave from Punta Sam, also near Cancún. More expensive passenger ferries, with less frequent departures, leave from the Playa Linda pier on Cancún Island.

COZUMEL   Mexico's principal Caribbean island, Cozumel is known as one of the world's top five dive destinations. It has also earned the dubious honor of being one of the world's top cruise ports of call. This allows hundreds of thousands each year to get a glimpse of the beauty of the place, but crowds clog the shops, streets, and restaurants from morning to mid-afternoon. Apart from diving and shopping, favored pastimes include fishing and exploring ruins on the island. For those staying in Cozumel, the ruins, cenote diving, and the beach villages of the mainland are a quick ferry ride away. Cozumel has a few luxury resorts, numerous hotels that cater to divers with special packages, plus many inexpensive places to stay.

A car/passenger ferry runs between Puerto Morelos (south of Cancún) and Cozumel. Passenger ferries also run between Playa del Carmen and Cozumel, the preferred way to go if you aren't flying directly from your home base.

THE COSTA TURQUESA   Signs pointing to brand-new, expensive resort developments are found all along Highway 307 from Cancún south to **Tulum,** a stretch known both as the "Tulum Corridor," referring to the distance from Cancún to Tulum, and as the "Costa Turquesa," south from Cancún to Chetumal on the Belize border. The character of the Corridor is changing, but there are still plenty of small beachfront hideaways, bargain bungalows, and luxury retreats a short distance from the highway. South of Tulum, almost 100 miles of this coast have been set aside as the Sian Ka'an Biosphere Reserve.

A trip down the coast is a great way to spend a day of a vacation centered in Cancún. The most popular agency-led tours out of Cancún are to the ruins of Tulum, followed by a stop at Xel-Ha for a swim and snorkeling in the beautiful clear lagoon; and to the ecological/archaeological theme park of Xcaret.

The Costa Turquesa is best experienced in a car. (See chapter 4, "Cancún," for information on rentals.) Highway 307 south of Cancún has just been expanded to four broad lanes between Cancún and the Playa del Carmen turnoff. It is bordered by jungle on both sides, except where there are beaches and beach settlements.

Here are some **drive times from Cancún:** Puerto Morelos (port for the car ferry to Cozumel and a sleepy beachside town), 45 minutes; Playa del Carmen (the very hip beachside village), 1 hour; Xcaret Lagoon and Paamul, 1¼ hours; Akumal, 1¾ hours; Xel-Ha and Tulum, around 2 hours; and Chetumal, about 5 hours.

THE PUNTA ALLEN & MAJAHUAL PENINSULAS   These two areas will appeal to people looking for totally off-the-beaten-track travel, or for world-class adventure sports. **Punta Allen's** saltwater fly-fishing is extraordinary, and the **Chinchorro Banks,** 22 miles off Majahual's little village of Xcalak, is perhaps the last example of a pristine Caribbean reef; the diving is spectacular. Both places are hard to get to, have beautiful beaches, are overrun by exotic bird life and jungle flora, and have a few laid-back, rustic inns to stay at.

THE RÍO BEC RUIN ROUTE   Between Lago Bacalar and Escárcega, in Campeche state, is the Río Bec ruin route, where several "new" sites are open to the public and others are available with special permission.

CHETUMAL   Though Chetumal is the capital of Quintana Roo state, it's best to think of it as a gateway to Guatemala, Belize, the several ruins near the city, and the excellent diving and fishing to be had off the Xcalak Peninsula. In 1995 a fantastic museum opened in Chetumal, and the re-excavation of many of the ruins near Chetumal may be a reason for a detour there, but Lago Bacalar is the preferred place to stay near Chetumal.

1 Isla Mujeres

10 miles N of Cancún

Isla Mujeres—the Island of Women. Was this really a place where 17th-century pirates stashed their women for safekeeping as they headed out to plunder and pillage? Or does the name of this tiny sliver of an island date back even further, to the time of the Maya, who possibly considered it a sanctuary for sacred virgins? A legacy of stony statues of women and shrines to Ixchel, their fertility goddess, was discovered by Spanish conquistadors upon their arrival.

Whatever its history, Isla Mujeres today is a serene respite from the nonstop glitz and action of Cancún, easily viewed across a narrow channel. Just 5 miles long and 2½ miles wide, it's known as the best value in the Caribbean, assuming you prefer your vacation laid-back and heavy on relaxation.

The streets have been paved in brick, and many original Caribbean-style clapboard houses remain, adding a colorful and authentic reminder of the island's past. Suntanned visitors hang out in open-air cafes and stroll streets lined with frantic souvenir vendors. Calling out for attention to their bargain-priced wares, they give a carnival atmosphere to the hours when tour-boat traffic is at its peak.

Days in "Isla"—as the locals call it—can alternate between adventurous activity and absolute repose. Trips to the Isla Contoy bird sanctuary are popular, as are the excellent diving, fishing, and snorkeling. In the evenings most people find the slow, relaxing pace one of the island's biggest draws. It is then that the island is bathed in a cool breeze, perfect for casual open-air dining and drinking in small street-side restaurants. Most people pack it in as early as 9 or 10pm, when most of the businesses close. Restless night owls, however, will find kindred souls at a few bars on Playa Norte that stay open late.

ESSENTIALS

GETTING THERE & DEPARTING   **Puerto Juárez,** just north of Cancún, is the dock for the passenger ferries to Isla Mujeres. The *Caribbean Queen* makes the 45-minute trip many times daily, and costs just under $2. The newer *Caribbean Express* makes the trip in 20 minutes and costs about $3, running every hour on the half hour between 6:30am and 8:30pm. Pay at the ticket office, or if the ferry is about to leave, you can pay aboard.

Taxi fares are now posted by the street where the taxis park; be sure to check the rate before agreeing to a taxi. Moped and bicycle rentals are also readily available as you depart the ferry boat.

Isla Mujeres is so small that a vehicle isn't necessary, but if you're taking one, you'll use the **Punta Sam** port a little beyond Puerto Juárez. The ferry runs the 40-minute trip five or six times daily all year except in bad weather (check with the tourist office in Cancún for a current schedule). Cars should arrive an hour in advance of the ferry departure to register for a place in line and pay the posted fee, which varies depending on weight and type of vehicle.

There are also ferries to Isla Mujeres from the **Playa Linda** pier in Cancún, but they're less frequent and more expensive than those from Puerto Juárez. The Playa Linda ferries simply don't run if there isn't a crowd. A new **Watertaxi** (☎ **98/ 86-4270** or 98/86-4847) to Isla Mujeres operates from Playa Caracol, between the Fiesta Americana Coral Beach Hotel and the Xcaret terminal on the island, with prices about the same as those from Playa Linda, about four times the cost of the public ferries from Puerto Juárez. Scheduled departures are 9 and 11am and 1 and 3pm with returns from Isla Mujeres at 10am, noon, 2pm, and 5pm. Adult fares are $13.50, kids 12 and under are half price, and those under 3 ride free.

To get to either Puerto Juárez or Punta Sam **from Cancún,** take any Ruta 8 city bus from avenida Tulum. If you're coming from Mérida, you can either fly to Cancún and then proceed to Puerto Juárez, or you can take a bus directly from the Mérida bus station to Puerto Juárez. **From Cozumel,** you can either fly to Cancún (there are daily flights) or take a ferry to Playa del Carmen (see the "Cozumel" section below for details), where you can travel to Puerto Juárez.

ORIENTATION   **Arriving**   Ferries arrive at the dock in the center of town. Most hotels are close by. Tricycle taxis are the least expensive and most fun way to

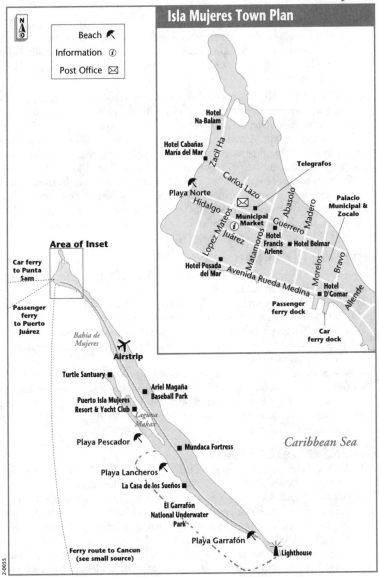

Isla Mujeres Town Plan

Beach 🏖
Information ⓘ
Post Office ✉

Hotel Na-Balam
Hotel Cabañas María del Mar
Zacil Ha
Carlos Lazo
Telegrafos
Playa Norte
Hidalgo
Palacio Municipal & Zocalo
Abasolo
Madero
López Mateos
Juárez
Municipal Market
Guerrero
Hotel Francis Arlene
Hotel Belmar
Matamoros
Hotel Posada del Mar
Avenida Rueda Medina
Morelos
Bravo
Hotel D'Gomar
Allende
Passenger ferry dock
Car ferry dock

Car ferry to Punta Sam
Area of Inset
Passenger ferry to Puerto Juárez
Bahía de Mujeres
Airstrip
Turtle Sanctuary
Ariel Magaña Baseball Park
Puerto Isla Mujeres Resort & Yacht Club
Laguna Makax
Playa Pescador
Mundaca Fortress
Caribbean Sea
Playa Lancheros
La Casa de los Sueños
El Garrafón National Underwater Park
Playa Garrafón
Lighthouse
Ferry route to Cancun (see small source)

2-0055

get to your hotel; you and your luggage pile in the open carriage compartment while the "driver" pedals through the streets. Regular taxis are always lined up in a parking lot to the right of the pier, with their rates posted.

Visitor Information   The **City Tourist Office** (☎ and fax **987/7-0316**) is on the second floor of the Plaza Isla Mujeres. You'll find it at the northern end of Juárez, between López Mateos and Matamoros. It's open Monday to Friday from 9am to 2:30pm and 7 to 9pm. Also look for *Islander*, a free publication with history, local information, advertisements, and list of events (if any).

Island Layout   Isla Mujeres is about 5 miles long and 2½ miles wide, with the town located at the northern tip of the island. The **ferry docks** are right at the center of town, within walking distance of most hotels, restaurants, and shops. The street running along the waterfront is **Rueda Medina,** commonly called the **Malecón.** The **market** (Mercado Municipal) is by the post office on **calle Guerrero,** an inland street at the north edge of town, which, like most streets in the town, is unmarked.

GETTING AROUND   A popular form of transportation on Isla Mujeres is the electric **golf cart,** available for rent at many hotels for $10 per hour or $50 per day. They don't go more than 20 miles per hour, so don't expect to speed around the island, but they're fun. Anyway, on Isla Mujeres you aren't there to hurry. Many people enjoy touring the island by moto, the local sobriquet for motorized bikes and scooters. Fully automatic versions are available for around $25 to $30 per day or $6 per hour. They come with seats for one person, but some are large enough for two. There's only one main road with a couple of offshoots, so you won't get lost. Be aware that the rental price does not include insurance, and any injury to yourself or the vehicle will come out of your pocket. **Bicycles** are also available for rent at some hotels for $5 per day.

FAST FACTS: ISLA MUJERES

Area Code   The area code of Isla Mujeres is **987.** The first digit for all telephone numbers on the island has been changed from 2 to 7.

Hospital   The Hospital de la Armada, on Medina at Ojon P. Blanco (☎ 987/7-0017). It's half a mile south of the town center.

Post Office/Telegraph Office   The correo is on calle Guerrero, by the market.

Telephone   Ladatel phones accepting coins and prepaid phone cards are found at the plaza and throughout town.

Tourist Seasons   Isla Mujeres's tourist season (when hotel rates are higher) is a bit different from that of other places in Mexico. High season runs December through May, a month longer than in Cancún; some hotels raise their rates in August and some hotels raise their rates beginning in mid-November. Low season is June through mid-November.

BEACHES & WATER SPORTS

THE BEACHES   The most popular beach in town used to be called Playa Cocoteros ("Cocos" for short). Then, in 1988, Hurricane Gilbert destroyed the coconut palms on the beach. Gradually, the name has changed to **Playa Norte,** referring to the long stretch of beach that extends around the northern tip of the island, to your left as you get off the boat. This is a truly splendid beach—a wide stretch of fine white sand and calm, translucent, turquoise-blue water. Topless sunbathing is allowed here. The beach is easily reached on foot from the ferry and from all downtown hotels. Water-sports equipment, beach umbrellas, and lounge chairs are available for rent. Those in front of restaurants usually cost nothing if you use the restaurant as your headquarters for drinks and food. New palms are sprouting all over Playa Norte, and it won't be long until it will be deserving of its previous name.

   Garrafón National Park is known best as a snorkeling area, but there is a nice stretch of beach on either side of the park. **Playa Lancheros** is on the Caribbean side of Laguna Makax. Local buses go to Lancheros, then turn inland and return downtown. The beach at Playa Lancheros is nice, but the few restaurants there are high priced.

WATER SPORTS   Swimming   Wide Playa Norte is the best swimming beach, with Playa Lancheros second. There are no lifeguards on duty on Isla Mujeres, and the system of water-safety flags used in Cancún and Cozumel isn't used here.

Snorkeling   By far the most popular place to snorkel is **Garrafón National Park,** at the southern end of the island, where you'll see numerous schools of colorful fish. The well-equipped park has beach chairs, changing rooms, rental lockers, showers, and a snack bar. Admission is $2. Also good for snorkeling is the **Manchones Reef,** which is just off shore and reached by boat, where a bronze cross was installed in 1994.

Another excellent location is around the lighthouse (*el faro*) in the **Bahía de Mujeres** at the southern tip of the island, where the water is about 6 feet deep. Boatmen will take you for around $10 per person if you have your own snorkeling equipment or $15 more if you use theirs.

Diving   Several dive shops have opened on the island, most offering the same trips. The traditional dive center is **Buzos de México,** on Rueda Medina at Morelos (☎ 987/7-0131), next to the boat cooperative. Dive instructor Carlos Gutiérrez, speaks English, French, and Italian and offers certification (5 to 6 days for $350), and resort courses ($80 with three dives), and makes sure all dives are led by certified dive masters. **Bahía Dive Shop,** on Rueda Medina 166 across from the car ferry dock (☎ and fax **987/7-0340**), is a full-service shop with dive equipment for sale and rent and resort and certification classes.

All 30- to 40-foot dives cost $45 to $65 for a two-tank trip; equipment rental costs $15. **Cuevas de los Tiburones** (Caves of the Sleeping Sharks) is Isla's most famous dive site and costs $70 to $80 for a two-tank dive at a depth of 70 to 80 feet (only advisable for experienced divers). There are actually two places to see the sleeping sharks: the Cuevas de Tiburones and La Punta. A storm collapsed the arch that was featured in a Jacques Cousteau film showing the sleeping sharks, but the caves are still there. Sharks have no gills, and so must constantly move to receive the oxygen they need. (Remember the line in *Annie Hall* equating relationships to sharks, "They must constantly move forward or die"?) The phenomenon here is that the high salinity and lack of carbon monoxide in the caves, combined with strong and steady currents, allow the sharks to receive the oxygen they need without moving. Your chance of actually seeing sleeping sharks, by the way, is about one in four; fewer sharks are present than in the past. The best time to see them is January to March.

Other dive sites include a wreck 9 kilometers offshore; Banderas reef, between Isla Mujeres and Cancún, where there's always a strong current; Tabos reef on the eastern shore; and Manchones reef, 1 kilometer off the southeastern tip of the island, where the water is 15 to 35 feet deep. The best season for diving is from June through August, when the water is calm.

Fishing   To arrange a day of fishing, ask at the **Sociedad Cooperativa Turística** (boatmen's cooperative; ☎ 987/7-0274) or the travel agency mentioned below, under "A Visit to Isla Contoy." The cost can be shared with four to six others and includes lunch and drinks. All year you'll find bonito, mackerel, kingfish, and amberjack. Sailfish and sharks (hammerhead, bull, nurse, lemon, and tiger) are in good supply in April and May. In winter, larger grouper and jewfish are prevalent. Four hours of fishing close to shore costs around $120; 8 hours farther out goes for $240. The cooperative is open Monday to Saturday from 8am to 1pm and 5 to 8pm, and Sunday from 7:30 to 10am and 6 to 8pm.

OTHER ATTRACTIONS
A TURTLE SANCTUARY   A worthwhile outing on the island is to this reserve dedicated to preserving Caribbean sea turtles and to educating the public about them.

As few as 20 years ago fishermen converged on the island nightly from May to September waiting for these monster-size turtles to lumber ashore to deposit their Ping-Pong-ball–shaped eggs. Totally vulnerable once they began laying their eggs, and exhausted when they finished, the turtles were easily captured and slaughtered for their highly prized meat, shell, and eggs. Then a concerned fisherman, Gonzalez Cahle Maldonado, began convincing others to spare at least the eggs, which he protected. It was a start. Following his lead, the fishing secretariat founded this **Centro de Investigaciones** 10 years ago; it's funded by both the government and private donations. Since then at least 28,000 turtles have been released and every year local schoolchildren participate in the event, thus planting the notion of protecting the turtles for a new generation of islanders.

Six different species of sea turtles nest on Isla Mujeres. An adult green turtle, the most abundant species, measures 4 to 5 feet in length and can weigh as much as 450 pounds when grown. At the center, visitors walk through the indoor and outdoor turtle pool areas, watching the creatures paddling around. The turtles are separated by age, from newly hatched up to 1 year. Besides protecting the turtles that nest on Isla Mujeres of their own accord, the program also calls for capturing the turtles at sea and bringing them to enclosed compounds to mate and later to be freed to nest on Isla Mujeres. They are tagged and then released. While in the care of the center these guests receive a high-protein diet and reportedly grow faster than in the wild. People who come here usually end up staying at least an hour, especially if they opt for the guided tour, which enhances a visit. The permanent shelter has large wall paintings of all the sea turtles of the area. The sanctuary is on a piece of land separated from the island by Bahía de Mujeres and Laguna Makax; you'll need a taxi to get there. Admission is $1; the shelter is open daily from 9am to 5pm.

A MAYA RUIN Just beyond the lighthouse, at the southern end of the island, is a pile of stones that formed a small Maya pyramid before Hurricane Gilbert struck. Believed to have been an observatory built to the moon goddess Ixchel, it's been reduced to a rocky heap. The location, on a lofty bluff overlooking the sea, is still worth seeing. If you're at Garrafón National Park and want to walk, it's not too far. Turn right from Garrafón. When you see the lighthouse, turn toward it down the rocky path.

A PIRATE'S FORTRESS The Fortress of Mundaca is about 2½ miles in the same direction as Garrafón, about half a mile to the left. The fortress was built by the pirate Mundaca Marecheaga, who in the early 19th century arrived at Isla Mujeres and proceeded to set up a blissful paradise in a pretty, shady spot while making money from selling slaves to Cuba and Belize. Island lore also says he decided to settle down and built this hacienda after being captivated by the charms of an island girl. However, she reportedly spurned his affections and left with another man, leaving him heartbroken and alone on Isla Mujeres.

A VISIT TO ISLA CONTOY If at all possible, plan to visit this pristine uninhabited island, 19 miles by boat from Isla Mujeres, that was set aside as a national wildlife reserve in 1981. The oddly shaped 3.8-mile-long island is covered in lush vegetation and harbors 70 species of birds as well as a host of marine and animal life. Bird species that nest on the island include pelicans, brown boobies, frigates, egrets, terns, and cormorants. Flocks of flamingos arrive in April. June, July, and August are good months to spot turtles that bury their eggs in the sand at night. Most excursions troll for fish (which will be your lunch), anchor en route for a snorkeling expedition, and skirt the island at a leisurely pace for close viewing of the birds without disturbing the habitat, then pull ashore. While the captain prepares lunch, visitors can swim, sun, follow the nature trails, and visit the fine nature museum. For a while the island was closed to visitors, but it's reopened now after rules for its use and safety were agreed to by fishermen and those bringing visitors. The trip from Isla Mujeres takes a minimum of 1½ hours one way, more if the waves are choppy. Because of the tight-knit boatmen's cooperative, prices for this excursion are the same everywhere: $30. You can buy a ticket at the **Sociedad Cooperativa Turística** (☎ **987/7-0274**) on avenida Rueda Medina, next to Mexico Divers and Las Brisas restaurant, or at one of several travel agencies, such as **La Isleña,** on Morelos between Medina and Juárez (☎ **987/7-0036**). La Isleña is open daily from 7am to 9pm and is a good source for tourist information. Contoy trips leave at 8:30am and return around 4pm.

Three types of boats go to Contoy. Small boats have one motor and seat eight or nine people. Medium-size boats have two motors and hold 10. Large boats have a toilet and hold 16 passengers. Most boats have a sun cover. The first two types are being phased out in favor of larger, better boats. Boat captains should respect the cooperative's regulations regarding capacity and should have enough life jackets to go around. Snorkeling equipment is usually included in the price, but double-check that before heading out.

SHOPPING

Shopping is a casual activity here. There are only a few shops of any sophistication. Otherwise you are bombarded by shop owners, especially on Hidalgo, selling Saltillo rugs, onyx, silver, Guatemalan clothing, blown glassware, masks, folk art, beach paraphernalia, and T-shirts in abundance. Prices are also lower than in Cancún or Cozumel, but with the overeager sellers, bargaining is necessary to achieve a satisfactory price.

WHERE TO STAY

There are plenty of hotels in all price ranges on Isla Mujeres. Rates are at their peak during high season, which is the most expensive and most crowded time to go. Elizabeth Wenger of **Four Seasons Travel** in Montello, WI (☎ **800/552-4550** or 608/297-2332) specializes in Mexico travel and especially books a lot of hotels in Isla Mujeres. Her service is invaluable in high season when hotel occupancy is high.

VERY EXPENSIVE

✪ **La Casa de los Sueños.** Carretera Garrafón s/n, 77400 Isla Mujeres, Q. Roo. ☎ **800/551-2558** in the U.S., or 987/7-0651. Fax 987/7-0708. www.lossuenos.com. E-mail: info@lossuenos.com. 9 units. A/C TV. High season $200–$290 double. Low season $120–$250 double. Breakfast included. AE, MC, V.

This "house of dreams" is easily Isla Mujeres' most sophisticated property, originally built as a private residence. Lucky for us, it opened in early 1998 as an upscale, adults-only B&B. Its location on the southern end of the island, adjacent to El Garrafón National Park, makes it ideal for snorkeling or diving enthusiasts. The excellent design features vivid colors and sculpted architecture, with a large, open interior courtyard, tropical gardens, and an infinity pool that melts into the cool Caribbean waters. All rooms have a balcony or terrace and face west, offering stunning views of the sunset and the night lights of Cancún. In addition, the rooms— which have names like Serenity, Passion, and Love—also have satellite TV, large, marble bathrooms, and luxury amenities. There's a small beach, palapa-shaded lounge area, private boat dock, and complimentary use of snorkeling equipment, kayaks, and bicycles for sightseeing around the island. Full American breakfast is included in the room price, and bar service and light lunches are also available.

Geared to a healthful, stress-free vacation, the B&B forbids smoking and encourages casual dress and no shoes. Meditation areas and daily massage services are also available. Private boat transportation from Cancún to the B&B's dock can be arranged on request.

Dining: The well-equipped kitchen and dining area serves breakfast, included, plus light lunches. There's also an outdoor palapa bar for refreshments.

Amenities: Swimming pool, meditation areas, massage service, free use of bicycles, private beach, boat dock, diving and snorkeling available.

Puerto Isla Mujeres Resort & Yacht Club. Puerto de Abrigo Laguna Macax, Isla Mujeres, Q. Roo. Reservation address: km 4.5 Paseo Kukulkán, 77500 Cancún, Q. Roo. ☎ **800/ 960-ISLA** in the U.S., 987/7-0413 or 987/7-0330, 98/83-1228 in Cancún. 25 units. A/C MINIBAR TV TEL. High season $265 suite. Low season $135 suite. Villas $190–$375. Rates include transportation from Cancún's offices in Playa Linda and daily continental breakfast. V, MC, AE.

The concept here—an exclusive glide-up yachting/sailing resort—is new not only to Isla Mujeres, but to all of Mexico. Facing an undeveloped portion of the glass-smooth mangrove-edged Macax Lagoon, Puerto Isla Mujeres is a collection of modern suites and villas with sloping white stucco walls and red-tile roofs spread across spacious palm-filled grounds. Beautifully designed with Scandinavian and Mediterranean elements, guest quarters feature tile, wood-beam ceilings, natural wood and marble accents, televisions with VCR, stereos with CD changer, and living areas. Villas have two bedrooms upstairs with a full bathroom and a small bathroom downstairs with a shower. Each villa also features a small, stylish kitchen area with dishwasher, microwave, refrigerator, and coffeemaker. A whirlpool is on the upper patio off the master bedroom. Since weather is of consideration to the boating crowd, nightly turndown service leaves the next day's weather forecast on the pillow beside the requisite chocolate. The beach club, with refreshments, is a water-taxi ride across the lagoon on a beautiful stretch of beach. A staff biologist can answer questions about birds and water life on Isla Mujeres. Even though the resort opened in 1995, more suites and villas are already on the drawing board.

Dining: Two excellent restaurants, one indoor and one outdoors by the pool, gourmet deli, small grocery store.

Amenities: Nearby beach club and free-form swimming pool with swim-up bar. Transportation is offered from the Cancún office at Playa Linda by boat to Isla Mujeres, plus there's a full-service marina with 60 slips for 30- to 60-foot vessels, short- and long-term dockage, fueling station, charter yachts and sailboats, and sailing school. Mopeds, golf carts, bicycles, and water-sports equipment for rent, and video and CD library. Laundry and room service.

EXPENSIVE

Hotel Na Balam. Zacil-Ha 118, 77400 Isla Mujeres, Q. Roo. ☎ **987/7-0279.** Fax 987/ 7-0446. E-mail: nabalam@cancun.rce.com.mx. 31 units. A/C. High season $125 suite. Low season $86 suite. AE, MC, V. Free unguarded parking.

This popular, two-story hotel near the end of Norte Beach has comfortable rooms on a quiet, ideally located portion of the beach. Rooms are in three sections, with some facing the beach and others across the street in a garden setting where there's a swimming pool. All rooms have either a patio or a balcony. Each fashionably furnished and spacious suite contains two double beds, a seating area, and folk-art decorations. Though other rooms are newer, the older section is well kept, with a bottom-floor patio facing the peaceful palm-filled sandy inner yard and Norte Beach. From Tuesday to Thursday yoga lessons are offered; ask about the time and price. The restaurant, **Zacil-Ha,** is one of the island's most popular (see "Where to Dine," below). To find the hotel from the pier, walk 5 blocks to López Mateos; turn right and walk 4 blocks to Lazo (the last street). Turn left and walk to the sandy road parallel to the beach and turn right. The hotel is half a block farther.

Dining: Zacil-Ha restaurant serving Mexican cuisine, seafood and health food; two bars—one adjacent to the restaurant and one on the beach.

Amenities: Swimming pool and beach; diving and snorkeling trips available; mopeds, golf carts, and bicycles for rent; library, rec room with TV and VCR, and Ping-Pong tables. Salon services including manicures, pedicures, massages, and facials, along with yoga classes.

MODERATE

Hotel Cabañas María del Mar. Av. Carlos Lazo 1, 77400 Isla Mujeres, Q. Roo. ☎ **800/ 223-5695** in the U.S., or 987/7-0179. Fax 987/7-0213 or 987/7-0156. 56 units. A/C. High season $70–$75 double. Low season $45–$50 double. Rates include continental breakfast. MC, V.

A good choice, the Cabañas María del Mar is located on Playa Norte, a half block from the Hotel Na Balam. There are three completely different sections to this hotel. The older two-story section behind the reception area and beyond the garden offers nicely outfitted rooms facing the beach, all with two single or double beds, refrigerators, and balconies with ocean views. Eleven single-story cabañas closer to the reception and pool are rather dark and are the lowest priced. The newest addition, **El Castillo,** is across the street and built over and beside Buho's restaurant. It contains all "deluxe" rooms, but some are larger than others. The five rooms on the ground floor all have large patios; upstairs rooms have small balconies. Most have one double bed. All have ocean views, blue-and-white tile floors, and tile lavatories and are outfitted in colonial-style furniture. There's a small pool in the garden. The owners also have a bus for tours and a boat for rental, as well as golf cart and *moto* (motorized bikes or scooters) rental.

To get here from the pier, walk left 1 block, then turn right on Matamoros. After 4 blocks, turn left on Lazo, the last street. The hotel is at the end of the block.

✪ Hotel Posada del Mar. Av. Rueda Medina 15, 77400 Isla Mujeres, Q. Roo. ☎ **800/ 544-3005** in the U.S., or 987/7-0044. Fax 987/7-0266. www.iminet.com/mexico/ posada.htm. E-mail: hposada@cancun.rce.com.mx. 40 units. A/C TEL. High season $54–$64 double. Low season $32–$36 double. AE, MC, V.

Attractively furnished, quiet, and comfortable, this long-established hotel faces the water and a wide beach 3 blocks north of the ferry pier, and it has one of the few swimming pools on the island. The very spacious rooms are in either a three-story building or one-story bungalow units. For the spacious quality of the rooms and the location, this is among the best values on the island. A wide, seldom used but appealing stretch of Playa Norte is across the street. An extremely appealing casual palapa-style bar and a lovely pool are set on the back lawn, and the popular restaurant **Pinguino** (see "Where to Dine," below) is by the sidewalk at the front of the property. From the pier, go left for 4 blocks; the hotel is on the right.

INEXPENSIVE

✪ Hotel Belmar. Av. Hidalgo 110, 74000 Isla Mujeres, Q. Roo. ☎ **987/7-0430.** Fax 987/7-0429. 11 units. A/C TV TEL. High season $56 double. Low season $28–$45 double. AE, MC, V.

Situated above Pizza Rolandi (consider the restaurant noise), this hotel is run by the same people who serve up those wood-oven pizzas. Each of the simple but stylish rooms comes with two twin or double beds and handsome tile accents. Prices are high for no views, but the rooms are very pleasant. On the other hand, this is one of the few island hotels with televisions (bringing in U.S. channels) in the room. There is a large suite with Jacuzzi and a patio. The hotel is between Madero and Abasolo, 3½ blocks from the passenger ferry pier.

Hotel D'Gomar. Rueda Medina 50, 77400 Isla Mujeres, Q. Roo. ☎ **987/7-0540.** 16 units. High season $30–$35 double. Low season $20–$25 double. No credit cards.

You can hardly beat this hotel for comfort at reasonable prices. Rooms, with rattan furniture, all have two double beds, pink walls and drapes, and a wall of windows with great breezes and picture views. The higher prices are for air-conditioning, which is hardly needed with fantastic breezes and ceiling fans. Manager Manuel Serano says, "We make friends of all our clients." The only drawback is that there are five stories and no elevator. But it's conveniently located catercorner (look right) from the ferry pier, with exceptional rooftop views. The name of the hotel is the most visible sign on the "skyline."

Hotel Francis Arlene. Guerrero 7, 77400 Isla Mujeres, Q. Roo. ☎ and fax **987/7-0310**; in Cancún 98/84-3302. 26 units. A/C (20 rooms). High season $41–$46 double. Low season $37–$42 double. No credit cards.

The Magaña family operates this neat little two-story inn behind the family home, which is built around a small, shady courtyard. You'll notice the tidy cream-and-white facade of the building from the street. Rooms are clean and comfortable, with tile floors and all-tile baths, and soap and towels laid out on your bed. Each downstairs room has a refrigerator and stove; each upstairs room comes with a refrigerator and toaster. All have either a balcony or a patio. Rates were substantially better if quoted in pesos and are reflected above. In dollars they are 15% to 20% higher. It's 5½ blocks inland from the ferry pier, between Abasolo and Matamoros.

WHERE TO DINE

The **Municipal Market,** next door to the telegraph office and post office on avenida Guerrero, has several little cookshops operated by obliging and hard-working women. At the **Panadería La Reyna,** at Madero and Juárez, you can pick up inexpensive sweet bread, muffins, cookies, and yogurt. It's open Monday to Saturday from 7am to 9:30pm.

As in the rest of Mexico, a **cocina económica** restaurant literally means "economic kitchen." Usually aimed at the local population, these are great places to find good food at rock-bottom prices. That's especially so on Isla Mujeres, where you'll find several.

MODERATE

✪ **Las Palapas Chimbo's.** Norte Beach. No phone. Breakfast $2–$3; sandwiches and fruit $2–$3.50; seafood $5–$8. No credit cards. Daily 8am–6pm. SEAFOOD.

If you're looking for a beachside palapa-covered restaurant where you can wiggle your toes in the sand while relishing fresh seafood, this is the best of them. Locals recommend it as their favorite on Norte Beach. Try the delicious fried fish (a whole one), which comes with rice, beans, and tortillas. You'll notice the bandstand and dance floor that's been added to the middle of the restaurant, and especially the sex-hunk posters all over the ceiling—that is, when you aren't gazing at the beach and the Caribbean. Chimbo's becomes a disco at night, and draws a motley crew of drinkers and dancers. (See "Isla Mujeres After Dark," below.) To find it from the pier, walk left to the end of the Malecón, then right onto the Playa Norte; it's about half a block on the right.

✪ **Pinguino.** In the Hotel Posada del Mar, av. Rueda Medina 15. ☎ **987/7-0300.** Breakfast $2–$3; main courses $3.75–$6.75; daily special $6. AE, MC, V. Daily 7:30am–10pm; bar open to midnight. MEXICAN/SEAFOOD.

The best seats on the waterfront are on the deck of this restaurant/bar, especially in late evening when islanders and tourists arrive to dance and party. This is the place to feast on lobster—you'll get a beautifully presented, large, sublimely fresh lobster tail with a choice of butter, garlic, and secret sauces. Breakfasts include fresh fruit, yogurt, and granola or sizable platters of eggs, served with homemade wheat bread. Pinguino is in front of the hotel, 3 blocks west of the ferry pier.

Pizza Rolandi. Av. Hidalgo. ☎ **987/7-0429.** Main courses $3.75–$27; pizza $6–$18. AE, MC, V. Daily 11am–11pm. ITALIAN.

Pizza Rolandi, the chain that saves the day with dependably good, reasonably priced food amid other expensive resorts, comes through in Isla Mujeres as well. In the casual dining room, in an open courtyard of the Hotel Belmar, you can savor plate-size pizzas, pastas, and calzones cooked in a wood oven. There's also a more expensive menu with fish, beef, and chicken dishes. Guitarists often perform in the evenings. It's 3½ blocks inland from the pier, between Madero and Abasolo.

✪ **Zacil-Ha.** At the Hotel Na Balam, Norte Beach. ☎ **987/7-0279.** Breakfast $3.50–$4.50; main courses $6–$9. AE, MC, V. Breakfast 7:30–10:30am, lunch 12:30–3:30pm, dinner 7–10pm. INTERNATIONAL.

At this restaurant you can enjoy some of the island's best food while sitting among the palms and gardens at tables on the sand. The serene environment is enhanced by the food—terrific pasta with garlic, shrimp in tequila sauce, fajitas, seafood pasta, and delicious mole enchiladas. Main courses come with vegetable and rice. Between the set hours for meals you can have all sorts of enticing food, such as blender vegetable and fruit drinks, tacos and sandwiches, ceviche, and terrific nachos. It's likely you'll stake this place out for several meals before you leave. It's at the end of Playa Norte and almost at the end of calle Zacil-Ha.

INEXPENSIVE

✪ **Cafecito.** Calle Matamoros 42, corner of Juárez. ☎ **987/7-0438.** Coffee drinks $1–$3; crêpes $1.75–$3.75; breakfast $2–$4; main courses $4.75–$7. No credit cards. Mon–Wed and Fri–Sat 8am–2pm and 6:30–10:30pm; Thurs and Sun 8am–2pm. CRÊPES/ICE CREAM/COFFEE/FRUIT DRINKS.

Sabina and Luis Rivera own this cute, Caribbean-blue corner restaurant where you can begin the day with flavorful coffee and a croissant and cream cheese, or end it with a hot-fudge sundae. Terrific crêpes are served with yogurt, ice cream, fresh fruit, or chocolate sauces, as well as ham and cheese. The two-page ice-cream menu satisfies most any craving, even one for waffles with ice cream and fruit. The three-course fixed-price dinner starts with soup, then a main course such as fish or curried shrimp with rice and salad, followed by dessert. It's 4 blocks from the pier at the corner of Juárez and Matamoros.

✪ **Chen Huaye.** Bravo 6. No phone. Breakfast $2–$3.50; main courses $1.75–$5. No credit cards. Wed–Mon 9am–11pm. YUCATECAN MEXICAN/HOME COOKING.

The Juanito Tago Trego family owns this large lunchroom where tourists and locals find a variety of pleasing dishes at equally pleasing prices. Light meals include empanadas, Yucatecan salubites, panucos, and quesadillas. The *tamal costado,* a tamal stuffed with chicken pieces and baked in a banana leaf, is a daily special. Main courses might include breaded pork chops, chicken in adobado, or fried chicken. The name, by the way, is Maya for "only here." It's between Guerrero and Juárez; you'll recognize it by the wagon wheel in front.

Cocina Económica Carmelita. Calle Juárez 14. ☎ **987/7-0136.** Meal of the day $3. No credit cards. Daily 12–3pm; and Dec–March 4pm–8pm. MEXICAN/HOME COOKING.

Few tourists find their way to this tiny restaurant, open only for lunch. But locals know they can get a filling, inexpensive, home-cooked meal prepared by Carmelita in the back kitchen and served by her husband at the three cloth-covered tables in the front room of their home. Two or three comida corridas are available each day and are served until they run out. They begin with black bean soup and include a fruit water drink. Common selections include paella or *cochinita pibil,* and fish-stuffed chiles; Sunday is *pozole* day. It's 2 blocks from the passenger ferry pier, between Bravo and Allende.

ISLA MUJERES AFTER DARK

Those in a party mood by day's end might want to start out at the beach bar of the **Hotel Na Balam** on Playa Norte, which hosts a crowd until around midnight. On Saturday and Sunday there's live music here between 4 and 7pm. **Las Palapas Chimbo's** restaurant on the beach becomes a jammin' dance joint with a live band from 9pm until whenever. Farther along the same stretch of beach, **Buho's,** the restaurant/beach bar of the Cabañas María del Mar, has its moments as a popular, low-key hangout. **Pinguino** in the Hotel Posada del Mar offers a convivial late-night hangout. There are two places to be: the restaurant/bar, where the manager, Miguel, whips up some potent concoctions and the band plays nightly during high season from 9pm to midnight; and the more tranquil but totally delightful poolside bar with swings under a giant palapa.

2 Cozumel

44 miles SE of Cancún

Cozumel is the original Caribbean destination in Mexico, a top cruise-ship port of call in the Americas and one of the world's top five dive destinations. Despite all this acclaim, Cozumel remains a laid-back, ocean-oriented village, infused with a mix of Maya and Mexican authenticity.

The largest island in the Mexican Caribbean, it is located just 12 miles offshore from Playa del Carmen, a 45-minute, $5 ferry ride away. The name comes from the Maya word *Cuzamil,* meaning "land of the swallows." Today, it remains the home of two species of birds found nowhere else: the Cozumel vireo and the Cozumel thrasher. Only 3% developed, this 28-mile long, 11-mile-wide island still has vast stretches of pristine jungle and uninhabited shoreline.

The only town is San Miguel de Cozumel, usually called just San Miguel. On the island, you'll find a mix of all the necessities for a good vacation: excellent snorkeling and scuba places, sailing and water sports, expensive resorts and modest hotels, elegant restaurants and taco shops, and even a Maya ruin or two. Due to the influx of cruise visitors, shopping is extensive, with many duty-free stores selling jewelry, perfumes, and designer wares. If after a while you do get restless, the ancient Maya city of **Tulum,** the lagoons of **Xel-Ha** and **Xcaret,** or the nearby village of **Playa del Carmen** provide convenient and interesting excursions.

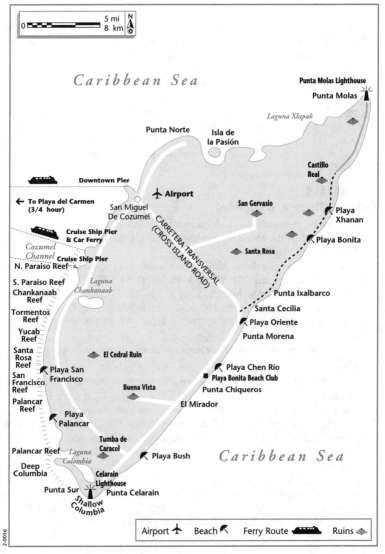

During pre-Hispanic times the island was one of three important ceremonial centers (Izamal and Chichén-Itzá were the other two). Maya women would travel the 12 miles by boat to the island at least once in their life to worship the goddess of fertility, Ixchel. More than 40 sites around the island containing shrines remain today, and archaeologists still uncover the small dolls regularly offered in the fertility ceremony.

Salt and honey, trade products produced on the island, further linked Cozumel with the mainland; they were brought ashore at the ruins we know today as Tulum. The site was occupied when Hernán Cortés landed here in 1519. Before his own boat docked, Cortés's men sacked the town and took the chief's wife and children captive. According to Bernal Díaz del Castillo's account, everything was returned. Diego de Landa's account says Cortés converted the Indians and replaced their sacred Maya figures with a cross and a statue of Mary in the main temple at Cozumel. After the Spanish Conquest the island was an important port; but foreign diseases decimated the population, and by 1570 it was almost uninhabited.

The inhabitants returned later, but the War of the Castes in the 1800s severely curtailed Cozumel's trade. Cozumel continued on its economic rollercoaster, and after the Caste War it again took its place as a commercial seaport. In the mid-1950s Cozumel's fame as a diving destination began to grow, and real development of the island as the site for a vacation resort evolved along with Cancún beginning in the mid-1970s.

ESSENTIALS
GETTING THERE & DEPARTING

BY PLANE   **Aerocozumel,** a Mexicana affiliate, has numerous flights to and from Cancún and Mérida. **Mexicana** flies from Mexico City. **Taesa** flies from Cancún, Chetumal, and Mérida.

Here are some telephone numbers for confirming departures to and from Cozumel: **Aerocozumel** (☎ **98/72-3456,** or 98/84-2002 in Cancún); **Continental** (☎ **800/231-0856** in the U.S., or 987/2-0847 in Cozumel); and **Mexicana** (☎ **800/531-7921** in the U.S.; 800/50-220-00 in Mexico; 987/2-0157 or 987/2-2945 at the airport; fax 987/2-2945); **Taesa** (☎ **01-800-904-6300** within Mexico).

Only colectivo vans are available from the airport into town, costing around $5 to $6. Taxis from town to the airport will run $8 to $12.

BY FERRY   Passenger ferries to Cozumel depart from Playa del Carmen on the mainland daily, with scheduled service. There is also a car ferry from Puerto Morelos. You can catch a bus to Playa del Carmen from Cancún.

The **Water Jet Service** (☎ **987/2-1508** or 987/2-1588), makes the trip between Cozumel and Playa del Carmen in 45 minutes. It costs $5 one-way, and is enclosed and air-conditioned, with cushioned seats, bar service, and video entertainment. Departures are almost hourly from 5am to 11pm. In Playa del Carmen, the ferry dock is 1½ blocks from the main square and from the bus drop-off point. Tickets are also sold in booths at the main pier in Cozumel. Since schedules change frequently, be sure to double-check them at the docks, especially the time of the last ferry back, if that's the one you intend to use. Storage lockers are available at the Cozumel dock for $2 per day. From Cozumel to Playa del Carmen, the ferry runs approximately every hour or hour and a half between 4am and 10pm, also at a cost of $5 one way.

For those who are considering a **car ferry,** the first thing to know is that you're better off without a car in Cozumel; parking is difficult. A solution is to drive to Playa del Carmen, find a reliable place to leave your car, and take the passenger ferry. If you do want to take your car over, the terminus in **Puerto Morelos** (☎ **987/1-0008**) is the largest establishment in town, and is very easy to find. The car-ferry schedule is complicated and may change, so double-check it before arriving in Puerto Morelos. On Monday, the ferry leaves at 6am, 9:30am, and 6pm; on Tuesday at 10am, 3pm, and 8pm; on Wednesday to Sunday one daily departure with varying hours. The crossing takes approximately 3 hours.

Cargo takes precedence over cars. Officials suggest that camper drivers stay overnight in the parking lot to be first in line for tickets. In any case, *always arrive at least 3 hours in advance of the ferry's departure to purchase a ticket and to get in line.*

Since passenger-boat service between Playa del Carmen and Cozumel is so fast and frequent, I don't recommend that foot passengers bother with this boat.

When returning to Puerto Morelos from Cozumel, the ferry departs from the international cruise-ship pier daily. Get in line about 3 hours before departure, and double-check the schedule by calling ☎ 987/2-0950. The fare is $45 for a car and $5 per passenger.

ORIENTATION

ARRIVING   Cozumel's **airport** is immediately north of downtown. Aero Transportes colectivo vans at the airport provide transportation into town and to the north or south hotel zone. Buy your ticket as you exit the terminal. Cozumel now has two **cruise-ferry docks,** with a third under controversial construction. The newest one, **Puerto Maya,** about a mile south of the older one (dubbed the **International Pier**) also stirred controversy because it was built over North Paradise Reef—the reef with the best shore diving and snorkeling possibilities. Dive operators, the town, and ecological preservation activists from around the world protested the building of this pier, without success.

VISITOR INFORMATION   The **State Tourism Office** (☎ and fax **987/2-0972** or 987/2-0218) is on the second floor of the Plaza del Sol commercial building facing the central plaza and is open daily from 8:30am to 3pm.

CITY LAYOUT   San Miguel's main waterfront street is called **avenida Rafael Melgar,** running along the western shore of the island. Passenger ferries dock right in the center, opposite the main plaza and Melgar. Car ferries dock south of town at the International Pier near the hotels Sol Caribe and La Ceiba. Cruise ships dock at the International Pier and at the New Puerto Maya Pier.

The town is laid out on a grid, with avenidas running north and south, calles running east and west. The exception is **avenida Juárez,** which runs right from the passenger-ferry dock through the main square and inland. Juárez divides the town into northern and southern halves.

Heading inland from the dock along Juárez, you'll find that the avenidas you cross are numbered by fives: 5a avenida, 10a avenida, 15a avenida. If you turn left and head north, calles are numbered evenly: 2a Norte, 4a Norte, 6a Norte. Turning right from Juárez heads you south, where the streets are numbered: 1a Sur (also called Adolfo Salas), 3a Sur, 5a Sur.

ISLAND LAYOUT   The island is cut in half by one road, which runs past the airport and the ruins of San Gervasio to the almost uninhabited southern coast of the island. The northern part of the island has no paved roads. It's scattered with small, badly ruined Maya sites, from the age when "Cuzamil" was a land sacred to the moon goddess Ixchel. San Gervasio is accessible by motor scooter and car.

Most inexpensive hotels are in the town of San Miguel. Moderate to expensive accommodations are north and south of town. Many cater to divers. Beyond the hotels to the south is **Chankanaab National Park,** centered on the beautiful lagoon of the same name. Beyond Chankanaab are **Playa Palancar** and, offshore, the **Palancar Reef** (*arrecife*). At the southern tip of the island are **Punta Celarain** and the lighthouse.

The eastern, seaward shore of the island is mostly surf beach, beautiful for walking but dangerous for swimming.

GETTING AROUND   You can walk to most destinations in town. However, getting to outlying hotels and beaches, including the Chankanaab Lagoon, requires a taxi.

Important Note ——————————————————————————————————

North/south streets have the right of way, and these drivers don't slow down.

Car rentals are as expensive here as they are in other parts of Mexico. International agencies have counters in the airport, or rentals can be arranged by your hotel tour desk or any local travel agency. See "By Car" under "Getting Around" in chapter 3 for specifics.

Moped rentals are all over the village and cost about $25 for 24 hours, but terms and prices vary. Carefully inspect the actual moped you'll be renting to see that all the gizmos are in good shape: horn, light, starter, seat, mirror. And be sure to note all damage to the moped on the rental agreement. Most important, read the fine print on the back of the rental agreement, which states that you are not insured, are responsible for paying any damage to the bike (or for all of it if it's stolen or demolished), and must stay on paved roads. It's illegal to ride a moped without a helmet (subject to a $25 fine).

Taxis: Here are a few sample fares: Island tour, $30; town to southern hotel zone, $4 to $8; town to northern hotels, $3 to $5; to Chankanaab from town, $6. Call ☎ 987/2-0236 for taxi pickup.

FAST FACTS: Cozumel

American Express   The local representative is Fiesta Cozumel, calle 11 no. 598 (☎ 987/2-0725).

Area Code   The telephone area code is **987.**

Climate   From October to December there can be strong winds all over the Yucatán, as well as some rain. In Cozumel, wind conditions in November and December can make diving dangerous. May to September is the rainy season.

Diving   If you intend to dive, remember to bring proof of your diver's certification. Underwater currents can be very strong here, and many of the reef drops are quite steep, making them excellent sites for experienced divers, but can be overly challenging for novice divers.

Post Office   The post office (*correo*) is on avenida Rafael Melgar at calle 7 Sur, at the southern edge of town; it's open Monday to Friday from 9am to 6pm and Saturday from 9am to noon.

Recompression Chamber   There are three recompression chambers (*cámaras de recompresión*). One is on calle 5 Sur, 1 block off Melgar between Melgar and avenida 5 Sur (☎ 987/2-2387 or 987/2-1848). Normal hours are 8am to 1pm and 4 to 8pm. The 24-hour Emergencies number is ☎ 987/2-1430. Another one is the **Hyperbaric Center of Cozumel** ☎ 987/2-3070.

Seasons   High season is Christmas to Easter, and in August.

EXPLORING THE ISLAND

For **diving** and **snorkeling** it's best to go directly to the recommended shops below. For **island tours, ruins tours** on and off the island, **glass-bottom boat tours, fiesta nights, fishing,** and other activities, I can recommend the travel agency **InterMar Cozumel Viajes,** calle 2 Norte, 101-B between avenidas 5 and 10. (☎ 987/2-1098; fax 987/2-0895; e-mail intermar@cozumel.czm.com.mx). The office is close to the main plaza between avenidas 5 and 10 Norte. But many of these you can do on your own without purchasing a tour.

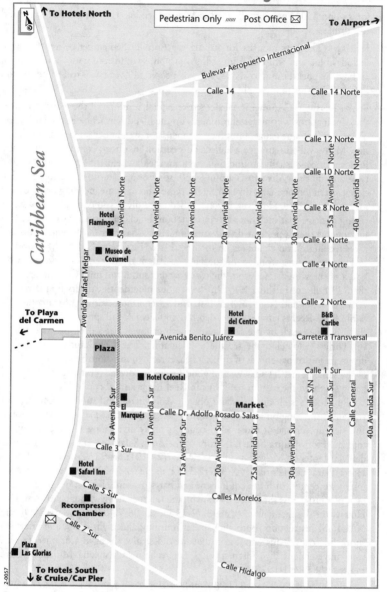

San Miguel de Cozumel

Pedestrian Only /////   Post Office ⊠

To Hotels North

To Airport →

N

Caribbean Sea

Bulevar Aeropuerto Internacional

Calle 14   Calle 14 Norte

Calle 12 Norte

Calle 10 Norte

Calle 8 Norte

Calle 6 Norte

Calle 4 Norte

Calle 2 Norte

5a Avenida Norte

10a Avenida Norte

15a Avenida Norte

20a Avenida Norte

25a Avenida Norte

30a Avenida Norte

35a Avenida Norte

40a Avenida Norte

Avenida Rafael Melgar

Hotel Flamingo

Museo de Cozumel

To Playa del Carmen ←

Hotel del Centro

B&B Caribe

Carretera Transversal

Avenida Benito Juárez

Plaza

Calle 1 Sur

Hotel Colonial

El Marqués

Calle Dr. Adolfo Rosado Salas

Market

5a Avenida Sur

10a Avenida Sur

15a Avenida Sur

20a Avenida Sur

25a Avenida Sur

30a Avenida Sur

35a Avenida Sur

Calle S/N

Calle General

40a Avenida Sur

Calle 3 Sur

Hotel Safari Inn

Calle 5 Sur

Recompression Chamber

⊠

Calle 7 Sur

Calles Morelos

Plaza Las Glorias

To Hotels South ↓ & Cruise/Car Pier

Calle Hidalgo

2-0057

A FESTIVAL

Carnaval (Mardi Gras) is Cozumel's most colorful fiesta. It begins the Thursday before Ash Wednesday with daytime street dancing and nighttime parades on Thursday, Saturday, and Monday (the best).

WATER SPORTS Boat Trips Boat trips are another popular pastime on Cozumel. Some excursions include snorkeling and scuba diving or a stop at a beach with lunch. Various types of tours are offered, including rides in glass-bottom boats for around $30. These usually start at 9am and end at 1pm and include beer and soft drinks.

Fishing   The best months for fishing are April to September, when the catch includes blue and white marlin, sailfish, tarpon, swordfish, dorado, wahoo, tuna, and red snapper. Fishing costs $450 for six people all day or $80 to $85 per person for a half day for four people.

Scuba Diving   Cozumel is Mexico's dive capital, and one of the world's premier dive destinations. Various establishments on the island rent scuba gear—tanks, regulator with pressure gauge, buoyancy compensator, weight belts, mask, snorkel, and fins. Many will also arrange a half-day expedition in a boat, complete with lunch, for a set price—usually around $40. Sign up the day before if you're interested. A two-tank morning dive costs around $50; some shops are now offering an additional afternoon one-tank dive for $9 for those who took the morning dives, or $25 for a one-tank dive. However, if you're a dedicated diver, you may save by buying a diving package that includes air transportation, hotel, and usually two dives a day. Cozumel is such a popular dive destination that it has over 60 dive operators and three recompression chambers on the island (see "Fast Facts: Cozumel," above).

The underwater wonders of the famous **Palancar Reef** are offshore from the beach of the same name. From the car-ferry pier south to Punta Celarain are more than 20 miles of offshore reefs. In the famous blue depths, divers find caves and canyons, small and large colorful fish, and an enormous variety of sea coral. The **Santa Rosa Reef** is famous for its depth, sea life, coral, and sponges. **San Francisco Reef,** off the beach by the same name south of town, has a drop-off wall, but it's still fairly shallow and the sea life is fascinating. The **Chankanaab Reef,** where divers are joined by schools of tropical fish, is close to the shore by the national park of the same name. It's shallow and good for novice divers. Next after Chankanaab going south on the eastern road, **Yucab Reef** has beautiful coral.

Numerous vessels on the island operate daily diving and snorkeling tours, so if you aren't traveling on a prearranged dive package, the best plan is to shop around and sign up for one of those. Of Cozumel's many dive shops, two are among the top: Bill Horn's **Aqua Safari,** in front of the Aqua Safari Inn and next to the Vista del Mar Hotel on Melgar at calle 5 (☎ **987/2-0101;** fax 987/2-0661); and in the Hotel Plaza Las Glorias (☎ **987/2-3362** or 987/2-2422), is a PADI five-star instructor center, with full equipment and parts, a good selection of books, and its own pier just across the street. They're on the Internet at www.aquasafari.com. **Dive House,** on the main plaza (☎ **987/2-1953;** fax 987/2-0368), offers PADI, and NAUI SSI instruction. Both shops offer morning and night dives, and afternoon snorkeling trips. Aqua Safari is one of the oldest dive shops in Cozumel. For private, independent dive instruction, I can recommend **Sheena Mulshaw, Divemaster** (☎ **984/1-1978**).

You can save money by renting your gear at a beach shop, such as the two mentioned above, and diving from shore. The shops at the Plaza Las Glorias and La Ceiba hotels are good for shore diving. It costs about $6 to rent one tank and weights; extra charges apply for regulator, BC, mask, and fins. The dives from shore are only worthwhile from San Francisco beach, Chankanaab, and La Ceiba beach. Even then it's a lot of work to haul your own gear. The sites are much better in the depths offshore, and it really is a lot easier to take a boat.

A new twist in underwater Yucatán is **cenote diving** and **snorkeling.** The peninsula's underground *cenotes* (say-noh-tehs) or sinkholes, which were sacred to the Maya, lead to a vast system of underground caverns. Here, the gently flowing water

In case you want to see the world.

At American Express, we're here to make your journey a smooth one. So we have over 1,700 travel service locations in over 120 countries ready to help. What else would you expect from the world's largest travel agency?

do more

AMERICAN
EXPRESS

Travel

In case you want to be welcomed there.

We're here to see that you're always welcomed at establishments everywhere. That's why millions of people carry the American Express® Card – for peace of mind, confidence, and security, around the world or just around the corner.

do more

AMERICAN EXPRESS

Cards

In case you're running low.

We're here to help with more than 118,000 Express Cash
locations around the world. In order to enroll, just call
American Express before you start your vacation.

do more

And just in case.

We're here with American Express® Travelers Cheques and Cheques *for Two.*® They're the safest way to carry money on your vacation and the surest way to get a refund, practically anywhere, anytime.

Another way we help you…

do more

AMERICAN EXPRESS

Travelers Cheques

is so clear divers appear to be floating on air through caves that look just like those on dry land, complete with stalactites and stalagmites, plus tropical fish, eels, and turtles. The caverns were formed millions of years ago during the last two glacial eras, but only in recent years has this other world been opened to certified divers. The experienced cave divers/owners of **Yucatech Expeditions** (☎ and fax **987/ 2-5659;** fax 987/2-1417; e-mail: yucatech@cozumel.czm.com.mx), offer this unique experience five times weekly from Playa del Carmen (you take the ferry with your gear and they meet you with vans there). Cenotes are 30 to 45 minutes from Playa and a dive in each cenote lasts around 45 minutes. Snorkelers paddle around the cenotes, while divers explore the depths. Dives are within the daylight zone, about 130 feet into the caverns and no more than 60 feet deep. There's plenty of natural light. Company owner German Yañez Mendoza, inspects diving credentials carefully and has a list of requirements divers must meet before cave diving is permitted. They also offer the equivalent of a resort course in cave diving and a full cave-diving course. A snorkeling trip to two cenotes runs around $65, while a two-cenote dive costs around $130, including transportation from Cozumel, tanks, weights, food and drinks (beers only after the dives).

Snorkeling   Anyone who can swim can snorkel. Rental of the snorkel (breathing pipe), goggles, and flippers should cost only about $4 for half a day; a 2-hour snorkeling trip costs $15. The brilliantly colored tropical fish provide a dazzling show. **Chankanaab Park** is one of the best places to go on your own for an abundant fish show.

Agency-arranged **snorkeling excursions** cost around $40 for a 10am to 3pm trip that includes snorkeling at three different reefs, lunch, beer, and soft drinks. Two-hour snorkeling trips through the dive shops recommended above cost $15 and usually leave around 2:30pm.

Windsurfing   One of Mexico's top windsurfing champions, **Raul de Lille** offers windsurfing classes and equipment rentals at the beach in front of Sol Cabañas del Caribe, on the north side. For information, call ☎ **987/2-0017;** fax 987/2-1942.

A TOUR OF THE ISLAND

Travel agencies can book you on a group tour of the island for around $35, depending on whether the tour includes lunch and a stop for snorkeling. A taxi driver charges $60 for a 4-hour tour. A 4-hour horseback tour of the island's interior to the ruins and jungle costs $60; call **Rancho Buenavista** (☎ **987/2-1537** or 987/2-4374). The trip leaves from the Neptuno Disco (call for schedule information), or the InterMar Viajes travel agency mentioned above. You can also easily rent a motorbike or car for half a day to take you around; see above under "Getting Around."

North of town, along avenida Rafael Melgar (which becomes Carretera Pilar), you'll pass a yacht marina and a string of Cozumel's first hotels as well as some new condominiums. A few of the hotels have nice beaches. This road ends just past the hotels; you can backtrack to the transversal road that cuts across the island from west (the town side) to east and links up with the eastern highway that brings you back to town.

The more interesting route begins by going south of town on Melgar (which becomes Costera Sur or Carretera a Chankanaab) past the Hotel Barracuda and Sol Caribe. After about 3 miles you'll see a sign pointing left down an unpaved road a short distance to the Rancho San Manuel, where you can rent horses. There are only seven horses here, but a guide and soft drink are included in the price. Rides cost $20 per hour. It's open daily from 8am to 4pm.

About 5 miles south of town you'll come to the Crowne Princess and La Ceiba hotels and also the car ferry dock for ferries to Puerto Morelos. Go snorkeling out in the water by the Hotel La Ceiba and you might spot a sunken airplane, put there for an underwater movie. Offshore, from here to the tip of the island at Punta Celarain, 20 miles away, is the Underwater National Park, so designated to protect the reef from damage by visitors. Dive masters warn not to touch or destroy the underwater growth.

CHANKANAAB NATIONAL PARK This lagoon and botanical garden is a mile past the big hotels and 5½ miles south of town. Known as a natural aquarium, it has long been famous for the color and variety of its sea life. The intrusion of sight-seers began to ruin the marine habitat, so now visitors must swim and snorkel in the open sea, not in the lagoon. The beach is wide and beautiful, with plenty of shady thatched umbrellas to sit under, and the snorkeling is good—lots of colorful fish. Arrive early to stake out a chair and palapa before the cruise-ship visitors arrive. There are rest rooms, lockers, a gift shop, several snack huts, a restaurant, and a snorkeling-gear-rental palapa.

Surrounding the lagoon, the botanical garden, with shady paths, has 352 species of tropical and subtropical plants from 22 countries and 451 species from Cozumel. Several Maya structures have been re-created within the gardens to give visitors an idea of Maya life in a jungle setting. There's a small natural history museum as well. Admission to the park costs $3; it's open daily from 8am to 5pm.

THE BEACHES

Ten miles past the Chankanaab National Park, you'll come to Playa San Francisco and, south of it, Playa Palancar. Besides the beach at Chankanaab Lagoon, they're the best on Cozumel. Food (usually overpriced) and equipment rentals are available. On the east side of the island, the Playa Bonita Beach Club, near Playa Chiqueros, has water sports and windsurfing-equipment rentals. The restaurant is open daily from 10am to 5pm.

PUNTA CELARAIN After Playa San Francisco, you plow through the jungle on a straight road for miles until you're 17½ miles from town. Finally, though, you emerge near the southern reaches of the island on the east coast. The lighthouse you see in the distance is at Punta Celarain, the island's southernmost tip. The sand track is unsuitable for motorbikes, but in a car you can drive to the lighthouse in about 25 minutes.

THE EASTERN SHORE The road along the east coast of the island is wonderful. There are views of the sea, the rocky shore, and the pounding surf. On the land side are little farms and forests. Exotic birds take flight as you approach, and monstrous (but harmless) iguanas skitter off into the undergrowth.

Most of the east coast is unsafe for swimming because the surf can create a deadly undertow. There are always cars pulled off along the road here, with the occupants spending the day on the golden beach dotted with limestone formations, but not in the churning waters. Three restaurants catering to tourists are along this part of the coast, complete with sombrero-clad iguanas for picture companions.

Halfway up the east coast, the paved eastern road meets the paved transversal road (which passes the ruins of San Gervasio) back to town, 9½ miles away. The east-coast road ends when it turns into the transversal, petering out to a narrow track of sandy road by a nice restaurant in front of the Chen Río Beach; vehicles, even motorbikes, will get stuck on the sand road. If you're a bird watcher, leave your vehicle on the highway here and walk straight down the sandy road. Go slowly and quietly and at the least you'll spot many herons and egrets in the lagoon on the left that parallels the path. Much farther on are Maya ruins.

OTHER ATTRACTIONS

MAYA RUINS   One of the most popular island excursions is to **San Gervasio** (100 B.C. to A.D. 1600). A road leads there from the airport, or you can continue on the eastern part of the island following the paved transversal road. The worn sign to the ruins is easy to miss, but the turnoff (left) is about halfway between town and the eastern coast. Stop at the entrance gate and pay the $1 road-use fee. Go straight ahead over the potholed road to the ruins about 2 miles farther and pay the $3.50 to enter; camera permits cost $4 for each still or video camera you want to bring in. A small tourist center at the entrance has cold drinks and snacks for sale.

When it comes to Cozumel's Maya remains, getting there is most of the fun, and you should do it for the mystique and for the trip, not for the size or scale of the ruins. The buildings, though preserved, are crudely made and would not be much of a tourist attraction if they were not the island's only cleared and accessible ruins. More significant than beautiful, the site was once an important ceremonial center where the Maya gathered, coming even from the mainland. The important deity here was Ixchel, known as the goddess of weaving, women, childbirth, pilgrims, the moon, and medicine. Although you won't see any representations of her at San Gervasio today, Bruce Hunter, in his *Guide to Ancient Maya Ruins,* writes that priests hid behind a large pottery statue of her and became the voice of the goddess speaking to pilgrims and answering their petitions. She was the wife of Itzamná, sun god and as such, preeminent among all Maya gods.

Tour guides charge $10 for a tour for one to six people. A better option is to find a copy of the green booklet *San Gervasio,* sold at local checkout counters or bookstores, and tour the site on your own. Seeing it takes 30 minutes. Taxi drivers offer a tour to the ruins for about $25; the driver will wait for you outside the ruins.

PARQUE ARQUEOLÓGICO   This park contains reproductions of many of Mexico's important archaeological treasures, including the 4-foot-high Olmec head and the Chaac-Mool seen at Chichén-Itzá. A Maya couple demonstrates the lifestyle of the Maya in a *nah,* or thatch-roofed oval home. The park is a nice addition to the island's cultural attractions and is well worth visiting, but wear bug repellent before you begin exploring. The park is open daily from 8am to 6pm; admission is $1.50. To get there, turn left on the unmarked road across from the International Pier, off Costera Sur just south of the La Ceiba hotel, then left on avenida 65 Sur and follow the signs.

A HISTORY MUSEUM   The **Museo de la Isla de Cozumel,** on avenida Melgar between calles 4 and 6 Norte (☎ **987/2-1475**), is more than just a nice place to spend a rainy hour. On the first floor an excellent exhibit showcases endangered species, the origin of the island, and its present-day topography and plant and animal life, including an explanation of coral formation. Upstairs, showrooms feature the history of the town, artifacts from the island's pre-Hispanic sites, and colonial-era cannons, swords, and ship paraphernalia. It's open daily from 9am to 5pm. Admission is $3.00; guided tours in English are free. There's a rooftop restaurant open long hours.

TRIPS TO THE MAINLAND

PLAYA DEL CARMEN & XCARET   Going on your own to the nearby seaside village of **Playa del Carmen** and the **Xcaret** nature park is as easy as a quick ferry ride from Cozumel (For ferry information, see "Getting There & Departing," above.) Both are covered in detail later in this chapter. Cozumel travel agencies offer an Xcaret tour that includes the ferry fee, transportation to the park, and the admission fee for $45.

CHICHÉN-ITZÁ, TULUM & COBÁ   Travel agencies can arrange day trips to the fascinating ruins of **Chichén-Itzá** either by air or by bus. Departure times vary depending on which transportation you choose. Since the ruins of **Tulum,** overlooking the Caribbean, and **Cobá,** in a dense jungle setting, are closer, they cost less to visit. They are a complete architectural contrast to Chichén-Itzá: Coba is a grandiose archaeological zone within a remote jungle setting, while Tulum is much smaller in actual dimensions. A trip to Cobá and Tulum, both of which have had less restorative attention given them than Chichén-Itzá, begins at 9am and returns around 6pm.

SHOPPING

Shopping has evolved from the ubiquitous T-shirt shops into stores that feature expensive resort wear, silver, and better decorative and folk art. Most stores are on avenida Melgar; the best shops for high-quality Mexican folk art are Los Cinco Soles, Talavera, and Playa del Angel. Prices for serapes, T-shirts, and the like are normally less expensive on the side streets off Melgar.

If you want to pick up some Mexican tapes and CDs, head to **Discoteca Hollywood,** at Juárez 421 (☎ **987/2-4090**); it's open Monday to Saturday from 9am to 10pm. Self-billed as the "Paradise of the Cassette," this store stocks a large selection.

WHERE TO STAY

Cozumel's hotels are in three separate locations: in the **central town,** and to the **north** and **south** of town. The older resorts, most of which are expensive, line beaches and coral and limestone outcroppings north and south of town; the more budget-oriented inns are in the central village. *Note:* There's a **central reservations number** for many (not all) of the island's hotels (☎ **800/327-2254** in the U.S. and Canada). As an alternative to a hotel, **Cozumel Vacation Villas and Condos,** av. 10 Sur no. 124, 77600 Cozumel, Q. Roo (☎ **800/224-5551** in the U.S., 987/2-0729, or 987/2-1375; e-mail; info@cozumel-villas.com) offers a wide range of accommodations and prices.

Because Cozumel is principally a destination for divers, there are numerous options that cater to this specialty market. Some are for serious, no-frills divers who only want a good bed and a hot shower for after the dive. These hotels usually don't have a pool or restaurant. There are others that are a little more upscale, often on the beach, that offer complete dive services in addition to rooms and facilities. The remaining properties are for divers traveling with non-divers.

NORTH OF TOWN

I'll start with the northernmost hotels going through town, and move onward to the end of the southern hotel zone. Like beaches south of town, those along the northern shore appear sporadically and some hotels have enclosed them with retaining walls. **Carretera Santa Pilar** is the name of Melgar's northern extension, so just take Melgar north and all the hotels are lined up in close proximity to each other on the Santa Pilar Beach a short distance from town and the airport.

Very Expensive

Hotel El Cozumeleño Beach Resort. Km 4.5 Carretera Santa Pilar (Apdo. Postal 53), 77600 Cozumel, Q. Roo. ☎ **987/2-0050** or 987/2-0049. Fax 987/2-0381. 100 units. A/C TEL TV. High season $200–$280 double; low season $140–$220 double. All inclusive. AE, MC, V.

The Cozumeleño all-inclusive resort is a five-story hotel (with elevator) on one of the nicest stretches of coral-free beach on the island. The expansive marble-floored lobby scattered with groupings of pastel chairs and couches is a popular gathering place. The glassed-in dining room looks out onto the Caribbean, as do all the spacious and nicely furnished guest rooms. The beach here is rocky, but their pleasant free-form pool and surrounding areas compensate with extensive gardens, a hot tub, and shade palapas.

Dining/Diversions: Two restaurants, one by the beach and pool and the other indoors, serve all three meals. A karaoke bar provides music to drink by.

Amenities: Palm-shaded pool, children's pool, tennis court, water-sports equipment, 19-hole miniature golf course, game room, gym, and diving center. Laundry and room service, travel agency, auto and moped rental.

Expensive

Playa Azul. Km 4 Carretera Pilar, 77600 Cozumel, Q. Roo. ☎ **987/2-0199** or 987/2-0043. Fax 987/2-0110. E-mail: playazul@cozumel.czm.com.mx. 30 units. A/C TEL. High season $110–$170 double. Low season $70–$130 double. MC, V.

This boutique hotel caters to divers and offers extra-clean, extremely spacious rooms, most with large balconies or terraces overlooking their white, sandy beach. Under new management, the hotel has recently been completely renovated, and offers new common services and facilities, including a second-floor lobby with pool table and video room, plus a library. The beachfront pool has cushioned lounges. There are shade palapas on the beach, plus a private dock for dive boat pick-ups. All rooms have either king or two double beds, with suites offering two convertible single sofas in the separate living room area. In-room safety deposit boxes and extra-large bathrooms are added features. All rooms are simply furnished, with tile floors. The friendly, on-site management assures top service.

Dining/Diversions: The **Playa Azul** restaurant specializes in seafood and Mexican cuisine and offers indoor or patio dining; there's room service available from 7am to 11pm. The beachfront palapa bar is open from 9am to 6pm.

Amenities: Beachfront pool with water-sports equipment; atrium lounge with video room and satellite TV. Laundry, dry cleaning, gift shop, room service, scooter and car rental. Massage service available.

Sol Cabañas del Caribe. Km 4.5 Carretera Santa Pilar (Apdo. Postal 9), 77600 Cozumel, Q. Roo. ☎ **888/341-5993** in the U.S., 987/2-0017, or 987/2-0072. Fax 987/2-1599. E-mail: paradisu@cozumel.czm.com.mz. 49 units. A/C. High season $168 double. Low season $69 double. Dive and honeymoon packages available. AE, MC, V. Free parking.

Built in two sections, the hotel gives you two choices of room styles. Standard rooms in the two-story section adjacent to the lobby are smallish (but very nice) and decorated in Southwest shades of apricot and blue. All have small sitting areas and either a porch or balcony facing the beach and pool. The one-story bungalow/cabaña section has a similar decor, but rooms are larger and have patios on the beach.

Dining/Diversions: The main restaurant is in a glassed-in terrace on the beach, and there's a poolside spot for snacks.

Amenities: Swimming pool; water-sports equipment for rent including sailboats, jetskis, and diving, snorkeling, and windsurfing equipment; pharmacy; gift shop; travel agency.

Moderate

Hotel Fontan. Km 2.5 Carretera San Juan, 77600 Cozumel, Q. Roo. ☎ **800/221-6509** in the U.S., or 987/2-0300. Fax 987/2-0105. 48 units. A/C TV TEL. High season $95–$125 double. Low season $80–100 double. No credit cards. Free unguarded parking.

Rooms on all four floors of this tan-colored hotel are well maintained and have private balconies; most have ocean views. Baths all have showers. There's a nice pool and Jacuzzi by the beach (held up by a retaining wall) that are surrounded by lounge chairs. There's a restaurant/bar, plus a dock for water sports. A scuba shop is located on site, and kayaks and mountain bikes are available for use by hotel guests. Their Restaurant Jardin Maya is open daily from 7am to 10:30pm. The hotel is an excellent value for your money.

IN TOWN
Very Expensive
✪ **Hotel Plaza Las Glorias.** Km 1.5 av. Rafael Melgar, 77600 Cozumel, Q. Roo. ☎ **800/342-AMIGO** in the U.S., or 987/2-2000. Fax 987/2-1937. 170 units. A/C MINI-BAR TV TEL. High season $252 double. Low season $168 double. AE, MC, V.

An all-suite hotel, this one offers the top-notch amenities of the expensive hotels farther out, but it's within 5 blocks of town. Beyond the expansive, lively lobby bar is the pool, with a swim-up bar, a multilevel deck, a shored-up beach, and the ocean. Most of the large, pleasantly furnished rooms have marble floors, separate sunken living rooms, and balconies with views. Standard in-room amenities include hair dryers, purified tap water, and in-room safety deposit boxes.

Dining/Diversions: There's usually a buffet at breakfast and dinner. The main restaurant features different specialties nightly. Palapa dining outside serves all meals (weather permitting), and the popular lobby bar features a large-screen TV that brings in major sports events. In high season there's often live entertainment (soft music) there as well and a happy hour with two-for-one drinks between 5 and 7pm.

Amenities: Swimming pool with Jacuzzi and swim-up bar by the beach, diving pier, organized pool games, recreational director, travel agency, concierge. Laundry and room service, travel agency, car rental, shopping arcade, and fully equipped dive shop with PADI and NAUI certification available.

Moderate
B&B Caribo. 799 av. Juárez, 77600 Cozumel, Q. Roo. ☎ **800/830-5558** in the U.S.; or ☎ and fax 987/2-3195. 12 units (10 with bathroom). $60–$80 double. Rates include continental breakfast. AE, MC, V.

This blue-and-white residence behind a short, white iron fence looks like one of the finer residences in this neighborhood. The 12 rooms continue the crisp blue-and-white decor and come with cool tile floors, white furniture, blue bedspreads, and big bottles of purified drinking water. Besides having fans, all rooms are air-conditioned. Ten rooms have private bathrooms. Two rooms have a shared bathroom in the middle, and these have fans but no air-conditioning. Rooms either have one or two double beds or a double and a single. The two most expensive rooms have kitchens. A bakery is located in the front of the house. To find the Caribo from the plaza, walk 6½ blocks inland on Juárez, and it's on the left.

Hotel Colonial. Av. 5 Sur no. 9 (Apdo. Postal 286), 77600 Cozumel, Q. Roo. ☎ **987/2-0209**, 987/2-4034, or 987/2-0506. Fax 987/2-1387. 28 units. A/C TV TEL. High season $54 studio, $64 suite. AE, MC, V.

Across the street from the El Marqués hotel is a collection of shops and this pleasant three-story hotel, with an elevator. It's a good deal for the money, especially if you like to spread out. The lobby is far back past the shops. You get a quiet, spacious, furnished studio or a one-bedroom apartment with red-tile floors on the first floor; second- and third-floor rooms have kitchenettes. The street is closed to traffic. From the plaza, walk half a block south on avenida 5 Sur; the hotel is on the left.

Inexpensive

✪ Hotel del Centro. Av. Juárez 501, 77600 Cozumel, Q. Roo. ☎ **987/2-5471.** Fax 987/2-0299. 24 units. A/C TV. High season $45 double. Low season $35 double. Suite w/kitchen $70. Discounts for weekly stays. MC, V.

Although this new, surprisingly stylish hotel is located 6 long blocks from the waterfront, it's a great bargain and one of the most attractive locations in town. The rooms are small, but modern and extra-clean, with decorative details, TV, and two double beds. Several suites with kitchenettes are also available. The rooms surround a garden courtyard with an oval pool framed by comfortable lounge chairs and a restaurant/bar.

Hotel El Marqués. Av. 5 Sur no. 180, 77600 Cozumel, Q. Roo. ☎ **987/2-0677.** Fax 987/2-0537. 39 units. A/C. High season $40 double. Low season $28 double. Discounts for 2 or more nights. MC, V.

Step back into the '60s in these sunny rooms with gold trim and Formica-marble countertops, French provincial overtones, gray-and-white tile floors, and two double beds. The junior suites have refrigerators; full suites have refrigerators, stoves, and sitting areas. Third-floor rooms have good views. The staff is friendly and attentive, and the price is right. To find it from the plaza, turn right (south) on avenida 5 Sur; the hotel is near the corner of Salas, on the right up the stairs next to Coco's restaurant.

✪ Hotel Flamingo. Calle 6 Nte. no. 81, 77600 Cozumel, Q. Roo. ☎ **800/806-1601** in th U.S. or 987/2-1264. Fax 987/2-6006. www.hotelflamingo.com. E-mail: dive@hotelflamingo.com. 22 units. TV. High season $35–$50 double. Low season $30–$40 double. Penthouse $99–$129. MC, V.

Completely remodeled in 1997, the Flamingo offers the best value in Cozumel, and caters to serious divers looking for extra-clean, basic accommodations. The Flamingo offers three floors of quiet rooms, a grassy inner courtyard, rooftop terrace, and very helpful new management. Second- and third-story rooms are spacious. All have white tile floors and new bathroom fixtures; 15 rooms have air-conditioning and some have mini-refrigerators. Rooms in the front of the building have balconies overlooking the street. All have two double beds and cable TV. The penthouse suite has a full kitchen and sleeps up to 6. Trade paperbacks are by the reception desk and a TV and complimentary coffee in the lobby are for guests. Special dive packages are available, and Spanish lessons are taught at the hotel. To find it, walk 5 blocks north on Melgar from the plaza and turn right on calle 6; the hotel is on the left between Melgar and avenida 5. Street parking is available.

✪ Hotel Safari Inn. Av. Melgar at calle 5 Sur (Apdo. Postal 41), 77600 Cozumel, Q. Roo. ☎ **987/2-0101.** Fax 987/2-0661. E-mail: dive@aquasafari.com. 12 units. A/C. $40 double. MC, V.

This pleasant budget hotel has a great location for divers: It's in town, above and behind the Aqua Safari Dive Shop. Natural colors and stucco pervade the interior of this three-story (no elevator) establishment. The huge rooms come with firm beds, built-in sofas, and tiled floors. The hotel caters to divers and offers some good dive packages through its dive shop Aqua Safari, one of the most reputable on the island. To find it from the pier, turn right (south) and walk 3½ blocks on Melgar; the hotel is on your left facing the Caribbean at the corner of calle 5 Sur.

SOUTH OF TOWN

The best beaches are south of town, but not all the best ones have hotels on them. Each hotel has either a swimming pool, a tiny cove, a dock, or all three. You'll be able to swim, sun, and relax at any of these hotels, and most are diver-oriented. **Costera Sur,** also called **Carretera a Chankanaab,** is the southern extension of Melgar, so just follow Melgar south through town to reach these hotels, which are, generally speaking, farther apart than those north of town, and a more expensive cab ride.

Very Expensive

✪ **Presidente Inter-Continental Cozumel.** Km 6 Costera Sur, 77600 Cozumel, Q. Roo. ☎ **800/327-0200** in the U.S., or 987/2-0322. Fax 987/2-1360. 253 units. A/C MINIBAR TV TEL. High season $240–$400 double. Low season $180–$330 double. Discounts and packages available. AE, DC, MC, V. Free parking.

Without a doubt, this is Cozumel's finest hotel in terms of style, on-site amenities, and excellence in service. Palatial in scale, it still retains a feeling of conviviality. The common areas display a masterful combination of marble with hot-pink stucco and stone. Located near the Chankanaab Lagoon, the hotel is surrounded by shady palms and spread out on a beautiful beach with no close neighbors. Rates vary widely, depending on your view and time of year you travel, even within seasons. There are four categories of rooms—some have balconies and garden views, while very spacious rooms come with balconies and ocean views. Deluxe beachfront rooms are the top choice, with expansive private patios and direct access to the beach on the ground floor; on the second floor there are balconies with ocean views. These deluxe rooms exude luxury; other rooms may be disappointing by comparison. No-smoking rooms are all on the fourth level, and two rooms are set aside for guests with disabilities.

Dining/Diversions: The **Arrecife** restaurant serves international specialties and is open daily from 6pm to midnight. **Caribeño,** by the pool and beach, is open from 7am to 7pm. Three bars, including a pool bar, and 24-hour room service. They offer a special in-room dining option for deluxe beachfront rooms, and will set up your service on your private patio for a romantic dinner, complete with serenading trio.

Amenities: Swimming pool, two tennis courts, water-sports equipment rental, dive shop and dive-boat pier, children's activities program, pharmacy, boutiques. Laundry and room service, travel agency, car and motorbike rental.

Expensive

La Ceiba Beach Hotel. Km 4.5 Costera Sur (Apdo. Postal 284), 77600 Cozumel, Q. Roo. ☎ **800/877-4383** in the U.S., or 987/2-0844. Fax 987/2-0065. 113 units. A/C MINIBAR TV TEL. High season $145–$180 double. Low season $96–$120 double. Diving packages available. AE, MC, V. Free parking.

Across from the Crown Paradisse Sol Caribe, on the beach side of the road, La Ceiba is named for the lofty and majestic tropical tree that was sacred to the Maya. It's a popular hotel with divers, and the large lobby seems to always be bustling with guests. The guest rooms, while not necessarily outfitted in the latest style, are nicely furnished, large, and comfortable; all have ocean views and balconies. The swimming pool is only steps from the beach.

The emphasis here is on water sports, particularly scuba diving, and if this is your passion, be sure to ask about the special dive packages when you call for reservations. Diving is available right from the hotel beachfront.

Dining/Diversions: The **Galleon Bar/Restaurant,** off the lobby, has walls shaped like an old ship and is open for all meals. **Chopaloca,** by the beach, is open daily from early morning until almost midnight.

Amenities: Small, rectangular swimming pool and hot tub by the beach with outdoor Jacuzzi; tennis court; gym and sauna; water sports; dive shop and dive-boat pier; roped-off area for snorkeling. Laundry and room service, travel agency.

WHERE TO DINE

Zermatt (☎987/2-1384), a terrific little bakery, is on avenida 5 at calle 4 Norte. On calle 2 Norte, half a block in from the waterfront, is the **Panificadora Cozumel,** excellent for a do-it-yourself breakfast or for picnic supplies. It's open from 6am to 9pm daily.

VERY EXPENSIVE

✪ **Café del Puerto.** Av. Melgar 3. ☎ **987/2-0316.** Reservations recommended. Main courses $15–$35. AE, MC, V. Daily 5pm–11pm. INTERNATIONAL.

For a romantic dinner with a sunset view, try this restaurant. After being greeted at the door, you can climb the spiral staircase to the main dining room or continue to a higher loft, overlooking the rest of the dining room. Soft piano music echoes in the background. The service is polished and polite, and the menu is sophisticated, with dishes like mustard steak flambé, shrimp brochette with bacon and pineapple, and prime rib. From the pier, cross the street and turn left on Melgar; it's almost immediately on your right.

Pepe's Grill. Av. Rafael Melgar at Salas. ☎ **987/2-0213.** Reservations recommended. Main courses $15–$30; children's menu $6.50. AE, MC, V. Daily 5–11:30pm. GRILLED SPECIALTIES.

Pepe's started the grilled-food tradition in Cozumel and continues as a popular trendsetter with low lights, soft music, solicitous waiters, and excellent food; the perpetual crowd is here for a reason. The menu is extensive, with flame-broiled specialties such as beef filet Singapore and shrimp Bahamas. The children's menu offers breaded shrimp and fried chicken. For dessert try the cajeta crêpes.

MODERATE

El Moro. 75 BIS Nte. 124. ☎ **987/2-3029.** Main courses $4–$12; margarita $3; beer $1.25. MC, V. Fri–Wed 1–11pm; closed Thurs. REGIONAL.

Crowds flock to El Moro for its wonderfully prepared food and service, but not the decor, which is orange, orange, orange, and Formica. And it's away from everything; a taxi is a must, costing around $1.50 one way. But you won't care as soon as you taste anything (and especially if you sip on one of their giant, wallop-packing margaritas). The pollo Ticuleño, a specialty from the town of Ticul, is a rib-sticking, delicious, layered plate of smooth tomato sauce, mashed potatoes, crispy baked corn tortilla, and batter-fried chicken breast, all topped with shredded cheese and green peas. Besides the regional food, other specialties of Mexico come out of the kitchen piping hot, such as enchiladas and seafood prepared many ways, plus grilled steaks, sandwiches, and, of course, nachos. El Moro is 12½ blocks inland from Melgar between calles 2 and 4 Norte.

La Choza. Salas 198 at av. 10 Sur. ☎ **987/2-0958.** Breakfast $2.80; main courses $8–$16. AE, MC, V. Daily 7:30am–11pm. YUCATECAN.

The filled tables looking out the big open-air windows on the corner of Salas and avenida 10 Sur announce that this is a favorite of both tourists and locals. It looks like a big Maya house with white stucco walls and a thatched roof. Platters of chiles stuffed with shrimp, *pollo en relleno negro* (chicken in a blackened pepper sauce), *puerco entometado* (pork stew), and beefsteak in a poblano pepper sauce are among the truly authentic specialties.

✪ **La Veranda.** Calle 4 Nte. ☎ **987/2-4132.** Reservations recommended in high season. Main courses $6–$16. MC, V. Daily 6pm–1am. SEAFOOD/INTERNATIONAL.

Nothing here is quite what you expect. La Veranda is in a new building that's architecturally like the old island frame houses with cut-out wood trim. It's a stylish restaurant with cloth-covered tables, good service, and terrific crispy fresh salads, curried chicken, large seafood platters, roast-beef sandwiches, fajitas, stir-fried vegetables, steaks, and an enormous Mexican combo including roasted chicken, rice, beans, guacamole, an enchilada, and a quesadilla. You can dine inside or on the veranda or patio in back overlooking the shaded garden. In the main room, casual couches and conversational areas are conducive to leisurely drinking, chatting, card playing, backgammon, or watching ESPN, CNN, WGN Chicago, or sporting events. (The television is played at low volume.) The gracious owners Anibal and Mercedes de Iturbide are almost always on hand. To get there from the plaza turn left (north) on avenida 5 Norte, walk 2 blocks, and turn right on calle 4 Norte; it's behind Zermatt bakery, on your right midway up the block.

✪ **Lobster House (Cabaña del Pescador).** Km 4 Carretera Pilar. ☎ **987/2-4132.** Lobster sold by weight $10–$30. No credit cards. Daily 6–10:30pm. LOBSTER.

If you do something well, then concentrate on that and forget the rest. This is the obvious rule to live by here, as the only item on this menu is their lobster dinner, served one way—steamed with a side of rice, vegetables, and bread. It's a flavorful meal, perfectly seasoned and flawlessly cooked—why bother with anything else when you've achieved perfection? The price of dinner is determined by the weight of the lobster you select, with side dishes provided at no charge. Dark wooden tables lit with candles add to the inviting atmosphere, surrounded by tropical gardens, fountains, and a small pond, complete with ducks. Owner Fernando adds to the welcoming feeling here, and will even send next door to his brother's restaurant, El Guacamayo, if you simply must have something other than lobster. The Lobster House is located across from the Playa Azul hotel.

✪ **Prima.** Calle Salas 109. ☎ **987/2-4242.** Pizzas $5–$14; pastas $5–$15; calzone $3.75–$5.25. AE, MC, V. Daily 4–11pm. ITALIAN.

One of the few good Italian restaurants in Mexico, Prima gets better every year. Everything is fresh—the pastas, calzones, vegetables, and sourdough pizza. Owner Albert Domínguez grows most of the vegetables in his hydroponic garden on the island. The menu changes daily and might include shrimp scampi, fettuccine with pesto, and lobster and crab ravioli with cream sauce. The fettuccine Alfredo is wonderful, as are the puff-pastry garlic "bread" and crispy house salad. Dining is upstairs on the breezy terrace. Next door is **Habanas Co.** with cigars and liquors. To get to either place from the pier, turn right (south) on Melgar and walk 2 blocks to calle 5 Sur and turn left. Prima is visible on your left between avenidas 5 and 10 Sur. Hotel delivery is available.

Pizza Rolandi. Av. Melgar, between calles 6 and 8 Nte. ☎ **987/2-0946.** Main courses $8–$13; pizza $9–$14; daily specials $5–$13. AE, MC, V. Mon–Sat 11am–11pm; Sun 5–11pm. ITALIAN.

Deck chairs and glossy wood tables make the inviting interior garden a restful place in daytime, and it becomes romantic with candlelight at night. The specialty here (as in their branches in Isla Mujeres and Cancún) is wood-oven–baked pizzas. But for a change, look for pasta prepared five ways and the weekly specials, which may be a special appetizer of sea bass carpaccio, pizza, pasta, or fish with an Italian twist. To get there from the pier, turn left (north) on Melgar and walk 4 blocks; it's on your right.

INEXPENSIVE

✪ **Café Caribe.** Av. 10 Sur 215. ☎ **987/2-3621.** Coffee and pastries $1.50–$4. No credit cards. Mon–Sat 7am–1pm and 6–10:30pm. PASTRIES & COFFEE.

This cute little cafe behind a facade of fuchsia and dark green may become your favorite place to start the day, finish it, or spend time in between. You'll find ice cream, milk shakes, fresh cheesecake and carrot cake, waffles, bagels, croissants, and biscuits filled with cheese and cream, ham and cheese, or butter and marmalade. Nine different coffees are served, including Cuban, cappuccino, espresso, and Irish. To get there from the plaza, turn right (south) on avenida 5 Sur, walk 1 block and turn left on calle Salas, then right on avenida 10; it's on your left.

Casa Denis. Calle 1 Sur. ☎ **987/2-0067.** Breakfast $1.75–$3.75; main courses $4.75–$12. No credit cards. Mon–Sat 7am–11pm; Sun 5pm to 11pm. REGIONAL/INTERNATIONAL.

This yellow wooden house holds a great home-style Mexican restaurant. Small tables are scattered outside on the pedestrian-only street and in two rooms separated by a foyer filled with family photos. More tables are set in the back on the shady patio. You can make a light meal from empanadas filled with potatoes, cheese, or fish, or go for the full comida of fried grouper, rice, and beans; or better yet, try one of the regional specialties such as pollo pibil or pork brochette seasoned with the subtle flavor of achiote. Groups of four or more can request a special meal in advance. To get there from the plaza, walk a half block inland up calle 1 Sur; it's on your right.

Coco's. Av. 5 Sur no. 180, at the corner of calle Salas. ☎ **987/2-0241.** Breakfast $3–$5.75. No credit cards. Tues–Sun 7am–noon. Closed the last 2 weeks of Sept and the first week of Oct. MEXICAN/AMERICAN.

Tended by owners Terri and Daniel Ocejo, Coco's is clean and welcoming to the tourist, right down to the free coffee refills. Plan to indulge in stateside favorites like hash browns, cornflakes and bananas, gigantic blueberry muffins, cinnamon rolls, and cream-stuffed rolls. Mexican specialties include huevos rancheros, huevos Mexicana, and eggs scrambled with chiles and covered with melted cheese. A gift section at the front includes gourmet coffee, local honey, bottles of hot peppers, chocolate, *rompope,* and vanilla. To get there from the plaza, turn right (south) on avenida 5 Sur. Coco's is on your right beside the entrance to the Hotel El Marqués.

Comida Casera Toñita. Calle Salas 265, between calles 10 and 15 Nte. ☎ **987/2-0401.** Breakfast $1.75–$3; main courses $3.75–$5; daily specials $3; fruit drinks $1.75. No credit cards. Mon–Sat 8am–6pm. HOME-STYLE YUCATECAN.

The owners have taken the living room of their home and made it into a comfortable dining room, complete with filled bookshelves and classical music playing in the background. Whole fried fish, fish fillet, fried chicken, and beefsteak prepared as you wish are on the regular menu. Daily specials give you a chance to taste authentic regional food, including a pollo a la naranja, chicken mole, pollo en escabeche, and pork chops with achiote seasoning. Their Sopa de Lima is one of the best in all of the Yucatán Peninsula, but their Pozole is consistently over-salted. To reach Toñita's, walk south from the plaza on avenida 5 Sur for 1 block, then turn left on calle Salas and walk east 1½ blocks; the restaurant is on your left.

Natural. Calle Rosado Salas 352. ☎ **987/2-5560.** Breakfast $1.75–$3.25; salads $1.75–$3; sandwiches $1.55–$3; fruit and vegetable juices 95¢–$1.55; coffee 75¢. No credit cards. Mon–Sat 7am–6pm. FRUIT/PASTRIES.

The sweet smell of fruit will greet you as you enter Frutas Selecta, the downstairs grocery store specializing in fresh fruit. Upstairs is the sleek and cheery restaurant with windows on two sides. Juices, licuados, "the best coffee in town," yogurt, veggie sandwiches, a salad bar, fruit shakes, baked potatoes with a variety of toppings, and pastries are served. From the plaza, turn right and walk 1 block south on avenida 5 Sur, then turn left on calle Salas and walk 3 blocks east. It's on your right between 15th and 20th Norte.

Jeanie's Waffle House. Av. Melgar. ☎ **987/2-4145**. Waffles $3.15–$5; breakfast $3.25–$4; main courses $5–$9. No credit cards. Daily 6am–10pm. BREAKFAST/DESSERTS/MEXICAN.

Tables are often full since the Waffle House has far more business than it has space to handle. The name is a bit misleading since you can order much more than waffles, and you can also have breakfast anytime. Jeanie De Lille, the island's premier pastry chef, bakes crisp, light waffles and serves them in many ways, including the waffle ranchero with eggs and salsa, the waffle Benedict with eggs and hollandaise sauce, and waffles with whipped cream and chocolate. Hash browns, homemade breads, and great coffee are other reasons to drop in for breakfast mornings and evenings. The menu has been expanded to include fried fish, tamales, carne asada tampiqueña, and several pasta dishes, and there is a full bar. To get there from the pier, turn right (south) on Melgar and walk 4 blocks; it's on your left between the Aqua Safari and the Hotel Vista del Mar.

COZUMEL AFTER DARK

Cozumel is a town frequented by divers and other actively inclined visitors who play hard all day and wind down at night. People sit in outdoor cafes around the zócalo (plaza) enjoying the cool night breezes until the restaurants close. **Carlos 'n' Charlie's, Planet Hollywood,** the **All Star Cafe,** and the **Hard Rock Cafe,** all located along Melgar, are among the liveliest and most predictable places in town. **Joe's Lobster Pub** on avenida 5 between Juárez and calle 2 Norte, is the most happening place for live music, with reggae and salsa their specialty. The other hot spot is **Raga**, with live and recorded reggae, rock, and dance music. It's located on avenida Rosado Salas, at 10 av. Sur. Other specialty bars include the **Hog's Breath Saloon,** imported from Key West, and located on the main highway across from the international Pier; and **Scruffy Murphy's Irish Pub,** across from the La Ceiba hotel.

3 Puerto Morelos & Environs

21 miles S of Cancún

Puerto Morelos remains a small and tranquil fishing town, with not a whole lot going on after dark. It's excellent for diving, snorkeling, and fishing, and for simply lying on the beach. Puerto Morelos was once important for the Maya: It was the spot where women departed on their pilgrimages to Cozumel, in order to pay homage to the goddess of fertility, and it was a key trading point with Cozumel and other islands. Today, most people come to Puerto Morelos in order to take the car-ferry to Cozumel, several hours away. The building boom in this area that was stalled following Hurricane Gilbert has been resumed.

ESSENTIALS

GETTING THERE   By Bus   Buses from Cancún's bus station going to Tulum and Playa del Carmen usually stop here, but be sure to ask in Cancún if your bus makes the Puerto Morelos stop.

By Car   Drive south from Cancún along Highway 307 to the km 31 marker, then turn east toward Puerto Morelos.

By the Puerto Morelos–Cozumel Car Ferry   The dock (☎ 987/1-0008), the largest establishment in town, is very easy to find. See the Cozumel section above for details on the car-ferry schedule, but several points bear repeating here: The car-ferry schedule is complicated and may change, so double-check it before arriving. And always arrive at least 3 hours in advance of the ferry's departure to purchase a ticket and to get in line.

ORIENTATION

On the highway, near the Puerto Morelos junction, you'll see a gas station with public phones (including Ladatel phones that accept prepaid phone cards) and a supermarket on the right.

EXPLORING IN & AROUND PUERTO MORELOS

Puerto Morelos is attracting more and more people who seek seaside relaxation without the crowds and high prices. Its beaches are as beautiful as any along the coast, but they don't look like it because the deposits of seaweed and other wave-brought debris mar the visual appeal. Also, except for **Los Pelicanos,** there are no seaside restaurants selling drinks and food and no thatched beach umbrellas. Though the village is attracting more resort development now, and other businesses are popping up too, you make your own fun here, which is precisely its appeal to some people. For **diving and fishing,** try **Sub Aqua Explorers** (☎ 987/1-0078; fax 987/1-0027). More than 15 dive sites are nearby and many are close to shore. A two-tank dive costs around $60 and night dives $55. Two hours of fishing costs around $80 and snorkeling excursions run around $5.

If you are traveling by car, there are a couple of worthwhile stops along Highway 307 on the way to Puerto Morelos from Cancún. **Croco Cun,** a zoological park where crocodiles are raised, is one of the most interesting attractions in the area—don't be put off by the comical name. Though far from grand, the park has exhibits of crocodiles in all stages of development, as well as animals of nearly all the species that once roamed the Yucatán Peninsula. The snake exhibit is fascinating, though it may make you think twice about roaming in the jungle. The rattlesnakes and boa constrictors are particularly intimidating, and the tarantulas are downright enormous. Children enjoy the guides' enthusiastic tours and are entranced by the spider monkeys and wild pigs. Wear plenty of bug repellent and allow an hour or two for the tour, followed by a cool drink in the restaurant. Croco Cun is open daily from 8:30am to 5:30pm. Admission is $5, and free for children under 6. The park is at km 31 on Highway 307.

About half a mile before Puerto Morelos is a 150-acre **jardín botánico,** opened in 1990 and named after Dr. Alfredo Barrera, a biologist who studied the selva (a common geographical term meaning "tropical evergreen broadleaf forest"). A natural, protected showcase for native plants and animals, it's open Tuesday to Sunday from 9am to 4pm. Admission is $3.75.

The park is divided into six parts: an **epiphyte area** (plants that grow on others); **Maya ruins;** an **ethnographic area,** with a furnished hut and typical garden; a **chiclero camp,** about the once-thriving chicle (chewing gum) industry; a **nature park,** where wild vegetation is preserved; and **mangroves.** Wandering along the marked paths, you'll see that the dense jungle of plants and trees is named and labeled in English and Spanish. Each sign has the plant's scientific and common names, use of the plant, and the geographic areas where it is found in the wild. It's rich in bird and animal life, too, but to catch a glimpse of something you'll have to move quietly and listen carefully.

WHERE TO STAY & DINE

Cabañas Puerto Morelos. Apdo. Postal 1524, 77501 Cancún, Q. Roo. ☎ **987/1-0004.**
E-mail: 102312.3506@compuserve.com. (For reservations: Niki Seach, 7912 NE Ochoa, Elk
River, MN 55330. ☎ and fax 612/441-7630. E-mail: 102301.2317@compuserve.com.)
4 units. High season $450–$750 per week, $70 per night. Low season $275–$450 per week,
$50 per night. No credit cards.

If you're looking for something comfortable and reasonable, away from the crowds
and near the beach, this is a good place to consider, especially for a long stay.
Connie and Bill Butcher created this shady hideaway with lots of extra touches. It
consists of three one-bedroom cabañas and a two-bedroom house. The cabañas, all
with tile floors, have kitchens equipped with coffeemakers and juicers, plus bottled
water, several beers, and soft drinks to get guests started. You'll also find paperback
books and colorful furniture with folk art accents. There's a shady place outside for
dining or lounging. The Butchers are known for their willingness to help guests
enjoy the area. Most rooms are booked in advance from the United States, but you
can take a chance on a vacancy if you're in the area. This spot is 12 miles from the
Cancún airport. To find it from the Puerto Morelos zócalo, turn left at the edge of
the zócalo as you come from the highway. Go 3 blocks and it's on the left behind a
white wall and gate. Ring the bell.

Caribbean Reef Club. Villa Marina, 77501 Puerto Morelos, Q. Roo. ☎ **800/3-CANCUN** in
the U.S., or 987/1-0191. Fax 987/1-0190. 45 units. A/C TV. High season $280–$300. Low
season $220–$240. Price is per couple, per night, all inclusive. MC, V. Adults only.

Opened in 1991, this is the nicest place to stay in Puerto Morelos, and it's right on
the beach. The units (called suites but they're really like upscale apartments) come
with marble floors, neutral-toned furniture, and windows on the garden all facing
the sea. All come with one bedroom (most with two double beds), combination
kitchenette with living room (and sleeper sofa), remote-control TV, and two bathrooms with showers (some have a combo tub/shower). Besides air-conditioning,
each also has a fan. There's a nice-size pool next to the beach. The hotel offers complimentary use of snorkeling gear, small sailboats, and windsurfer boards. A comfortable and breezy beachfront restaurant on the property serves all three meals daily
between 8am and 10pm—it's the best restaurant in Puerto Morelos. To find it
follow directions through Puerto Morelos to the ferry pier and the complex is just
beyond it.

Los Pelicanos. On the ocean side behind and to the right of the zócalo. ☎ **987/1-0014.**
Main courses $5.50–$16; lobster $25. MC, V. Daily 10am–11pm. SEAFOOD.

Since this village has few restaurants, Los Pelicanos holds almost a captive audience
for central village beachside dining. You'll notice the inviting restaurant down a
block to the right of the plaza on the street paralleling the ocean. Select a table
inside under the palapa or outside on the terrace (wear mosquito repellent in the
evenings). From the terrace you have an easy view of pelicans swooping around the
dock. The seafood menu has all the usual offerings, from ceviche to conch made
three ways to shrimp, lobster, and fish. There are grilled chicken and steak for those
who don't want seafood.

Posada Amor. Apdo. Postal 806, 77580 Cancún, Q. Roo. ☎ **987/1-0033.** 20 units (8 with
bathroom). $28 double without bathroom; $35 double with bathroom; $38.50 for a room
with 4 beds and bathroom. No credit cards.

The simple, cheery little rooms at the Posada Amor, with screens and mosquito netting, are plain but adequate (and overpriced for what you receive). They're clustered

The Yucatán's Upper Caribbean Coast

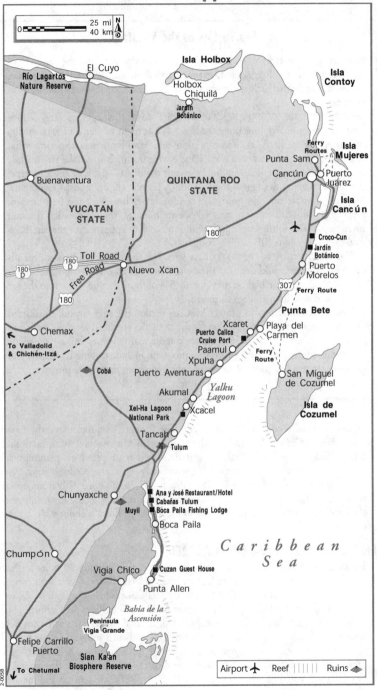

Sea Turtles of the Yucatán

At least four species of endangered marine turtles nest on the beaches of Quintana Roo: the **loggerhead, green, hawksbill,** and **leatherback** varieties. Of these, the leatherback is almost nonexistent, and the loggerhead is the most abundant.

Most turtles return to the beach of their birth to lay their eggs, as often as three times in a season. Strolling along the beach late at night in search of giant turtles (prime egg-laying hours are between 10pm and 3am) is a special experience that will make you feel closer to the Yucatán's environment. It may take you a while to get used to the darkness, but don't use your flashlight—lights of any kind repel the turtles. Laying the eggs is tough work. A female will dig nonstop with back flippers for more than an hour; the exercise leaves her head and legs flushed. Depositing the 100 or more eggs takes only minutes, then she makes the nest invisible by laboriously covering it with sand and disappears into the sea. Each soft-shelled egg looks like a Ping-Pong ball.

Hatchlings scurry to the sea 45 days later, but successful incubation depends on the temperature and depth of the nest. When conditions are right, the hatch rates of fertile eggs are high; however, only 5% of those that do make it to the sea escape predators long enough to return.

Despite recent efforts to protect Mexico's turtles, the eggs are still considered an aphrodisiac, and there's a market for them; turtles are killed for their shells and meat as well. Since turtle life expectancy is more than 50 years, killing one turtle kills thousands more. Costly protection programs include tagging the female and catching the eggs as they are deposited and removing them to a protected area and nest of identical size and temperature.

around a patio in back of the restaurant. The Posada's restaurant is newly remodeled rustic and quaint like an English cottage, with whitewashed walls, small shuttered windows, and open rafters, and decorated with primitive paintings and flowers on each table. The food is tasty, with many regional specialties, sandwiches, a comida corrida for $4, and a Sunday buffet for $5.75. It's open daily from 7:30am to 11pm. To get here, when you enter town, turn right; with the town square on the left, follow the main street leading to the ferry; the hotel is about a block down on the right.

EN ROUTE TO PLAYA DEL CARMEN

Heading south on Highway 307 from Puerto Morelos, it's only 20 miles to Playa del Carmen, so you'll be there in half an hour or less. However, you'll pass several small beach resorts en route. The two more upscale places below are run by the reputable Turquoise Reef Group. And less than 3 miles before Playa del Carmen, you'll pass several roads that head out to the relaxed, isolated small hotels at **Punta Bete,** which is the name of a beach—not a town. If you turn left and follow a small unpaved trail at the km 52 marker and PUNTA BETE sign, you'll find two small inexpensive groups of bungalows at the end of the trail and on a fine stretch of beach, which you'll have almost to yourself. Two of these are spartan and inexpensive (yet comfortable) at $25 to $35 per double, with a few individual bungalows on the beach and a restaurant at each one. **Cabañas Bahía Xcalacoco,** has two cabañas (Apdo. Postal 176, 77710 Playa del Carmen, Q. Roo). **Cabañas Xcalacoco** has seven cabañas (Apdo. Postal 176, 77710 Playa del Carmen, Q. Roo). There's no electricity, but all rooms have private baths. There's another group of cabañas to the left of the Cabañas Xcalacoco, with nearly the same name, but the upkeep and service are undependable, and I don't recommend it.

If you come here between July and October, you can walk the beach at night to watch for **turtles** lumbering ashore to lay their eggs, or watch the eggs hatch and the tiny vulnerable turtles scurry to the ocean in the last 2 months.

WHERE TO STAY & DINE FARTHER ALONG HIGHWAY 307

La Posada del Capitán Lafitte. Km 62 Carretera Cancún–Tulum, 77710 Playa del Carmen, Q. Roo. ☎ **800/538-6802** or 303/674-9615 in the U.S., or 987/3-0214. Fax 987/3-0212. 62 units. High season $170 double. Low season $120 double. Christmas, New Year's, Thanksgiving, and part of Feb are higher. Minimum 3-night stay. Rates include breakfast and dinner. AE, MC, V. Free parking.

Continuing on Highway 307, a few miles beyond the Punta Bete turnoff, you'll see a large sign on the left to the entrance to La Posada del Capitán Lafitte. From the highway, drive a mile down a rough dirt road that heads toward the ocean. Here you can enjoy the feeling of being on a private, nearly deserted island, but enjoy all the amenities of a relaxing vacation. The numerous cabañas of Capitán Lafitte stretch out along a huge portion of powdery white beach with space enough between them to feel luxuriously separate from other guests. The one- and two-story white stucco bungalows are smallish but very comfortable, stylishly furnished, and equipped with tile floors, small tiled bathrooms, either two double or one king-size bed, and an oceanfront porch. Twenty-nine bungalows have air-conditioning; the rest have fans. There's 24-hour electricity (a plus you learn to value on isolated stretches of this coast). If you wish, coffee can be served in the room as early as 6:30am. There's a turtle patrol in which guests can participate during summer on nearby beaches where green and loggerhead turtles nest. Divers from North America make up a sizable portion of the clientele here, as well as repeat visitors who come annually just for the peace, quiet, beach, and relaxation.

Dining/Diversions: One restaurant takes care of all meals, and the chef will prepare your catch. There's also a poolside bar and swinging chair bar.

Amenities: You'll find a large raised swimming pool and sunning deck, well-equipped game room, and excellent dive shop with PADI instruction. Laundry and room service, and travel agency.

Shangri-La Caribe. Km 69.5 Carretera Cancún–Tulum (Apdo. Postal 253), 77710 Playa del Carmen, Q. Roo. ☎ **800/538-6802** or 303/674-9615 in the U.S., or 987/3-0611. Fax 987/3-0500. 85 units. High season $177 ocean-view double; $227 beachfront double. Low season $127 ocean-view double; $177 beachfront double. Book well in advance during high season. AE, MC, V. Free parking.

After Punta Bete and La Posada del Capitán Lafitte—and only a mile or so before you reach Playa del Carmen on Highway 307—you'll see the Volkswagen Plant and a huge sign for the Shangri-La Caribe and another resort called Las Palapas. Turn left at the VW building, and you'll find the Shangri-La a mile straight ahead on a semipaved road. The two-story, high-domed, palapa-topped bungalows meander to the ocean linked by sidewalks and edged by tropical vegetation. Accommodations are quaint, but all come with two double beds, nice tile bathrooms, and an inviting hammock strung on the patio or balcony. Windows are screened, and a ceiling fan circulates the breeze. Prices get higher the closer you get to the beach and are higher for two-bedroom casas. Though you're very close to Playa del Carmen, hotel guests are the only ones using the beach, and the feeling is one of being many relaxing miles from civilization. You'll share this beachside retreat with lots of European vacationers, meaning topless sunbathing is the norm.

Dining: One restaurant serves all three meals, and the bar is open long hours. Rates include breakfast.

Amenities: The large inviting pool is surrounded by a sundeck, and there are horses for rent at $25 an hour. The absence of coral on the beach makes it an ideal place for windsurfing and swimming, less ideal for snorkeling. The **Cyan-Ha Diving Center** on the premises offers diving, snorkeling, and fishing trips, and equipment rental for these sports. May and June are best for fishing with abundant marlin, sailfish, and dorado. Car rental and bus or taxi tours to nearby lagoons and to Tulum, Cobá, and Chichén-Itzá.

4 Playa del Carmen

20 miles SW of Puerto Morelos, 44 miles SW of Cancún, 6.5 miles N of Xcaret, 8 miles N of Puerto Calica

Playa del Carmen has become, in my opinion, the ultimate Mexican beach vacation today. It's definitive *nuevo hip*, with an intriguing mix of smaller, eclectic accommodations and entertainment, set alongside amazing beach beauty. Already discovered by European travelers, this place sizzles with style.

Once this was little more than a very authentic launch for fishing boats and the Cozumel ferry. Playa now rivals Cozumel and her northern neighbor of Cancún in vacation appeal. Playa's location is the best on the Caribbean coast: It's an hour from the many flights arriving into Cancún's airport, a 45-minute ferry ride from Cozumel, and less than an hour to the Tulum ruins and other worthy coastal explorations.

Accommodations here are dominated by one-of-a-kind inns, B&Bs, and cabañas. Currently, almost 80% of the visitors here come from the E.U., which gives Playa an offbeat, global attitude. Snippets of conversation in various languages float in the constant sea breeze. Playa attracts a chic, young crowd that enjoys the growing number of coffee shops, reggae bars, and new-age vegetarian restaurants that are appearing along the pedestrian-only avenida 5.

A couple of larger resorts have joined the small guest houses. The Continental Plaza Playacar was the first major hotel to open here in 1991, followed by the Diamond Resort, Royal Maeva, and the Fisherman's Village. In addition, new sewage and water lines, telephone service, and more brick-paved streets have been added, but still, Playa's a small town undergoing substantial growth.

The wide, clear stretches of beach and calm, aquamarine water are the main draws here. The strong European influence means that topless sunbathing (nominally against the law in Mexico) is a nonchalantly accepted practice, including leisurely topless strolling anywhere there's a beach.

Locals anticipate that Playa del Carmen won't remain a secret for long, and that a greater number of Americans soon will be strolling beside Europeans on the beach. Before all this changes the feel of Playa, book a trip now and enjoy this stylish, welcoming, easy-paced place.

ESSENTIALS
GETTING THERE & DEPARTING

BY CAR　The turnoff to Playa del Carmen from Highway 307 is plainly marked, and you'll arrive on the town's widest street, avenida Principal, also known as avenida Benito Juárez (not that there's a street sign to that effect).

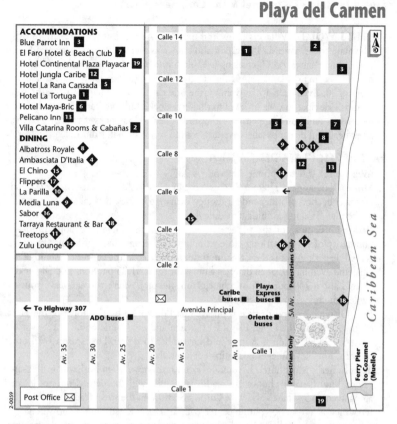

ACCOMMODATIONS
Blue Parrot Inn 3
El Faro Hotel & Beach Club 7
Hotel Continental Plaza Playacar 19
Hotel Jungla Caribe 12
Hotel La Rana Cansada 5
Hotel La Tortuga 1
Hotel Maya-Bric 6
Pelicano Inn 13
Villa Catarina Rooms & Cabañas 2

DINING
Albatross Royale 8
Ambasciata D'Italia 4
El Chino 15
Flippers 17
La Parilla 10
Media Luna 9
Sabor 16
Tarraya Restaurant & Bar 18
Treetops 11
Zulu Lounge 14

Calle 14
Calle 12
Calle 10
Calle 8
Calle 6
Calle 4
Calle 2

Post Office ✉

← To Highway 307
ADO buses ■
Avenida Principal
Caribe buses ■
Playa Express buses ■
Oriente buses ■
Pedestrians Only
5A Av.
Calle 1
Calle 1

Av. 35
Av. 30
Av. 25
Av. 20
Av. 15
Av. 10

Ferry Pier to Cozumel (Muelle)
Pedestrians Only

Caribbean Sea

2-0059

BY THE PLAYA DEL CARMEN–COZUMEL PASSENGER FERRY See the Cozumel section "Getting There & Departing" above, for details.

BY TAXI Taxi fares from the Cancún airport are high—about $60 one way, but they're the fastest, most immediate form of travel. Colectivos from the Cancún airport can reduce this to about $30. Returning to the airport, there is a service offering shared taxi rides for $14 per person. Check at your hotel or at the Caribe Maya restaurant on avenida 5 at calle 8 for information and reservations.

BY BUS There are three bus stations in Playa del Carmen, all on avenida Principal (the main street): Transportes de Oriente, Playa Express, and ATS are a half block north of the plaza and avenida 5 on avenida Principal; Expreso Oriente is on the corner of avenida 5 and avenida Principal; and the ADO station is 4 blocks west of the plaza.

Buses travel to and from Cancún with regularity, as well as to Xcaret, Tulum, Cobá, Chetumal, Chichén-Itzá, and Mérida.

ORIENTATION

ARRIVING The ferry dock in Playa del Carmen is 1½ blocks from the main square and within walking distance of hotels. **Buses** are along avenida Principal, a short distance from hotels, restaurants, and the ferry pier. **Tricycle taxis** are the only vehicles allowed between the bus stations and avenida 5 and the ferry. A number of these efficient taxis meet each bus and ferry and can transport you and your luggage to any hotel in town. The New Puerto Calica cruise pier is almost 8 miles south of Playa del Carmen; Playa taxis meet each ship.

CITY LAYOUT   Villagers know and use street names, but few street signs exist. The main street, **avenida Principal,** also known as avenida Benito Juárez, leads into town from Highway 307, crossing avenida 5 one block before it ends at the beach next to the main plaza, or **zócalo.** Traffic is diverted from avenida Principal at avenida 10. **Avenida 5** (5th Avenue), the other main artery (closed to traffic from avenida Principal to calle 6) leads to the ferry dock, 2 blocks from the zócalo; most restaurants and hotels are either on avenida 5, or a block or two off of it. The village's beautiful beach parallels avenida 5 and is only a block from it.

FAST FACTS: PLAYA DEL CARMEN

Area Code   The telephone area code is **987.**

Money Exchange   There are several major banks and branches in Playa, along with a collection of independent money-exchange houses. Several are located close to the pier, or along avenida 5 at calle 8.

Parking   Because of the pedestrian-only blocks and increasing population and popularity of Playa, parking close to hotels has become more difficult. The most accessible parking lot is the **Estacionamiento Mexico** at the corner of avenida Principal and avenida 10, open daily 24 hours; the fee is $1.25 per hour and $8 per day. There's also a 24-hour lot just a block from the pier, where you can leave your car while you cross over to Cozumel.

Post Office   The post office is on avenida Principal 3 blocks north of the plaza, on the right past the Hotel Playa del Carmen and the launderette.

Seasons   High season is August and December to Easter. Low season is all other months, but November is becoming very popular.

Telephones   Most hotels have phones and faxes now; often both are on the same phone line. Ladatel phones are readily available, with numerous phones located along avenida 5. There's also **The Calling Station** on the street leading up from the ferry pier, a full-service phone center with air-conditioned booths, no surcharges, fax service, and a bulletin board where you can leave messages for friends. It's open Monday to Saturday from 8am to 11pm, and Sunday from 9am to 10pm.

WHAT TO SEE & DO IN PLAYA

Playa is for relaxing. But beyond that, the island of **Cozumel** is a $5, 45-minute ferry ride away; **Tulum, Xel-Ha, Xcaret,** and **Xcalacoco** are easy excursions.

Avenida 5 is lined with dozens of trendy, small shops selling imported batik clothing, Guatemalan fabric clothing, premium tequilas, Cuban cigars, masks, pottery, hammocks, and a few T-shirts. There's even a couple of tattoo salons in the mix.

Reef diving can be arranged through **Tank-Ha Dive Center** (☎ and fax **987/3-0302;** fax 987/3-1355; mayanriviera.com/diving/tankha; e-mail: tankha@playadelcarmen.com). The friendly owner, Alberto Leonard, came to Playa by way of Madrid, and is now offering cave and cenote diving excursions. You can also book his trips at the Hotel Maya Bric and at the Royal Albatros. Snorkeling trips cost $25 and include soft drinks and equipment. Two-tank dive trips are $55; resort courses are available for $65 with PDIC and PADI instructors. For **cavern diving,** see "Scuba Diving" in "Cozumel," above, where small groups meet in Playa del Carmen for this new one-of-a-kind experience.

An 18-hole championship **golf course** (☎ 987/3-0624), designed by Robert Von Hagge, is open adjacent to the Continental Plaza Playacar. Greens fees are $99 (includes golf cart), caddie $20, club rental $20, and the price includes tax. Two

tennis courts are also available at the club. If your hotel is a member of the golf club, greens fees may be reduced to as low as $20.

WHERE TO STAY
VERY EXPENSIVE

Continental Plaza Playacar. Km 62.5 Frac. Playacar, 77710 Playa del Carmen, Q. Roo ☎ **800/88-CONTI** in the U.S., or 987/3-0100. Fax 987/3-0105. 185 units. A/C MINIBAR TV TEL. High season $280–$485 double. Ask about off-season rates and special packages. AE, DC, MC, V.

The village's most upscale resort hotel opened in 1991 on 308 acres that spread out along the beach beyond the ferry pier. Almost 200 Maya ruins were found during development of the resort, many of which decorate the grounds and common areas. The entrance of this five-story, pale pink hotel leads you through a wide marble lobby beyond which you see the meandering pool with swim-up bar, and the beach. The large, nicely furnished rooms all have in-room safety deposit boxes, purified tap water, tile floors, large bathrooms, wet bars with refrigerators, and balconies with sea views. Rates vary depending on your view—garden, ocean, parking lot, or brick wall—and on whether you have one or two bedrooms. To find it from the ferry pier, turn left when you get off the ferry and follow the road a short distance until you see the Playacar sign. If you're driving in, turn right at the last street before the main street dead-ends and you'll see signs to the hotel about 2 blocks ahead.

   Dining/Diversions: La Pergola, with pool, beach, and ocean view, serves international food daily for breakfast and dinner. **La Sirena** is the poolside restaurant. The stylish and welcoming lobby bar is open between 6pm and 1am daily.

   Amenities: Oceanside pool with swim-up bar, water-sports equipment, one lighted tennis court. Laundry and room service, baby-sitting, gift shop and boutiques, travel agency, and tours to nearby archaeological zones and lagoons.

EXPENSIVE

Blue Parrot Inn. Calle 12 Nte. and the beachfront (Apdo. Postal 64), 77710 Playa del Carmen, Q. Roo. ☎ **800/634-3547** from the U.S., or 987/3-0083; ☎ and fax 987/3-0049. 45 units. High season: $65–$75 double; $125–$160 suites; $155–$175 villas. Low season: $45–$55 double; $75–$105 suites; $100–$110 villas. AE, MC, V.

One of the original beachfront inns in Playa, the Blue Parrot has evolved along with the town, each year offering improvements and additions in rooms and services. It has arguably the best beach location, and its three bars and beachfront pool have made it a favorite place in town for evening entertainment. Rooms are clean and comfortable, though a bit worn, with white walls and very basic Mexican decor. Mattresses are on the thin side in some of the older units. Some rooms have small kitchenettes, and the beachfront villa sleeps up to eight people. Several of the newer units come with air-conditioning. A main restaurant serves fresh seafood and Mexican favorites, and a new Japanese restaurant recently opened, serving sushi as well. Live music plays every weekend in the on-site jazz club. There's also a dive center and massage service on the premises. Overall, it's a casual, friendly place to meet other visitors and indulge in the many pleasures of being on such an exquisite beach.

   Dining/Diversions: Beachfront restaurant serving international and Mexican cuisine, open from 7am to midnight. There's also the World Famous Beach Bar.

   Amenities: Broad beachfront and pool; dive shop; plus snorkeling and ocean kayaking available. Some rooms have their own pools.

✪ **El Faro Hotel and Beach Club.** On the beach at calle 10 Nte., 77710 Playa del Carmen, Q. Roo. ☎ **888/243-7413** from the U.S., or 987/3-0970. Fax 987/3-0968. 72 units. High season $145–$205 double. Low season $105–$175 double. Rates include breakfast. AE, MC, V. Limited free guarded parking available.

This hotel is also becoming the town's landmark, for the graceful, swirling lighthouse that borders the northern edge of its beachfront location. El Faro ("the lighthouse") is the work of German Bernd Durrmeier, who explains that this is the only privately owned, official operating lighthouse in the world, and also the only official lighthouse with guest accommodations inside. He calls it the "Honeymoon Suite," because newlyweds probably won't mind the very cozy accommodations as much. The remaining rooms and suites are spread around the spacious property graced by tall palms and tropical gardens fronting 75 meters of sandy beachfront. A small but stunning pool (heated in winter months) has islands of palms inside, and is bordered by cushioned lounges and a palapa-topped bar for libations. The entire property has a cool, clean feel to it, with its white and cream stucco facade. The spacious rooms, in two-story buildings, have clay-tile floors, marble baths, and either one king or two double beds. Decor is quality Mexican folk art with rustic wood furnishings, and all have ocean views, plus a large balcony or terrace. Rates vary according to the dominant view—garden, sea, or beachfront—the size of the room, and the time of year. The property has many ecologically friendly extras that you can't see—the owners use solar heat and recycled water to maintain their exquisite gardens. The restaurant, supervised by a Swiss chef, is open 7:30am to 6pm, serving guests their choice of continental or American breakfast in the mornings, and tasty choices for lunch and snacks throughout the day. European spa services are in the process of being added. Above all, the exceptional standard of service and the warm hospitality is a winning and rare combination for this area.

Dining/Diversions: Beachfront restaurant serving Mexican and international cuisine. Open for breakfast and lunch, 8am to 6pm. Palapa poolside bar is open 8am to 8pm.

Amenities: Swimming pool, beach, massage services, free guarded parking.

MODERATE

Albatros Royale. Calle 8 (Apdo. Postal 31), 77710 Playa del Carmen, Q. Roo. ☎ **800/ 538-6802** in the U.S. and Canada, or 987/3-0001. 31 units. High season $80 double. Low season $60 double. Rates include breakfast. AE, MC, V.

This "deluxe" sister hotel to the neighboring Pelicano Inn rises up on a narrow bit of land facing the beach. The two stories of rooms all have tile floors, tile bathrooms with marble vanities and showers, balconies or porches, and most have ocean views. Most have two double beds, but seven have queen-size beds. Breakfast is taken almost next door at the Pelicano Inn. To get here from the corner of avenida 5 and calle 8 (where you'll see the Rincón del Sol center), turn toward the water on calle 8; it's midway down the block on your left. Street parking is scarce.

✪ **Hotel Jungla Caribe.** Av. 5 Nte. at calle 8 (Apdo. Postal 180), 77710 Playa del Carmen, Q. Roo. ☎ **987/3-0650.** 26 units. A/C TV. High season $60–$80 double; $100–$120 suite. Low season 30% off high-season prices. AE, MC, V.

Located right in the heart of 5th Avenue action, "La Jungla" is an inventive inn, with high-styled decor that mixes neo-classical with Robinson Crusoe. For the creativity and quality, it's an excellent value. Rolf Albrecht, the mastermind behind the hotel, envisioned a lot of space and comfort for guests, so even the standard rooms are expansive, with gray-and-black marble floors, the occasional Roman column, and large bathrooms. There's a catwalk to the "tower" section of suites. There's an attractive pool on the first level and an excellent restaurant infused with tropical plants that overlooks calle 8.

La Tortuga. #732 av. 10, corner of calles 12 and 14, 77710 Playa del Carmen, Q. Roo. ☎ and fax **987/3-1484.** hotel_la_tortuga@bigfoot.com. 15 units. A/C MINIBAR TV TEL. High season $75–$80 double. Low season $65–$70 double. No credit cards.

This new and stylish inn is already enjoying success due to its clean, elegant rooms and quiet location. There's a small, central swimming pool, with a grassy area surrounding it to take in the sun. Rooms are decorated in a rustic Southwestern style with Mexican accents. The higher-priced rooms have a private Jacuzzi, and all have cable TV. Room service is available from the neighboring Tucan restaurant. It's located 2 large blocks off the beach, on the main north/south avenue in town.

INEXPENSIVE

Hotel Maya-Bric. Av. 5 Nte., 77710 Playa del Carmen, Q. Roo. ☎ and fax **987/3-0011.** 29 units. High season $45 double. Low season $30 double. MC, V; 6% commission charged for using credit cards. Free guarded parking.

Flowers and a colorful exterior will draw your eye to this two-story beachfront inn. Each of the well-kept rooms has recently been redecorated, and has two double beds with fairly firm mattresses; some have ocean views. The buildings frame a small pool where guests gather for card games and conversation. The pool was repainted last year, with new landscaping added to the surrounding garden.

The Maya-Bric is well supervised and is frequented by loyal guests who return annually. The gates are locked at night, and only guests are allowed to enter. A small restaurant by the office sometimes serves breakfast and snacks during the high season. Air-conditioning is being added to all rooms. The on-site dive shop, **Tank-Ha** (See "What to See & Do in Playa," above), rents diving and snorkeling gear and arranges trips to the reefs.

La Rana Cansada. #732 calle 10, 77710 Playa del Carmen, Q. Roo. ☎ and fax **987/3-0389.** 15 units. High season $55 double. Low season $25 double. No credit cards.

The "Tired Frog" is one of the most simply pleasant inns in the village, though it's a bit overpriced in high season. Behind an elegant hacienda-style wall and handsome iron gate, clean, plainly furnished rooms face an inner courtyard with a small snack bar under a large thatched palapa. Hammocks are strung on the covered porch outside the row of rooms. Some rooms have concrete ceilings and others a thatched roof, and all have well-screened doors and windows. New rooms are on the drawing board as well as a small pool and breakfast service. Paperbacks are available at the front desk, and manager John Swartz is very accommodating with tips on seeing the area. It's 1½ blocks inland from the beach. To find it from the main plaza, walk 5 blocks north on avenida 5 and turn left on calle 10; the hotel is on the left.

Treetops. Calle 8 s/n, 77710 Playa del Carmen, Q. Roo. ☎ and fax **987/3-0351.** E-mail: treetops@linux.pya.com.mx. 14 units. High season $45–$75 double. Low season $35–$55 double. Rates include continental breakfast. MC, V.

Set in a small patch of undisturbed jungle, with bungalows linked by stone pathways, this place is cooler than any in town and comes complete with its own cenote and swimming pool. The older bungalows (each a separate unit) are rustic but comfortable and come with small charms like thatched roofs and rock walls and unusual architecture—no two are alike. Two bungalows have kitchens. The new rooms, in a two-story fourplex, have a choice of air-conditioning or fan, refrigerators, and nice balconies or patios. The new air-conditioned **Safari Restaurant** is situated in the treetops above the pool. The restaurant offers a short menu of charcoal-broiled hot dogs and hamburgers (with U.S. beef), club sandwiches, homemade potato salad, Tex-Mex chili, and tacos. The **Safari Bar,** to the left after you enter, is a good place to go for an evening drink and to meet fellow travelers. The bar is open daily from 3pm to midnight. Happy hour is from 5 to 7pm. There's satellite TV broadcasting U.S. channels in the reception area and bar. From the avenida Principal, walk 4 blocks north on avenida 5, then turn right for half a block on calle 8; the hotel is on the left, half a block from the beach.

✪ **Villa Catarina Rooms & Cabañas.** Calle Privada Nte. between 12 and 14, 77710 Playa del Carmen, Q. Roo. ☎ **987/3-0970.** Fax 987/3-0968. 15 units. High season $55–$75 double. Low season $33–$45 double. No credit cards.

Hammocks are stretched in front of each of the stylishly rustic rooms and cabañas here, nestled in a grove of palms and fruit trees. Each of the clean, tastefully furnished rooms has one or two double beds on wooden bases, with brick floors underneath. Some units have a small loft for reading and relaxing; others have palapa roofs or terraces. Furnishings and Mexican folk art accent decorations are very high quality, especially considering the room prices. Bathrooms are detailed with colorful tiles, and some of the larger rooms have sitting areas. There's good cross-ventilation through well-screened windows. Complimentary coffee is served every morning. There's limited street parking available.

WHERE TO DINE

Restaurants are constantly opening and closing in Playa, so you may find many new ones besides those listed below.

EXPENSIVE

Ambasciata D'Italia. Av. 5 at calle 12. No phone. Main courses $6–$20. No credit cards. Daily 6–11:30pm. ITALIAN.

The predominately Italian crowd filling the tables here is a telling sign that the food is authentic and delicious. Entrees cover a range of homemade pasta and northern Italian specialties, with seafood prominently featured. There's an admirable selection of wines and an exceptional espresso is served. The ambiance is lively and sophisticated.

Flippers. Av. 5 at calle 4. No phone. Grilled specialties $7–$17; seafood platter $22. No credit cards. Daily 3–10:30pm. MEXICAN/GRILLED MEAT.

There's almost always something happening at Flippers, which stands out for its nautical theme, created by fishnets and ropes under a thatched palapa. There's an extensive bar list as well as a varied menu that includes grilled specialties from sea and land plus hamburgers, poc chuc, and beef tampiqueña. Happy hour, when drinks are two for the price of one, runs from 5 to 11pm and live music draws a crowd most evenings between 7 and 10pm.

✪ **La Parrilla.** Av. 5 at calle 8. ☎ **987/3-0687.** Main courses $6.25–$25. AE, MC, V. Daily noon–2am. MEXICAN/GRILLED MEATS.

The Rincón del Sol plaza is one of the prettiest buildings in Playa, and now it houses one of the most popular restaurants in town. The dining room is set in two levels above the street with the open kitchen in back. The aroma of grilling meat permeates the air. The huge chicken fajitas come with plenty of homemade tortillas and beans, and if you want to feast on lobster, this is one place to do it. The tables fill quickly in the evening, but there are smaller bar tables set out in the plaza's courtyards, where you can wait.

MODERATE

El Chino. Calle 4 at av. 15. ☎ **987/3-0015.** Breakfast $2.25–$3.50; main courses $4–$9. No credit cards. Daily 8am–11pm. YUCATECAN/MEXICAN.

Despite its name, there's not a Chinese dish on the menu. But locals highly recommend this place. Though slightly off the popular avenida 5 row of restaurants, it has its own clean, cool ambiance, with tile floors and plastic-covered polished wood tables set below a huge palapa roof with whirring ceiling fans. The open-air side patio is good for evening meals. The standard breakfast menu applies, plus you can order fresh blended fruit drinks. Main courses include such regional favorites as poc chuc, chicken pibil, and Ticul-style fish, plus shrimp-stuffed fish and beef, chicken, and shrimp borcettes. Other selections are lobster and shrimp crêpes, fajitas, and ceviche.

✪ **Media Luna.** Av. 5, corner of calle 8. No phone. Breakfast $2.50–$5; main courses $2.50–$10. No credit cards. Daily 7:30am–11:30pm. INTERNATIONAL.

Few restaurants have such mouthwatering aromas coming from the kitchen. When you read the menu you'll know why. The spinach-and-mushroom breakfast crêpes arrive with fabulous herb-, onion-, and garlic-flavored potatoes. Other crêpes are filled with fresh fruit. For dinner there are savory Greek salads, black bean quesadillas, giant shrimps with polenta, grilled shrimp salads, fresh grilled fish, and pastas with fresh herbs and sauces, plus other entrees featuring Indian, Italian, Mexican, and Chinese specialties. Decorated in muted textiles from Guatemala, it's a casual, inviting place, with sidewalk dining facing festive 5th Avenue and soft taped guitar music in the background.

Pelicano Inn. On the beach, at calle 6. ☎ **987/3-0997.** Buffet breakfast $6; main courses $3–$30. AE, MC, V. Buffet breakfast daily 7–11am; lunch daily 11:30am–6pm (happy hour noon–1pm and 4–6pm). MEXICAN/AMERICAN.

Located on the beach, this is a good place to meet Americans who live here and while away some hours munching and people-watching. The food is dependably good. The breakfast buffet is all you can eat, so arrive hungry. Apart from breakfast you have a choice of peel-your-own Cajun-flavored shrimp with U.S.-style tartar and shrimp sauce, hamburgers, hot dogs, quesadillas, pastries, ice cream, beer, wine, and coffee. From avenida Principal, walk 4 blocks north on avenida 5, turn right half a block on calle 8 to a marked Pelican Inn pathway, and turn right, or go to the beach and turn right; the hotel/restaurant is on the beach.

✪ **Zulu Lounge.** Av. 5, between calles 6 and 8. ☎ **987/3-0056.** Main courses $4–$9. AE. Daily 5:30–11:30pm. THAI/VEGETARIAN.

Inspired by Thai flavors and decor, this fetching restaurant offers a casual, relaxing space for dining on flavorful food. Broken tile–topped tables add a Mexican touch to the smartly decorated interior accented by bamboo and Thai fabrics. Asian jazz and techno recorded music underscores the hip ambience, and plays a little louder in the back room, where there's a couple of pool tables and a few rooms for rent. Standard Thai favorites include Pad Thai and vegetarian spring rolls. Their yellow curry is invitingly spicy. Most dishes are prepared with your choice of seafood, chicken, beef, or vegetarian. Full bar service and excellent espresso drinks are available.

INEXPENSIVE

Sabor. Av. 5 between calles 2 and 4. No phone. Yogurt and granola $1.50–$2.75; sandwiches $2–$3; vegetarian plates $2.25–$4; pastries 95¢–$1.50. No credit cards. Daily 8am–11pm. BAKERY/HEALTH FOOD.

A patio that's always full of patrons attests to the popularity of this modest restaurant. The list of hot and cold drinks includes espresso and cappuccino, café frappe, hot chocolate, tea, and fruit and vegetable drinks, and Sabor now has Blue Bell ice cream (a favorite of Texans) and light vegetarian meals. Try a cup of something with a slice of pie and watch village life stroll by.

⭐ **Tarraya Restaurant/Bar.** Calle 2 Nte. at the beach. No phone. Main courses $4–$7; whole fish $5.75. No credit cards. Daily noon–9pm. SEAFOOD.

"The restaurant that was born with the town," proclaims the sign. This is also the restaurant locals recommend as the best for seafood. Since it's right on the beach, with the water practically lapping at the foundations, and since the owners are fishermen, the fish is so fresh it's practically still wiggling. The wood hut doesn't look like much, but you can have fish fixed almost any way imaginable. If you haven't tried the Yucatecan specialty, Tik-n-xic fish, this would be a good place. It's on the beach opposite the basketball court.

PLAYA DEL CARMEN AFTER DARK

It seems like everyone in town is out on avenida 5 or Juárez across from the square until 10 or 11pm; there's pleasant strolling, meals and drinks at streetside cafes, huskers to watch and listen to, and shops to duck into. Later in the evening your choices move to the beach or to bars located mostly above street level: a **Señor Frog's** down by the ferry dock, dishing out its patented mix of thumping dance music, Jell-O shots, and frat-house antics; on the beach at 4th street, the pirate-ship designed **Captain Tutils** has a large bar area, dance floor, and live entertainment nightly; the **Safari Bar** at the Treetops hotel always has a congenial crowd gathered around the bar and television until midnight; and then there's the beachside bar at the **Blue Parrot,** which seems to draw most of the European and American expatriate community with its sultry jazz music, has swings for bar stools, and stays open late (somewhere around 2 to 3am). **Pancho's Mexican Cafe,** one of Playa's most popular restaurants, is known for its oversized margaritas and lively, open-air ambience. It's located on calle 12, just off of 5th Avenue. (They're also adding a second courtyard bar and have 40 rooms for rent in back of the original bar/restaurant.) **Espiral,** on 5th Avenue near the bus station, is the newest addition, playing recorded techno dance music.

5 Highway 307 from Xcaret to Xel-Ha

This section of the mainland coast between Playa del Carmen and Tulum is right on the front lines of the Caribbean coast's transformation from idyllic backwater to developing tourist destination. South of Playa del Carmen along Highway 307 is a succession of new commercial nature parks, planned resort communities, and for now, anyway, a few rustic beach hideaways and unspoiled coves. From north to south, this section will cover Xcaret, Paamul, Xpuha, Puerto Aventuras, Akumal, and Xel-Ha. Puerto Calica, the new cruise-ship pier, is 2½ miles south of Xcaret and 8 miles south of Playa del Carmen.

Of the fledgling resorts south of Playa del Carmen, **Akumal** is one of the most attractive and complete, with moderately priced hotels and bungalows scattered among the graceful palms that line the beautiful, soft beach and gorgeous bay. **Puerto Aventuras** is a privately developed, growing resort city aimed at affluent travelers and private-condo owners. **Paamul** and **Xpuha** offer inexpensive inns on gorgeous beaches 2½ miles apart. If the offbeat beach life is what you're after, grab it now before it disappears. (Other little-known and inexpensive getaways can be found on the **Punta Allen Peninsula** south of Tulum, and the **Majahual Peninsula** south of Felipe Carillo Puerto; see the next section· for details.) Two water theme parks offer entertaining ways to spend the day immersed in the beauty of this region. One is centered around the crystal-clear series of cenotes and lagoons at **Xel-Ha.** The other is the immensely popular park development of **Xcaret.** Popular day trips from Cancún, they are open to anyone traveling along this coast.

EN ROUTE SOUTH FROM PLAYA DEL CARMEN   The best way to travel this coast is in a rental car. Bus transportation from Playa del Carmen south exists but is not great. Buses depart fairly regularly from Playa headed toward Chetumal, stopping at every point of interest along the way; however, remember—it can be a long walk to the coast and to your final destination. There's also bus service to and from Cobá three times a day. Another option is to hire a car and driver; costs run around $10 to $12 per hour, or an all-day rate can be negotiated. Find a driver you like and whose English is good; remember, you'll be with him all day.

XCARET: A DEVELOPED NATURE PARK

Six and a half miles south of Playa del Carmen (and 50 miles south of Cancún) is the turnoff to Xcaret (pronounced *ish*-car-et), a specially built, ecological and **archaeological theme park** that is one of the area's most popular tourist attractions, designed as a place to spend the day. It's open Monday to Saturday from 8:30am to 8:30pm and Sunday from 8:30am to 5:30pm. Without exaggeration, everywhere you look in Cancún are signs advertising Xcaret, or someone is handing you a leaflet about it. They even have their own bus terminal to take tourists from Cancún at regular intervals, and they've added an evening extravaganza.

Xcaret may celebrate Mother Nature, but its builders rearranged quite a bit of her handiwork in completing it. If you're looking for a place to escape the commercialism of Cancún, this may not be it; it's expensive and may even be very crowded, thus diminishing the advertised "natural" experience. Children, however, love it, and the jungle setting and palm-lined beaches are beautiful. Once past the entrance booths (built to resemble small Maya temples) you'll find pathways that meander around bathing coves, the snorkeling lagoon, and the remains of a group of Maya temples. You'll have access to swimming beaches with canoes and pedal boats; limestone tunnels to snorkel through; marked palm-lined pathways; a wild bird breeding aviary; a charro exhibition; horseback riding; scuba diving; a botanical garden and nursery; a sea turtle nursery where the turtles are released after their first year; a pavilion showcasing regional butterflies; a tropical aquarium where visitors can touch underwater creatures such as manta rays, starfish, and octopi; and a "Dolphinarium" where visitors swim with the dolphins for an extra charge of $80. The opportunity to swim with the dolphins is limited in number each day, and no reservations are taken—it's strictly a first-come, first-served basis. There is also a visitor's center with lockers, first aid, and gifts. Visitors aren't allowed to bring in food or drinks, so you're limited to the rather high-priced restaurants on site. No personal radios are allowed, and you must remove all suntan lotion if you swim in the lagoon, as the chemicals in lotion will poison the lagoon habitat.

The price of $35 per person entitles you to all the facilities—boats, life jackets, and snorkeling equipment for the underwater tunnel and lagoon, and lounge chairs and other facilities. Other attractions, such as horseback riding, scuba diving and the Dolphin Swim, cost extra. However, there may be more visitors than equipment (such as beach chairs), so bring a beach towel and your own snorkeling gear. Travel agencies in Cancún offer Xcaret as a day trip (departing at 8am and returning at 6pm) that includes transportation and admission plus guide, for $50. You can also buy a ticket to the park at the **Xcaret Terminal** (☎ 98/83-0654 or 98/83-3143) next to the Hotel Fiesta Americana Coral Beach on Cancún Island. Xcaret's nine colorfully painted buses transport people to and from Cancún. "Xcaret Day & Night" includes round-trip transportation from Cancún, a charreada festival, lighted pathways to Maya ruins, dinner, and folkloric show; for a price of $69 for adults and $45 for children ages 5 to 11. Xcaret buses leave its terminal at 9 and 10am daily, with the "Day & Night" tour returning at 9:30pm.

PAAMUL: A BEACH HIDEAWAY

About 10 miles south of Xcaret, 16 miles south of Cozumel, 62 miles southwest of Cancún, and half a mile east of the highway is Paamul (also written Pamul), which in Maya means "a destroyed ruin." Turn when you see the Minisuper (a place to pick up reasonably priced snacks and drinks), which is also owned by the Cabañas Paamul (see below). At Paamul you can enjoy a beautiful beach and a safe cove for swimming; it's an idyllic place to leave the world behind. Thirty years ago the Martin family gave up coconut harvesting on this wide stretch of land, which includes a large, shallow bay, gained title to the land, and established this comfortable out-of-the-way respite. They plan soon to build more rooms on the unoccupied portion of the bay.

Scuba Max (☎ 987/3-0667; fax 987/4-1729) is a fully equipped, PADI-, NAUI-, and SSI-certified dive shop here, located next to the cabañas. Using three 38-foot boats, they take guests on dives 5 miles in either direction. If it's too choppy, the reefs in front of the hotel are also excellent. They also offer a night dive in Paamul, which is considered the best night dive in the Mexican Caribbean. The cost per dive is $30 to $35 if you have your own equipment, plus $20 to $25 if you rent their gear. The snorkeling is also excellent in this protected bay and the one next to it.

WHERE TO STAY & DINE

✪ **Cabañas Paamul.** Km 85 Carretera Cancún–Tulum (Apdo. Postal 83), 77710 Playa del Carmen, Q. Roo. ☎ **99/25-9422** in Mérida. Fax 99/25-6913. (Reservations: av. Colón 501-C, Depto. D-211 x 6 y 62 97000 Mérida, Yuc.) 7 bungalows; 190 trailer spaces (all with full hookups). July–Aug and Dec–Feb $60 double. March–June and Sept–Nov $50 double. RV space with hookups $16 per day, $360 per month. No credit cards.

When you reach this isolated, relaxing hotel you'll see an extremely tidy lineup of mobile homes and beyond them a row of coral-and-white beachfront bungalows with covered porches, just steps away from the Caribbean. Despite the number of mobile homes (which are occupied more in winter than any other time), there's seldom a soul on the beautiful little beach. Each bungalow contains two double beds, tile floors, rattan furniture, ceiling fans, hot water, and 24-hour electricity. A large, breezy palapa-topped restaurant serves delicious food at more than reasonable prices. Saturdays the happy hour starts at 6pm with country music, and Sundays at 6pm there's a buffet dinner. Try the Pescado Paamul or Shrimp Paamul; both are wonderful baked medleys devised by the gracious owner Eloiza Zapata. For stays longer than a week, ask for a discount, which can sometimes be as much as 10%. The trailer park isn't what you might expect—some trailers have decks or patios and thatched palapa shade covers. Trailer guests have access to 12 showers and separate bathrooms for men and women. Laundry service is available nearby. Turtles nest here June to September. The Paamul turnoff is clearly marked on the highway; then it's almost a mile on a straight, narrow, paved-but-rutted road to the bungalows. Visitors not staying here are welcome to use the beach, though the owners request that they not bring in drinks and food and use the restaurant instead.

PUERTO AVENTURAS: A RESORT COMMUNITY

About 2½ miles south of Paamul (65 miles southwest of Cancún), you'll come to the new city-size development of Puerto Aventuras on Chakalal Bay. Though it's on 900 oceanfront acres, you don't see the ocean unless you walk through one of the three hotels. A complete resort, it includes a state-of-the-art marina, hotels, several restaurants, and multitudes of fashionable condominiums winding about the grounds and around the marina. The golf course has nine holes open for play, plus there are numerous options for sportfishing. I don't recommend this resort for a vacation at this time because it's so far from anything, and there are better options along this coast. And, if you're touring this part of the world you won't see much of it by staying here. Architecturally sophisticated, it's like the island of Cancún without the crowds or nightlife. It's targeted more as a resort community for Mexican nationals who've purchased condominiums here, than at foreign tourists who've come to experience the Yucatecan culture.

Even if you don't stay here, the **Museo CEDAM** on the grounds is worth a stop. CEDAM stands for Center for the Study of Aquatic Sports in Mexico, and the museum houses displays on the history of diving on this coast from pre-Hispanic times to the present. Besides dive-related memorabilia, there are displays of pre-Hispanic pottery, figures, copper bells found in the cenotes of Chichén-Itzá, shell fossils, and sunken ship contents. It's open daily from 10am to 1pm and 2 to 6pm. Donations are requested. If you're hungry, there's a restaurant opposite the museum.

XPUHA: ANOTHER BEACH HIDEAWAY

Almost 3 miles beyond Paamul, east of the highway, is an area known as Xpuha (ish-poo-*hah*) consisting of an incredibly beautiful wide bay and fine stretch of sand. Some of this heavenly beach is interrupted by several restaurants and the all-inclusive Robinson Club at the far southern end. If you're looking for something totally offbeat and clean, but not at all posh, then consider two of the humble inns on this beach. These are on a nicely kept stretch of beach that still has an uninhabited appeal. Finding them can be confusing, since from Highway 307 several crude signs mark entrance down even cruder, narrow rutted roads cutting through the jungle. To get to these hotels and the best portion of beach, take the one marked "Villas Xpuha."

The **restaurant** of the Villas Xpuha offers home-style cooking with a simple-but-varied menu and several fish entrees from which to choose. It's open daily from 7am to 8pm. It's ideal for day-trippers who want to spend the day on the beach and have restaurant facilities, too; they request that visitors not bring food. As long as you use the restaurant of the Villas Xpuha, there's no charge for the two public bathrooms and showers. Besides the beach, a huge lagoon is within walking distance, and the reef is not far offshore.

WHERE TO STAY & DINE

Villas del Caribe Xpuha. Km 88 Carretera Cancún–Tulum, 77710 Playa del Carmen, Q. Roo. No phone. 9 units. High season $35 double. No credit cards.

Not quite as nice as its neighbor (see "Villas Xpuha," below), this inn is still a good choice. The two stories of rooms face the beach, with communal porches for lounging. Rooms have blue-tile floors and matching blue walls, and each comes with one or two double beds, an all-tile bath, and windows facing the beach; one room has a kitchen. There's 24-hour electricity and hot water here, too. The management has radio communication with the Hotel Flores in Cozumel (☎ 987/2-1429), so if you're there, you can reserve a room ahead (or vice versa).

Villas Xpuha and Restaurant. Km 88 Carretera Cancún–Tulum (Apdo. Postal 115), 77710 Playa del Carmen, Q. Roo. No phone. 5 units. High season $40 double. Low season $32 double. No credit cards.

The five rooms here line up in a row of blue buildings; four have a porch area on the beach and ocean, and one is an island-style wooden structure. The rooms are plain but clean, each with nice tile floors, two windows, two single beds, two plastic chairs, hammock hooks, and a place for a suitcase, but no closet. A single bare bulb in the center of each ceiling provides light. Count on 24-hour electricity and hot water. The hotel has a dive shop offering diving and snorkeling trips and kayak rentals.

AKUMAL: A RESORT ON A LAGOON

Continuing south on Highway 307 a short distance, you'll come to Akumal, a small, modern, and ecologically oriented community built around and named after a beautiful lagoon. It's one of those places foreigners discover, explore, fall in love with, and return to live. Signs point the way in from the highway, and the white arched Akumal gateway is less than half a mile toward the sea. The resort complex here consists of five distinct establishments sharing the same wonderful, smooth palm-lined beach and the adjacent Half Moon Bay and Yalku Lagoon. The hotel's signs and white entrance arches are clearly visible from Highway 307. On the way in to Akumal, a Visitor's Information and Reception Center (generally open afternoons, 2pm to 7pm) will assist you with help on where to stay and what to do in town. It's sponsored by a local real estate office, and although the information may not be completely unbiased, I still found it to be a friendly and helpful service.

You don't have to be a guest to enjoy the beach, swim in the beautiful clear bay, and eat at the restaurants. It's an excellent place to spend the day while on a trip down the coast. Besides the excellent snorkeling, ask at the reception desk about **horseback rides on the beach.** Equipment rental for snorkeling and windsurfing is readily available. For **scuba diving,** two completely equipped dive shops with PADI-certified instructors serve the hotels and bungalows in this area. Both are located between the two hotels. There are almost 30 dive sites in the region (from 30 to 80 feet), and two-tank dives cost around $65. Both shops offer resort courses as well as complete certification. **Lagoon snorkeling** is best on the left side of the lagoon, the side by the big circular restaurant and a bit farther out. **Fishing trips** can also be arranged through the dive shops. You're only 15 minutes from good fishing. Two hours (the minimum period) costs $100, and each additional hour is $35 for up to four people with two fishing lines.

WHERE TO STAY

Club Akumal Caribe/Hotel Villas Maya Club. Km 104 Carretera Cancún–Tulum (Hwy. 307). ☎ 987/5-9012. (For reservations, P.O. Box 13326, El Paso, TX 79913; ☎ 800/351-1622 in the U.S., 800/343-1440 in Canada, or 915/584-3552.) 70 units. A/C. High season $90 bungalow, $110 hotel room, $140–$397 villa/condo. Low season $76 bungalow, $100 hotel room, $120–$233 villa/condo. AE, MC, V for reservations only; cash only at the resort.

The white arches you drive under and the entrance are not impressive, but the lodging selection is. The 41 spacious **Villas Maya Bungalows** have beautiful tile floors and comfortable, nice furniture, all with fully equipped kitchens. The 21 rooms in the new three-story **beachfront hotel** are similarly furnished but with small kitchens (no stove), a king-size or two queen-size beds, pale tile floors, and stylish Mexican accents. The **Villas Flamingo** are four exquisitely designed and luxuriously (but comfortably) furnished two-story homes facing Half Moon Bay. Each has one, two, or three bedrooms; large living, dining, and kitchen areas; and a lovely furnished patio just steps from the beach. The hotel has its own pool separate from other facilities on the grounds. Akumal's setting is truly relaxing and there's a restaurant facing the beach and lagoon, plus a **grocery store** with all the common necessities. If you're traveling with children, ask about the **children's program** that functions during specific times of year (extra charge of $15 per child, per day; with pre-pay discounts available). The hotel has recently upgraded the decor in the rooms; and the pools, restaurant, and Kid's Club were all remodeled in late 1997.

WHERE TO DINE

La Buena Vida. Media Luna Bay, Akumal. ☎ **987/5-9060.** Main courses $3–$7.50. MC, V. Daily 11am–11:30pm. CASUAL MEXICAN/GRILLED SPECIALTIES.

La Buena Vida is the town's most popular beachfront restaurant and bar, a laid-back place for passing the day and reveling in the otherwise tranquil Akumal nights. Tables on the beach are set for enjoying the casual and consistently good fare. Sandwiches, fish fillets, and chicken dishes are more popular items. The shrimp tacos come with generous servings of jumbo shrimp and freshly made guacamole. Lounge chairs and beach set-ups are an extra bonus for daytime patrons. A large, round bar with swing chairs and satellite TV serves as the locally favorite gathering place, where you catch up with the goings-on around town.

A CAVERN TOUR/SCUBA DIVING OPERATOR

On the right side of the road (if you're coming from Cancún), about 11½ miles south of Xcacel (and about 9 miles north of Tulum), is **Divers of the Hidden Worlds** (☎ 987/4-4081; it's a cellular phone in Cancún). Experienced divers lead certified divers, snorkelers, and hikers on a variety of unusual trips, with two-tank dives ranging in price from $60 to $90, depending on the type of dive and location. Some require hiking in the jungle to dry caves; others have divers penetrating the underground world of watery caves with glass-clear water. Snorkelers investigate the *cenotes* (sinkholes leading to underground caves). Some dives are for more advanced divers, and some trips last all day, while others consume half a day. They also offer reef dives, resort courses, and cave-diving certification. They'll provide transportation from Cancún.

XEL-HA: SNORKELING & SWIMMING

The Caribbean coast of the Yucatán is carved by the sea into hundreds of small *caletas* (coves) that form the perfect habitat for tropical marine life, both flora and fauna. Many caletas remain undiscovered and pristine along the coast, but Xel-Ha, 8 miles south of Akumal, is enjoyed daily by throngs of snorkelers and scuba divers who come to luxuriate in its warm waters and swim among its brilliant fish. Xel-Ha (shell-*hah*) is a swimmers' paradise, with no threat of undertow or pollution. It's a beautiful, completely calm cove that's a perfect place to bring kids for their first snorkeling experience (experienced snorkelers may be disappointed—the crowds here seem to have driven out the living coral and a lot of the fish; you can find more abundant marine life and avoid an admission charge by going to Akumal, among other spots).

The entrance to Xel-Ha is half a mile from the highway. Admission is $15 per adult and $7 for children ages 5 to 12, and includes use of inner tubes, life vest, and shuttle train to the river. It's open daily from 8:30am to 5:30pm, and offers free parking with admission.

Once in the 10-acre park, you can rent snorkeling equipment and an underwater camera—but you may also bring your own. Food and beverage service, changing rooms, showers, and other facilities are all available. For non-snorkelers, platforms have been constructed that allow decent sealife viewing. When you swim, be careful to observe the SWIM HERE and NO SWIMMING signs. (The greatest variety of fish can be seen right near the ropes marking off the no-swimming areas and near any groups of rocks.)

Just south of the Xel-Ha turnoff on the west side of the highway, don't miss the **Maya ruins** of ancient Xel-Ha. You'll likely be the only one there as you walk over limestone rocks and through the tangle of trees, vines, and palms. There is a huge, deep, dark cenote to one side and a temple palace with tumbled-down columns, a jaguar group, and a conserved temple group. A covered palapa on one pyramid guards a partially preserved mural. Admission is $2.50.

Xel-Ha is close to the ruins at Tulum—it's a good place for a dip when you've finished climbing these Maya ruins. A very popular day trip from Cancún combines the two (see "Excursions & Organized Tours" in chapter 4). You can even make the short 8-mile hop north from Tulum to Xel-Ha by bus. When you get off at the junction for Tulum, ask the restaurant owner when the next buses come by; otherwise you may have to wait as long as 2 hours on the highway.

6 Tulum, Punta Allen & Sian Ka'an

Tulum (80 miles southwest of Cancún) and the Punta Allen Peninsula (110 miles southwest of Cancún at its tip) are the southernmost points many travelers reach in their wanderings down the Caribbean coast (although there is more to discover farther on). The walled Maya city of Tulum is a large Postclassic Maya site that dramatically overlooks the Caribbean. It's a natural beacon to visitors to Quintana Roo, and within a 2-hour drive of Cancún. Tour companies and public buses make the trip regularly from Cancún and Playa del Carmen. And for those who want to leave the modern world a long, long way behind, Punta Allen (which can take between 1½ to 3 hours to reach from Tulum, depending on the current road conditions) may be the ultimate. It's a place without the crowds, frenetic pace, or creature comforts of the resorts to the north—down here, the generator shuts down at 10pm (if there is one). What you will find is great fishing and snorkeling, the natural and archaeological riches of the Sian Ka'an Biosphere Reserve, and a chance to rest up at what truly feels like the end of the road. A few beach cabañas now offer reliable power, telephones, and hot showers.

ORIENTATION   When traveling south of Highway 307, get your bearings on Tulum by thinking of it as several distinct areas: First, on your left will be the junction of Highway 307 and the old access road to the Tulum ruins (it no longer provides access); here you'll find two small hotels, two restaurants, and a Pemex gas station. Next, a few feet south of the old road on Highway 307, also on the left, is the new Tulum ruins access road, leading to a large parking lot. And a few feet farther along 307 is the left turn onto the road leading to the hotels and campgrounds south of the ruins.

AT&T

AT&T Direct℠ Service

Steps to follow for easy calling worldwide:

1. Just dial the AT&T Access Number for the country you are calling from.
2. Dial the phone number you're calling.
3. Dial your card number.

AT&T Access Numbers

Anguilla +	1-800-872-2881	Brit. Vir. Isl +	1-800-872-2881
Antigua +	1-800-872-2881	**Canada**	**1 800 CALL ATT**
Argentina	0-800-54-288	Cayman Isl +	1-800-872-2881
Aruba	800-8000	**Chile**	**800-800-311**
Bahamas	1-800-872-2881	**Colombia**	**980-11-0010**
Barbados +	1-800-872-2881	Costa Rica	0-800-0-114-114
Belize ▲	811	Dominica +	1-800-872-2881
Belize †	555	Dom. Rep. ★ □	1-800-872-2881
Bermuda +	1-800-872-2881	**Ecuador ▲**	**999-119**
Bolivia ●	**0-800-1112**	**El Salvador○**	**800-1785**
Brazil	**000-8010**	Grenada +	1-800-872-2881

AT&T

AT&T Direct℠ Service

Steps to follow for easy calling worldwide:

1. Just dial the AT&T Access Number for the country you are calling from.
2. Dial the phone number you're calling.
3. Dial your card number.

AT&T Access Numbers

Anguilla +	1-800-872-2881	Brit. Vir. Isl +	1-800-872-2881
Antigua +	1-800-872-2881	**Canada**	**1 800 CALL ATT**
Argentina	0-800-54-288	Cayman Isl +	1-800-872-2881
Aruba	800-8000	**Chile**	**800-800-311**
Bahamas	1-800-872-2881	**Colombia**	**980-11-0010**
Barbados +	1-800-872-2881	Costa Rica	0-800-0-114-114
Belize ▲	811	Dominica +	1-800-872-2881
Belize †	555	Dom. Rep. ★ □	1-800-872-2881
Bermuda +	1-800-872-2881	**Ecuador ▲**	**999-119**
Bolivia ●	**0-800-1112**	**El Salvador○**	**800-1785**
Brazil	**000-8010**	Grenada +	1-800-872-2881

AT&T Access Numbers

Guatemala ○✕	99-99-190		Paraguay ▲2	008-11-800
Guyana ✦	165		Peru ▲	0-800-50000
Haiti	**183**		**Puerto Rico**	**1 800 CALL ATT**
Honduras	800-0-123		St. Kitts/Nevis✦	1-800-872-2881
Jamaica □	872		St. Vincent△	1-800-872-2881
Mexico ▽1	**01-800-288-2872**		**Suriname**△	**156**
Montserrat	1-800-872-2881		Turks & Caicos✦	1-800-872-2881
Neth. Ant.⊙	**001-800-872-2881**		Uruguay	000-410
Nicaragua	**174**		**U.S. Virgin Isl.**	**1 800 CALL ATT**
Panama	**109**		**Venezuela**	**800-11-120**

For access numbers not listed ask any operator for **AT&T Direct℠** Service.
In the U.S., call 1-800-331-1140 for a wallet card listing all worldwide AT&T Access Numbers.

Visit our Web site at: www.att.com/traveler
Bold-faced countries permit country-to-country calling outside the U.S.

● Public phones and select hotels.
✦ + Public phones require coin or card deposit.
✕ May not be available from every phone/public phone.
★ Collect calling only.
♦ Available from select hotels.
○ Available from select hotels.
✕ From St. Maarten or phones at Bobby's Marina, use 1-800-872-2881.
⊙ Public phones require local coin payment during call.
△ When calling from public phones, use phones marked "Ladatel."
▽ Available from public phones only.
□ If call card calls available from select hotels.
1 If call does not complete, use 001-800-462-4240.
2 From Asuncion only.

When placing an international call *from* the U.S., dial 1 800 CALL ATT.

© 5/98 AT&T

AT&T Access Numbers

Guatemala ○✕	99-99-190		Paraguay ▲2	008-11-800
Guyana ✦	165		Peru ▲	0-800-50000
Haiti	**183**		**Puerto Rico**	**1 800 CALL ATT**
Honduras	800-0-123		St. Kitts/Nevis✦	1-800-872-2881
Jamaica □	872		St. Vincent△	1-800-872-2881
Mexico ▽1	**01-800-288-2872**		**Suriname**△	**156**
Montserrat	1-800-872-2881		Turks & Caicos✦	1-800-872-2881
Neth. Ant.⊙	**001-800-872-2881**		Uruguay	000-410
Nicaragua	**174**		**U.S. Virgin Isl.**	**1 800 CALL ATT**
Panama	**109**		**Venezuela**	**800-11-120**

For access numbers not listed ask any operator for **AT&T Direct℠** Service.
In the U.S., call 1-800-331-1140 for a wallet card listing all worldwide AT&T Access Numbers.

Visit our Web site at: www.att.com/traveler
Bold-faced countries permit country-to-country calling outside the U.S.

● Public phones and select hotels.
✦ + Public phones require coin or card deposit.
✕ May not be available from every phone/public phone.
★ Collect calling only.
♦ Available from select hotels.
○ Available from select hotels.
✕ From St. Maarten or phones at Bobby's Marina, use 1-800-872-2881.
⊙ Public phones require local coin payment during call.
△ When calling from public phones, use phones marked "Ladatel."
▽ Available from public phones only.
□ If call card calls available from select hotels.
1 If call does not complete, use 001-800-462-4240.
2 From Asuncion only.

When placing an international call *from* the U.S., dial 1 800 CALL ATT.

© 5/98 AT&T

(go down in history)

drop down to Mexico without an **AT&T Direct**® Service wallet guide. It's a list of access numbers you need to call

fast and clear from around the world, using an AT&T Calling Card or credit card. What an amazing culture we live in.

For a list of **AT&T Access Numbers,** take the attached wallet guide.

's all within your reach. **AT&T**

For
Travelers
who want more than
the Official Line

Macmillan Publishing USA

Also Available:

- The Unofficial Guide to Branson
- The Unofficial Guide to Chicago
- The Unofficial Guide to Cruises
- The Unofficial Disney Companion
- The Unofficial Guide to Disneyland
- The Unofficial Guide to the Great Smoky & Blue Ridge Mountains
- The Unofficial Guide to Miami & the Key
- Mini-Mickey: The Pocket-Sized Unofficial Guide to Walt Disney World
- The Unofficial Guide to New York City
- The Unofficial Guide to San Francisco
- The Unofficial Guide to Skiing in the West
- The Unofficial Guide to Washington, D.C

This last road is the road south along the narrow **Punta Allen Peninsula** to **Boca Paila,** a portion of the **Sian Ka'an Biosphere Reserve,** and **Punta Allen,** a lobstering/fishing village at the tip's end. Though most of this 30-mile-long peninsular stretch of sandy, potholed road is uninhabited, there are several rustic inns along a fabulous beach south of the ruins.

Across the highway from the turnoff to the Punta Allen Peninsula on Highway 307 is the road to Cobá, another fascinating Maya city 40 miles inland. See "Cobá," below, for details.

Finally, south of the Punta Allen road on Highway 307 is the **village of Tulum.** The highway here is lined with businesses, including the bus stations, auto repair shops, markets, and pharmacies. The village of Tulum, by the way, increasingly has the look of an up-and-coming place, with sidewalks and restaurants it's never sported before.

EXPLORING THE TULUM ARCHAEOLOGICAL SITE

Located 8 miles south of Xel-Ha, Tulum is a Maya fortress overlooking the Caribbean. By A.D. 900, the end of the Classic period, Maya civilization began to decline and most of the large ceremonial centers were deserted. During the Postclassic period (A.D. 900 to the Spanish Conquest), small rival states developed with a few imported traditions from north-central Mexico. Tulum is one such walled city-state; built in the 10th century, it functioned as a seaport. Aside from the spectacular setting, Tulum is not an impressive city when compared to Chichén-Itzá or Uxmal. There are no magnificent pyramidal structures as are found in the Classic Maya ruins. The primary god here was the diving god, depicted on several buildings as an upside-down figure above doorways. Seen at the Palace at Sayil and Cobá, this curious, almost comical figure is also known as the bee god.

The most imposing building in Tulum is the large stone structure on the cliff called the **Castillo** (castle), actually a temple as well as a fortress, once covered with stucco and painted. In front of the Castillo are several unrestored palacelike buildings partially covered with stucco. And on the **beach** below, where the Maya once came ashore, tourists swim and sun, combining a visit to the ruins with a dip in the Caribbean.

The **Temple of the Frescoes,** directly in front of the Castillo, contains interesting 13th-century wall paintings, but entrance is no longer permitted. Distinctly Maya, they represent the rain god Chaac and Ixchel, the goddess of weaving, women, the moon, and medicine. On the cornice of this temple is a relief of the head of the rain god. If you get a slight distance from the building you'll see the eyes, nose, mouth, and chin. Notice the remains of the red-painted stucco on this building—at one time all the buildings at Tulum were painted a bright red.

Much of what we know of Tulum at the time of the Spanish Conquest comes from the writings of Diego de Landa, third bishop of the Yucatán. He wrote that Tulum was a small city inhabited by about 600 people, who lived in dwellings situated on platforms along a street and who supervised the trade traffic from Honduras to the Yucatán. Though it was a walled city, most of the inhabitants probably lived outside the walls, leaving the interior for governors, priestly hierarchy, and religious ceremonies. Tulum survived about 70 years after the Conquest, when it was finally abandoned.

Because of the excess of visitors this site receives, it is no longer possible to climb all of the ruins. In many cases, visitors are asked to remain behind roped-off areas to view them.

In late 1994 a new entrance to the ruins was constructed about a 10-minute walk from the archaeological site. Cars and buses enter a large parking lot; some of the public buses from Playa del Carmen go directly to the visitors' center, where there are artisans' stands, a bookstore, a museum, a restaurant, several large rest rooms, and a ticket booth for Inter-Playa buses, which depart for Playa del Carmen and Cancún frequently between 7:40am and 4:40pm. After walking through the center, visitors pay the admission fee to the ruins ($2; free on Sunday), and another fee ($1) if you choose to ride an open-air shuttle to the ruins and, if you're driving, another fee ($1) to park. You can easily walk, however. There's an additional charge of $4 for a permit to use a video camera at the site. Licensed guides have a stand by the path to the ruins and charge $20 for a 45-minute tour in English, French, or Spanish for up to four persons. They will point out many architectural details you might otherwise miss.

WHERE TO STAY & DINE IN TULUM

There are three places to stay near the entrance to the Tulum ruins, at the old cross-roads entrance. The Hotel Acquario and Cabañas Cristinas are owned by the same family and offer an array of clean, comfortable accommodations in the broadest range of prices. The **Motel Crucero** is across the street. I much prefer the two-story **Hotel Aquario,** which offers 35 rooms, all with TV, air conditioning, and ceiling fans, plus screened windows. The best rooms are a selection of newly redecorated rooms that face the street on the second floor. These are more modern and include in-room security boxes. Rates range from $37.50 to $75 a night per double during high season; and $19 to $50 in low season. There's even a small pool. The Acquario's ground-floor restaurant and bar offers an eclectic mix of services for this remote part of Mexico: There's e-mail and Internet access, *The New York Times* daily delivery, and excellent cappuccino. Basic needs are also met, including a small tobacco shop, public phones, and laundry service. Owner Felipe Ramirez will supply details about the ruins or surrounding attractions, including locating area cenotes. Next door, their Cabañas Cristinas offers more basic, rustic accommodations, which are nonetheless very clean and comfortable. Each room comes with two double beds (or an equivalent combination), a bathroom with hot water, ceiling fans, and screened windows under a palapa roof. Rates are $22.50, double, cash only. They also have a Minisuper for basic supplies, plus a restaurant with TV. For reservations, call ☎ **987/1-2194** or 987/1-2195; e-mail: tulum@cancun.rce.com.mx.

THE PUNTA ALLEN PENINSULA

About 3 miles south of the Tulum ruins on the Punta Allen Road, the pavement ends and the road becomes narrow and sandy, with many potholes during the rainy season. Beyond this point is a 30-mile-long peninsula called Punta Allen, split in two at a cut called Boca Paila, where a bridge connects the two parts of the penin-sula and the Caribbean enters a large lagoon on the right. It's part of the far eastern edge of the 1.3-million-acre **Sian Ka'an Biosphere Reserve** (see below). Along this road you'll find several cabaña-type inns, all on beautiful beaches facing the Caribbean. Taxis from the ruins can take you to most of these; then you can find a ride back to the junction at the end of your stay.

EXPLORING THE PUNTA ALLEN PENINSULA

The natural environment is the peninsula's marquee attraction, whether your tastes run to relaxing on the beaches or going on bird-watching expeditions (these are available between June and August, with July being best). Sea turtles nest on its beaches from May to October. The turtles lumber ashore at night, usually between 10pm and 3am. *A note about provisions:* Since the Punta Allen Peninsula is rather

The Sian Ka'an Biosphere Reserve

Down the peninsula a few miles south of the Tulum ruins, you'll pass the guard-house of the Sian Ka'an Biosphere Reserve. The Reserve is a tract of 1.3 million acres set aside in 1986 to preserve tropical forests, savannas, mangroves, coastal and marine habitats, and 70 miles of coastal reefs. The area is home to jaguars, pumas, ocelots, margays, jaguarundis, spider and howler monkeys, tapirs, white-lipped and collared peccaries, manatees, brocket and white-tailed deer, croco-diles, and green, loggerhead, hawksbill, and leatherback sea turtles. It also protects 366 species of birds—you might catch a glimpse of an ocellated turkey, a great curassow, a brilliantly colored parrot, a toucan or trogon, a white ibis, a roseate spoonbill, a jabiru (or wood stork), a flamingo, or one of 15 species of herons, egrets, and bitterns.

The park is separated into three parts: a "core zone" restricted to research; a "buffer zone," where visitors and families already living there have restricted use; and a "cooperation zone," which is outside the reserve but vital to its preserva-tion. If you drive on Highway 307 from Tulum to an imaginary line just below the Bahía (bay) of Espíritu Santo, all you see on the Caribbean side is the reserve; but except at the ruins of Muyil/Chunyaxche, there's no access. At least 22 archaeological sites have been charted within Sian Ka'an. The best place to sample the reserve is the Punta Allen Peninsula, part of the "buffer zone." The inns were already in place when the reserve was created. Of these, only the Cuzan Guest House (see "Where to Stay & Dine" under "The Punta Allen Peninsula," below) offers trips for birding. But bring your own binoculars and birding books and have at it—the bird life here is rich. At the Boca Paila bridge you can often find fishermen who'll take you into the lagoon on the landward side, where you can fish and see plenty of bird life; but it's unlikely the boatman will know bird names in English or Spanish. Birding is best just after dawn, especially during the April to July nesting season.

Day trips to the Sian Ka'an are led by the Friends of Sian Ka'an from the Restaurant y Cabañas Ana y José just south of the Tulum ruins on Monday, Tuesday, Friday, and Saturday for $50 per person using their vehicle or $40 per person if you drive yourself. Trips start from the Cabañas at 9:30am and return there around 2:30pm. For reservations, contact **Amigos de Sian Ka'an** (☎ 98/84-9583; fax 98/87-3080) in Cancún. Or you may be able to book the tour once you've arrived at the Restaurant y Cabañas Ana y José (see "Where to Stay & Dine" under "The Punta Allen Peninsula," below) if the tour, limited to 19 people, isn't full.

remote and there are no stores, handy provisions to bring along include a flashlight, mosquito repellent, mosquito coils, water, and snacks. Most hotels along here charge for bottled water in your room and for meals. From October to December winds may be accompanied by nippy nights, so come prepared—some hotels don't have blankets.

Lodgings here vary in quality; some are simple but quite comfortable, while others are a lot like camping out. One or two have electricity for a few hours in the evening, but shut it off around 10pm, and there are no electrical outlets; most don't have hot water. The first one is half a mile south of the ruins, and the farthest is 30 miles down the peninsula.

The following hotels are listed in the order you'll find them as you drive south on the Punta Allen road (from Tulum). To reach the first one you'll need to take the Punta Allen exit from Highway 307, then turn left when it intersects the coastal road. The rest of the hotels are to the right.

WHERE TO STAY & DINE

Restaurant y Cabañas Ana y José. Punta Allen Peninsula, km 7 Carretera Punta Allen (Apdo. Postal 15), 77780 Tulum, Q. Roo. ☎ **987/1-2004,** or 98/80-6022 in Cancún. E-mail: anayjose@cancun.rce.com.mx. 16 units. High season $60–$70 double. Low season $50–$60 double. No credit cards. Free unguarded parking.

This place started as a restaurant and blossomed into a comfortable inn on the beach. All rooms have tiled floors, one or two double beds, baths with cold-water shower, patios or balconies, and electricity between 5:30 and 10:30pm. The rock-walled cabañas in front are a little larger, and some face the beautiful wide beach just a few yards off, but these are also the most expensive rooms. New rooms have been added on a second level in back. The only drawback is the lack of cross venti-lation in some of the lower rooms in the back section, which can be extremely uncomfortable at night without electricity to power fans. The inn also offers bicycle and kayak rentals, trips through Maya canals and to little-known ruins, snorkeling, and dive trips. Biologist-led boat excursions, organized by the Friends of Sian Ka'an headquartered in Cancún, to the Sian Ka'an Biosphere Reserve begin here at 9:30am Monday, Tuesday, Friday, and Saturday (weather permitting) for $50 per person. (See Sian Ka'an box above, and "Road Trips from Cancún" in chapter 4, for details on making reservations for the Biosphere Reserve trip).

The excellent, screened-in restaurant, with sand floors under the palapa, offers modest prices and is open daily from 8am to 9pm. The hotel is 4 miles south of the Tulum ruins. Reservations are a must in high season, or arrive very early in the day before it fills up.

Cabañas Tulum. Punta Allen Peninsula, km 7 Carretera Tulum (Apdo. Postal 63), 77780 Tulum, Q. Roo. No phone. 18 units. $40 double. No credit cards.

Next door to Ana y José's (above) is a row of bungalows facing a heavenly stretch of ocean and beach. Each bungalow includes a hot-water shower, two double beds, screens on the windows, a table, one electric light, a nice-size tiled bathroom, and a veranda where you can hang a hammock. Mattresses, which rest on a cement plat-form, are too thin to cushion against the hard surface. Flat top sheets, which are also used as bottom sheets, immediately work off the mattress, leaving guests either wrestling with them all night or giving up to settle in on the bare mattress. A small restaurant serves beer, soft drinks, and all three meals for reasonable prices—just don't expect a gourmet meal. In fact for any meal other than breakfast, you're better off taking meals at Ana y José or at Zazil Kin. The cabañas are often full between December 15 and Easter and July and August, so arrive early or make reservations. It's 4 miles south of the ruins.

Boca Paila Fishing Lodge. Km 25 Carreterra Tulum–Punta Allen (Apdo. Postal 59), 77600 Cozumel, Q. Roo. ☎ **987/2-5944** or 987/2-1176. Fax 987/2-0053. (For reservations con-tact Frontiers, P.O. Box 959, 100 Logan Rd., Wexford, PA 15090; ☎ **800/245-1950** in the U.S., or 412/935-1577; fax 412/935-5388.) 8 cabañas. High season (Dec 3–June 2) $2,150 per person double. Low season $1,750 per person double. Rates are for 6 days and 7 nights, including all meals and a private boat and bonefishing guide for each cabaña. Ask about prices for a nonangler sharing a double with an angler. Nonfishing drop-in prices July–Sept, $210 per person double with 3 meals; $300 1–2 people for day of fishing with lunch but no overnight. No credit cards on site, however if prepaying while reserving with Frontiers, all major credit cards are accepted.

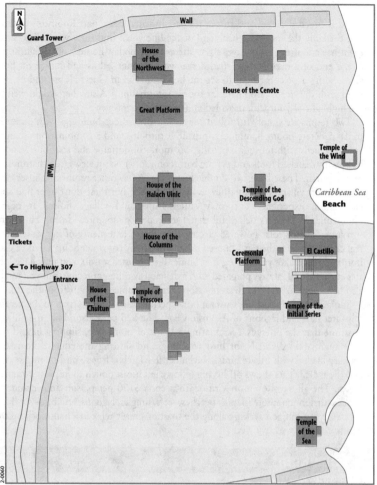

Easily a top contender for the nicest spot along this road, the white stucco cabañas offer friendly beachside comfort. Spread out on the beach and linked by a pleasant walkway, each individual unit has a mosquito-proof palapa roof, large tiled rooms comfortably furnished with two double beds, rattan furniture, hot water in the bathrooms, wall fans, 24-hour electricity, and a comfortable screened porch. The Boca Paila attracts a clientele that comes for saltwater fly-fishing in the flats, mostly for bonefish. Prime fishing months are March to June. But when occupancy is low, nonfishing guests can be accommodated with advance notice. Overnight non-fishing rates are priced high as a discouragement to drop-ins. The lodge is about midway down the Punta Allen Peninsula, just before the Boca Paila bridge.

✪ **Cuzan Guest House.** Punta Allen. (For reservations contact Apdo. Postal 24, 77200 Felipe Carrillo Puerto, Q. Roo.) ☎ **983/4-0358.** Fax 983/4-0383 in Felipe Carrillo Puerto. 8 units. $40–$65 double. All-inclusive 7-day fly-fishing package $1,599. Rates include all meals. No credit cards.

About 30 miles south of the Tulum ruins is the end of the peninsula and Punta Allen, the Yucatán's best-known lobstering and fishing village, planted on a palm-studded beach. Isolated and rustic, it's part Indiana Jones, part Robinson Crusoe, and certainly the most laid-back end of the line you'll find for a while. The small town has a lobster cooperative, a few streets with modest homes, and a lighthouse at the end of a narrow sand road dense with coconut palms and jungle on both sides. So it's a welcome sight to see the beachside Cuzan Guest House and its sign in English that reads "stop here for tourist information." A stay here could well be the highlight of your trip, provided you're a flexible traveler.

Two rooms are simply furnished Maya-style oval stucco buildings with thatched roofs, concrete floors, hammocks, private bathrooms, and a combination of single and king beds with mosquito netting. Six more comfortable and spacious wooden huts, with thatched roofs and private bathrooms, offer ocean views from hammocks on the porch. These have two double beds each. A few other rooms or houses elsewhere in the village are sometimes available for rent, but these don't offer that special Cuzan experience and may suffer from loud village noises at night. Unfortunately, Cuzan's delightful thatched teepees disappeared during Hurricane Roxanne. There's solar-powered electricity at night, and plenty of hot water. The real charmer here is the sand-floored restaurant run by co-owner Sonja Lilvik, a Californian who makes you feel right at home. If it's lobster season, you may have lobster at every meal, always prepared with a deliciously different recipe. But you might also be treated to a pile of heavenly stone crabs or some other gift from the sea.

Sonja arranges fly-fishing trips for bone, permit, snook, and tarpon to the nearby saltwater flats and lagoons of Ascension Bay. The $25 per person boat tour of the coastline that she offers is a fascinating 3 hours of snorkeling, slipping in and out of mangrove-filled canals for bird watching, and skirting the edge of an island rookery loaded with frigate birds. November to March is frigate bird mating season and the male frigate shows off his big billowy red breast pouch to impress potential mates. The all-day Robinson Crusoe Tour costs $100 per person and includes a boat excursion to remote islands, beaches, reefs, jungles, lagoons, and bird-watching areas. Or you can go kayaking along the coast or simply relax in a hammock on the beach.

7 Cobá Ruins

105 miles SW of Cancún

From the turnoff at the Tulum junction, you travel inland an hour or so to arrive at these mystical ruins jutting up from the forest floor.

The impressive Maya ruins at Cobá, deep in the jungle, are a worthy detour from your route south. You don't need to stay overnight to see the ruins, but there are a few hotels. The village is small and poor, gaining little from the visitors who pass through to see the ruins. **Used clothing** (especially for children) would be a welcome gift.

ESSENTIALS
GETTING THERE & DEPARTING
BY CAR   The road to Cobá begins in Tulum, across Highway 307 from the turnoff to the Punta Allen Peninsula. Turn right when you see the signs to Cobá and continue on that road for 40 miles. When you reach the village, proceed straight until you see the lake; when the road curves right, turn left. The entrance to the ruins is at the end of that road past some small restaurants. Cobá is also about a 3-hour drive south from Cancún.

BY BUS   Several buses a day leave Cobá for Tulum and Playa del Carmen.

ORIENTATION

The highway into Cobá becomes one main paved street through town, which passes El Bocadito restaurant and hotel on the right (see "Where to Stay & Dine," below) and goes a block to the lake. If you turn right at the lake you reach the Villas Arqueológicas a block farther. Turning left will lead you past a couple of primitive restaurants on the left facing the lake, and to the ruins, straight ahead, the equivalent of a block.

EXPLORING THE COBÁ RUINS

The Maya built many breathtaking cities in the Yucatán, but few were grander in scope than Cobá. However, much of the 42-square-mile site, on the shores of two lakes, is unexcavated. A 60-mile-long *sacbe* (a pre-Hispanic raised road or causeway) through the jungle linked Cobá to Yaxuná, once a large and important Maya center 30 miles south of Chichén-Itzá. It's the Maya's longest-known sacbe, and there are at least 50 or more shorter ones from here. An important city-state, Cobá, which means "water stirred by the wind," flourished between A.D. 632 (the oldest carved date found here) until after the founding of Chichén-Itzá, around 800. Then Cobá slowly faded in importance and population until it was finally abandoned. Scholars believe Cobá was an important trade link between the Yucatán Caribbean coast and inland cities.

Once in the site, keep your bearings—it's very easy to get lost on the maze of dirt roads in the jungle. If you're into it, bring your bird and butterfly books; this is one of the best places to see both. Branching off from every labeled path you'll notice unofficial narrow paths into the jungle, used by locals as shortcuts through the ruins. These are good for scouting for birds, but be careful to remember the way back.

The **Grupo Cobá** boasts a large, impressive pyramid, the **Temple of the Church** (La Iglesia), which you'll find if you take the path bearing right after the entrance. Walking to it, notice the unexcavated mounds on the left. Though the urge to climb the temple is great, the view is better from El Castillo in the Nohoc Mul group farther back at the site.

From here, return back to the main path and turn right. You'll pass a sign pointing right to the ruined *juego de pelota* (ball court), but the path is obscure.

Continuing straight ahead on this path for 5 to 10 minutes, you'll come to a fork in the road. To the left and right you'll notice jungle-covered, unexcavated pyramids, and at one point you'll cross a raised portion crossing the pathway—this is the visible remains of the sacbe to Yaxuná. Throughout the area, intricately carved stelae stand by pathways, or lie forlornly in the jungle underbrush. Though protected by crude thatched roofs, most are so weatherworn as to be indiscernible.

The left fork leads to the **Nohoch Mul Group,** which contains **El Castillo,** the tallest pyramid in the Yucatán (rising even higher than the great El Castillo at Chichén-Itzá and the Pyramid of the Magician at Uxmal). So far, visitors are still permitted to climb to the top. From the magnificent lofty position you can see unexcavated jungle-covered pyramidal structures poking up through the forest all around. The right fork (more or less straight on) goes to the **Conjunto Las Pin-**

For Your Comfort at Cobá

Because of the heat, visit Cobá in the morning or after the heat of the day has passed. Mosquito repellent, drinking water, and comfortable shoes are imperative.

Wings & Stings

The mosquito and fly population is fierce, but this is one of the best places along the coast for birding—go early in the morning.

---

turas. Here, the main attraction is the **Pyramid of the Painted Lintel,** a small structure with traces of the original bright colors above the door. You can climb up to get a close look. Though maps of Cobá show ruins around two lakes, there are really only two excavated buildings to see after you enter the site.

Admission is $2; children under 12 enter free daily, and Sunday and holidays it's free to everyone. Camera permits are $4 for each video. The site is open daily from 8am to 5pm.

WHERE TO STAY & DINE

El Bocadito. Calle Principal, Cobá, Q. Roo. No phone. For reservations contact Apdo. Postal 56, 97780 Valladolid, Yuc. 8 units. $16–$21 double. No credit cards. Free unguarded parking.

El Bocadito, on the right as you enter town, could take advantage of being the only game in town besides the much more expensive Villas Arqueológicas, but it doesn't. Next to the hotel's restaurant of the same name, the rooms are arranged in two rows facing an open patio. They're simple, each with tile floors, two double beds, no bed-spreads, a ceiling fan, and a washbasin separate from the toilet and cold-water shower cubicle. It's agreeable enough and always full by nightfall, so arrive no later than 3pm to secure a room.

The clean, open-air restaurant offers good meals at reasonable prices, served by a friendly, efficient staff. Busloads of tour groups stop here at lunch (always a sign of approval). I enjoy the casual atmosphere of El Bocadito, and there's a bookstore and gift shop adjacent to the restaurant.

✪ **Villas Arqueológicas Cobá.** Cobá, Q. Roo. ☎ **800/258-2633** in the U.S., or 5/203-3086 in Mexico City. 44 units. A/C. $90 double, room only including tax. Half board (choice of breakfast or lunch) available for an additional $12 per person; full board (3 meals) available for an extra $25 per person. Rates include all charges and taxes. AE, MC, V. Free guarded parking.

Operated by Club Med but nothing like a Club Med Village, this lovely lakeside hotel is a 5-minute walk from the ruins. The hotel has a French polish, and the restaurant is top-notch, though expensive. A room rate including meals is available. The rooms, built around a plant-filled courtyard and beautiful pool, are stylish and soothingly comfortable. The hotel also has a library on Mesoamerican archaeology (with books in French, English, and Spanish). Make reservations—this hotel fills with touring groups.

To find it, drive through town and turn right at the lake; the hotel is straight ahead on the right.

EN ROUTE TO FELIPE CARRILLO PUERTO: MUYIL & CHUNYAXCHE

From Tulum you continue along the main Highway 307 past the Cobá turnoff; it heads southwest through Tulum village. About 14 miles south of Tulum village are the ruins of **Muyil** (ca. A.D. 1–1540) at the settlement of **Chunyaxche,** on the left side. Although archaeologists have done extensive mapping and studies of the ruins, only a few of the more than 100 or so buildings, caves, and subterranean temples have been excavated; it's actually more historically significant than it is interesting,

Coba Ruins

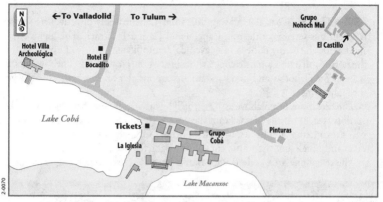

and for most people it may not be worth the time or admission price. Birding in the early morning, however, is quite worthwhile. New excavations take place off and on, so keep checking the progress. One of the objects of this research is to find evidence of an inland port, since canals link the site to the Caribbean 9 miles east of the Boca Paila cut.

Admission is $2; free for children under 12 and free for everyone on Sunday and festival days. It's open daily from 8am to 5pm.

The **Friends of Sian Ka'an** in Cancún (see the box, "Sian Ka'an Biosphere Reserve," above) organizes trips through the canals from Boca Paila. The **Restaurant y Cabañas Ana y José** south of the Tulum ruins (see the listing under "Where to Stay & Dine," under "The Punta Allen Peninsula," above) also guides visitors here through the lagoons and canals.

After Muyil and Chunyaxche, Highway 307 cuts through 45 miles of jungle to Felipe Carrillo Puerto.

8 Felipe Carrillo Puerto

134 miles SW of Cancún

Felipe Carrillo Puerto (pop. 47,000) is a busy crossroads in the jungle along the road to Ciudad Chetumal. It has gas stations, a market, a small ice plant, a bus terminal, and a few modest hotels and restaurants. Since the main road intersects the road back to Mérida, Carrillo Puerto is the turning point for those making a "short circuit" of the Yucatán Peninsula. Highway 184 heads west from here to Ticul, Uxmal, Campeche, and Mérida.

As you pass through, consider its strange history: This was where the rebels in the War of the Castes took their stand, guided by the "Talking Crosses." Some remnants of that town (named Chan Santa Cruz) are still extant. Look for signs in town pointing the way.

Last Gas

Felipe Carrillo Puerto is the only place to buy **gasoline** between Tulum and Chetumal, although if you're desperate, the tire repairman's family in Limones might sell you a liter or two. Look for the big tire leaning against the fence.

ESSENTIALS Coastal Highway 307 from Cancún leads directly here. There's frequent bus service south from Cancún and Playa del Carmen. The highway goes right through the town, becoming avenida Benito Juárez in town. Driving in from the north, you'll pass a traffic circle with a bust of the great Juárez. The town market is here. Small hotels and good restaurants are located on the highway as it goes through town.

The directions given above assume you'll be driving. If you arrive by bus, the **bus station** is right on the plaza. From there it's a 10-minute walk east down calle 67, past the cathedral and banks, to avenida Juárez. Turn left onto Juárez to find restaurants and hotels and the traffic circle I use as a reference point.

The telephone **area code** is **983. Banks** here don't exchange foreign currency.

9 Majahual, Xcalak & the Chinchorro Reef

In recent years, a tremendous amount of commercial attention has been focused on this remote part of Quintana Roo, with developments rumored to be going in both north of the Majahual turnoff and in the tiny village of Xcalak itself. Several small inns have also opened between Majahual and Xcalak. But the peninsula is still a little-known area, at least for the moment. A roll-with-the-punches kind of traveler will savor its rustic and remote appeal, especially those preferring this coast's offbeat offerings, divers looking for new underwater conquests, bird lovers seeking an abundance of colorful tropical bird life, and anyone looking for quiet, beachfront relaxation. Your destination is the **Costa de Cocos Dive Resort** and the nearby fishing village of **Xcalak** near the end of the peninsula. Offshore reefs and the exceptional yet little-known Chinchorro Reef offer great diving possibilities. The village of Xcalak once had a population as large as 1,200 before the 1958 hurricane; now it has only 200 inhabitants. You'll pass many down-and-out places on the way, so the clean Costa de Cocos will stand out when you see it.

ORIENTATION

ARRIVING By Car Driving south from Felipe Carrillo Puerto, you'll come to the turnoff (left) onto Highway 10, 1½ miles after Limones, then it's a 30-mile drive to the coastal settlement of **Majahual** (mah-*hah*-wahl), and another 35 miles to the end of the peninsula and the tiny fishing village of Xcalak (eesh-*kah*-lahk). To orient you further, the turnoff from Highway 307 is 163 miles southwest of Cancún and 88 miles southwest of Tulum.

Driving from the turnoff at Highway 307 to Xcalak takes around 2 hours. At Majahual, where you turn right (south), there's a military guard station. Tell the guard your destination and continue on the new paved highway for 35 more miles, about a half hour. *Slow down at settlements. Residents aren't expecting much traffic, and dogs and children play on the road.*

By Plane A new, 4,500-ft. airstrip opened in early 1998, and regular, twice-weekly air service from Cancún was expected to be put in place. Check with the **State Tourism Office** in Chetumal (☎ **983/20855** or 983/25073) about the status of this service.

By Bus From Chetumal's bus station, two full-size **buses** daily go to Xcalak. There's combi (minivan) transportation from behind the Holiday Inn, but they cram in twice as many passengers as will fit comfortably and may carry a pig or goat on top as well.

The Yucatán's Lower Caribbean Coast

To Valladolid ↖

To Cancún ↗

Chumpón

Tulum

Restaurant & Cabañas Ana y José

Laguna San Felipe

Cabañas Tulum

Boca Paila Fishing Lodge

Punta Allen

Cuzan Guest House

To Ticul & Uxmal ↖

295

307

Bahía de la Ascensión

Peninsula Vigia Grande

Polyuc

184

Felipe Carrillo Puerto (Chan Santa Cruz)

Sian Ka'an

Biosphere

Reserve

Pta. Sta. Rosa

Bahía del Espíritu Santo

Pta. Herrero

QUINTANA ROO

Mosquitero

Los Limones

Placer

Cafetal

10

307

Cayo Norte

Laguna Bacalar

Bahía de San José

Rancho Encantado

Bacalar

Calderitas

Majahual

Banco Chinchorro (Chinchorro Reef)

Cenote Azul

Chetumal

Cayo Lobos

186

Bahía Chetumal

To Escárcega ←

Costa de Cocos Dive Resort

Xcalak

BELIZE

Caribbean Sea

LEGEND

Airport ✈

0   25 mi
     40 km

N

2-0093

By Ferry   A year ago, ferry docks and two 20-car **ferries** (with passenger space) were being prepared to run between Chetumal and Xcalak, eliminating the tedious road trip through Limones and Majahual. Again, check with the **State Tourism Office** in Chetumal (☎ **983/20855** or 983/25073) about the status of this service. To date, there is only passenger service aboard a 30-passenger ferry that takes you 6 miles north of Xcalak; cost is $5 each way.

DIVING THE CHINCHORRO REEF

The **Chinchorro Reef Underwater National Park** is a 24-mile-long, 8-mile-wide oval-shaped reef with a depth of 3 feet on the reef's interior to 3,000 feet on the exterior. Locals claim it's the last virgin reef system in the Caribbean. It's invisible from the ocean side; one of its diving attractions is the number of shipwrecks, at least 30 of them, along the reef's eastern side. One is on top of the reef. Divers have counted 40 cannons at one wreck site. On the west side are walls and coral gardens, but it's too rough to dive there.

Aventuras Chinchorro is the fully equipped dive shop for Sandwood Villas and Villa Caracol (see below) as well as for other establishments in the area. Local diving just off shore costs $45 per diver for a two-tank dive. Chinchorro Banks diving costs between $25 and $65 per person, depending on how long you stay, how far you go, and how many divers are in the group. Fishing and snorkeling excursions and trips into Belize can also be arranged, as well as rental of kayaks and horses. For diving reservations or for rooms at the above-mentioned inns, contact **Aventuras Chinchorro,** 812 Garland Ave., Nokomis, FL 34275 (☎ **800/480-4505** or 941/488-4505). Credit cards are only accepted when prepaying reservations from the U.S.

WHERE TO STAY & DINE

Besides the Costa de Cocos Dive Resort described below, there are two other small, cozy inns about a half a mile from each other and near the village of Xcalak. **Sandwood Villas** are four two-bedroom apartments renting for $55 per person; the **Villa Caracol,** where rooms rent for $65 per person, is a four-room inn with air-conditioning, balconies, 24-hour electricity, hot water, free snorkeling and fishing equipment, and a beachside bar and grill. Rates at both places include breakfast and dinner, and lunch is available. Discounts are offered for stays of a week or more. Thirteen RV hookups are also available, at $15 per night for one or two people, but no camping is permitted. Contact **Aventuras Chinchorro,** listed above, for reservations.

Aside from those connected to the establishments mentioned here, a couple of restaurants in Xcalak offer good seafood meals—ask at your hotel which one is the current favorite.

Important Note about Provisions

Since this is a remote part of the world, travelers should expect inconveniences. When things break down or food items run out, replacements are a long way off. You might arrive to find that the dive boat's broken, or that there's no beer, or that the generator powering the water pumps, toilets, and electricity is off for hours or days. Needless to say, a flashlight might come in handy. Bring a large quantity of strong mosquito repellent with DEET as a main ingredient—the mosquitoes are undaunted by anything else. You might want to stow a package or two of mosquito coils to burn at night.

Costa de Cocos Dive Resort. Km 52 Carretera Majahual–Xcalak, Q. Roo. (For reservations contact ☎ **800/538-6802**; www.northcoast.com/~brown/CostadeCocos.html; e-mail: ccocos@gte.net.) 12 cabañas. High season $120 double with 1 or 2 beds. Low season $100 double. Dive rates and packages available; e-mail your request. Rates include breakfast and dinner. No credit cards.

Far and away the most sophisticated hostelry along this route, this place will seem a welcome respite. It's located in a palm grove just before the fishing village of Xcal-ak, which is a half mile beyond. The beautifully constructed thatch-roofed cabañas are fashioned after Maya huts, but have sophisticated details like limestone walls, handsomely crafted mahogany-louvered and screened windows, beautiful wood plank floors in the bedroom, large tile bathrooms, comfortable furnishings, shelves of paperback books, hot water, and mosquito netting. They have 24-hour wind and solar power, and reverse-osmosis purified tap water. Nice as it is, it still won't hurt to inspect your shoes daily for hidden critters—this is the jungle, after all.

All dive equipment is available and included in dive packages or rented separately for day guests. The resort operates a 40-foot dive boat for diving Chinchorro. Water-sports equipment for rent includes ocean kayaks and Windsurfer boards, and they now offer day or overnight sea-kayaking trips to Belize, inside the reef. Fly-fishing for bonefish, tarpon, and snook inside Chetumal Bay with experienced, English-speaking guides is a popular way to spend the day, as is bird watching at their sanctuary island. NAUI resort or open-water certification can be arranged for an additional fee. Beer and soft drinks are sold at the resort, but bring your own liquor and snacks. The casual restaurant features home-style cooking, usually with a choice of one or two main courses at dinner, sandwiches at lunch, and regular breakfast fare in the morning.

Anytime the sea gets choppy, your planned dive at **Chinchorro Reef** (22 miles offshore) may be grounded. However, diving 5 minutes offshore from the Costa de Cocos Resort is highly rewarding during these postponements.

10 Lago Bacalar

65 miles SW of Felipe Carrillo Puerto, 23 miles NW of Chetumal

Bacalar offers another offbeat alternative in this part of the Yucatán. The crystal-clear spring-fed waters of Lake Bacalar form Mexico's second largest lake at slightly over 65 miles long. Known as the Lake of Seven Colors, mismanagement of the nat-ural mixture of spring and seawater in recent years changed the characteristic varied deep blue colors. It's still beautiful to gaze upon, and the colors range from crystal clear and pale blue to deep blue-green and Caribbean turquoise. Spaniards fleeing coastal pirates used Maya pyramid stones to build a fort in Bacalar, which is now a modest museum. The area is very quiet—it's the perfect place to swim and relax. At least 130 species of birds have been spotted in the area. If you're in a car, take a detour through the village of Bacalar and down along the lakeshore drive. To find the lakeshore drive, go all the way past town on Highway 307, where you'll see a sign pointing left to the lake. When you turn left, that road is the lakeshore drive. You can double back along the drive from there to return to the highway. The Hotel Laguna is on the lakeshore drive. From here it's a 30-minute drive to Chetumal and to the Corozol Airport in Belize. Besides its location on Lago Bacalar, this area is also perfect for launching excursions into the Río Bec ruin route, described below.

ORIENTATION   If driving, signs into Bacalar are plainly visible from Highway 307. Buses going south from Cancún and Playa del Carmen stop here, and there are frequent buses from Chetumal.

WHERE TO STAY

Hotel Laguna. Costera de Bacalar 143, 77010 Lago Bacalar, Q. Roo. ☎ **983/2-3517** in Chetumal. 34 units. $30 double. $55 bungalow for 5 persons. No credit cards.

The Laguna is off the beaten path, so there are almost always rooms available, except in winter, when Canadians seem to fill the place. Rooms overlook the pool and have a lovely view of the lake. The water along the shore is very shallow, but you can dive from the hotel's dock into 30-foot water. The hotel's restaurant offers main courses costing about $4 to $8. It's open daily from 8am to 8pm. To find it, go through town toward Chetumal. Just at the edge of town you'll see a sign pointing left to the hotel and lakeshore drive.

✪ **Rancho Encantado Cottage Resort.** Km 3 Carretera Felipe Carrillo Puerto–Chetumal (Apdo. Postal 233), 77000 Chetumal, Q. Roo. ☎ and fax **983/8-0427.** (For reservations contact P.O. Box 1256, Taos, NM 87571; ☎ **800/505-MAYA** in the U.S.; fax 505/776-2102; www.encantado.com; e-mail: mpstarr@laplaza.org.) 12 casitas. Dec–Apr $150 double; May–Nov $120 double; both including continental breakfast and dinner. Villa $1,100 week (discount for longer villa stays). Rates for casitas only, without food service, are $17.50 less per person. AE, MC, V.

What an Edenic, serene place in which to unwind! Rancho Encantado's immaculate white stucco individual casitas/cottages are spread out on a shady manicured lawn beside the smooth Lago Bacalar. Each spacious, sublimely comfortable, and beautifully kept room has mahogany-louvered windows, a shiny red-tile floor, mahogany dining table and chairs, a living room or sitting area, a porch with chairs, and hammocks strung between trees. Some have a blue-tile kitchenette and others have a coffee area; coffeemakers and coffee are provided in each room. Some rooms have cedar ceilings and red-tiled roofs and others have thatched roofs. All are decorated with folk art, murals inspired by Maya ruins, foot-loomed pastel-colored bedspreads, and Zapotec rugs from Oaxaca. The newest rooms are the four waterfront casitas (rooms 9 through 12) with white stucco walls, thatched roofs, and fabulous hand-painted murals inspired by those at Bonampak. Two of these have a striking, rust-colored plaster face resembling the faces at nearby Kohunlich. The owners' villa on the lake is also available several months a year.

An open-air conference center, with a soaring palapa roof, sits next to the water and near the restaurant. The large palapa-topped restaurant overlooks the lake and serves all three meals. There's no beef on the menu, but plenty of chicken, fish, vegetables, and fresh fruit. The honey here is from Rancho hives. You can swim from the hotel's dock, and kayaks and canoes are available for guest use. Orange, lime, mango, sapote, ceiba, banana, palm, and oak trees, wild orchids, and bromeliads on the expansive grounds make great bird shelter, attracting flocks of chattering parrots, turquoise-browed motmots, toucans, and at least 100 more species, many of which are easy to spot outside your room. Ask the manager, Luis Tellez, for a copy of the extensive birding list.

Tellez also keeps abreast of developments at the nearby archaeological sites and is the only source of current information before you reach the ruins. He's developed a lot of knowledge about the sites and leads several trips himself. Almost a dozen excursions are available through the hotel. Among them are day trips to the **Río Bec** ruin route, an extended visit to **Calakmul,** a ruins visit and lunch with a local family (a guest favorite), outings to the **Majahual Peninsula,** and a riverboat trip to the Maya ruins of **Lamanai** deep in a Belizian forest. Mirabai Starr offers 8-day "Writing at the Ruins" workshops in January and June. *Note:* This is the only hotel offering guided trips to the Río Bec ruins, many of which are available only by special permit, which Tellez can obtain. Several ruins are easily reachable from the road, and others are so deep in the jungle that a guide is necessary to find them and a four-wheel-drive vehicle is a must. With advance notice, the hotel can arrange guides and the hotel has transportation. They also work with Río Bec specialist Serge Rìou (see "Touring the Ruins with a Guide," below). Excursions range in price from $55 to $115 per person, depending on the length and difficulty of the trip, and several have a three-person minimum. Groups interested in birding, yoga, archaeology, and the like are invited to bring a leader and use Rancho Encantado as a base. Special packages and excursions can be arranged in advance from the hotel's U.S. office. To find the Rancho, look for the hotel's sign on the left about 1 mile before Bacalar.

WHERE TO EAT

Besides the lakeside restaurant of **Rancho Encantado** (see above), you may enjoy the **Restaurant Cenote Azul,** a comfortable open-air thatched-roof restaurant on the edge of the beautiful Cenote Azul. In both places, main courses cost from $5 to $12. To get to Restaurant Cenote Azul, follow the highway to the south edge of town and turn left at the restaurant's sign; follow that road around to the restaurant. At Rancho Encantado you can swim in Lago Bacalar, and at the Restaurant Cenote you can take a dip in placid Cenote Azul, but without skin lotion of any kind, because it poisons the cenote.

SIDE TRIPS FROM BACALAR: THE RÍO BEC RUIN ROUTE

A few miles west of Bacalar begins the Yucatán's **southern ruin route,** generally called the Río Bec region, although other architectural styles are present. Until recently the region enjoyed little attention. However, all that is rapidly changing. Within the last several years, the Mexican government has spent millions of pesos to build a new highway, conserve previously excavated sites, and uncover heretofore unexcavated ruins.

This is an especially ruin-rich, but little-explored, part of the peninsula. With the opening in late 1994 of **Dzibanché** (an extensive "new" site), paved-road access to **Calakmul** in 1994, and the **Museo de la Cultura Maya** in 1995 in Chetumal, together with other "new sites" and discoveries at existing ruins, the region is poised to become the peninsula's newest tourist destination. With responsible guides, other jungle-surrounded but difficult-to-reach sites may also be available soon. A new four-lane highway leads from close to Bacalar for several miles before it becomes two-lane again; construction crews are continuing to work widening the road even further. Tourist services (restaurants, hotels) are slowly being added along the route, but informed guides must be arranged before you arrive, and there are no visitors' centers. Rancho Encantado trucks in water to the bathrooms at the ruins of Kohunlich, making them the only public rest rooms on the route. Part of what makes this area so special is the feeling of pioneering into unmarked land, and with that comes a bit of inconvenience. However, this area is definitely worth watching and visiting now.

BIRD & ANIMAL LIFE   The fauna along the entire route is especially rich. Toucans fly across the highway, and orioles are extremely common. Gray fox, wild turkey, tesquintle (a bushy-tailed plant-eating rodent), the raccoon relative coatimundi (with its long tapered snout and tail), and armadillos will surely cross your path. At Calakmul a family of howler monkeys resides in the trees overlooking the parking area.

THE ROUTE'S STARTING POINT   The route begins just 9 miles from the edge of Bacalar where there's the turnoff from Highway 307 to Highway 186, which leads to the Río Bec ruin route as well as to Escarcega, Villahermosa, and Palenque. *A reminder:* On your return, if you are going back to Bacalar (or north on Highway 307), the guards at the government inspection station at the Reforma intersection will ask to see your travel papers (birth certificate or passport) and tourist permit. It is the intersection you pass after turning from Highway 186 north on Highway 307 toward Bacalar. You can divide your sightseeing into several day trips. If you get an early start, many of the ruins mentioned below can be easily visited in a day from Bacalar. These sites will be changing, though, since swarms of laborers are still busy with further exploration.

Evidence shows that these ruins, especially Becán, were part of the **trade route** linking the Caribbean coast at Cobá to Edzná and the Gulf coast and with Lamanai in Belize and beyond. Once this region was dense with Maya cities, cultivated fields, lakes, and an elaborate system of rivers that connected the region with Belize and Central America. Today many of these ancient cities hide under cover of jungle, which has overtaken the land from horizon to horizon.

FACILITIES, OR LACK THEREOF   There are no visitor facilities or refreshments at these sites, so bring your own water and food. However, in the village of Xpujil (just before the ruins of Xpujil), the **Restaurant Posada Calakmul** (☎ 983/2-9162) is open daily from 6am to 1am. Under the watchful eye of Doña María Cabrera, it serves excellent home-style food and caters to ruins enthusiasts—hung about the room are photos and descriptions of little-known sites written by Río Bec specialist Serge Rìou (see below). The new **hotel rooms** behind the restaurant cost $20 for a double and are clean and comfortable, with tile floors, private bathrooms with hot water, good beds, and a small porch.

Because phone service is so limited in this area, note the number (☎ 983/2-8863) for **Caseta Telefónica** in Xpujil Campeche, where residents make phone calls and where tourists can receive messages.

Near the entrance to the Chicanná ruins, on the north side of the road, is the new **Ramada Inn Eco Village,** km 144 Carretera Excarcega (☎ 981/6-2233 in Campeche for reservations; the hotel has no phone). Though the name suggests an ecological bent, approximately 20 acres of jungle were completely leveled to build an as-yet unpaved parking lot for all the buses and cars that will one day come, a swimming pool, a restaurant, and 28 nicely furnished rooms in sets of two stories. Manicured lawns with flower beds and pathways link the rooms, which have a Polynesian architecture. There are no ecologically oriented tours. For the moment, the hotel attracts primarily bus tours and individual travelers. Electricity is generated between 6pm and 10am. Restaurant prices are high, and don't include the 15% tax. A 15% service charge might also be added. Double rooms go for $100, including breakfast. American Express, MasterCard, and Visa are accepted.

Luis Tellez at Rancho Encantado, at Bacalar (see "Where to Stay," under "Lago Bacalar," above), is the best source of information about the status of these sites and any new ones. Entry to each site is $2 to $4, and all are free on Sunday. Informational signs at each building within the sites are in Mayan, Spanish, and English. Wear loads of mosquito repellent. The following list of sites is in order if you're driving from Bacalar or Chetumal.

For a map of this area, consult the Yucatán Peninsula map earlier in this chapter.

TOURING THE RUINS WITH A GUIDE   If you're coming to this part of the Yucatán specifically to see the Río Bec ruins, the services of Serge Rìou, "Maya

Lowland Specialist," will probably be indispensable to you. Several years ago young Mr. Rìou visited the Río Bec ruin route on a vacation from France. He fell so in love with the culture, romance, and history of the ruins that he returned to live and learn all that was possible about these little-known ruins. Living in Xpujil, he hiked the forests daily in search of ruins, worked with archaeologists on the trail of new sites, photographed the ruins, attended conferences of Maya specialists, and read everything he could find on Mexican archaeology. Today his encyclopedic knowledge of the nearby ruins makes him the most informed guide. He speaks excellent English and Spanish and charges around $75 to $100 per person a day to guide up to three people to a variety of sites. The higher price is for **Calakmul,** the farthest site from Chetumal. He can arrange necessary permits to unopened sites. You can contact him directly (Apdo. Postal 298, 77000 Chetumal, Q. Roo; ☎ **983/2-4514** or 983/2-1251) or arrange for his services through **Rancho Encantado** at Lago Bacalar (see "Where to Stay," under "Lago Bacalar," above), which has all the necessary types of vehicles, or contact him through the **Holiday Inn** in Chetumal (see "Where to Stay & Dine," under "Chetumal," below).

ADDITIONAL INFORMATION   To make the most of your visit, background reading might include *A Forest of Kings: The Untold Story of the Ancient Maya* by Linda Schele and David Friedel (William Morrow, 1990), *The Blood of Kings: Dynasty and Ritual in Maya Art* by Linda Schele and Mary Ellen Miller (George Braziller, 1968), and *The Maya Cosmos* by David Freidel and Linda Schele (William Morrow, 1993). *Arqueología Mexicana* magazine devoted its July–August 1995 issue to the Quintana Roo portion of the Río Bec ruin route. Last, though it lacks historic and cultural information, and many sites have expanded since it was written, Joyce Kelly's *An Archeological Guide to Mexico's Yucatán Peninsula* (University of Oklahoma, 1993), is the best companion book to have. For a crash course, focus your learning on the meaning of the jaguar, Xibalba (the underworld), and the earth monster.

DZIBANCHÉ

Dzibanché (or Tzibanché) means "place where they write on wood." Exploration began here in 1993, and it opened to the public in late 1994. Scattered over 26 square miles (though only a small portion is excavated), it's both a Preclassic and a Postclassic site (A.D. 300–900) that was occupied for around 700 years.

TEMPLES & PLAZAS   Two enormous adjoining plazas have been cleared. The site shows influence from Río Bec, Petén, and Teotihuacán. **The Temple of the Owl,** on the Plaza de Xibalbá, has a miniature version of Teotihuacán-style *talud tablero* (slant and straight facade) architecture flanking the sides of the main stairway leading to the top with its lintel and entrance to an underground tomb. (Teotihuacán ruins are near Mexico City, but their influence was strong as far as Guatemala.) Despite centuries of an unforgiving wet climate, a wood lintel, in good condition and with a date carving, still supports a partially preserved corbeled arch on top of this building. Inside the temple, a tomb was discovered, making this the second known temple in Mexico built over an underground tomb (the first discovered is the Temple of Inscriptions at Palenque). A diagram of this temple shows interior steps leading from the top, then down inside the pyramid to ground level, just as at Palenque. The stairway is first reached by a deep, well-like drop that held remains of a sacrificial victim and which was sacked during pre-Hispanic times. Uncovered at different levels of the stairwell were a number of beautiful polychromed lidded vessels, one of which has an owl painted on the top handle, with its wings spreading onto the lid. White owls were messengers of the gods of the underworld in the Maya religion. This interior stairway isn't open to the public, but you can clearly see the lintel just behind the entrance to the tomb. Further exploration of the tomb awaits stabilization of interior walls.

Opposite the Temple of the Owl is the **Temple of the Cormorant,** so named after a polychromed drinking vessel found here picturing a cormorant. Here, too, archaeologists have found evidence of an interior tomb similar to the one in the Temple of the Owl, but excavations of it have not begun. Other magnificently preserved pottery pieces found during excavations include an incense burner with an almost three-dimensional figure of the diving god attached to the outside, and another incense burner with an elaborately dressed figure of the god Itzamná attached.

The site also incorporates another section of ruins called **Kinichná** (keen-eech-*nah*), which is about 1½ miles north and is reachable only by a rutted road that's impassable in the rainy season. There, an Olmec-style jade figure was found.

NO ROAD—YET A formal road to these ruins has not been built, but there's a sign pointing to the right turn to Morocoy approximately 18 miles from the Highway 307 turnoff. You follow that paved road, which turns into an unpaved road, and pass the small settlement (not really a town) of Morocoy to another rough dirt road to the right (there's a sign to the ruins there), and follow it for about a mile to the ruin entrance. Ask at Rancho Encantado, near Bacalar (see "Where to Stay," under "Lago Bacalar," above), about the condition of the unpaved portion of road.

KOHUNLICH

Kohunlich (koh-*hoon*-leek), 26 miles from the intersection of highways 186 and 307, dates from around A.D. 100 to 900. Turn left off the road, and the entrance is 5½ miles ahead. From the parking area you enter the grand parklike site, crossing a large and shady ceremonial area flanked by four large conserved pyramidal edifices. Continue walking, and just beyond this grouping you'll come to Kohunlich's famous **Pyramid of the Masks** under a thatched covering. The masks, actually enormous plaster faces, date from around A.D. 500 and are on the facade of the building. Sporting an elongated face and undulating lips, the masks show vestiges of blue and red paint. Note the carving on the pupils, which show a cosmic connection, possibly with the night sun that illuminated the underworld. It's speculated that masks covered much of the facade of this building, which is built in the Río Bec style with rounded corners, a false stairway, and a false temple on the top. At least one theory is that the masks are a composite of several rulers at Kohunlich. During recent excavations of buildings immediately to the left after you enter, two intact pre-Hispanic skeletons and five decapitated heads were uncovered that were once probably used in a ceremonial ritual. To the right after you enter (follow a shady path through the jungle) is another recently excavated plaza. It's thought to have housed elite citizens, due to the high quality of pottery found there and the fine architecture of the rooms. Scholars believe that Kohunlich became overpopulated, leading to its decline. The bathrooms here are the only ones at any site on the route.

CHACAN BACAN

Chacan Bacan (chah-*kahn* bah-*kahn*), which dates from around 200 B.C., was first discovered in 1980 with excavation beginning in 1995. It's scheduled to open sometime in 1999, with 30 to 40 buildings uncovered. The discovery of huge **Olmec-style heads** on its facade should make future digs exciting. The heads, showing from the middle of the skull forward, have helmetlike caps similar in style to the

Maya Construction Styles

Río Bec Style   Found particularly in the states of Campeche and Quintana Roo, and south in Guatemala, the style takes its name from the ruins of Río Bec, located south of Xpuhil on Highway 186 between Chetumal and Escárcega. Río Bec architecture is characterized by roofcombs, which adorn rooftops like lattice-work false fronts. Frequently, doorways are elaborate stonework mouths of Chaac, also called "monster mouths." Steep pyramids are frequently almost cone-shaped, with such narrow stairs leading to the top that they are difficult to climb. Examples of the Río Bec style are at Xpuhil, Becán, Chicaná, and Calakmul. Away from the traditional Río Bec area, roofcombs also appear in several places such as Palenque, Uxmal, and Kabah.

Chenes Style   The baroque examples of Maya architecture, Chenes buildings have facades that are elaborately embellished from top to bottom with separately cut stone pieces, often with many representations of Chaac, the Maya rain god. As with the Río Bec style, doorways are often open mouths of a fierce-looking Chaac with pointed teeth representing the "monster mouth" entrance to Xibalba, the Maya underworld. Though the Chenes heartland is in the states of Campeche and Quintana Roo, Yucatán's ruins also have excellent Chenes-style buildings. Good examples are the Nunnery Annex at Chichén-Itzá, and the high-up doorway on the Temple of the Magician at Uxmal, and at Kabah where 250 Chaac masks cover the stunning facade of the Codz Poop. Chenes, or "well country" style, is the name given to a region that contains many wells or that features this type of architecture.

Puuc Style   The name Puuc refers to a region, a culture, and an architectural style. The Yucatán's only hilly area, south of Mérida, is known as the Puuc (Maya for hills or mountains), and gives the architecture its name. Architecturally elaborate stonework, often in the style of mosaics, generally begins from the top of the doorline to the roofline and includes many masks of Chaac, appearing with an elephant trunklike hook nose. In other places, these masks appear on the facade as well as ornamental corner ends of buildings. Puuc buildings are also embellished with a series of short stone columns, giving the buildings a beautiful, almost Greek appearance.

full multiton Olmec heads unearthed in Veracruz and Tabasco on Mexico's Gulf Coast, where the Olmecs originated. These heads are thought to be older than the figures at both Kohunlich and Balamkú. The exact size of the site hasn't been determined, but it's huge. In a densely forested setting, with thousands of tropical hardwood trees, plants, birds, and wild animals, it's been earmarked as an ecological/touristic center. Though not yet open to the public, it's about 50 miles and a 1½-hour drive from Bacalar. The turnoff (left) to it is at Caoba, where you follow a paved road for about 1½ miles, then turn left on an unmarked path. From the paved portion you can look left and see the uncovered pyramid protruding over the surrounding jungle. Ask Luis Tellez at Rancho Encantado at Lago Bacalar about the accessibility of this site.

XPUJIL

Xpujil (also spelled Xpuhil) means either "cattail" or "forest of kapok trees" and flourished between A.D. 400 and 900. Ahead on the left after you enter, you'll see a rectangular ceremonial platform 6½ feet high and 173 feet long holding three once-ornate buildings. These almost conical edifices resemble the towering ruins of Tikal in Guatemala and rest on a lower building with 12 rooms. Unfortunately, they are so ruined you can only ponder how it might have been. To the right after you enter are two newly uncovered structures, one of which is a large acropolis. From the highway, a small sign on the right points to the site that is just a few yards off the highway and 49 miles from Kohunlich.

BECÁN

Becán (bay-*kahn*), about 4½ miles beyond Xpujil and once surrounded by a moat, means "canyon filled by water" and dates from early Classic to late Postclassic (600 B.C. to A.D. 1200). The moat, which isn't visible today, once had seven bridges leading to the seven cities that were pledged to Becán. Following jungle paths beyond the first visible group of ruins, you'll find at least two recently excavated **acropolises.** Though the site was abandoned by A.D. 850, ceramic remains indicate there may have been a population resurgence between A.D. 900 and 1000, and it was still used as a ceremonial site as late as A.D. 1200. Becán was a governmental and ceremonial center with political sway over at least seven other cities in the area, including Chicanná, Hormiguero, and Payan.

To really understand this site, you need a good guide. But for starters, the first plaza group you see after you enter was the center of grand ceremonies. From the highway you see the backside of a pyramid (Temple 1) with two temples on top. From the highway you can see between the two pyramid-top temples to Temple 4, which is opposite Temple 1. When the high priest appeared through the mouth of the earth monster in the center of Temple 4 (which he reached via a hidden side stairway that's now partly exposed), he was visible from what is now the highway. It's thought that commoners had to watch ceremonies from outside the ceremonial plaza; thus the site was positioned for good viewing purposes. The backside of Temple 4 is believed to have been a civic plaza where rulers sat on stone benches while pronouncing judgments. The second plaza group dates from around A.D. 850 and has perfect twin towers on top, where there's a big platform. Under the platform are 10 rooms that are thought to be related to Xibalba (shee-*bahl*-bah), the underworld. Earth monster faces probably covered this building (and they appeared on other buildings as well). Remains of at least one ball court have been unearthed. Becán is about 4½ miles beyond Xpujil and is visible on the right side of the highway, about half a mile down a rutted road.

CHICANNÁ

Slightly over a mile beyond Becán, on the left side of the highway, is Chicanná, which means "house of the mouth of snakes." Trees loaded with bromeliads shade the central square surrounded by five buildings. The most outstanding edifice features a monster-mouth doorway and an ornate stone facade with more superimposed masks. As you enter the mouth of the earth monster, note that you are walking on a platform which functions as the open jaw of the monster with stone teeth on both sides.

CALAKMUL

This area is both a massive Maya archaeological zone with at least 60 sites and a 178,699-acre rain forest designated in 1989 as the Calakmul Biosphere Reserve, which includes territory in both Mexico and Guatemala.

THE ARCHAEOLOGICAL ZONE   Since 1982, archaeologists have been excavating the ruins of Calakmul, which dates from 100 B.C. to A.D. 900. It's the largest of the area's 60 known sites. Nearly 7,000 buildings have been discovered and mapped. At its zenith at least 60,000 people may have lived around the site, but by the time of the Spanish Conquest of Mexico in 1519, there were fewer than 1,000 inhabitants. Discoveries include more stelae than any other site. By Building 13 is a stelae of a woman dating from A.D. 652. Of the buildings, Temple 3 is the best preserved. In it were found offerings of shells, beads, and polychromed tripod pottery. The tallest, at 178 feet, is Temple 2. From the top of it you can see the outline of the ruins of El Mirador, 30 miles across the forest in Guatemala. Temple 4 charts the line of the sun from June 21 when it falls on the left (north) corner, to September 21 and March 21, when it lines up in the east behind the middle temple on the top of the building, to December 21 when it falls on the right (south) corner. Numerous jade pieces, including spectacular masks, were uncovered here, most of which are on display in the Museo Regional in Campeche. Temple 7 is largely unexcavated except for the top, where in 1984 the most outstanding jade mask yet to be found at Calakmul was uncovered. In *A Forest of Kings,* Linda Schele and David Freidel tell of wars between Calakmul, Tikal, and Naranjo (the latter two in Guatemala) and how Ah-Cacaw, king of Tikal (75 miles south of Calakmul) captured King Jaguar-Paw in A.D. 695 and later Lord Ox-Ha-Te Ixil Ahau, both of Calakmul. From January to May the site is open Tuesday to Sunday from 7am to 7pm. The site gets so wet during the rainy season from June to October that it's best not to go.

CALAKMUL BIOSPHERE RESERVE   Set aside in 1989, this is the peninsula's only high forest *selva,* a rain forest that annually records as much as 16 feet of rain. Among the plants are cactus, epiphytes, and orchids. Endangered animals include the white-lipped peccary, jaguar, and puma. So far more than 250 species of birds have been recorded. At the moment there are no guided tours in the reserve, and no overnight stays or camping are permitted. But a hint of the region can be seen around the ruins. Howler monkeys are often peering down on visitors as they park their cars near the entrance to the ruins.

The turnoff on the left for Calakmul is located approximately 145 miles from the intersection of Highways 186 and 307, just before the village of Conhuas. There's a guard station there where you pay to enter the road/site. From the turnoff it's a 1½-hour drive on a paved, but very narrow and somewhat rutted road that may be difficult during the rainy season from May to October.

BALAMKÚ

Balamkú (bah-lahm-*koo*) was literally snatched from the incredibly destructive hands of looters by Instituto de Antropología e Historia (INAH) archaeologist Florentino García Cruz in October 1990. Amateur archaeologist and guide Serge Rìou was close behind him to photograph the site before looters hit one last time, destroying the head of one of the figures. An uncharted site at the time, it was saved by García, who had been alerted by locals that looters were working there.

Today it's open to the public, and though small, it's worth the time to see it since the facade of one building is among the most unusual on this route. When you reach the clearing, about 2 miles from the highway via a narrow dirt path through the jungle, there are two buildings, one on the right and one on the left. The right

A Driving Caution

Numerous curves in the road make seeing oncoming traffic (what little there is) difficult, and there have been head-on collisions.

building is really three continuous, tall, but narrow, pyramids dating from around A.D. 700. The left building, which dates from around A.D. 400, holds the most interest because of the cross-legged figures resembling those found at Copan, in Honduras. Originally there were four of these regal figures (probably representing kings), seated on crocodiles or frogs above the entrance to the underworld, but looters destroyed two on each end and further disfigured the others.

Still, enough remains to see the beauty; the whole concept of this building, with its molded stucco facade, is of life and death. On the head of each almost three-dimensional figure are the eyes, nose, and mouth of a jaguar figure, followed by the full face of the human figure, then a neck formed by the eyes and nose of another jaguar, and an Olmec-like face on the stomach, its neck decorated by a necklace, then the crossed legs of the figure seated upon a frog or crocodile. The earth monster is represented by a half-snake, half-crocodile animal, all symbols of death, water, and life. The May 1992 issue of *Mexico Desconocido* features the discovery of Balamkú written by Florentino García Cruz.

11 Chetumal

85 miles S of Felipe Carrillo Puerto, 23 miles S of Lago Bacalar

Quintana Roo became a state in 1974, and Chetumal (pop. 170,000) is its capital. While Quintana Roo was still a territory, it was a free-trade zone to encourage trade and immigration between neighboring Guatemala and Belize. The old part of town, down by the river (Río Hondo), has a Caribbean atmosphere and wooden buildings, but the newer parts are modern Mexican. There is lots of noise and heat, so your best plan would be not to stay—it's not a particularly interesting or friendly town. It is, however, worth a detour to see the wonderful **Museo de la Cultural Maya,** especially if your trip involves seeing the Río Bec ruin route described above.

ESSENTIALS
GETTING THERE & DEPARTING

BY PLANE   **Aerocaribe** (Mexicana; ☎ **983/2-6336** or 983/2-6675) has daily flights to and from Cancún and flights several times weekly between Chetumal and the ruins of Tikal in Guatemala. **Avio Quintana** (☎ **983/2-9692**) flies Monday to Friday to Cancún in a 19-passenger plane for around $50 one way.

BY CAR   It's a 2½-hour ride from Felipe Carrillo Puerto. If you're heading to Belize you'll need a passport and special auto insurance, which you can buy at the border. You can't take a rental car over the border, however.

To get to the ruins of Tikal in Guatemala you must first go through Belize to the border crossing at Ciudad Melchor de Mencos.

BY BUS   The bus station of **Autotransportes del Caribe** (no telephone) is 20 blocks from the town center on Insurgentes at Niños Héroes. Buses go to Cancún, Tulum, Playa del Carmen, Puerto Morelos, Mérida, Campeche, Villahermosa, and Mexico City. **Omniturs del Caribe** (☎ **983/2-7889** or 983/2-8001) has deluxe buses to Mérida.

To Belize: Two companies make the run from Chetumal (through Corozal and Orange Walk) to Belize City. **Batty's Bus Service** runs 10 buses per day, and **Venus Bus Lines** (☎ **983/2-2132** in Corozal) has seven daily buses. Though it's a short distance from Chetumal to Corozal, it may take as much as 1½ hours, depending on how long it takes the bus to pass through Customs and Immigration. (See "Onward from Chetumal," below, for more Customs information.)

To Limones, Majahual, and Xcalak: Two buses a day run between these destinations.

BY FERRY   The docks are ready, but the new ferry was too big and ferry service has been delayed between Chetumal and the Xcalak/Majahual Peninsula. However, check with the **State Tourism Office** in Chetumal (☎ **983/20855;** fax 983/2-5073) about the status of this service. To date, there is only passenger service aboard a 30-passenger ferry that takes you 6 miles north of Xcalak; the cost is $5 each way.

VISITOR INFORMATION

The State Tourism Office (☎ **983/2-0266** or 983/2-0855; fax 983/2-5073 or 983/2-6097) is at avenida Hidalgo 22, at the corner of Carmen Ochoa.

ORIENTATION

The telephone **area code** is **983.** Chetumal has many "no left turn" streets, with hawk-eyed traffic policemen at each one. Be alert—they love to nail visitors and may even motion you into making a traffic or pedestrian violation, then issue a ticket, or take a bribe instead.

You'll arrive following Obregón into town. Niños Héroes is the other main cross street. When you reach it, turn left to find the hotels mentioned below.

A MUSEUM NOT TO MISS

Chetumal is really the gateway to Belize or to the Río Bec ruins, and not a touristically interesting city. But it's worth a detour to Chetumal to see the **Museo de la Cultura Maya.** If you can arrange it, see the museum before you tour the Río Bec ruins, since it will all make more sense after getting it in perspective here.

Museo de la Cultura Maya. Av. Héroes s/n. ☎ **983/2-6838.** Admission $2; children $1. Tues–Thurs 9am–7pm, Fri and Sat 9am–8pm, Sun 9am–2pm. It's on the left between Colón and Gandhi, 8 blocks from av. Obregón, past the Holiday Inn.

Sophisticated, impressive, and informative, this new museum unlocks the complex world of the Maya. Push a button and an illustrated description appears explaining the medicinal and domestic uses of plants with their Maya and scientific names, another describes the five social classes of the Maya by the way they dress, and yet another shows how the beauty signs of cranial deformation, crossed eyes, and facial scarification were achieved. An enormous screen flashes moving pictures taken from an airplane flying over more than a dozen Maya sites from Mexico to Honduras. Another large television shows the architectural variety of Maya pyramids and how they were probably built. Then a walk on a glass floor takes you over representative ruins in the Maya world, clearly showing the variety of pyramidal shapes and particular sites. And, finally, one of the most impressive sections is the three-story stylized sacred ceiba tree, which the Maya believed represented the underworld (Xibalba) (on the bottom floor of the museum), earth (the middle floor of the museum), and the 13 heavens (the third floor of the museum). From this you'll have a better idea of the significance of the symbolism on the pyramids in the Maya world. Plan no less than 2 hours here. Even then, especially if your interest is high, you may want to take a break and return—there's a lot to see and learn. What a museum!

WHERE TO STAY & DINE

Hotel Holiday Inn Caribe. Niños Héroes 171, 77000 Chetumal, Q. Roo. ☎ **800/ 465-4329** in the U.S., or 983/2-1100. Fax 983/2-1676. 75 units. A/C TV TEL. $60–$85 double. AE, DC, MC, V. Free parking.

This modern hotel (formerly the Hotel Continental) across from the central market was remodeled in 1995 and became a Holiday Inn. The hotel has a good-size pool (a blessing in muggy Chetumal) and a good restaurant. The hotel is only 2 blocks from the Museo de la Cultura Maya. You can contact Río Bec specialist Serge Rìou through the travel agency here. To find it as you enter the town on Obregón, turn left on Niños Héroes, go 6 blocks and look for the hotel on the right, opposite the market.

Hotel Nachancan. Calz. Veracruz 379, 77000 Chetumal, Q. Roo. ☎ **983/2-3232.** 20 units. A/C TV. $20 double, $28 suite. No credit cards.

Opposite the new market, this hotel offers rooms that are plain but clean and comfortable. A restaurant is off the lobby. It's relatively convenient to the bus station, but not close enough to walk if you arrive by bus. It is, however, within walking distance of the Museo de la Cultura Maya. To find it from avenida Obregón, turn left on Calzada Veracruz and follow it for at least 10 blocks; the hotel will be on the right.

ONWARD FROM CHETUMAL

From Chetumal you have several choices. The Maya ruins of Lamanai are an easy day trip into Belize if you have transportation (not a rental car); you can explore the Río Bec ruin route north of the city; and north of Bacalar you can cut diagonally across the peninsula to Mérida or retrace your steps to Cancún. You can take Highway 186 west to Escarcega, Villahermosa, and Palenque, but I don't recommend it and neither does the U.S. State Department: It's a long, hot, and lonely trip on a highway that is often riddled with potholes after you cross into Campeche state. Permanent "zona de deslave" signs warn motorists that parts of the roadbed are missing entirely or are so badly dipped they might cause an accident. Road conditions improve from time to time, but annual rains cause constant problems. And from time to time bandits have robbed travelers. At the Campeche state line there's a military guard post with drug-sniffing dogs; every vehicle is searched. A military guard post at the Reforma intersection just before Bacalar requires motorists to present the identification you used to enter Mexico (birth certificate or passport), plus your tourist permit. Other photo identification may be required, as well as information on where you're staying or where you're headed. The whole procedure should take only minutes.

Mérida & the Maya Cities   6

Ask most people about the Yucatán, and they think of Cancún and the Caribbean coast, Chichén-Itzá, and perhaps Uxmal. In fact, there's so much to do in the Yucatán, and such variety, that you'll find something different and exciting at every stop. One day you can be climbing a pyramid, another day descending into a cave or cenote (deep natural well), another day walking on a deserted beach (and dancing in the streets in Mérida that night), and the next day heading out in a small boat to pay a visit to a giant colony of pink flamingos. The Yucatecan people are warm and helpful, and their way of life is a fascinating mix of Mexican and Caribbean cultures—with a strong dose of Maya heritage.

EXPLORING THE YUCATÁN'S MAYA HEARTLAND

The best way to see the Yucatán is by car. The terrain is flat, the highways and towns are laid out in a simple manner, there is little traffic on the highways, and the main roads are in great shape. Off the beaten path, the roads are narrow and rough, but hey—we're talking rental cars. Rentals are pricey compared with the U.S., but some promotional deals are available. See "By Car," in the Mérida section below. Regular buses ply the roads between the main towns, and there are plenty of tour buses going to the ruins—but buses to out-of-the-way destinations are much less common than in the rest of Mexico. One giant bus company (ADO) controls almost all the first-class bus service. The key to comfortable bus travel is air-conditioning, and this is the main difference between first and second class.

The Yucatán is *tierra caliente* (the hotlands). The coolest weather is from December to February; the hottest is from May to June when the air is still, and to a lesser degree from July to October, due to the rainy season. September and October can go either way. Never travel in this region without sunblock and mosquito repellent! High season is seldom as crowded in the interior of the peninsula as in Cancún, and most hotels have dropped the two-tiered pricing system. Even in the off-season, tourism from Europe is heavy from May to August (a fact that astounds most Yucatecans), and July and August are the traditional vacation months for Mexicans—when the residents of Mérida flock to the the port of Progreso.

From the many available options, here's my pick of essential stops in Yucatán:

MÉRIDA   There's a lot to do in this vibrant and tropical-style colonial city; it's the place to buy hammocks, guayaberas, Panama hats, and native embroidered dresses, or *huipils.*

CHICHÉN-ITZÁ & VALLADOLID   These two towns 25 miles apart are about midway between Mérida and Cancún. It's about 2 hours by car from Mérida to Chichén on the new toll road, or *autopista.* You can spend a day at the beautifully restored ruins, then stay at one of the nearby hotels—or drive 25 miles south to Valladolid, a quiet but charming colonial town with a pleasant central square. Valladolid features two eerie but accessible cenotes, and the spectacular ruins at Ekbalam are only 25 miles to the north. Also nearby is the Río Lagartos nature preserve, teeming with flamingos and other native birds that shelter there.

CELESTÚN NATIONAL WILDLIFE REFUGE   This flamingo sanctuary wetlands reserve is an offbeat sand-street fishing village on the Gulf coast, a 1½-hour drive from Mérida. Plan a long day, with a very early start. Travelers looking for solitude might find this a welcome respite for a week.

DZIBILCHALTÚN   This Maya site, now a national park, is located 9 miles north of Mérida along the Progreso Road. Here you'll find a number of pre-Hispanic structures, nature trails, and the new Museum of the Maya. Make this a half-day trip in the cool of the morning.

PROGRESO   A modern city and Gulf coast beach escape 21 miles north of Mérida, Progreso has a beautiful oceanfront drive and a wide beach lined with coconut palms that's popular on the weekends. Plan a full-day trip if you like beaches, but there's not much else to see.

UXMAL   Smaller than Chichén, but architecturally more striking and mysterious. It's about 50 miles to the south of Mérida and can be seen in a day. Several other nearby sites comprise the Puuc route, and can be explored on the following day. It's also possible, though a bit rushed, to see Uxmal and the other ruins on a 1-day trip by special excursion bus from Mérida. Sunday is a good day to go, since admission is free to the archaeological sites.

CAMPECHE   This beautiful walled colonial city has been so meticulously restored that it's a delight just to stroll down the streets. Campeche is about 3 hours southwest of Mérida in the direction of Palenque; a full day should give you enough time to see its architectural highlights and museums.

1 Mérida: Gateway to the Maya Heartland

900 miles E of Mexico City; 200 miles W of Cancún

Mérida is the capital of the state of Yucatán and has been the dominant city in the region since the Spanish Conquest. The colonial historic center is large but easy to navigate. Mérida is also the only city in the interior that has a nightlife to speak of, and it's more varied and authentic than Cancún's. People here know how to have a good time; there's something happening every night, making Mérida the preferred place to stay overnight while making day trips to nearby attractions.

ESSENTIALS

GETTING THERE & DEPARTING   By Plane   Aeromexico and **Mexicana** have direct nonstop flights from Miami. **Aviateca** has a direct nonstop from

Houston. Otherwise, you will have to get here through Cancún, Cozumel, or Mexico City. **Mexicana** (☎ **99/24-6633** or 99/24-6910) flies from Mexico City. **Aeromexico** (☎ **99/27-9277** or 99/27-9433) flies to and from Cancún and Mexico City. **Aerocaribe** (☎ **99/28-6786**), a Mexicana affiliate, provides service to and from Cozumel, Cancún, Oaxaca, Tuxtla Gutiérrez, San Cristóbal, Veracruz, Villahermosa, and points in Central America. **Taesa** (☎ **99/46-1826** at the airport) flies in from Monterrey and Mexico City. **Aviateca** (☎ **99/46-1312**) flies from Guatemala City. **Aviacsa** (☎ **99/26-9087**) provides service from Cancún, Monterrey, Villahermosa, Tuxtla Gutiérrez, Tapachula, Oaxaca, and Mexico City. Taxis to and from the city to the airport run about $6.

By Car   Highway 180 from Cancún, Chichén-Itzá, or Valladolid enters Mérida at calle 65, past the market and within 1 block of the Plaza Mayor. **Highway 261** from Uxmal (via Muna and Uman) becomes avenida Itzáes; if you arrive by 261, turn right on calle 59 (first street after the zoo). If you arrive from Uxmal via Ticul and the ruins of Mayapán, you can get to Highway 180 into Mérida from the town of Kanasín.

A traffic loop or *periférico* encircles Mérida, making it possible to skirt the city and head for a nearby city or site. Directional signs are generally good into the city, but going around the city on the loop requires constant vigilance.

The federal highway (carretera federal) between Mérida and Cancún is labeled 180. The trip takes 5 to 6 hours, and the road is in decent shape. There is a new four-lane divided **toll road** (known as the *cuota* or *autopista*) that parallels highway 180. It starts at the town of Kantunil, 35 miles east of Mérida. By avoiding small towns and a multitude of annoying speed bumps, the autopista cuts up to 2 hours from the journey between Mérida and Cancún; one-way tolls cost about $20. See "En Route to Uxmal," below, at the end of the Mérida section, for suggested routes from Mérida.

By Bus   The first-class bus station, **CAME,** is on calle 70, between calles 69 and 71 (see "City Layout," below). When you get there you'll see the names and logos of a number of different bus lines—ADO, Premier, Expresso, Maya de Oro, Linea Dorada—these all belong to the same company. To buy a ticket, find your destination on the big board above the ticket counter and go to the ticket agent directly below it. The ticket agent might give you a couple of options with different prices for either first class or deluxe. The main difference between the two is that deluxe has more legroom; both are air-conditioned. Unless it's a really long ride, I choose the bus that has the most convenient departure time. Tickets can be purchased in advance.

To/from Chichén-Itzá: Four buses per day plus all the *de paso* buses. Also, check out tours operating from the hotels in Mérida and Valladolid.

To/from Valladolid and Cancún: There is a bus every hour.

To/from Playa del Carmen, Tulum, and Chetumal: There are 10 departures per day for Playa del Carmen; three for Tulum; four for Chetumal. **Caribe Express** is the only non-affiliated, first-class bus line, and it has service to Chetumal four times per day. Buses leave from the second-class bus station (see below).

To/from Campeche: There is service to Campeche every hour between 6am and 10pm

To/from Palenque and San Cristóbal de las Casas: There is first-class service to Palenque twice daily.

For shorter trips, such as to Uxmal, go to the **second-class bus station,** next block over, on calle 68 between calles 69 and 71.

To/from Uxmal: Four buses per day. The last departure from Uxmal leaves before the popular English version of the nightly sound-and-light show. You can hook up with various tour buses through most hotels or any travel agent/tour operator in town. There's also one bus per day that combines Uxmal with the other sites to the south (Kabah, Sayil, Labná, and Xlapak route—known as the Puuc route) and does the whole round trip in a day. It stops for 2 hours at Uxmal and 30 minutes at each of the other sites. Tour bus companies cover this route as well.

To/from Progreso, Dzibilchaltún, and Celestún: Buses to these places depart from the **Progreso Station** at calle 62 no. 524, between calles 65 and 67.

ORIENTATION   Arriving by Plane   Mérida's airport is 8 miles from the city center on the southwestern outskirts of town where Highway 180 enters the city. The airport has desks for renting a car, reserving a hotel room, and getting tourist information.

Taxi tickets to town are sold outside the airport doors, under the covered walkway. A **colectivo** (group van or minibus) ticket is less expensive, but you'll need to wait for a group of five to assemble. Colectivos are $6; private taxis, $2.

City bus no. 79 ("Aviación") operates between the town center and the airport, but the buses do not have frequent service. Other city buses run along avenida Itzáes, just outside the airport precincts, heading for downtown.

Visitor Information   You'll find two sources of tourist information: One is run by the city, the other by the state. Each has different materials. The principal **state office** is the downtown branch in the Teatro Peón Contreras, on calle 60 between calles 57 and 59 (☎ **99/24-9290**). It's open Monday through Sunday from 8am to 8pm, as are the information booths at the airport (☎ **99/46-1300**), the bus station, and on calle 62 next to the Palacio Municipal. Mérida's **visitor information office** is on calle 59 between calles 60 and 62 (☎ **99/23-0883**). Hours are from 9am to 2pm and from 4 to 8pm.

City Layout   Mérida has the standard layout for towns in the Yucatán: streets running north-south are even numbers; those running east-west are odd numbers. The numbering begins on the north and the east sides of town so that if you are walking on an odd-numbered street and the even numbers of the cross streets are increasing, then you know that you are heading west; likewise, if you are on an even-numbered street and are crossing streets with odd numbers that are increasing,, then you know you are going south.

Another useful tip is that address numbers don't tell you anything about what cross street to look for, so you really can't be sure of where your destination is on the city grid. This is why in addition to an address, you will often see cross streets listed, usually like this: "calle 60 no. 549 x 71 y 73." The "x" is actually a multiplication sign—a short way of saying the word "por" (meaning "by") and "y" ("and"). Thus, you know that the place is on calle 60 between calles 71 and 73.

The center of town is the bright, busy **Plaza Mayor** (sometimes called the Plaza Principal, but most often referred to simply as *El Centro*). It's bordered by calles 60, 62, 61, and 63. The Plaza always has a big, cheerful crowd in and around it, but it's really hopping on Sundays—when the city closes off the crossing streets to traffic, and the Plaza becomes an instant festival. (See the box on "Festivals & Special Events in Mérida," below.) Around the Plaza Mayor are the cathedral, the Palacio de Gobierno (state government headquarters), the Palacio Municipal, and the Casa de Montejo. Within a few blocks are several smaller plazas, the University of Yucatán, and the bustling market district.

Mérida's most fashionable district is the broad tree-lined boulevard called Paseo de Montejo and its surrounding neighborhood. The Paseo de Montejo begins 7 blocks northwest of the Plaza Mayor and runs north-south. There are a number of trendy restaurants and a few clubs here, some gorgeous mansions built during the boom times of the henequen industry, the new international hotels, and offices for various banks and airlines. Where the Paseo intersects avenida Colón, you'll find the two fanciest hotels in town: the Hyatt and the Fiesta Americana.

GETTING AROUND   By Car   In general, reserve your car in advance from the U.S. to get the best weekly rates. During peak high season (December to January), you may be able to get a better price in Mérida than in Cancún; check prices for both. Rental cars are expensive, averaging $40 to $90 per day. If you want to rent for only a day or two, you can avoid the high cost of parking lots in Mérida. These *estacionamentos* charge one price for the night and double that if you leave your car for the following day. Many hotels offer free parking, but make sure they include daytime parking in the price. The local rental companies are very competitive and have promotional deals you can get only if you are there on the spot. When comparing, make sure it's apples to apples; ask if the price quote includes the IVA tax and insurance coverage. (Practically everybody offers unlimited free mileage.) For tips on saving money on car rentals by renting in advance from your home country see "Getting Around," in chapter 3. Also, you may want to look into a special rental deal offered by Mayaland Tours if you stay at its hotels in Chichén-Itzá and Uxmal. Ask about pickup or drop-off in Cancún if your trip starts or ends there. For information contact Mayaland Resorts, av. Colón 502, 97000 Mérida, Yuc.; ☎ 800/235-4079 in the U.S., or 99/25-2122; fax 99/25-7022.

By Taxi   Taxis are easy to come by and are cheaper than in Cancún, but still expensive by Mexican standards.

By Bus   Bus travel within the heart of downtown isn't necessary, since everything is within walking distance of the main plaza. However, to get to the large, shady Parque Centenario on the western outskirts of town, a bus is available. Look for a white bus of the same name ("Centenario") on calle 64. Most buses on calle 59 go to Mérida's ambitious zoological park, or to the Museum of Natural History. "Central" buses stop at the bus station, and any bus marked "Mercado" or "Correo" (post office) will take you to the market district. For quick trips, take the Volkswagen minivans (usually painted white) that run out in several directions from the main plaza along simple routes. Known as combis, colectivos, or *peseros,* they're easy to spot along the side streets next to the plaza.

FAST FACTS: Mérida

American Express   Paseo de Montejo no. 492 (☎ 99/42-8200).

Area Code   The telephone area code is **99.**

Bookstore   The Librería Dante, calle 60 at calle 57 (☎ **99/24-9522**), has a selection of English-language cultural-history books on Mexico. It's open Monday through Friday from 8am to 9:30pm, Saturday from 8am to 2pm and 5 to 9pm, and Sunday from 10am to 2pm and 4 to 8pm.

Climate   From November through February, the weather can be chilly and windy. In other months, it's just hot, especially during the day. Rain can occur anytime of year but usually occurs in the July-to-November rainy season and follows the pattern of afternoon tropical showers.

Festivals & Special Events in Mérida

Many Mexican cities offer weekend concerts in the park, but Mérida surpasses them all with almost-daily public events, most of which are free and fun to watch.

Sunday   Each Sunday from 9am to 9pm, there's a fair called Domingo en Mérida (Sunday in Mérida). The main plaza and a section of calle 60 from El Centro to Plaza Santa Lucía are blocked off from traffic. This was done by initiative of the municipal government, which wanted to get tourists to stay in the city longer, but the local populace quickly made the party its own. Parents come with their children to stroll around and take in the scene. There are booths selling food and drink, along with a lively little flea market and used-book fair. There are children's art classes, educational booths, and concerts of all kinds. At 11am in front of the Palacio del Gobierno, musicians play everything from jazz to classical and folk music. Also at 11am, the police orchestra performs Yucatecan tunes at the Santa Lucía park. At 11:30am, you'll find bawdy comedy acts at the Parque Cepeda Peraza (Parque Hidalgo) on calle 60 at calle 59. There's a lull in mid-afternoon, and then the plaza fills up again as people walk around the plaza and visit with friends. Around 7pm in front of the *Ayuntamiento,* a large band starts playing mambos, rumbas, and cha-cha-chas with great enthusiasm; you may see a thousand people dancing there in the street. Then everyone is invited into the Ayuntamiento to see folk ballet dancers reenact a typical Yucatecan wedding. All events are free.

Monday   The City Hall Folklore Ballet and the Police Jaranera Band perform at 9pm in front of the Palacio Municipal. The music and dancing celebrate the Vaquerías feast, which occurs after the branding of cattle on Yucatecan haciendas. Among the featured performers are dancers with trays of bottles or filled glasses on their heads—a sight to see. Admission is free.

Tuesday   The theme for the Tuesday entertainment, held at 9pm in Parque Santiago, on calle 59 at calle 72, is Musical Memories. Music includes popular South American and Mexican as well as North American songs from the 1940s. Admission is free.

Wednesday   At 9pm in the Teatro Peón Contreras on calle 60 at calle 57, the University of Yucatán Folklore Ballet presents "Yucatán and Its Roots." Admission is $5.

Thursday   Typical Yucatecan music and dance are presented at the Serenata in Parque Santa Lucía at 9pm. Admission is free.

Friday   At 9pm in the patio of the University of Yucatán, calle 60 at calle 57, the University of Yucatán Folklore Ballet often performs typical regional dances from the Yucatán. Admission is free.

Saturday   "Noche Mexicana" at the park at the beginning of Paseo de Montejo begins at 9pm. It features several performances of various kinds of traditional music and dance of Mexico. Some of the performers are amateurs who acquit themselves reasonably well; others are professional musicians and dancers who thoroughly know their craft. There are some food stands selling very good antojitos, as well as drinks and ice cream.

Also, on the evening of the first Friday of each month, Dennis LaFoy of the **Yucatán Trails Travel Agency** (☎ **99/28-2582**) invites those in the English-speaking community to a casual get-together. They usually gather at the Hotel Mérida Misión Park Plaza on calle 60, across from the Hotel Casa del Balam, but call Dennis to confirm the location.

Complaints   Tourists who encounter difficulties with public officials such as police officers can call ☎ **01-800/0-0148** in Mexico to report incidents. If you have problems with Customs officials at the airport, report them to SEDOCAM, which is the Comptroller and Administrative Development Secretariat (☎ **01-800/0-0148** in Mexico).

Consulates   The **American consulate** is at Paseo de Montejo no. 453 and avenida Colón (☎ **99/25-5409** or 25-5011). The **British Vice-Consulate** is at calle 53 no. 498 at the corner of calle 58 (☎ **99/28-6152**). Office hours are 9am to 1pm. The vice-consul fields questions about travel to Belize as well as matters British.

Currency Exchange   Most banks in Mérida are a mess to deal with and do not offer outstanding exchange rates to offset the hassle. More times than not, casas de cambio in Mérida offer better rates and no wait. Try **Mérida Consultoria Finex** (☎ **99/24-1842**), open every day from 8am to 8pm. It is in the Parque Hidalgo, next door to the Caribe Hotel.

Hospitals   **Hospital O'Horan** is on avenida Itzáes at avenida Jacinto Canek (☎ **99/24-4111**), north of the Parque Centenario.

Post Office   Mérida's main post office (correo) is located in the midst of the market at the corner of calles 65 and 56. A branch office is located at the airport. Both are open Monday through Friday from 8am to 7pm and Saturday from 9am to 12pm.

Seasons   There are two high seasons: one in July and August, when the weather is very hot and humid, and when Mexicans most commonly take their vacations; and another between November 15 and Easter Sunday, when northerners flock to the Yucatán to escape winter weather, and the weather is significantly cooler.

Spanish Classes   Maya scholars, Spanish teachers, and archaeologists from the United States are among the students at the **Centro Idiomas del Sureste,** calle 14 no. 106 at calle 25, Colonia México, 97000 Mérida, Yuc. (☎ **99/26-1155;** fax 99/26-9020). The school has two locations: in the Colonia México, a northern residential district, and on calle 66 at calle 57 in the downtown area. Students live with local families or in hotels; sessions running 2 weeks or longer are available for all levels of proficiency and areas of interest. For brochures and applications, contact Chloe Conaway de Pacheco, Directora.

Telephones   There are long-distance *casetas* at the airport, the bus station, at calle 57 corner with calle 60, calle 59, corner with calle 62, and at calle 60 between calles 55 and 53. To use the public Ladatel phones, buy a card from just about any newsstand or store. (To call long-distance from a Ladatel phone, you'll also need a separate long-distance card.) Also see "Telephone/Fax" in "Fast Facts: Mexico," in chapter 3.

EXPLORING MÉRIDA

In addition to the special events and festivals enumerated in the box above, Mérida has a number of attractions, most of which are within walking distance of each other in the downtown area.

WALKING TOUR
Mérida

Start: Plaza Mayor.
Finish: Palacio Cantón.
Time: Allow approximately 2 hours, not counting time for browsing or refreshment.
Best Times: Wednesday through Sunday before noon.
Worst Times: Monday, when the Anthropology Museum is closed; Tuesday when the Museo de Arte Contemporáneo is closed.

Downtown Mérida is a great example of a lowland colonial city. There is a casual, homey feel to the town. Buildings lack the severe baroque features that characterize central Mexico; most are finished in stucco and painted in tropical colors. Mérida's gardens add to this relaxed, tropical atmosphere. The gardeners here do not seek the kind of garden where all is exactly in its place and is obviously a display of the gardener's control over nature. Natural exuberance is the ideal, with plants growing in a wild profusion that disguises human intervention. A perfect example is the patio in the Palacio Montejo, which is one of our first stops. Mérida's plazas are a slightly different version of this aesthetic: Unlike the highland plazas, with their carefully sculpted trees and shrubs, Mérida's squares are typically built around giant laurel trees, surrounded by beds of native ornamentals. Usually you'll see a part of the plaza dedicated to a small, thoroughly manicured area or topiary showing that the gardener could work in the highland style, if he chose. Begin this walk at the:

1. **Plaza Mayor.** It has had many names over the years; this one finally stuck for its simplicity. Simpler still is El Centro, which is how most people refer to it. Even when there's no formal event in progress, the park is full of people sitting on the benches talking with friends or taking a casual stroll. A plaza like El Centro is a great advantage for a big city such as Mérida; there's a personal feel and a sense of community that combat the modern bustle of urban life. Notice the beautiful scale and composition of the major buildings surrounding the plaza. The most prominent of these is the:

2. **Cathedral.** Built between 1561 and 1598, it's celebrating its 400th anniversary with concerts and fiestas all the way into 1999. Much of the stone in the cathedral's walls came from the ruined buildings of Tihó, the former Maya city. This building, too, was once finished with stucco, and you can still see where it remains in places. People like the look of the unfinished walls, which show the cathedral's age. Notice how the two top levels of the bell towers are built off-center from their bases—an uncommon feature. Inside, decoration is sparse, with altars draped in fabric colorfully embroidered like a Maya woman's shift. The most notable feature is a picture over the right side door of Ah Kukum Tutul Xiú visiting the Montejo camp.

    To the left of the main altar is a smaller shrine with a curious statue of Jesus recovered from a burned-out church in the town of Ichmul. The figure was carved in the 1500s by a local artist from a miraculous tree that was hit by lightning and burst into flames—but did not char. The statue blistered as the flames destroyed the church, but the figure of Jesus survived the fire. In 1645 it was moved to the cathedral in Mérida, where the locals named it Cristo de las Ampollas (Christ of the Blisters). Take a look in the side chapel (open from 8 to 11am and 4:30 to 7pm), which contains a life-size diorama of the Last Supper. The Mexican Jesus is covered with prayer crosses brought by supplicants asking for intercession.

To the right (south) of the cathedral is the:

3. **Museo de Arte Contemporáneo Ateneo de Yucatán (MACAY)** (☎ **99/28-3236**). The city's contemporary art museum is housed in the former seminary on the site of the archbishop's palace. The palace was torn down during the Mexican Revolution in 1915, but the remaining building is a stately architectural gem. Inside its two stories, built around a patio, 17 exhibition rooms show works by contemporary artists from the Yucatán and around the world. Nine of the rooms hold the museum's permanent collection, while eight rooms showcase changing exhibits. One area includes a display of the building's history and Yucatecan embroidery. It's open Wednesday through Monday from 10am to 6pm (closed Tuesday). Admission $2.50; free Sunday. On the south side of the Plaza Mayor is the:

4. **Palacio Montejo (Casa de Montejo).** Conquering the Yucatán was the Montejo family business, begun by Francisco Montejo the Elder and continued by his son and his nephew, also named Francisco. Construction of the house started in 1542 under Francisco Montejo El Mozo, ("The Younger"; the elder Montejo's illegitimate son). Bordering the entrance is a politically incorrect figure of the conqueror standing on the heads of the vanquished—borrowed, perhaps, from the pre-Hispanic custom of portraying victorious Maya kings treading on their defeated foes. The posture of the conquistador—and his expression of wide-eyed dismay—makes him less imposing than perhaps he would have wished. This building is now occupied by a bank, and you can enter the courtyard and see for yourself what a charming residence it must have been for the descendants of the Montejos, who lived here until as recently as the 1970s. If we continue circling the plaza in the same direction, on the west side, facing the cathedral is the:

5. **Palacio Municipal (City Hall).** More commonly known as the *Ayuntamiento,* with its charming clock tower, here you can look out over the plaza and see the hall that serves for public meetings of the city council. On the north side of the Plaza Mayor is the:

6. **Palacio de Gobierno,** dating from 1892. Large murals painted by the Meridiano artist Fernando Pacheco Castro between 1971 and 1973 decorate the interior walls. Scenes from Maya and Mexican history abound, and the painting over the stairway depicts the Maya spirit with ears of sacred corn, the "sunbeams of the gods." Nearby is a painting of the mustachioed Lázaro Cárdenas, who as president in 1938 expropriated 17 foreign oil companies and was hailed as a Mexican liberator. The palace is open Monday through Saturday from 8am to 8pm and Sunday from 9am to 5pm.

🌀 **TAKE A BREAK**   Revive your batteries with a cup of coffee and some pastries or a bolillo from the **Pan Montejo** on the southwest side of the plaza on the corner of calles 63 and 62. Add a glass of fresh orange or papaya juice from Jugos California next door, take a seat at the plaza, and enjoy the morning sun.

EXPLORING CALLE 60   Continuing north from the Plaza Mayor up calle 60, you'll see many of Mérida's old churches and little parks. Several stores catering to tourists along calle 60 sell gold-filigree jewelry, pottery, clothing, and folk art. A stroll along this street leads to the Parque Santa Ana and continues to the fashionable boulevard Paseo de Montejo and its Museo Regional de Antropología. On your right as you leave the northeast corner of the Plaza, turn right on calle 61 for a block to the corner of calle 61 and calle 58 and the:

7. **Museo de la Ciudad.** Occupying a former convent and hospital, the museum collection relates the city's past in the form of photographs, drawings, and dioramas. It's open Tuesday through Saturday from 9am to 8pm, Sunday 9am to 1pm. Admission is $2. Backtrack to calle 60; ahead on your right is the:

8. **Teatro Daniel de Ayala.** This theater offers a busy schedule of performing artists from around the world. Inquire within. A few steps beyond and across the street is the:

9. **Parque Cepeda Peraza (Parque Hidalgo).** Named for the 19th-century general Manuel Cepeda Peraza, the parque was part of Montejo's original city plan. Small outdoor restaurants front hotels on the parque, making it a popular stopping-off place at any time of day.

TAKE A BREAK Any of the several outdoor restaurants on the Parque Cepeda Peraza makes an inviting respite. My favorite is **Giorgio,** where you can claim a table and write postcards; barter for hammocks, amber jewelry, and baskets displayed by wandering artisans; or just watch the people go by. It's in front of the Gran Hotel.

Bordering Parque Cepeda Peraza across calle 59 is the:

10. **Iglesia de Jesús, or El Tercer Orden (the Third Order).** Built by the Jesuit order in 1618, this is the favorite spot in Mérida for getting hitched. You might come across a wedding in progress. The entire block on which the church stands belonged to the Jesuits, who are traditionally known as great educators, and their schools developed into the Universidad de Yucatán. Walk east on calle 59, 5 blocks past the Parque Cepeda Peraza and the church, and you'll see the former:

11. **Convento de la Mejorada.** This convent is a late-1600s work by the Franciscans. While here, go half a block farther on calle 59 to the Museo Regional de Artes Populares (see "Crafts," below). Backtrack to calle 60 and turn north. Just beyond the church (Iglesia de Jesús) is the:

12. **Parque de la Madre (Parque Morelos).** The park contains a modern statue of the Madonna and Child; the statue is a copy of the work by Renoir that stands in the Luxembourg Gardens in Paris. Beyond the Parque de la Madre and across the pedestrian way is:

13. **Teatro Peón Contreras.** This enormous beige edifice was designed by Italian architect Enrico Deserti in the early years of this century. In one corner you'll see a branch of the State Tourist Information Office facing the Parque de la Madre. The main theater entrance, with its Carrara marble staircase and frescoed dome, is a few steps farther. Domestic and international performers appear here frequently. On the west side of calle 60, at the corner of calle 57, is the:

14. **Universidad de Yucatán.** The university was founded in the 19th century by Felipe Carrillo Puerto with the help of General Cepeda Peraza. The founding is illustrated by a fresco (1961) by Manuel Lizama.

A block farther on your left, past the Hotel Mérida Misión Park Inn, is the:

15. **Parque Santa Lucía.** Surrounded by an arcade on the north and west sides, the park once was where visitors first alighted in Mérida after arriving in their stagecoaches. On Sunday, Parque Santa Lucía holds a used-book sale and small swap meet, and several evenings a week it hosts popular entertainment. On Thursday nights performers present Yucatecan songs and poems. A block west from the parque on calle 55 at the corner of calle 62 is:

Walking Tour—Mérida

1. Plaza Mayor
2. Cathedral
3. Museo Contemporáneo
4. Palacio Montejo
5. Palacio Municipal
6. Palacio de Gobierno
7. Museo de la Ciudad
8. Teatro Daniel de Ayala
9. Parque Cepeda Peraza
10. Iglesia de Jesús
11. Convento de la Mejorada
12. Parque de la Madre
13. Teatro Peón Contreras
14. Universidad de Yucatán
15. Parque Santa Lucía
16. Biblioteca Cepeda Peraza
17. Iglesia de Santa Lucía
18. Parque Santa Ana
19. Paseo de Montejo
20. Palacio Canton/Museo Regional de Antropología

16. **Biblioteca Cepeda Peraza.** This library was founded by the general in 1867. Head back to the Parque Santa Lucía. Facing the park is the ancient:

17. **Iglesia de Santa Lucía (1575).** To reach Paseo de Montejo, continue walking north on calle 60 to the:

18. **Parque Santa Ana,** 4 blocks up calle 60 from the Parque Santa Lucía. Turn right here on calle 47 for 1½ blocks; then turn left onto the broad, busy boulevard known as the:

19. **Paseo de Montejo.** This tree-lined thoroughfare has imposing banks, hotels, and several 19th-century mansions erected by henequen barons, generals, and other Yucatecan potentates. It's Mexico's humble version of the Champs-Elysèes.

WINDING DOWN Before or after tackling the Palacio Cantón (see below), stop for a break at the Dulcería y Sorbetería Colón, on Paseo de Montejo 1 block north of the Palacio between calles 39 and 41. Baked goods, ice cream, and candy are displayed in a long glass counter. Unfortunately, coffee and tea are not available.

At the corner of calle 43 is the:

20. **Palacio Cantón.** This palace, with an entrance on calle 43, houses the ✪ **Museo Regional de Antropología** (Anthropology Museum; ☎ **99/23-0557**). Designed and built by Enrico Deserti, the architect who designed the Teatro Peón Contreras, this is the most impressive mansion on Paseo de Montejo and the only one open to the public. It was constructed between 1909 and 1911, during the last years of the Porfiriato as the home of General Francisco Cantón Rosado. The general enjoyed his palace for only 6 years before he died in 1917. The house was converted into a school and later became the official residence of the governor of the Yucatán.

The Palacio became an interregional museum covering not only the state of Yucatán but also the rest of the peninsula and Mexico. Its exhibits include cosmology; a pre-Hispanic time computation and comparative timeline; musical instruments; weaving examples and designs; and stone carvings from all over the country.

On the right as you enter is a room used for changing exhibits, usually featuring "the piece of the month." After that are the permanent exhibits with captions mostly in Spanish. Starting with fossil mastodon teeth, the exhibits take you through the Yucatán's history, paying special attention to the daily life of its inhabitants. You'll see how the Maya tied boards to babies' heads in order to give them the slanting forehead that was then a mark of great beauty, and how they filed teeth to sharpen them or drilled teeth to implant jewels. Enlarged photos show the archaeological sites, and drawings illustrate the various styles of Maya houses and how they were constructed. The one of Mayapán, for instance, clearly shows the city's ancient walls. Even if you know only a little Spanish, the museum provides a good background for explorations of Maya sites. The museum is open Tuesday through Saturday from 8am to 8pm and Sunday from 8am to 2pm. Admission is $3; free on Sunday. There's a museum bookstore on the left as you enter.

HORSE-DRAWN CARRIAGE TOURS

For a tour by horse-drawn carriage, look for a line of *coches de caleta* near the cathedral and in front of the Hotel Casa del Balam. Haggle for a good price.

ECOTOURS & ADVENTURE TRIPS

Recently there's been an explosion of companies that organize nature and adventure tours of the Yucatán Peninsula. One outfit with a long track record is **Ecoturismo Yucatán,** calle 3 no. 235, Col. Pensiones, 97219 Mérida, Yuc. (☎ **99/25-2187;** fax 99/25-9047; www.imagenet.com.mx/EcoYuc/Home.html; e-mail: ecoyuc@minter.cieamer.conacyt.mx). It is run by Alfonso and Roberta Escobedo, who can create an itinerary to meet just about any special and general interests you have for going to the Yucatán, or southern Mexico. Alfonso has been creating adventure and nature tours for more than a dozen years.

Another specialty tour agency is **Yucatán Trails,** calle 62 no. 482 (☎ **99/28-2582**). Canadian Dennis LaFoy, well known and active in the English-speaking community, is a font of information and can arrange a variety of individualized tours or answer any questions about travel.

SHOPPING

Mérida is known for **hammocks, guayaberas** (lightweight men's shirts that are worn untucked), and **Panama hats.** And there are good buys in **baskets** made in the Yucatán and **pottery,** as well as crafts from all over Mexico, especially at the **central market.** Mérida is also the place to pick up prepared **achiote,** a paste-like mixture of ground achiote seeds (annatto), oregano, garlic, masa, and other spices used in Yucatecan cuisine. When mixed with sour orange to a soupy consistency, it makes a great marinade, especially on grilled meat and fish. It can be found bottled in this form. It's also the sauce that makes baked chicken and cochinita pibil.

Mérida's bustling **market district,** bounded by calles 63 to 69 and calles 62 to 54, is a few blocks southeast of the Plaza Mayor. The streets surrounding the market are as busy and crowded as the market itself. Heaps of prepared achiote are sold in the food section.

CRAFTS

Casa de las Artesanías. Calle 63 no. 513, between calles 64 and 66. ☎ **99/28-6676.**

This store is in the front part of a restored monastery. Here you can find a wide selection of crafts from throughout Mexico. Stop by here before going to the various crafts markets to see what high-quality work looks like. The monastery's back courtyard is used as a gallery, with rotating exhibits on folk and fine arts. It's open Monday through Saturday from 9am to 8pm, Sunday 9am to 1pm.

Crafts Market. In a separate building of the main market, calle 67 at calle 56.

Look for a large pale-green building behind the post office. Climb the steps and wade into the clamor and activity while browsing for leather goods, hammocks, Panama hats, Maya embroidered dresses, men's formal guayabera shirts, and craft items of all kinds.

Museo Regional de Artes Populares. Calle 59 no. 441, between calles 50 and 48. No phone.

A branch of the Museo Nacional de Artes y Industrias Populares in Mexico City, this museum displays regional costumes and crafts in the front rooms. Upstairs is a large room full of crafts from all over Mexico, including filigree jewelry from Mérida, folk pottery, baskets, and wood carving from the Yucatán. Open Tuesday through Saturday from 8am to 8pm and Sunday from 9am to 2pm. Admission is free.

GUAYABERAS

Business suits are hot and uncomfortable in Mérida's soaking humidity, so business-men, politicians, bankers, and bus drivers alike wear the guayabera, a loose-fitting shirt that buttons up, is decorated with narrow tucks, pockets, and sometimes em-broidery and is worn over the pants rather than tucked in. Mérida is famous as the best place to buy guayaberas, which can be purchased for under $10 at the market or for over $50 custom-made by a tailor. A guaya-bera made of Japanese linen can set you back about $65. Most are made of cot-ton but can be had in various kinds of shirting material, and the traditional color is white. Connoisseurs have very definite opinions on color, the type of tucks that will run down the front, and embroidery.

Most shops display ready-to-wear shirts in several price ranges. Guayabera makers pride themselves on being innovators. I have yet to enter a shirt-maker's shop in Mérida that did not present its own updated version of the guayabera. When looking at guayaberas, here are few things to keep in mind. When Yucate-cans say *seda*, they do not mean silk but polyester; *lino* is linen. Take a close look at the stitching and the way the tucks line up over the pockets, etc.; with guayaberas the details are everything.

Jack Guayaberas. Calle 59 no. 507A. ☎ **99/28-6002.**

The craftsmanship here is very good, the place has a reputation to maintain, and some of the sales people can speak English. Prices are marked. This will give you a good basis of comparison should you want to hunt for a bargain. If they do not have the style and color of shirt you want, they will make it for you in about 3 hours. This shop also sells regular shirts and women's blouses. The shop is open Monday through Saturday 10am to 8pm; Sunday 10am to 2pm.

HAMMOCKS

I am an aficionado of hammocks, having slept in every variety across the length and breadth of Latin America. None is so comfortable as those of the Yucatán, which are woven with local cotton string in a fine mesh. For most of us, of course, the hammock is the equivalent of lawn furniture, something to relax in for an hour or so in the afternoon. But for the vast majority of Yucatecans, hammocks are their beds—what they sleep in at night. Many well-to-do Meridianos keep a bed just for show. I know a hotel owner who has 150 beds in his establishment, but will not sleep on a single one of them. He complains that when he does so, he wakes up unrested and sore.

My advice to the hammock buyer is this: The woven part should be cotton; it should be made with fine string; and the strings should be so numerous that when you get in it and stretch out at an angle, the gaps between the strings remain small. Don't pay attention to the words used to describe the size of a hammock; they have become practically meaningless. Good hammocks don't cost a lot of money ($15 to $30). If you want a superior hammock, ask for one made with "hilo de crochet de cuatro cajas" (the word *crochet* is also bandied about loosely). This should set you back about $80.

Nothing beats a tryout when you're shopping for this indispensable item; the two shops mentioned below will gladly hang a hammock for you to test-drive. When it's up, look to see that there are no untied strings. You can also see what street vendors are offering, but you have to know what to look for—or they are likely to take advantage of you.

Maquech—The Legendary Maya Beetle

One of the most unusual items for sale in the Yucatán is the live maquech beetle. Storekeepers display bowls of the large, dusty-brown insects with long black legs and backs sprinkled with multicolored glass "jewels" attached to small gold chains. The chain hooks to a small safety pin, and behold—you have a living brooch to wear.

One version of the maquech legend features a Maya princess who became the forbidden love object of a Maya prince. Without her knowledge, he crept into her garden one night, and just as they met, he was captured by the princess's guards. To save the prince, a sorceress turned him into a beetle and placed him on a decaying tree at the site of his capture. When the princess recovered from her faint, she looked for the prince where she had last seen him and found the bejeweled beetle instead; in an instant she recognized her lover. With a few strands of her long hair, she harnessed the beetle and kept it over her heart forever. Another version has it that the prince asked a sorceress to keep him close to the heart of his beloved princess, and (because he was very rich) she transformed him into a bejeweled beetle pin.

No matter which legend you believe, a purchased beetle comes with a piece of its favorite wood, a nice little box with air holes to carry it in, and a chain and safety pin. U.S. Customs, however, doesn't permit the beetle to cross the border, so plan to find it a home before you leave Mexico.

Hamacas El Aguacate. Calle 58 no. 604, corner with calle 73. ☎ **99/28-6429.**

El Aguacate sells hammocks wholesale and retail. It has the greatest variety and is the place to get a really expensive hammock. A good hammock is the size #6 in cotton; it runs $26. The store is open Monday to Friday 8am to 7pm, Saturday from 8am to 5pm. The store is about 6 blocks south of the main square.

Tejidos y Cordeles Nacionales. Calle 56 no. 516-B, between calles 63 and 65. ☎ **99/28-5561.**

This place is near the municipal market. The only hammocks it sells are cotton, and they are sold on the basis of weight—a pretty good practice because hammock lengths are standard. The prices here are better than at El Aguacate, and the difference in quality is slight. My idea of a good hammock weighs about 1½ kilos and runs about $18.

PANAMA HATS

Another useful and popular item is this soft, pliable hat made from the fibers of the jipijapa palm in several towns along Highway 180, especially Becal, in the neighboring state of Campeche. There's no need to journey all the way to Campeche, however, since Mérida sells the hats in abundance. They're just the thing to shade you from the fierce Yucatecan sun, and the hats can be rolled up and carried in a suitcase for the trip home.

Jipi hats come in three grades determined by the quality (pliability and fineness) of the fibers and closeness of the weave. The difference in weave is easily seen. A fine weave improves the shape of a hat. It has more body and regains its shape better. The best deals are in the Mercado or the artesanías market next to it; go from stall to stall until you find the specific shape and size of hat you are looking for.

WHERE TO STAY

Mérida is easier on the budget than Yucatán resort cities. Most hotels offer at least a few air-conditioned rooms, and some also have pools. You may find every room taken in July and August, when Mexicans vacation. In Mérida, free parking is a relative concept—for some hotels free parking means only at night; during the day there is a charge.

VERY EXPENSIVE

Hyatt Regency Mérida. Calle 60 no. 344, 97000 Mérida, Yuc. ☎ **800/228-9000** in the U.S., 99/25-6722, or 99/42-0202. Fax 99/25-7002. 300 units. A/C MINIBAR TV TEL. Weekday $110–$125 double. Ask about "supersaver rates"; rates may be cheaper if reserved from the U.S. AE, DC, MC, V.

At these prices perfection is the standard, and the fanciest, most comfortable hotel in town is still working out some minor details. The large, modern rooms have channels on satellite TV, 24-hour room service, direct-dial long-distance phone service, and personal safes. Trying to retrieve e-mail at the business center is problematic; ice machines may not be working; and room thermostats are a bit unpredictable. Regency Club rooms take up the top two floors; guests in these rooms receive complimentary continental breakfast, evening cocktails, and hors d'oeuvres; special concierge service; and access to private lounges and boardrooms. The hotel is at the intersection of calle 60 and avenida Colón.

Dining/Diversions: Several restaurants and bars.

Amenities: Business center, travel agency, and shops. Pool with swim-up bar; fitness equipment.

EXPENSIVE

✪ **Hotel Casa del Balam.** Calle 60 no. 488, 97000 Mérida, Yuc. ☎ **800/624-8451** in the U.S., or 99/24-8844. Fax 99/24-5011. 57 units. A/C MINIBAR TV TEL. $85 double. AE, DC, DISC, MC, V. Free parking.

This hotel is popular and centrally located. Most of the rooms are large and bright. The rooms are in two sections, which form two sides to the colonial style courtyard. The quietest are in the three-story section and the top floors of the six-story section. Rooms are stylishly decorated with folk art, dark furniture, iron headboards, and tile floors with area rugs. There's a travel agency and a rental-car agency in the lobby, as well as a popular restaurant and bar with a guitar trio playing in the evenings. The tables scattered around the courtyard have become a favorite romantic spot for evening cocktails and appetizers.

The owners also run the hotel **Hacienda Chichén,** at the ruins of Chichén-Itzá; you can make arrangements here to stay there. To find the hotel, walk 2 blocks north on calle 60 from the main square.

MODERATE

✪ **Casa Mexilio Guest House.** Calle 68 no. 495, 97000 Mérida, Yuc. ☎ **800/538-6802** in the U.S.; ☎ and fax 99/28-2505. 8 units. $55–$65 double. Rates include breakfast. MC, V. Parking on street.

This bed-and-breakfast is unlike any other I know. The owners show a genius for playing with space in an unexpected and delightful manner. Rooms are at different levels—creating private spaces joined to each other and to roof-top terraces by stairs and cat walks. Rooms are large and comfortable; most of the central patio is taken up by a small pool and whirlpool and exuberant vegetation. Breakfast fare is wonderful. The hotel is connected with the Turquoise Reef Group, which runs inns on

Mérida Accommodations & Dining

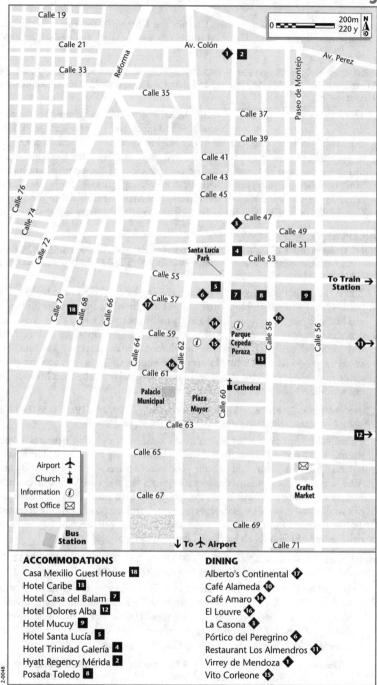

0 ———— 200m
———— 220 y
N

Calle 19
Calle 21
Calle 33
Reforma
Calle 35
Av. Colón **1** **2**
Paseo de Montejo
Av. Perez
Calle 37
Calle 39
Calle 41
Calle 43
Calle 45
Calle 76
Calle 74
Calle 72
Calle 47 **3**
Calle 49
Calle 51
Santa Lucía Park **4**
Calle 53
Calle 55
Calle 57 **5**
Calle 70
Calle 68
Calle 66
18
17
6 **7** **8** **9**
To Train Station →
Calle 64
Calle 59
14
10
Calle 62
16
15
ⓘ
Parque Cepeda Peraza
Calle 58
Calle 56
11 →
Calle 61
13
Calle 60
✝ Cathedral
Palacio Municipal
Plaza Mayor
12 →
Calle 63
Calle 65
Calle 67
Calle 69
Calle 71
Airport ✈
Church ✝
Information ⓘ
Post Office ✉
Crafts Market ✉
Bus Station
↓ To ✈ Airport

2-0048

ACCOMMODATIONS
Casa Mexilio Guest House **18**
Hotel Caribe **13**
Hotel Casa del Balam **7**
Hotel Dolores Alba **12**
Hotel Mucuy **9**
Hotel Santa Lucía **5**
Hotel Trinidad Galería **4**
Hyatt Regency Mérida **2**
Posada Toledo **8**

DINING
Alberto's Continental **17**
Café Alameda **10**
Café Amaro **14**
El Louvre **16**
La Casona **3**
Pórtico del Peregrino **6**
Restaurant Los Almendros **11**
Virrey de Mendoza **1**
Vito Corleone **15**

193

Mexico's Caribbean coast between Cancún and Chetumal. You can make reservations here for those inns. The hotel is 4 blocks west of the plaza between calles 57 and 59.

Hotel Caribe. Calle 59 no. 500, 97000 Mérida, Yuc. ☎ **99/24-9022.** Fax 99/24-8733. 54 units. A/C TV TEL. $38–$42 double; $55 suite for 2 with A/C. AE, MC, V. Free guarded parking.

This hotel is very popular for several reasons. It is located back from the street on the Plaza Hidalgo; rooms are comfortable and quiet; and the prices are good. Like most hotels in Mexico, rooms are not lit brightly enough for American tastes. All rooms are built around a three-story, covered courtyard. From the top floor, where there's a small pool and sundeck, there are nice views of the cathedral and town. Most doubles and suites come with air-conditioning. Parking during the day is extra. To get to the hotel from the Plaza Mayor, walk a half block to the Parque Cepeda Peraza. The hotel is in the back right corner of the park.

INEXPENSIVE

Hotel Dolores Alba. Calle 63 no. 464, 97000 Mérida, Yuc. ☎ **99/28-5650.** Fax 99/28-3163. E-mail: asanchez@Yucatan.com.mx. 46 units. A/C. $25–$28 double. No credit cards. Free guarded parking.

This is the perfect place to stay if you are traveling by car and are on a budget. The hotel is family-owned and -operated and was built from a converted Spanish colonial house. It has a large open court and a smaller courtyard with a clean pool, sundeck, and gardens. The rooms, half of which have air-conditioning, are decorated with local crafts. A small dining room opens for breakfast between 7 and 9am. The owners also operate the **Hotel Dolores Alba** outside Chichén-Itzá; you can make reservations at one hotel for the other. To find this hotel from the Plaza Mayor, walk east on calle 63 for 3½ blocks; it's between calles 52 and 54.

✪ **Hotel Mucuy.** Calle 57 no. 481, 97000 Mérida, Yuc. ☎ **99/28-5193.** Fax 99/23-7801. 22 units. $12 double. No credit cards.

This is half the price of other budget hotels listed here, and what separates it from the other $12 hotels in this city is the effort of the family that runs it. The Mucuy is named for a small dove said to bring good luck to places where it alights. Owners Alfredo and Ofelia Comín strive to make guests feel welcome with conveniences such as a communal refrigerator in the lobby, and for a small extra charge the use of a washer and dryer. This place stays pretty full, and reservations are not accepted. To find the hotel from the Plaza Mayor, walk 2 blocks north on calle 60, then turn right on calle 57 and go 1½ blocks; it's between calles 56 and 58.

Hotel Santa Lucía. Calle 55 no. 508, 97000 Mérida, Yuc. ☎ and fax **99/28-2662.** 51 units. A/C TV TEL. $24 double. MC, V. Free guarded parking nearby.

This small hotel opened in 1990. The rooms are in a three-story building with windows facing the inner hallways or the courtyard, which contains a long, inviting pool. Rooms are quiet, but mattresses are thin. The management is very helpful, providing information on tours, restaurants, and sights. It also runs the **Hotel San Clemente** in Valladolid. The hotel faces Parque Santa Lucía, just off calle 60.

Hotel Trinidad Galería. Calle 60 no. 456, 97000 Mérida, Yuc. ☎ **99/23-2463.** Fax 99/24-2319. 31 units. $20 double; $25 suite with A/C and TV. AE. Limited free parking.

Once an enormous home, this rambling hotel offers its guests a small shaded pool, a communal refrigerator, a shared dining room, original art and antiques, and lots of relaxing nooks with comfortable furniture. Upstairs, a covered porch decorated with antiques and plants runs the length of the hotel, providing yet another place to read or converse. Rooms are rather dark and simply furnished, and most don't have windows, but the overall ambience of the hotel is comparable to that of more expensive inns. To find the hotel from the Plaza Mayor, walk 5 blocks north on calle 60; it's at the corner of calle 51, 2 blocks north of the Santa Lucía Park.

Posada Toledo. Calle 58 no. 487, 97000 Mérida, Yuc. ☎ **99/23-1690.** Fax 99/23-2256. E-mail: hptoledo@pibilfinred.com.mx. 23 units. A/C TEL. $40–$45 double. MC, V. Free parking next door.

This colonial inn was once a private mansion. It's now a cross between a garden dripping with vines and a fading museum with beautifully kept antique furnishings. Two of the grandest rooms have been remodeled into a suite with ornate cornices and woodwork. Most rooms have no windows, but high ceilings, and appropriately creaky hardwood floors are standard. The highest rates are for air-conditioned rooms. The rooftop lounge area is excellent for viewing the city. Five rooms have TVs. To find the inn from the Plaza Mayor, walk 2 blocks north on calle 60, then right 1 block on calle 57 to calle 58; it's on the left.

WHERE TO DINE

Calle 62 between the Plaza Mayor and calle 57 contains a short string of small budget food shops. To make your own breakfast, try the **Panificadora Montejo,** at the corner of calles 62 and 63 on the southwest corner of the Plaza Mayor. For those who can't start a day without fresh orange juice, juice bars have sprouted up all over Mérida, and several are on or near the Plaza Mayor.

EXPENSIVE

Alberto's Continental. Calle 64 no. 482. ☎ **99/28-5367.** Reservations recommended. Main courses $8–$19. AE, MC, V. Daily 1pm–11pm. LEBANESE/YUCATECAN/ITALIAN.

Created from a fine old town house, the large and elegantly furnished rooms are built around a plant- and tree-filled patio that's framed in Moorish arches. Cuban floor tiles from a bygone era, along with antique furniture and sideboards, create an Old World mood. The eclectic menu features Lebanese, Yucatecan, and Italian specialties. There's a sampler plate of four Lebanese favorites, plus traditional Yucatecan specialties, such as pollo pibil and fish Celestún (bass stuffed with shrimp). Polish off your selections with Turkish coffee. Alberto's is at the corner of calle 57.

✪ **Virrey de Mendoza.** Calle 60 no. 327. ☎ **99/25-3082.** Main courses $7–$10. AE, MC, V. Daily 12:30–11:30. YUCATECAN/MEXICAN. Parking available.

Across the street from the Hyatt, Virrey is the most polished and contemporary restaurant in Mérida. The food and service are superb, while other essential matters— furniture, lighting, and surroundings—are all handled well. Try any of the Yucatecan specialties, like the pepper stuffed with crab; the filet mignon with cilantro, mushrooms, and olive oil; or the Huitlacoche crepes. My one reservation is that Virrey (like most restaurants throughout the Yucatán) thinks very highly of gouda cheese and uses it in dishes that are better suited to stronger domestic cheeses.

MODERATE

✪ **La Casona.** Calle 60 no. 434. ☎ **99/23-8348.** Reservations recommended. Pasta courses $5–$9; meat courses $5–$12. AE, MC, V. Daily 1pm–midnight. ITALIAN/ REGIONAL.

A gracious old Mérida house and its lush interior garden make a charming and romantic restaurant. The cuisine is Yucatecan and Italian, so you can choose among such dishes as pollo pibil, filet mignon with brandy and cream, linguine with mushrooms, and lasagna. The pollo en escabeche scored a hit on our latest visit. It's also a fine place to wind up the day sipping espresso or cappuccino. La Casona is 6 blocks north of the Plaza Mayor near the corner of calles 60 and 47. Free valet parking.

✪ **Restaurant Los Almendros.** Calle 50A no. 493. ☎ **99/28-5459.** Main courses $4–$9; daily special $5–$8. AE, MC, V. Daily 9am–11pm. YUCATECAN.

For traditional homestyle Yucatecan food, this is the place that comes to mind. It is practically an institution in Mérida. The colorful chairs and tables make for a festive mood. Ask to see the menu with color photographs of their dishes accompanied by descriptions in English. Los Almendros is known for its poc chuc—grilled pork with marinated onions. To reach the restaurant from the Parque Cepeda Peraza, walk east on calle 59 for 5 blocks, then left on calle 50A; it's half a block on the left facing the Parque de la Mejorada.

✪ **El Pórtico del Peregrino.** Calle 57 no. 501. ☎ **99/28-6163.** Reservations recommended. Main courses $6–$10. AE, MC, V. Daily noon–11pm. MEXICAN/INTERNATIONAL.

El Pórtico is a favorite among locals and visitors alike. It exudes local charm and comfort with a distinctive Mérida flavor. The interior is a lovely garden with three dining areas—two air-conditioned rooms and a patio (one room is nonsmoking, a rarity in Mexico). The menu offers soup, fish fillet, grilled gulf shrimp, spaghetti, pollo pibil, baked eggplant with chicken and cheese, and coconut ice cream topped with Kahlúa. The restaurant is 2 blocks north of the main square between calles 60 and 62.

INEXPENSIVE

Café Alameda. Calle 58 no. 474. ☎ **99/28-3635.** Breakfast $2.75–$3.25; main courses $3–$5. No credit cards. Daily 7:30am–6pm. MIDDLE EASTERN/MEXICAN.

The trappings are simple and informal, and the trick here is figuring out the Spanish names for popular Middle Eastern dishes. Kibbe is "quebbe bola," not "quebbe cruda," hummus is "garbanza," and shish kebab is "alambre." I leave it to you to figure out what a spinach pie is called (and they're excellent). Café Alameda is a treat for vegetarians, and the umbrella-shaded tables in the patio are perfect for morning coffee and pastries. The cafe is 3 blocks north and 1 block east of the Plaza Mayor, between calles 57 and 59.

Café Amaro. Calle 59 no. 507 interior 6. ☎ **99/28-2451.** Breakfast $2–$3; main courses $3–$4.50. No credit cards. Mon–Sat 8:30am–11pm. REGIONAL/VEGETARIAN.

This restaurant serves food in a pleasant courtyard beneath the branches of a large orchid tree. The crema de calabacitas (pumpkin) soup is delicious, as is the apple salad. The cafe is well known for its avocado pizza. There is also a limited menu of meat and chicken dishes; try the Yucatecan chicken. To find it from the Plaza Mayor, walk 1 block north on calle 60 and turn left on calle 59.

El Louvre. Calle 62 no. 499. ☎ **99/24-5073.** Main courses $2.75–$4; comida corrida $3.75. No credit cards. Daily 24 hours (comida corrida served 1–5pm). MEXICAN.

This big, open restaurant feeds everybody from farm workers to townspeople. There's also an English menu. The comida corrida might include beans with pork on Monday, pork stew on Tuesday, and so on, plus there are sandwiches, soups, and other full meals. From the Palacio Municipal, cross calle 61 and walk north on calle 62 a few steps; it's near the corner of calle 61.

Vito Corleone. Calle 59 no. 508 between calles 60 and 62. ☎ **99/28-5777.** Main courses $2–$5. No credit cards. Daily 9:30am–11:30pm. PIZZA/SPAGHETTI.

Aside from the food, the most impressive aspect of this tiny pizza parlor is the interesting use of *ollas* (clay pots) embedded in the wall above the hand-painted tile oven. The oven's golden-yellow tiles are as handsome as those that decorate church domes. The tables by the sidewalk are the only bearable places to sit when it's warm, since the oven casts incredible heat. Another section upstairs in the back is also tolerable. The thin-crusted pizzas are smoky and savory, and on Thursdays there's a two-for-one pizza special. To find it from the Plaza Mayor, walk north 1 block on calle 60 and turn left on calle 59; it's half a block ahead.

MÉRIDA AFTER DARK

For nighttime entertainment, see "Festivals & Special Events in Mérida," above, or check out the theaters included below.

Teatro Peón Contreras, at calles 60 and 57, and **Teatro Ayala,** on calle 60 at calle 61, both feature a wide range of performing artists from around the world. Stop in and see what's showing.

If nothing strikes your fancy, do not despair; Mérida has plenty of variety in its nightlife. Most of the discos are in the big hotels or on Paseo de Montejo. The most popular one at present is **Vatzya,** in the Fiesta Americana Hotel on the corner of calle 60 and avenida Colón (across from the Hyatt). For live music and entertainment, try one or more of the places listed below.

✪ **Ciudad Maya.** Calle 84 no. 506, 1 block west of the Plaza Mayor. ☎ **99/24-3313.** 1pm to 1am; no shows on Mon. $6 minimum.

Where else can you find a club that combines massive archaeological exhibits with a nightclub that combines massive replicas of Maya architecture with a racy, Latin-style floor show featuring scantilyclad Cuban dancers? This bar/restaurant has a Cuban floor show at 8 and 10pm; the six-member Cuban band puts Ricky Ricardo to shame, and costumes have the requisite big headdresses. There are two shows: "Streets of My Havana" and "Under the Mayan Sky"; call ahead to find out which is being performed. Between dance numbers, magicians, and acrobats entertain the audience. Ciudad Maya serves drinks, steaks, and antojitos, but the main attraction is the show. One more note of interest: Meridianos regard the club as a family place—don't be surprised to see little kids there.

El Trovador Bohemio. Calle 55 no. 504. ☎ **99/23-0385.** 9pm to 3am. Cover $1.25.

It's hard to overstate the importance of *música de trio* in Mexican popular culture. Boleros may have been at their most popular in the 1940s and 50s, but every new heartthrob in Mexican pop music feels compelled to release a new version of the classics at some point in his career. I like the originals best, and so do most Mexicans. If you know something of this music and are curious about it, El Trovador is your chance to hear how the music should be played. And if you understand colloquial Spanish, all the better; the language of boleros is vivid, passionate, and quite Mexican—definitely a unique cultural experience. El Trovador is small and dark, and everything is red, including diamond-tufted upholstered walls. The best time to go is Thursday through Saturday. This place faces the Santa Lucía Park.

Pancho's. Calle 59 no. 509. ☎ **99/23-0949.** 6pm to 3am. 3-drink minimum if you do not order food.

If you take this place seriously, you won't like it. Waiters in bandoliers and oversized sombreros, walls adorned with blow-ups of Revolution-era photos, and assorted emblems of Mexican identity—Pancho's, which serves Tex-Mex, is a parody of the tourist attraction, a place for drinking beer and loosing the occasional *grito*. Live music is performed in the courtyard, beginning at 9 on most nights, 10:30 on Saturdays. The five-piece band is quite good, with its large repertoire of cover tunes; it'll crank up salsa, rock, and jazz.

ROAD TRIPS FROM MÉRIDA
CELESTÚN NATIONAL WILDLIFE REFUGE: FLAMINGOS & OTHER WATERFOWL

This flamingo sanctuary and offbeat sand-street fishing village on the Gulf coast is a 90-minute drive from Mérida. To get here, take Highway 281 (a two-lane road) past numerous old henequen haciendas. **Autobuses de Occidente** schedules 10 buses per day bound for Celestún from the terminal at calles 50 and 67.

One telephone at the **Hotel Gutiérrez** (☎ **99/28-0419**) serves as the public phone for the entire village. You'll find a bank, two gas stations (but no unleaded gas), and a grocery store. Bus tickets are purchased at the end of the row of market stalls on the left side of the church. Celestún hotels don't furnish drinking water, so bring your own or buy it in town.

December 8 is the **Feast Day of the Virgen de Concepción,** the patron saint of the village. On the Sunday that falls nearest to July 15, a colorful procession carries Celestún's venerated figure of the Virgen de Concepción to meet the sacred figure of the Virgen de Asunción on the highway leading to Celestún. Returning to Celestún, they float away on decorated boats and later return to be ensconced at the church during a mass and celebration.

SEEING THE WATERFOWL   The town is on a narrow strip of land separated from the mainland by a lagoon. Crossing over the lagoon bridge, you'll find the 14,611-acre wildlife refuge spreading out on both sides without visible boundaries. You'll notice small boats moored on both sides waiting to take visitors to see the flamingos. In addition to flamingos, you will probably see frigate birds, pelicans, cranes, egrets, sandpipers, and other waterfowl feeding on shallow sandbars at any time of year. Of the 175 bird species that come here, some 99 are permanent residents. At least 15 duck species have also been counted. Flamingos are found here all year; nonbreeding flamingos remain year-round, and the larger group of breeding flamingoes takes off around April to nest on the upper Yucatán Peninsula east of Río Lagartos.

A 90-minute flamingo-sighting trip costs around $25 for four people or twice that much if you stay half a day. The best time to go is around 7am; the worst is midafternoon, when sudden storms come up. Be sure not to allow the boatmen to get close enough to frighten the birds; they've been known to do it for photographers, but it will eventually cause the birds to permanently abandon the habitat. Your tour will take you a short distance into the massive mangroves that line the lagoon to a sulfur pool, where the boatman kills the motor and poles in so you can experience the stillness and density of the jungle, feel the sultry air, and see other birds.

WHERE TO STAY   To find restaurants and hotels, follow the bridge road a few blocks to the end. On the last street, calle 12, paralleling the oceanfront, you'll find restaurants and hotels, all of which have decent rooms but marginal housekeeping standards. Always try to bargain for lower rates, which can go down by as much as 30% in the off-season.

Hotel María del Carmen. Calle 12 no. 111, 97367 Celestún, Yuc. ☎ **99/28-0152.** 9 units. $14 double. No credit cards.

Built in 1992, this three-story hotel on the beach stands out among Celestún's modest accommodations lineup. Spare but clean and large, each room has terrazzo floors, two double beds with sheets but no bedspread, screened windows (check screens for holes), and a small balcony or patio facing the ocean. Best of all, there's hot water in the bathrooms (not necessarily a hallmark of other Celestún hotels), but not always toilet seats. Lorenzo Saul Rodríguez and María del Carmen Gutiérrez own the hotel and are actively involved in local conservation efforts, particularly in protecting the sea turtles that nest on the beach in early summer. Look for the sign for Villa del Mar, the hotel's restaurant; the rooms are behind it across the parking area.

WHERE TO DINE Calle 12 is home to several rustic seafood restaurants aside from the place listed below. All have irregular hours of operation.

✪ **Restaurant Celestún.** Calle 12 no. 101, on the waterfront. ☎ **99/16-2031.** Main courses $3.75–$7. Daily 10am–6pm (sometimes). SEAFOOD/MEXICAN.

I highly recommend this ocean-view restaurant, owned by Elda Cauich and Wenseslao Ojeda; the service is friendly and swift. Tables and chairs fill a long room that stretches from calle 12 to the beach. The house specialty is a delicious shrimp, crab, and squid omelet (called a torta). But if you're a fan of stone crabs (manitas de cangrejo on the menu), this is definitely the place to chow down. Trapped in the gulf by Celestún fishermen, they come freshly cooked and seasoned with lime juice. Also popular during the fall season is pulpo (octopus). Other local specialties include liza (mullet) and caviar de Celestún (mullet eggs). To find the restaurant, follow the bridge road to the waterfront (calle 12); turn left and the restaurant is immediately on the right.

DZIBILCHALTÚN: MAYA RUINS

This Maya site, now a national park, located 9 miles north of Mérida along the Progreso road and 4½ miles east off the highway, is worth a stop. Dzibilchaltún was founded about 500 B.C. and flourished around A.D. 750, was in decline long before the coming of the conquistadors, but may have been occupied until A.D. 1600, almost 100 years after the arrival of the Spaniards. Since its discovery in 1941, more than 8,000 buildings have been mapped. The site, which was probably a center of commerce and religion, covers an area of almost 10 square miles with a central core of almost 65 acres. At least 12 sacbeob (causeways), the longest of which is 4,200 feet, have been unearthed. Dzibilchaltún means "place of the stone writing," and at least 25 stelae have been found, many of them reused in buildings constructed after the original ones were covered or destroyed.

Today, the most interesting buildings are grouped around the Cenote Xlacah, the sacred well, and include a complex of buildings around Structure 38; the **Central Group** of temples; the raised **causeways;** and the **Seven Dolls Group,** centered on the **Temple of the Seven Dolls.** It was beneath the floor of the temple that seven weird little dolls (now in the museum) showing a variety of diseases and birth defects were discovered. The Yucatán State Department of Ecology has added nature trails and published a booklet (in Spanish) of birds and plants seen at various points along the mapped trail. The booklet tells where in the park you are likely to see specific plants and birds.

The federal government has spent over a million pesos for the **Museum of the Maya** on the grounds of Dzibilchaltún. The museum, which opened in 1995, is a replica of a Maya village of houses, called nah, staffed by Maya demonstrating traditional cooking, gardening, and folk-art techniques.

To get to Dzibilchaltún by bus from Mérida, go to the Progreso bus station at calle 62 no. 524, between calles 65 and 67. There are five buses per day Monday through Saturday to the pueblo of Chanculob; it's a 1-kilometer walk to the ruins from there. On Sunday there are only three buses to Chanculob. The return bus schedule is posted at the ticket window next to the ruins.

The site and nature trails are open daily from 8am to 5pm. Admission is $4, free on Sunday; video camera use costs $4.

PROGRESO: GULF COAST CITY

For another beach escape, go to Progreso, a modern city facing the Gulf less than an hour from Mérida. This is where Meridianos have their weekend houses and where they come in large numbers for the months of July and August. At other times there are no crowds, no traffic, just the sea. Here, the Malecón, a beautiful oceanfront drive, borders a wide beach lined with coconut palms. The water here is not blue as on the Caribbean side, but it is clean. A long pier, or *muelle* (pronounced *mway*-yay), extends several miles into the bay to service oceangoing ships. Progreso is part-time home to some Americans and Canadians who come to escape northern winters.

Along or near the Malecón are several restaurants and hotels, including **Le Saint Bonnet** (Malecón at calle 78), ☎ **993/5-2299,** where locals dine on fresh seafood; try the pescado al ajillo.

From Mérida, buses to Progreso leave the special bus station at calle 62 no. 524, between calles 65 and 67, every 15 minutes during the day, starting at 5am. The trip takes 45 minutes.

In Progreso, the bus station is about 4 blocks south of calle 19, or Malecón, which runs along the beach.

EN ROUTE TO UXMAL

There are two routes to Uxmal, about 50 miles south of Mérida. The most direct is Highway 261 via Uman and Muna. From downtown, take calle 65 to avenida Itzáes and make a left. If you have the time and would like a more scenic route, try the meandering State Highway 18. See below.

HIGHWAY 261: YAXCOPOIL & MUNA Ten miles beyond Uman along Highway 261 is Yaxcopoil (yash-koh-poe-*eel*), the tongue-twisting Maya name of a fascinating 19th-century hacienda on the right side of the road between Mérida and Uxmal. It's difficult to reach by bus.

This hacienda, dating from 1864, was originally a cattle ranch comprising over 23,000 acres. Around 1900, it was converted to growing henequen (for the manufacture of rope). Take half an hour to tour the house (which boasts 18-foot ceilings and original furniture), factory, outbuildings, and museum. You'll see that such haciendas were the administrative, commercial, and social centers of vast private domains; they were almost little principalities carved out of the Yucatecan jungle. It's open Monday through Saturday from 8am to 6pm and Sunday from 9am to 1pm.

From Mérida via Uman, it's 20 miles to the Hacienda Yaxcopoil and 40 miles to Muna on Highway 261. Uxmal is 10 miles from Muna.

HIGHWAY 18: KANASÍN, ACANCEH, MAYAPÁN & TICUL Taking calle 67 east, head out of Mérida toward Kanasín (kahn-ah-*seen*) and Acanceh (ah-*kahn*-keh), for about 12 miles. When calle 67 ends, bear right, then go left at the next big intersection. Follow the wide divided highway with speed bumps. At Mérida's periférico (the road that circles the city), you'll see signs to Cancún. You can either cross the periférico and go straight into Kanasín or turn and follow the Cancún signs for a short distance and then follow the signs into Kanasín. In **Kanasín,** watch for signs that say CIRCULACIÓN or DESVIACIÓN. As in many Yucatán towns, you're being redirected to follow a one-way street through the urban area. Go past the market, church, and the main square on your left and continue straight out of town. The next village you come to, at km 10, is **San Antonio Tehuit,** an old henequen hacienda. At km 13 is **Tepich,** another hacienda-centered village, with those funny little henequen-cart tracks crisscrossing the main road. After Tepich comes **Petectunich** and finally **Acanceh.**

Across the street from and overlooking Acanceh's church is a partially restored pyramid. From Acanceh's main square, turn right (around the statue of a smiling deer) and head for **Tecoh** with its huge crumbling church (5½ miles farther along Highway 18) and Telchaquillo (7 miles farther). This route takes you past several old Yucatecan haciendas, each with a big house, chapel, factory with smokestack, and workers' houses.

Shortly after the village of Telchaquillo, a sign on the right side of the road will point to the entrance of the ruins of Mayapán.

RUINS OF MAYAPÁN

Founded, according to Maya lore, by the man-god Quetzalcoatl (Kukulkán in Maya) in about A.D. 1007, Mayapán ranked in importance with Chichén-Itzá and Uxmal and covered at least 2½ square miles. For more than 2 centuries, it was the capital of a Maya confederation of city-states that included Chichén and Uxmal. But before the year 1200, the rulers of Mayapán ended the confederation by attacking and conquering Chichén and by forcing the rulers of Uxmal to live as vassals in Mayapán. Eventually a successful revolt by the captive Maya rulers brought down Mayapán, which was abandoned during the mid-1400s.

After all this history, what you find at the site is a disappointment. There is some debate about why a city so powerful and important lacks more impressive architecture. Some believe this is evidence of social decay in the last years of Maya civilization.

The site is open daily from 8am to 5pm. Admission is $2; free on Sunday; use of a personal video camera is $4.

FROM MAYAPÁN TO TICUL   The road is a good one, but directional signs through the villages are almost nonexistent; stop and ask directions frequently. From Mayapán, continue along Highway 18 to **Tekit** (5 miles), turn right and you'll come to **Mama** on a road as thrilling as a roller-coaster ride (4⅓ miles). Then turn right again for Chapab (8 miles). After Chapab you reach Ticul (6¼ miles), the largest town in the region.

TICUL

Best known for the cottage industry of *huipil* embroidery and for the manufacture of ladies' dress shoes, Ticul isn't the most exciting stop on the Puuc route—but it's a convenient place to wash up and spend the night. It's also a center for large-size commercially produced pottery; most of the widely sold sienna-colored pottery painted with Maya designs comes from here. If it's a cloudy, humid day, the potters may not be working, since part of the process requires sun drying, but they still welcome visitors to purchase finished pieces.

One place worth a visit is **Arte Maya,** calle 23 no. 301, Carretera Ticul Muna (☎ **997/2-1095;** fax 997/2-0334). It is owned and operated by Luis Echeverría and Lourdes Castillo. This shop and gallery produces museum-quality art in alabaster, stone, jade, and ceramics. Much of the work is done as it was in Maya times; soft stone or ceramic is smoothed with the leaf of the siricote tree, and colors are derived from plant sources. If you buy from them, hang onto the written description of your purchase—their work looks so authentic that U.S. Customs has delayed entry of people carrying their wares, thinking that they're smuggling real Maya artifacts into the States.

Ticul is only 12 miles northeast of Uxmal, so thrifty tourists stay here instead of the more expensive hotels at the ruins. Try the **Hotel Bougambillias Familiar,** calle 23 no. 291A, 97860 Ticul, Yuc. (☎ **997/2-0761**). This place, with 20 rooms ($12 to $15 double) is motel-like, with parking outside the rooms. The half-circle drive into the arched entrance is lined with plants and pottery from the owner's local factory. High windows don't let in much light, the rooms have saggy beds, and bathrooms come without shower curtains and toilet seats. But the cool tile floors and ready hot water are attractions. In back is the hotel's pretty restaurant, **Xux-Cab,** but it has a limited menu. To find the hotel, follow calle 23 through Ticul on the road to Muna. It's on the right before you leave town, past the Santa Elena turnoff.

A SIDE TRIP: SPELUNKING IN THE YAXNIC CAVES

Just outside the village of Yotolín (also spelled Yohtolín), between Ticul and Oxkutzcab (along Highway 184), are some impressive caves called Yaxnic (*yash-neek*), on the grounds of the old, private Hacienda Yotolín. Virtually undeveloped and full of colored stalactites and stalagmites, the caves are visited by means of a perilous descent in a basket let down on a rope.

Arranging this spelunking challenge takes time, but the thrill may be worth it. Here's the procedure: Several days (or even weeks, if that's possible) before your intended cave descent, go to Yotolín and ask for the house of the *comisario,* a village elder. He will make the proper introductions to the hacienda owners, who in turn will tell you how to prepare for the experience.

FROM TICUL TO UXMAL

From Ticul to Uxmal, follow the main street (calle 23) west through town. Turn left at the sign to Santa Elena. It's 10 miles to Santa Elena; then, at Highway 261, cut back right for about 2 miles to Uxmal. The easiest route to follow is via Muna, but it's also longer and less picturesque. To go this way, drive straight through Ticul 14 miles to Muna. At Muna, turn left and head south on Highway 261 to Uxmal, 10 miles away.

2 The Ruins of Uxmal

50 miles SW of Mérida; 12 miles W of Ticul; 12 miles S of Muna

One of the highlights of a vacation in the Yucatán, the ruins of Uxmal—noted for their rich geometric stone facades—are the most beautiful on the peninsula. Remains of an agricultural society indicate that the area was occupied possibly as early as 800 B.C. However, the great building period took place 1,000 years later, between A.D. 700 and 1000, during which time the population probably reached 25,000. Then Uxmal fell under the sway of the Xiú princes (who may have come from the Valley of Mexico) after the year 1000. In the 1440s, the Xiú conquered

Mayapán, and not long afterward the glories of the Maya ended when the Spanish conquistadors arrived.

Close to Uxmal, four other sites—Sayil, Kabah, Xlapak, and Labná —are worth visiting. With Uxmal, these ruins are collectively known as the Puuc route, for the Puuc hills of this part of the Yucatán. See the "Puuc Maya Sites" section, below, if you want to explore these sites.

ESSENTIALS

GETTING THERE & DEPARTING By Car Two routes to Uxmal from Mérida, via Highway 261 or via State Highway 18, are described in "En Route to Uxmal," at the end of the Mérida section above. *Note:* There's no gasoline at Uxmal.

By Bus See "Getting There & Departing" in "Mérida," above, for information about bus service between Mérida and Uxmal. To return, wait for the bus on the highway at the entrance to the ruins. To see the sound-and-light show, sign up with one of the tour operators in Mérida.

ORIENTATION Uxmal consists of the archaeological site and its visitor center, five hotels, and a highway restaurant. The visitor center, open daily from 8am to 9pm, has a restaurant (with good coffee); toilets; a first-aid station; and shops selling soft drinks, ice cream, film, batteries, and books, and a state-run Casa de Artesanía. There are no phones except at the hotels. The food at the hotel restaurants is iffy and expensive. Most public buses pick up and let off passengers on the highway at the entrance to the ruins. The site itself is open daily from 8am to 5pm. Admission to the archaeological site of Uxmal is $4, but a Sunday visit will save money since admission is free to Uxmal and other recommended sites nearby. There's a $4 charge for each video camera you bring in. (Save your receipt; it's good for other area sites on the same day.) Parking costs $1.

Guides at the entrance of Uxmal give tours in a variety of languages and charge $20 for either a single person or a group. The guides frown on unrelated individuals joining a group. As usual, they'd rather charge you as a solo visitor, but you can ask other English speakers if they'd like to join you in a tour and split the cost. As at other sites, the guides vary in quality, but you will see areas and architectural details you might otherwise miss.

A 45-minute **sound-and-light show** is staged each evening in Spanish for $3 at 7pm and in English for $4 at 9pm. The bus from Mérida is scheduled to leave near the end of the Spanish show; confirm the exact time with the driver. If you stay for the English show, the only return to Mérida is via an expensive taxi. After the impressive show, the chant *Chaaac, Chaaac* will echo in your mind for weeks.

A TOUR OF THE RUINS

The Pyramid of the Magician As you enter the ruins, note the chultún, or cistern, where Uxmal stored its water. Unlike most of the major Mayan sites, Uxmal has no river or cenote to supply fresh water—perhaps the most mystifying feature of what was once a large and populous city.

Just beyond the chultún, the remarkable Pyramid of the Magician (also called Pyramid of the Dwarf) looms majestically on the right. The name comes from a legend about a mystical dwarf who reached adulthood in a single day after being hatched from an egg, and who built this pyramid in one night. Beneath it are five temples, since it was common practice for the Maya to build new structures atop old ones as part of a prescribed ritual.

The pyramid is unique because of its rounded sides, height, steepness, and the doorway on the opposite (west) side near the top. The doorway's heavy ornamentation, a characteristic of the Chenes style, features 12 stylized masks of the rain god Chaac, and the doorway itself is a huge open-mouthed Chaac mask.

The steep and risky climb to the top is worth it for the view. From on top you can see Uxmal's entire layout. Next to the Pyramid of the Magician, to the west, is the Nunnery Quadrangle, and left of it is a partially restored ball court, south of which are several large complexes. The biggest building among them is the Governor's Palace, and behind it lies the massive, largely unrestored Great Pyramid. In the distance is the Dovecote (House of the Doves), a small building with a lacy roof comb (false front) that looks like the perfect apartment complex for pigeons. From this vantage point, note how Uxmal is unique among Maya sites for its use of huge terraces constructed to support the buildings; look closely and you'll see that the Governor's Palace is not on a natural hill but rather on a giant platform, like the nearby Nunnery Quadrangle.

The Nunnery Quadrangle   The 16th-century Spanish historian Fray Diego López de Cogullado gave the building its name because it resembled a Spanish monastery. Possibly it was a military academy or a training school for princes, who may have lived in the 70-odd rooms. The buildings were constructed at different times: The northern one was first, then the southern, then the eastern, then the western. The western building has the most richly decorated facade, composed of intertwined stone snakes and numerous masks of the hook-nosed rain god Chaac.

The corbeled archway on the south was once the main entrance to the Nunnery complex; as you head toward it out of the quadrangle to the south, look above each doorway in that section for the motif of a Maya cottage, or *nah*, looking just like any number of cottages you'd see throughout the Yucatán today.

The Ball Court   A small ball court is conserved to prevent further decay, but compare it later on your trip to the giant, magnificently restored court at Chichén-Itzá.

The Turtle House   Up on the terrace south of the ball court is a little temple decorated with colonnade motif on the facade and a border of turtles. Though it's small and simple, its harmony is one of the gems of Uxmal.

The Governor's Palace   In its size and intricate stonework, this rivals the Temple of the Magician as Uxmal's masterwork—an imposing three-level edifice with a 320-foot-long mosaic facade done in the Puuc style. Puuc means "hilly country," the name given to the hills nearby and thus to the predominant style of pre-Hispanic architecture found here. Uxmal has many examples of Puuc decoration, characterized by elaborate stonework from door tops to the roofline. Fray Cogullado, who named the Nunnery, also gave this building its name. The Governor's Palace may have been just that—the administrative center of the Xiú principality, which included the region around Uxmal. It probably had astrological significance as well. For years, scholars pondered why this building was constructed slightly turned from adjacent buildings. Originally they thought the strange alignment was because of the *sacbe* (ceremonial road) that starts at this building and ends 11 miles distant at the ancient city of Kabah. But recently scholars of archaeoastronomy (a relatively new science that studies the placement of archaeological sites in relation to the stars), discovered that the central doorway, which is larger than the others, is in perfect alignment with Venus.

Before you leave the Governor's Palace, note the elaborately stylized headdress patterned in stone over the central doorway. As you stand back from the building on the east side, note how the 103 stone masks of Chaac undulate across the facade like a serpent and end at the corners where there are columns of masks.

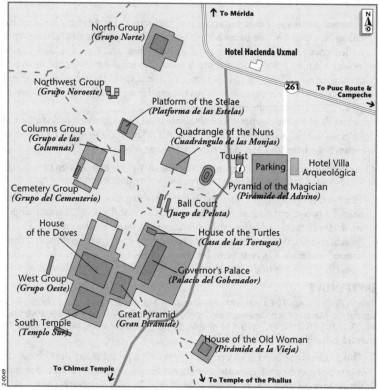

The Great Pyramid   A massive, partially restored nine-level structure, it has interesting motifs of birds, probably macaws, on its facade, as well as a huge mask. The view from the top is wonderful.

The Dovecote   It wasn't built to house doves, but it could well do the job in its lacy roof comb, a kind of false front on a rooftop. The building is remarkable in that roof combs weren't a common feature of temples in the Puuc hills, although you'll see one (of a very different style) on El Mirador at Sayil.

WHERE TO STAY

Unlike Chichén-Itzá, which has several classes of hotels from which to choose, Uxmal has (with one exception) only one type: comfortable but expensive. If occupancy is low, you might get a deal. Less expensive rooms are also available in nearby Ticul, but you'll need a car, as bus service is limited.

MODERATE

☼ **Hotel Hacienda Uxmal.** Km 80 Carretera Mérida–Uxmal, 97840 Uxmal, Yuc. ☎ 99/23-0275. (Reservations: Mayaland Resorts, av. Colón 502, 97000 Mérida, Yuc.; ☎ **800/235-4079** in the U.S., or 99/25-2122; fax 99/25-7022.) 79 units. A/C (in 21 units). High season $133 double. Low season $110 double. AE, MC, V. Free guarded parking.

One of my favorites, this is also the oldest hotel in Uxmal. Located on the highway across from the ruins, it was built as the headquarters for the archaeology staff years ago. Rooms are large and airy, exuding an impression of a well-kept yesteryear, with patterned tile floors, heavy furniture, and well-screened windows. All rooms have ceiling fans, and TVs are being added. Guest rooms surround a handsome central garden courtyard with towering royal palms, a bar, and a pool. Other facilities include a dining room and gift shop. A guitar trio usually plays on the open patio in the evenings. Checkout time is 1pm, so you can spend the morning at the ruins and take a swim before you hit the road again. It's on the highway just before you get to the entrance to the ruins.

Mayaland Resorts, owner of the hotel, offers tour packages that include discount car rental for the nights you spend in its hotels. Mayaland also has a transfer service between the hotel and Mérida for about $30 one way.

✪ **Villa Arqueológica.** Ruinas Uxmal, 97844 Uxmal, Yuc. ☎ **800/258-2633** in the U.S., or 99/28-0644. 43 units. A/C. $74 double. AE, MC, V. Free guarded parking.

This hotel is operated by Club Med, but it is nothing more than a hotel. It offers a beautiful two-story layout around a plant-filled patio and a pool. At guests' disposal are a tennis court, a library, and an audiovisual show on the ruins in English, French, and Spanish. Each of the serene rooms has two oversize single beds. French-inspired meals are à la carte only. It's easy to find—follow the signs to the Uxmal ruins, then turn left to the hotel just before the parking lot at the Uxmal ruins.

INEXPENSIVE

Rancho Uxmal. Km 70 Carretera Mérida–Uxmal, 97840 Uxmal, Yuc. No local phone. (Reservations: Sr. Macario Cach Cabrera, calle 26 no. 156, Ticul, Yuc., 97860; ☎ **99/49-0526** or 99/23-1576.) 20 units. A/C. $30–$36 double; $6 per person campsite. No credit cards. Free guarded parking.

This modest little hotel is an exception to the high-priced places near Uxmal, and it gets better every year. Air-conditioning has been added to 10 of the rooms, all of which have good screens, hot-water showers, and 24-hour electricity. The restaurant is good; a full meal of poc chuc, rice, beans, and tortillas costs about $5, and breakfast is $2.25 to $3. It's a long hike to the ruins from here, but the manager may help you flag down a passing bus or combi or even drive you himself if he has time. A primitive campground out back offers electrical hookups and use of a shower. The hotel is 2¼ miles north of the ruins on Highway 261.

WHERE TO DINE

Besides the hotel restaurants mentioned above and the restaurant at the visitor's center, there are few other dining choices.

Café-Bar Nicte-Ha. In the Hotel Hacienda Uxmal. ☎ **99/23-0275.** Soups and salads $2–$5; main courses $5–$8; fixed-price lunch $9. AE, MC, V. Daily 1–8pm. MEXICAN.

This small restaurant attached to the Hotel Hacienda Uxmal is visible from the crossroads entrance to the ruins. The food is decent, though the prices tend to be high. If you eat here, take full advantage of the experience and spend a few hours by the pool near the cafe: Its use is free to customers. This is a favorite spot for bus tours that fill the place to overcrowding, so come early.

Las Palapas. Hwy. 261. No phone. Breakfast $3; comida corrida $3.75; soft drinks $1. No credit cards. Daily 9am–6pm (comida corrida served 1–4pm). MEXICAN/YUCATECAN.

Three miles north of the ruins on the road to Mérida, you'll find this pleasant restaurant with open-air walls and large thatched palapa roof. The amiable owner, María Cristina Choy, has the most reasonable dining prices around. Individual diners can sometimes become lost in the crowd if a busload of tourists arrives, but otherwise the service is fine and the food quite good. There's also a small gift shop with regional crafts and a few books.

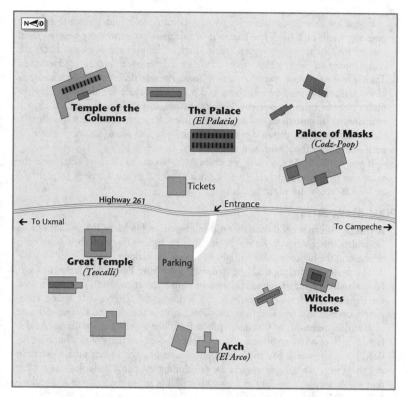

THE PUUC MAYA ROUTE & VILLAGE OF OXKUTZCAB

South and east of Uxmal are several other Maya cities worth exploring. Though smaller in scale than either Uxmal or Chichén-Itzá, each contains gems of Maya architecture. The facade of masks on the Palace of Masks at **Kabah,** the enormous palace at **Sayil,** and the fantastic caverns of **Loltún** may be among the high points of your trip. Also along the way are the **Xlapak** and **Labná ruins** and the pretty village of **Oxkutzcab.**

Kabah is 17 miles southeast of Uxmal. From there it's only a few miles to Sayil. Xlapak is almost walking distance (through the jungle) from Sayil, and Labná is just a bit farther east. A short drive beyond Labná brings you to the caves of Loltún. And Oxkutzcab is at the road's intersection with Highway 184, which can be followed west to Ticul or east all the way to Felipe Carrillo Puerto.

Tips on Seeing Puuc Maya Sites

All these sites are currently undergoing excavation and reconstruction, and some buildings may be roped off when you visit. And for photographers: You'll find afternoon light the best. The sites are open daily from 8am to 5pm. Admission is $2 each for Sayil, Kabah, and Labná; $1.25 for Xlapak; and $3 for Loltún. All except the caves of Loltún are free on Sunday. Use of a video camera at any time costs $4, but if you're visiting Uxmal in the same day, you pay only once for video permission and present your receipt as proof at each ruin. The sites are open daily from 8am to 5pm.

If you are driving, between Labná and Loltún you'll find a road and a sign pointing north to Tabí. A few feet west of this road is a narrow dry-weather track leading into the seemingly impenetrable jungle. A bit over a mile up this track, the jungle opens to the remains of the fabulous old henequen-producing **Hacienda Tabí.** The hewed-rock, two-story main house extends almost the length of a city block, with the living quarters above and storage and space for carriages below. In places it looks ready to collapse. Besides the house, you'll see the ruined chapel, remnants of tall chimneys, and broken machinery. Though not a formal public site, the caretaker will ask you to sign a guest book and allow you to wander around the hulking ruins, without climbing to the second story.

If you aren't driving, a daily bus from Mérida goes to all these sites, with the exception of Loltún and Tabí. (See "By Bus" under "Getting There & Departing," in Mérida, above, for more details.)

Puuc Maya Sites

KABAH If you're off to Kabah, head southwest on Highway 261 to Santa Elena (8½ miles), then south to Kabah (8 miles). The ancient city of Kabah is on both sides along the highway. Make a right turn into the parking lot.

The most outstanding building at Kabah is the huge **Palace of Masks,** or Codz Poop ("rolled-up mat"), named for a motif in its decoration. You'll notice it first on the right up on a terrace. Its outstanding feature is the Chenes-style facade, completely covered in a repeated pattern of 250 masks of the rain god Chaac, each one with curling remnants of Chaac's elephant-trunklike nose. There's nothing like this facade in all of Maya architecture. For years, stone-carved parts of this building lay lined up in the weeds like pieces of a puzzle awaiting the master puzzle-maker to put them into place. Now workers are positioning the parts, including the broken roof comb, in place. Sculptures from this building are in the museums of anthropology in Mérida and Mexico City.

Once you've seen the Palace of Masks, you've seen the best of Kabah. But you should take a look at the other buildings. Just behind and to the left of the Codz Poop is the **Palace Group** (also called the East Group), with a fine Puuc-style colonnaded facade. Originally it had 32 rooms. On the front you see seven doors, two divided by columns, a common feature of Puuc architecture. Recent restoration has added a beautiful L-shaped colonnaded extension to the left front. Further restoration is under way at Kabah, so there may be more to see when you arrive.

Across the highway, a large, conical dirt-and-rubble mound (on your right) was once the **Great Temple,** or Teocalli. Past it is a **great arch,** which was much wider at one time and may have been a monumental gate into the city. A sacbe linked this arch to a point at Uxmal. Compare this corbeled arch to the one at Labná (below), which is in much better shape.

SAYIL Just about 3 miles south of Kabah is the turnoff (left, which is east) to Sayil, Xlapak, Labná, Loltún, and Oxkutzcab. And 2½ miles along this road are the ruins of Sayil (which means "place of the ants").

Sayil is famous for **El Palacio.** This tremendous palace of more than 100 rooms is impressive for its size alone, but what makes it a masterpiece of Maya architecture is the building's facade that stretches across three terraced levels. Its rows of columns give it a Minoan appearance. On the second level, notice the upside-down stone figure of the diving god of bees and honey over the doorway; the same motif was used at Tulum several centuries later. The top of El Palacio affords a great view of the Puuc hills. Sometimes it's difficult to tell which are hills and which are unrestored pyramids, since little temples peep out at unlikely places from the jungle.

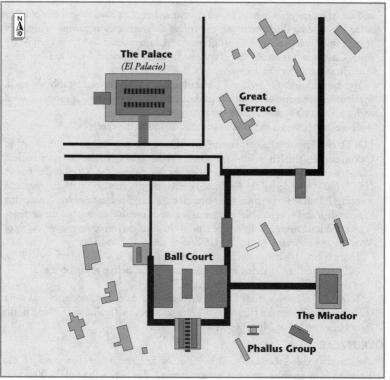

The large circular basin on the ground below the palace is an artificial catch basin for a chultún (cistern) because this region has no natural cenotes (wells) to catch rainwater.

In the jungle past El Palacio is **El Mirador,** a small temple with an oddly slotted roof comb. Beyond El Mirador, a crude **stela** (tall, carved stone) has a phallic idol carved on it in greatly exaggerated proportions.

XLAPAK Xlapak (*shla*-pahk) is a small site with one building; it's 3½ miles down the road from Sayil. The Palace at Xlapak bears the masks of the rain god Chaac.

LABNÁ Labná, which dates to between A.D. 600 and 900, is 18 miles from Uxmal and only 1¾ miles past Xlapak. Like other archaeological sites in the Yucatán, it's also undergoing significant restoration and conservation. Descriptive placards fronting the main buildings are in Spanish, English, and German.

The first thing you see on the left as you enter is **El Palacio,** a magnificent Puuc-style building much like the one at Sayil but in poorer condition. There is an enormous mask of Chaac over a doorway with big banded eyes, a huge snout nose, and jagged teeth around a small mouth that seems on the verge of speaking. Jutting out on one corner is a highly stylized serpent's mouth out from which pops a human head with an unexpectedly serene expression. From the front, you can gaze out to the enormous grassy interior grounds flanked by vestiges of unrestored buildings and jungle.

From El Palacio, you can walk across the interior grounds on a newly reconstructed sacbe leading to Labná's **corbeled arch,** famed for its ornamental beauty and for its representation of what many such arches must have looked like at other sites. This one has been extensively restored, although only remnants of the roof comb can be seen, and it was part of a more elaborate structure that is completely gone. Chaac's face is on the corners of one facade, and stylized Maya huts are fashioned in stone above the doorways.

You pass through the arch to **El Mirador,** or El Castillo, as the rubble-formed, pyramid-shaped structure is called. Towering on the top is a singular room crowned with a roof comb etched against the sky.

There's a refreshment/gift stand with rest rooms at the entrance.

LOLTÚN   The caverns of Loltún are 18½ miles past Labná on the way to Oxkutzcab, on the left side of the road. The fascinating caves, home of ancient Maya, were also used as a refuge and fortress during the War of the Castes (1847–1901). Inside, while you should examine the statuary, wall carvings and paintings, chultúns (cisterns), and other signs of Maya habitation, you'll note that the grandeur and beauty of the caverns alone are impressive. In front of the entrance is an enormous **stone phallus.** The cult of the phallic symbol originated south of Veracruz and appeared in the Yucatán between A.D. 200 and 500.

Tours lasting 1½ hours are given in Spanish daily at 9:30 and 11am and 12:30, 2, and 3pm and are included in the admission price. Before going on a tour, confirm these times at the information desk at Uxmal.

To return to Mérida from Loltún, drive the 4½ miles to Oxkutzcab and from there head northwest on Highway 184. It's 12 miles to Ticul, and (turning north onto Highway 261 at Muna) 65 miles to Mérida.

OXKUTZCAB

Oxkutzcab (ohsh-kootz-*kahb*), 7 miles from Loltún, is the heartland of the Yucatán's fruit-growing region. Oranges abound. The tidy village of 21,000, centered around a beautiful 16th-century church and the market, is worth a stop if for no other reason than to see the church and eat at Su Cabaña Suiza (see below) before heading back to Mérida, Uxmal, or Ticul.

During the last week in October and the first week in November is the **Orange Festival,** when the village turns exuberant with a carnival and orange displays in and around the central plaza.

A DINING DETOUR

✪ **Su Cabaña Suiza.** Calle 54 no. 101. ☎ **997/5-0457.** Main courses $3.50; soft drinks or orange juice 75¢. No credit cards. Daily 7:30am–6:30pm. CHARCOAL-GRILLED MEAT/MEXICAN.

It's worth a trip from Loltún, Ticul, or Uxmal just to taste the delicious charcoal-grilled meat at this unpretentious restaurant draped in colorful plants. Park in the gravel courtyard, then take a seat at one of the metal tables either under the palapa roof or outdoors where caged birds sing. Señora María Antonia Puerto de Pacho runs the spotless place with an iron hand, and family members provide swift, friendly service. The primary menu items include filling portions of charcoal-grilled beef, pork, or chicken served with salad, rice, tortillas, and a bowl of delicious bean soup. But you can also find a few Yucatecan specialties, such as costillas entomatadas, escabeche, queso relleno, and pollo pibil. The restaurant is between calles 49 and 51 in a quiet neighborhood 3 blocks south of the main square.

EN ROUTE TO CAMPECHE

From Oxkutzcab, head back 27 miles to Sayil and then drive south on Highway 261 to Campeche (78 miles). Along the way are several ruins and caves worth visiting.

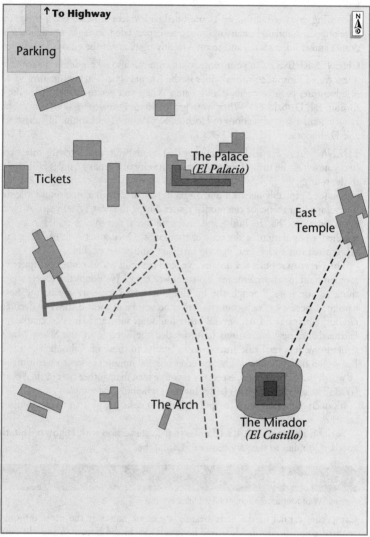

XTACUMBILXUNA CAVES Highway 261 heads south for several miles, passing through a lofty arch marking the boundary between the states of Yucatán and Campeche. Continue on through Bolonchén de Rejón (Bolonchén means "nine wells").

About 1¾ miles south of Bolonchén, a sign points west to the Grutas de Xtacumbilxuna, though the sign spells it XTACUMBINXUNAN. Another sign reads: IT'S WORTH IT TO MAKE A TRIP FROM NEW YORK TO BOLONCHÉN JUST TO SEE XTACUMBILXUNA CAVES (JOHN STEPHENS—EXPLORER). The caves are open whenever the guide is around, which is most of the time. Follow him down for the 30- or 45-minute tour in Spanish, after which a $1 to $3 tip is customary.

Legend has it that a Maya girl escaped an unhappy love affair by hiding in these vast limestone caverns—which wouldn't be hard to do, as you'll see. Unlike the fascinating caves at Loltún, which are filled with traces of Maya occupation, these have only the standard bestiary of limestone shapes: a dog, an eagle, a penguin, a Madonna and child, a snake, and so on—mostly figments of the guide's imagination.

CHENES RUINS   On your route south, you can also take a detour to see several unexcavated, unspoiled ruined cities in the Chenes style. These visits involve a bit of adventure; pack some food and water. When you get to Hopelchén, take the turnoff for Dzibalchén. When you get back to Dzibalchén (25½ miles from Hopelchén), ask for directions to Hochob, San Pedro, Dzehkabtún, El Tabasqueño, and Dzibilnocac.

EDZNÁ   From Hopelchén, Highway 261 heads west, and after 26 miles you'll find yourself at the turnoff for the ruins of the city of Edzná, 12 miles farther along to the south.

Founded probably between 600 and 300 B.C. as a small agricultural settlement, it developed into a major ceremonial center during the next 1,500 years. Archaeologists estimate that to build and maintain such a complex center must have required a population in the tens of thousands. Once a network of Maya canals crisscrossed this entire area, making intensive cultivation possible.

The **Great Acropolis** is a unique five-level pyramid with a temple complete with roofcomb on top. Edzná means "house of wry faces." No doubt there were some of those at one time. Though the buildings at Edzná were mostly in the heavily baroque Chenes, or "well-country," style, no vestige of these distinctive decorative facades remains at Edzná. Several other buildings surround an open central yard. Farther back, new excavations have revealed the **Temple of the Stone Mask,** a structure with several fine stucco masks similar to those of Kohunlich in the Río Bec region near Chetumal. The site takes only 30 minutes or less to see; it may not be worth the price of entry, especially if you've seen many other sites in the Yucatán. (*Note:* The afternoon light is better for photographing the temple.)

It's open daily from 8am to 5pm. Admission costs $3, plus $4 to use your video camera.

Back on Highway 261, it's 12 miles to the intersection with Highway 180, then another 26 miles to the very center of Campeche.

3 Campeche

157 miles SW of Mérida; 235 miles NE of Villahermosa

Campeche, capital of the state bearing the same name, is the most thoroughly restored colonial city in Mexico. The facades to all the houses in the old part of town have been repaired and painted. All electrical and telephone cables have been routed underground, and the streets have been paved with stones or bricks. It is so lovely that you just want to stroll about aimlessly and see what you come upon.

If you are a real ruins-hound or outdoors person, Campeche is a good place from which to strike out for Calakmul, the Río Bec ruins, and the surrounding ecological park. (See chapter 5.)

From the Río Bec area it is simple to cross over to Yucatán's southern Caribbean coast. For additional information, see the tourist offices for brochures. You might talk with an outfit called **Destino Maya** at av. Miguel Alemán no. 162, Despacho 106 (☎ **981/1-0934**). They are flexible and have up-to-date information.

Campeche first had contact with white men when Francisco de Córdoba landed here while passing through. Francisco de Montejo the Elder established a settlement here in 1531, but it did not last. Finally, it was refounded by Montejo the Younger in 1540. The town grew and became prosperous, but was pillaged by a ruthless Dutch pirate who was the original Peg Leg. It was attacked again through the joint efforts of several pirates and constantly harassed. The Campechanos grew tired of playing host to pirate parties and erected walls around the city, showing as much industry then as they now show in renovating their historic district. The area originally enclosed within the walls was quite large and the walls had a number of bastions; two forts, complete with moats and drawbridges, were built on the hills flanking the city on the north and south sides. The pirates never cared to return. Early in this century the wall around the city was razed, but the bastions and main gates were left intact.

ESSENTIALS
GETTING THERE & DEPARTING

BY PLANE   Aeromexico (☎ **981/6-6656** at the airport) flies once daily to and from Mexico City.

BY CAR   Highway 180 goes south from Mérida, passing near the basket-making village of Halacho and near Becal, known for Panama-hat weavers. At Tenabo, take the shortcut (right) to Campeche rather than going farther to the crossroads near Chencoyí. The longer way from Mérida is along **Highway 261** past Uxmal. From Uxmal, Highway 261 passes near some interesting ruins and the Xtacumbilxuna caves (see "En Route to Campeche" in the preceding section).

When driving the other direction, toward Celestún and Mérida, use the **Vía Corta** (short route) by going north on avenida Ruíz Cortínez, bearing left to follow the water (this becomes avenida Pedro Sainz de Baranda, but there's no sign). Follow the road as it turns inland to Highway 180, where you turn left (there's a gas station at the intersection). The route takes you through Becal and Halacho. Stores in both villages close between 2 and 4pm.

If you're leaving Campeche for Edzná and Uxmal, go north on either Cortínez or Gobernadores and turn right on Madero, which becomes **Highway 281.** To Villahermosa, take Cortínez south; it becomes **Highway 180.**

BY BUS   ADO (☎ **981/6-2802**) offers a first-class *de paso* bus to Palenque five times a day and buses to Mérida every hour or less from 5:30am to midnight.

ARRIVING   The **airport** is several miles northeast of the town center, and you'll have to take a taxi into town. The **ADO bus station,** on avenida Gobernadores, is 9 long blocks from the Plaza Principal. Turn left out the front door and walk 1 block. Turn right (calle 49) and go straight for 5 blocks to calle 8. Turn left here, and the Plaza Principal is 3 blocks ahead. Taxis are readily available outside the station.

INFORMATION   The **State of Campeche Office of Tourism** (☎ **981/6-6767;** fax 981/6-6068) is in the Plaza Turística, avenida Ruíz Cortínez s/n, 24000 Campeche, Camp. This is one of the modernist state buildings between the historic center and the shore. There are also information offices in Santa Rosa, San Carlos, and Santiago. The tourism offices here are better prepared and more helpful than in many other cities. They keep regular office hours: 9am to 2pm and 4 to 7pm.

> ### Bus Travel Warning
>
> There have been some bus holdups on highways in the state of Campeche, though none recently. All occurred at night. The U.S. State Department recommends avoiding traveling at night.

CITY LAYOUT   Most of your time in Campeche will be spent in the historic district. The administrative center of town is the modernist **Plaza Moch-Couoh** on avenida 16 de Septiembre near the waterfront. Next door to the plaza rises the modern office tower called the **Edificio Poderes,** or **Palacio de Gobierno—** headquarters for the state of Campeche. Beside it is the futuristic **Cámara de Diputados** or **Casa de Congreso** (state legislative chamber), which looks like an enormous square clam. Just behind it, the **Parque Principal** (central park) on calle 8 will most likely be your reference point for touring.

Campeche's system of street numbering is much like that of Yucatán's cities except that the number of north-south streets goes from west to east instead of the other direction.

GETTING AROUND   Most of the recommended sights, restaurants, and hotels are within walking distance of the Parque Principal, except for the two fort-museums. Campeche isn't easy to negotiate by bus, so I recommend taxis for anything beyond walking distance.

FAST FACTS: CAMPECHE

American Express   Local offices are at calle 59 no. 4–5 (☎ **981/1-1010**), in the Edificio Belmar, a half block toward town from the Ramada Inn. They're open Monday through Friday from 9am to 2pm and 5 to 7pm, and Saturday from 9am to 1:30pm. They do not cash traveler's checks.

Area Code   The telephone **area code** is **981.**

Post Office   The post office (correo) is in the Edificio Federal at the corner of avenida 16 de Septiembre and calle 53 (☎ **981/6-2134**), near the Baluarte de Santiago; it's open Monday through Saturday from 7:30am to 8pm. The telegraph office is here as well.

EXPLORING CAMPECHE

With such beautiful surroundings, friendly people, easy pace, and orderly traffic, Campeche is a lovely city worthy of at least a day on your itinerary. There are a couple of good museums, good restaurants, and several shops worth investigating.

INSIDE THE CITY WALLS

A good place to begin is the pretty zócalo, or **Parque Principal,** bounded by calles 55 and 57 running east and west and calles 8 and 10 running north and south. Construction of the church on the north side of the square began in 1650 and was finally completed a century and a half later.

For a good introduction to the city, turn south from the park on calle 8 and walk 5 blocks to the **Museo de la Ciudad** (city museum).

Baluarte de la Soledad. Calle 57 and calle 8, opposite the Plaza Principal. No phone. Admission 50¢, Sunday free. Tues–Sat 8am–8pm, Sun 8am–6pm.

This bastion houses the Sala de Estelas, a display of Maya votive stones brought from various sites in this ruins-rich state. Many are badly worn, but the excellent line drawings beside the stones allow you to admire their former beauty. Three additional rooms also have interesting artifacts; each room is dedicated to a different Maya scholar.

Baluarte de San Carlos/Museo de la Ciudad. Circuito Baluartes and av. Justo Sierra. No phone. Voluntary contributions. Tues–Sat 8am–8pm; Sun 8am–1pm.

This museum features a permanent exhibition of photographs and plans about the city and its history. The model of the city shows how it looked in its glory days and

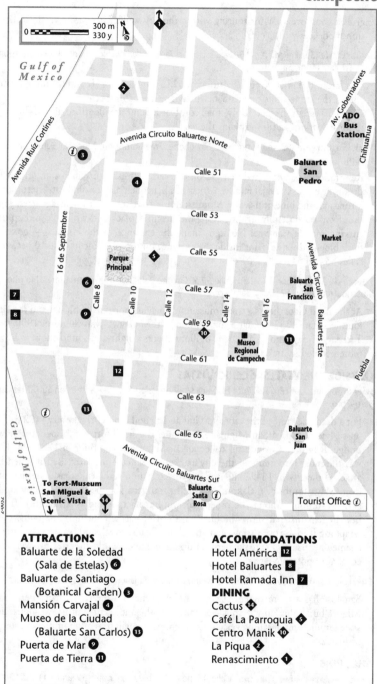

Campeche

Gulf of Mexico

Avenida Ruíz Cortines

Av. Gobernadores

ADO Bus Station

Chihuahua

Avenida Circuito Baluartes Norte

Baluarte San Pedro

Calle 51

16 de Septiembre

Calle 53

Market

Calle 55

Parque Principal

Calle 57

Baluarte San Francisco

Calle 8

Calle 10

Calle 12

Calle 14

Calle 16

Calle 59

Museo Regional de Campeche

Avenida Circuito Baluartes Este

Calle 61

Puebla

Calle 63

Calle 65

Avenida Circuito Baluartes Sur

Baluarte San Juan

Gulf of Mexico

To Fort-Museum San Miguel & Scenic Vista

Baluarte Santa Rosa ⓘ

Tourist Office ⓘ

ATTRACTIONS
Baluarte de la Soledad
  (Sala de Estelas) ❻
Baluarte de Santiago
  (Botanical Garden) ❸
Mansión Carvajal ❹
Museo de la Ciudad
  (Baluarte San Carlos) ⓭
Puerta de Mar ❾
Puerta de Tierra ⓫

ACCOMMODATIONS
Hotel América ⓬
Hotel Baluartes ❽
Hotel Ramada Inn ❼

DINING
Cactus ⓮
Café La Parroquia ❺
Centro Manik ❿
La Piqua ❷
Renascimiento ❶

gives a good overview for touring within the city walls. There are several excellent ship models as well.

Baluarte de Santiago. Av. 16 de Septiembre and calle 49. No phone. Free admission. Mon–Fri 7am–4pm, Sat 9am–4pm.

The Jardín Botánico Xmuch'haltun grows in a jumble of exotic and common plants within the stone walls of this baluarte. More than 250 species of plants and trees share what seems like a terribly small courtyard. Some are identified and, if the projector is working, a film explains the garden.

Mansión Carvajal. Calle 10 no. 584. No phone. Free admission. Mon–Sat 9am–2pm and 4–8pm.

Restoration was completed in 1992 on this early–20th-century mansion, originally the home of the Carvajal family, owners of a henequen plantation. In its latest transformation, the blue-and-white Moorish home contains government agencies. Join the crowd purposefully striding along the gleaming black-and-white tile and up the curving marble staircase. No signs mark the entrance to the building—look for fresh blue-and-white paint inside the entrance on the west side of calle 10 between calles 53 and 51.

Puerta de Tierra (Land Gate). Calle 59 at Circuito Baluartes/av. Gobernadores. No phone. Museum free, show $2. Daily 8am–9pm.

At the Land Gate there's a small museum displaying portraits of pirates and the city founders. The 1732 French 5-ton cannon in the entryway was found in 1990. On Tuesday, Friday, and Saturday at 8:30pm there's a light-and-sound show if 15 or more people buy tickets.

OUTSIDE THE WALLS: SCENIC VISTAS

Fuerte-Museo San Miguel. Ruta Escénica s/n. Admission 50¢; free admission Sun. Tues–Sun 8am–7pm.

For a dramatic view of the city and Gulf and a good museum, take a cab ($2 to $3) up to Fuerte-Museo San Miguel. San Miguel is a small fort with moat and drawbridge. It houses a wonderful collection of Maya artifacts. Built in 1771, this fort was the most important of the city's defenses. Santa Anna later used it when he attacked the city in 1842. The pride of the collection is the jade masks and jewelry from Maya tombs at Calakmul—a site in southern Campeche undergoing study and excavation. Among the other Calakmul artifacts found in structure VII are human remains that show the burial custom of partially burning the body, then wrapping it in a woven straw mat and cloth. Beans, copal, and feathers—all items deemed necessary to take the person through the underworld after death—were discovered in pottery vessels.

Fuerte-Museo San José el Alto. Av. Morazán s/n. Admission 50¢. Tues–Sun 8am–8pm.

San José has a more sweeping view of Campeche and the coast than Fuerte San Miguel but holds only a small exhibit of 16th- and 17th-century weapons and scaled miniatures of sailing vessels. On the way, you will pass by an impressive statue of Juárez.

SHOPPING

Casa de Artesanías Tukulna. Calle 10 no. 333 (between calles 59 and 61). ☎ **981/ 6-9088.** Mon–Sat 9am–2pm and 5–8pm.

This store run by DIF (a government family assistance agency) occupies a restored mansion. There is an elaborate display of regional arts and crafts in the back.

Everything that is produced in the state is represented in the showrooms. There are quality textiles, clothing, and locally made furniture. It's open Monday through Saturday from 9am to 2pm and 5 to 8pm.

WHERE TO STAY

It's ironic that in this wonderful colonial city there isn't a single good colonial-style hotel. The most comfortable hotels are outside the historic center; the most economical are inside.

EXPENSIVE

✪ **Ramada Inn.** Av. Ruíz Cortínes 51 (Apdo. Postal 251), 24000 Campeche, Camp. ☎ **800/854-7854** in the U.S., or 981/6-2233. Fax 981/1-1618. 120 units. A/C TV TEL. $105 double. AE, MC, V. Free parking.

Extensively remodeled in 1990, the handsomely furnished rooms at the Ramada Inn all have tile floors and balconies facing the Gulf of Mexico. The restaurant, bar, and coffee shop are popular with local citizens—always a good recommendation. There's a large swimming pool, a discotheque, and a fenced parking lot behind the hotel. It's on the main oceanfront boulevard, 2 blocks west of the Plaza Principal and next to the Hotel Baluartes.

MODERATE

Hotel Baluartes. Av. Ruíz Cortines 61, 24000 Campeche, Camp. ☎ **981/6-3911.** Fax 981/6-2410. 100 units. A/C TV TEL. $55 double. AE, MC, V. Free parking.

Opposite the Gulf of Mexico and next door to the Ramada Inn, this was the city's original luxury hotel. It's still a nice place but not refurbished and modern like the Ramada. Many of the rooms have a Gulf view. The swimming pool is refreshing after a day of touring. The Baluartes, which has a restaurant and bar on the first floor, is at the corner of calle 61, 2 blocks west of the Plaza Principal.

INEXPENSIVE

Hotel América. Calle 10 no. 252, 24000 Campeche, Camp. ☎ **981/1-2994.** 52 units, 4 with A/C. TV. $20 double. No credit cards. Free guarded parking 3 blocks away.

This is the best of the central hotels. It is old and worn but clean. The three stories of rooms (no elevator) have one, two, or three double beds and come with tile floors. Corner rooms are quieter than those with windows on the street. To find the hotel from the Parque Principal, walk south on calle 10 for 2½ blocks; it's on the right between calles 61 and 63.

WHERE TO EAT

Campeche's cooking is primarily seafood with some local versions of Mexican favorites. For regional food, try *colados* (which are delicious tamales), *tacos de salchicha* (an unusual pastry), *cazón de Campeche* (a tasty shark stew), and *pan de cazón* (another shark dish for those with more adventurous palates).

MODERATE

Cactus. Av. Malecón Justo Sierra. ☎ **981/1-1453.** Main courses $5–$9. No credit cards. Daily 7am–2am. STEAKS/MEXICAN.

If seafood isn't to your taste, try this steak house. It's a favorite with the locals. The rib-eyes are good, as is everything but the arrachera, which is the same cut of meat as fajitas and very tough.

✪ **La Pigua.** Av. Miguel Alemán no. 179A. ☎ **981/1-3365.** Main courses $6–$8. AE, DISC, MC, V. Daily noon–6pm. SEAFOOD/MEXICAN.

La Pigua is the best restaurant in the city. The dining area is in an air-conditioned version of the traditional Yucatecan house, but with the walls made of glass surrounded by thick and green vegetation. It's lovely. There are not many tables, so it is a good idea to make a reservation. The menu is in a sharkskin folder and is peppered with Spanish nautical terms. I can't even keep English nautical terms straight, so this menu poses a real challenge. But the owner is happy to help out his customers. The most unusual dishes are chiles rellenos stuffed with shark and coconut batter-fried shrimp served with applesauce. The crab claws are a house specialty. But the cook can prepare your favorite seafood in any style you want. To reach La Pigua from the Plaza Principal, walk north on calle 8 for 3 blocks. Cross the avenida Circuito by the botanical garden, where calle 8 becomes Miguel Alemán. The restaurant is 1½ blocks north, on the east side of the street.

Renacimiento. Calle 10 no. 90. ☎ **981/1-4257.** Main courses $4–$8. No credit cards. Tues–Sun noon–midnight. REGIONAL/ANTOJITOS.

This is a great place to come for traditional supper fare of tacos, tostadas, and other antojitos. It's in the arcade in the Plaza of San Francisco, the oldest barrio in town. And, if the locals are to be believed, this is where the Spaniards first came ashore in circumstances that allowed the celebration of Mass—the first on the continent. Contemplate this as you munch down a few antojitos. I recommend the turkey sincronizadas and the tacos al pastor. With the antojitos come several types of pico de gallo. The cabbage/habañero pico is for the sincronizadas, and the pineapple pico is for the tacos al pastor (again, according to locals, who I believe are right on target in this matter). The restaurant is a few blocks outside the north wall. Just ask anybody for San Francisco.

INEXPENSIVE

Centro Manik. Calle 59 no. 22 (between 12 and 14). ☎ **981/6-2448.** Breakfast $3; main dishes $2. No credit cards. Mon–Sat 8am–2pm, 6pm–midnight. VEGETARIAN.

This place specializes in vegetarian versions of popular foods—burgers, pizzas, and tamales. It also gets some of its inspiration from local and traditional recipes, such as pozole and brazo de reina. The restaurant makes its own bread and cakes and can serve them with a cappuccino. The interior is simple and pleasant; most of the tables are in a courtyard or a side room. The restaurant is frequented not just by college-age people, but also by business sorts. There is a small bookstore and a gallery, and some organic local products such as honey are sold.

La Parroquia. Calle 55 no. 9. ☎ **981/6-8086.** Breakfast $1–$3; main courses $2.75–$6; comida corrida $3.50. No credit cards. Daily 24 hours (comida corrida served 1–4pm). MEXICAN.

La Parroquia, a popular local hangout, has friendly waiters and offers excellent, inexpensive fare. Here, you can enjoy great breakfasts and colados, the delicious regional tamal. Selections on the comida corrida might include pot roast, meatballs, pork or fish, rice or squash, beans, tortillas, and fresh-fruit–flavored water.

4 The Ruins of Chichén-Itzá

112 miles W of Cancún; 75 miles E of Mérida

The fabled pyramids and temples of Chichén-Itzá (no, it doesn't rhyme with chicken pizza; it's pronounced chee-*chin* eat-*zah*) are the Yucatán's best-known ancient monuments. The ruins are plenty hyped, but Chichén is truly worth seeing. Walking among these stone platforms and pyramids and ball courts gives an appreciation for this ancient civilization that cannot be had from reading books. It evokes a tremendous sense of wonder; the amount of open space surrounding the Pyramid of Kukulkán, prompts you to ponder the kinds of mass celebrations or rituals that occurred here a millenium ago. Remember that much of what is said about the Maya (especially by tour guides) is merely educated guessing; even the Mayan alphabet is still poorly understood by scholars.

This Postclassic Maya city was established by Itzáes perhaps sometime during the 9th century A.D. Linda Schele and David Friedel, in *A Forest of Kings* (Morrow, 1990), have cast doubt on the legend that Kukulkán (called Quetzalcoatl by the Toltecs—a name also associated with a legendary god) came here from the Toltec capital of Tula (in north-central Mexico), and, along with Petén Maya coastal traders, built a magnificent metropolis that combined the Maya Puuc style with Toltec motifs (the feathered serpent, warriors, eagles, and jaguars). Not so, say Schele and Friedel. Readings of Chichén's bas-reliefs and hieroglyphs fail to support that legend, they say, and instead show that Chichén-Itzá was a continuous Maya site influenced by association with the Toltecs but not by an invasion. Not all scholars, however, embrace this new thinking, so the idea of a Toltec invasion still holds sway.

Though it's possible to make a round-trip from Mérida to Chichén-Itzá in 1 day, it will be a long, tiring, and very rushed day. Try to spend at least 1 night at Chichén-Itzá (most hotels are actually in the nearby village of Pisté).

ESSENTIALS

GETTING THERE & DEPARTING   **By Plane**   Day trips on charter flights from Cancún and Cozumel can be arranged by travel agents in the United States or in Cancún or Cozumel.

By Car   Chichén-Itzá is on the main Highway 180 between Mérida and Cancún. You can also take the autopista.

By Bus   From Mérida, there are four first-class **ADO** buses per day, and a couple that go to Valladolid will stop here. Also, there are several second-class buses per day. If you go round-trip in a day (a 2½-hour trip one way), take the 8:45am bus and reserve a seat on the return bus. *De paso* buses to Mérida leave hourly day and night, as do those to Valladolid and Cancún.

ORIENTATION   **Arriving**   If coming by bus, you'll arrive in the village of Pisté, at the station next to the Pirámide Inn. From Pisté, there's a sidewalk to the archaeological zone, which is a mile or so east of the bus station.

City Layout   The small town of **Pisté,** where most hotels and restaurants are located, is about a mile and a half from the ruins of Chichén-Itzá. Public buses from Mérida, Cancún, Valladolid, and elsewhere discharge passengers here. A few hotels are at the edge of the ruins, and one, the Hotel Dolores Alba (see "Where to Stay," below), is out of town about 1½ miles from the ruins on the road to Valladolid.

EXPLORING THE RUINS

The site occupies 4 square miles, and it takes a full, strenuous day (from 8am to noon and 2 to 5pm) to see all the ruins, which are open daily from 8am to 5pm. Service areas are open from 8am to 10pm. Admission is $4, free for children under 12 and free for all on Sunday and holidays. A permit to use your own video camera costs an additional $4. Parking is extra. *You can use your ticket to reenter on the same day, but you'll have to pay again for an additional day.* Chichén-Itzá's light-and-sound show was completely revamped in 1993 and is well worth seeing. The Spanish version is shown nightly at 7pm and costs $3.50; the English version is at 9pm and costs $4. The show may be offered in French and German as well. Ask at your hotel.

The large, modern visitor center, at the main entrance where you pay the admission charge, is beside the parking lot and consists of a museum, an auditorium, a restaurant, a bookstore, and rest rooms. You can see the site on your own or with a licensed guide who speaks either English or Spanish. These guides are usually waiting at the entrance and charge around $30 for one to six people. Although the guides frown on it, there's nothing wrong with your approaching a group of people who speak the same language and asking if they would like to share a guide with you. The guide, of course, would like to get $30 from you alone and $30 each from other individuals who don't know one another and still form a group. Be wary of some of what the history guides spout—some of it is just plain out-of-date, but the architectural details they point out are enlightening.

There are actually two parts of Chichén-Itzá (which dates from around A.D. 600 to 900). There's the northern (new) zone, which shows distinct Toltec influence, and the southern (old) zone, which is mostly Puuc architecture.

El Castillo   As you enter from the tourist center, the beautiful 75-foot El Castillo pyramid (also called the Pyramid of Kukulkán) will be straight ahead across a large open area. It was built with the Maya calendar in mind. There are 364 stairs plus a platform to equal 365 (days of the year); 52 panels on each side (which represent the 52-year cycle of the Maya calendar); and 9 terraces on each side of the stairways (for a total of 18 terraces, which represents the 18-month Maya solar calendar). If this isn't proof enough of the mathematical precision of this temple, come for the **spring** or **fall equinox** (March 21 or September 21 between 3 and 5pm). On those days, the seven stairs of the northern stairway and the serpent-head carving at the base are touched with sunlight and become a "serpent" formed by the play of light and shadow. It appears to descend into the earth as the sun hits each stair from the top, ending with the serpent head. To the Maya this was a fertility symbol: The golden sun had entered the earth, meaning it was time to plant the corn.

El Castillo was built over an earlier structure. A narrow stairway at the western edge of the north staircase leads into the structure, where there is a sacrificial altar-throne—a red jaguar encrusted with jade. The stairway is open at 11am and 3pm and is claustrophobic, usually crowded, humid, and uncomfortable. A visit early in the day is best. Photos of the figure are not allowed.

Main Ball Court (Juego de Pelota)   Northwest of El Castillo is Chichén's main ball court, the largest and best preserved anywhere, and only one of nine ball courts built in this city. Carved on both walls of the ball court are scenes showing Maya figures dressed as ball players decked out in heavy protective padding. The carved scene also shows a headless player kneeling with blood shooting from the neck; the player is looked upon by another player holding the head.

Players on two teams tried to knock a hard rubber ball through one or the other of the two stone rings placed high on either wall, using only their elbows, knees, and hips (no hands). According to legend, the losing players paid for defeat with their lives. However, some experts say the victors were in fact the only appropriate sacrifices for the gods. One can only guess what the incentive for winning might be in such case. Either way, the game must have been riveting, heightened by the perfect acoustics of the ball court.

The North Temple   Temples are found at both ends of the ball court. The North Temple has sculptured pillars and more sculptures inside, as well as badly ruined

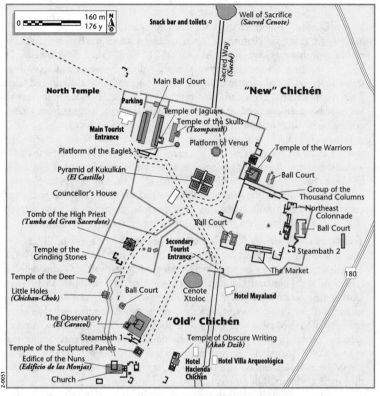

murals. The acoustics of the ball court are so good that from the North Temple, a person speaking can be heard clearly at the opposite end about 450 feet away.

Temple of Jaguars   Near the southeastern corner of the main ball court is a small temple with serpent columns and carved panels showing warriors and jaguars. Up the flight of steps and inside the temple, a mural was found that chronicles a battle in a Maya village.

Temple of the Skulls (Tzompantli)   To the right of the ball court is the Temple of the Skulls, with rows of skulls carved into the stone platform. When a sacrificial victim's head was cut off, it was impaled on a pole and displayed in a tidy row with others. Also carved into the stone are pictures of eagles tearing hearts from human victims. The word Tzompantli is not Mayan but came from central Mexico. Reconstruction using scattered fragments may add a level to this platform and change the look of this structure by the time you visit.

Platform of the Eagles   Next to the Tzompantli, this small platform has reliefs showing eagles and jaguars clutching human hearts in their talons and claws, as well as a human head emerging from the mouth of a serpent.

Platform of Venus   East of the Tzompantli and north of El Castillo near the road to the Sacred Cenote is the Platform of Venus. In Maya–Toltec lore, Venus was represented by a feathered monster or a feathered serpent with a human head in its mouth. It's also called the tomb of Chaac-Mool because a Chaac-Mool figure was discovered "buried" within the structure.

Sacred Cenote   Follow the dirt road (actually an ancient sacbe, or causeway) that heads north from the Platform of Venus; after 5 minutes you'll come to the great natural well that may have given Chichén-Itzá (the Well of the Itzáes) its name. This well was used for ceremonial purposes, not for drinking water, and according to legend, sacrificial victims were drowned in this pool to honor the rain god Chaac. Anatomical research done early this century by Ernest A. Hooten showed that bones of both children and adults were found in the well. Judging from Hooten's evidence, they may have been outcasts, diseased, or feeble-minded.

Edward Thompson, who was the American consul in Mérida and a Harvard professor, purchased the ruins of Chichén early this century and explored the cenote with dredges and divers. His explorations exposed a fortune in gold and jade. Most of the riches wound up in Harvard's Peabody Museum of Archaeology and Ethnology—a matter that continues to disconcert Mexican classicists today. Later excavations in the 1960s unearthed more treasure, and studies of the recovered objects detail offerings from throughout the Yucatán and even farther away.

Temple of the Warriors (Templo de los Guerreros)   Due east of El Castillo is one of the most impressive structures at Chichén: the Temple of the Warriors, named for the carvings of warriors marching along its walls. It's also called the Group of the Thousand Columns for the rows of broken pillars that flank it. During the recent restoration, hundreds more of the columns were rescued from the rubble and put in place, setting off the temple more magnificently than ever. A figure of Chaac-Mool sits at the top of the temple, surrounded by impressive columns carved in relief to look like enormous feathered serpents. South of the temple was a square building that archaeologists called the **Market** (mercado); its central court is surrounded by a colonnade. Beyond the temple and the market in the jungle are mounds of rubble, parts of which are being reconstructed.

The main Mérida–Cancún highway once ran straight through the ruins of Chichén, and though it has now been diverted, you can still see the great swath it cut. South and west of the old highway's path are more impressive ruined buildings.

Tomb of the High Priest (Tumba del Gran Sacerdote)   Past the refreshment stand to the right of the path is the Tomb of the High Priest, which stood atop a natural limestone cave in which skeletons and offerings were found, giving the temple its name.

The tomb has been reconstructed, and workers are unearthing other smaller temples in the area. As the work progresses, some buildings may be roped off and others will open to the public for the first time. It's fascinating to watch the archaeologists at work, meticulously numbering each stone as they take apart what appears to be a mound of rocks, then reassembling the stones into a recognizable structure.

Temple of the Grinding Stones (Casa de los Metates)   This building, the next one on your right, is named after the concave corn-grinding stones used by the Maya.

Temple of the Deer (Templo del Venado)   Past the House of Metates is this fairly tall though ruined building. The relief of a stag that gave the temple its name is long gone.

Little Holes (Chichan-chob)   This next temple has a roof comb with little holes, three masks of the rain god Chaac, three rooms, and a good view of the surrounding structures. It's one of the older buildings at Chichén, built in the Puuc style during the Late Classic period.

The Maya Calendar

To understand Chichén-Itzá fully, you need to know something about the unique way in which the Maya kept time on several simultaneous calendars.

Although not more accurate than our own calendar, the intricate Maya calendar systems begin, according to many scholars, in 3114 B.C.—before Maya culture even existed. From that date, the Maya could measure time—and their life cycle—to a point 90 million years in the future! The Maya conceived of world history as a series of cycles moving within cycles.

The Solar Year   The Maya solar year measured 365.24 days. Within that solar year there were 18 "months" of 20 days each, for a total of 360 days, plus a special 5-day period.

The Ceremonial Year   A ceremonial calendar, completely different from the solar calendar, ran its "annual" cycle at the same time, but this was not a crude system like the Gregorian calendar, which has saints' days, some fixed feast days, and some movable feasts. It was so intricate that the ordinary Maya depended on the priests to keep track of it. Complex and ingenious, the ceremonial calendar system consisted of 13 "months" of 20 days; within that cycle of 260 days was another of 20 "weeks" of 13 days. The Maya ceremonial calendar interlaced exactly with the solar calendar. Each date of the solar calendar had a name, and each date of the ceremonial calendar also had a name; therefore, every day in Maya history has two names, which were always quoted together.

The Double Cycle   After 52 solar years and 73 ceremonial "years," during which each day had its unique, unduplicated double name, these calendars ended their respective cycles simultaneously on the very same day; then a brand-new, identical double cycle began. Thus, in the longer scheme of things, a day would be identified by the name of the 52-year cycle, the name of the solar day, and the name of the ceremonial day.

Mystic Numbers   Several numbers were of great significance to the system. The number 20 was perhaps most important, as calendar calculations were done with a number system with base 20. There were 20 "suns" (days) to a "month," 20 years to a katun, and 20 katuns (20 times 20, or 400 years) to a baktun.

The number 52 was also of tremendous importance, for it signified, literally, the "end of time"—the end of the double cycle of solar and ceremonial calendars. At the beginning of a new cycle, temples were rebuilt for the "new age," which is why so many Maya temples and pyramids hold within them the structures of earlier, smaller temples and pyramids.

The Maya Concept of Time   The Maya considered time not as "progress" but as the wheel of fate, spinning endlessly, determining one's destiny by the combinations of attributes given to days in the solar and ceremonial calendars. The rains came on schedule, the corn was planted on schedule, and the celestial bodies moved in their great dance under the watchful eye of Maya astronomers and astrologers. *The Blood of Kings* (see "Recommended Books & Recordings" in chapter 2) has an especially good chapter on the Maya calendar. As evidence of the Maya obsession with time, Chichén's most impressive structure, El Castillo, is in fact an enormous timepiece.

Observatory (El Caracol)   Construction of the Observatory, a complex building with a circular tower, was carried out over centuries; the additions and modifications reflected the Maya's careful observation of celestial movements and their need for increasingly exact measurements. Through slits in the tower's walls, Maya astronomers could observe the cardinal directions and the approach of the all-important spring and autumn equinoxes, as well as the summer solstice. The temple's name, which means "snail," comes from a spiral staircase within the structure.

On the east side of El Caracol, a path leads north into the bush to the Cenote Xtoloc, a natural limestone well that provided the city's daily water supply. If you see any lizards sunning there, they may well be xtoloc, the lizard for which the cenote is named.

Temple of Panels (Templo de los Tableros)   Just to the south of El Caracol are the ruins of a steam bath (temazcalli) and the Temple of Panels, named for the carved panels on top. This temple was once covered by a much larger structure, only traces of which remain.

Edifice of the Nuns (Edificio de las Monjas)   If you've visited the Puuc sites of Kabah, Sayil, Labná, or Xlapak, the enormous nunnery here will remind you at once of the "palaces" at the other sites. Built in the Late Classic period, the new edifice was constructed over an older one. Suspecting that this was so, Le Plongeon, an archaeologist working earlier in this century, put dynamite in between the two and blew away part of the exterior, thereby revealing the older structures within. You can still see the results of Le Plongeon's indelicate exploratory methods.

On the eastern side of the Edifice of the Nuns is an **annex (Anexo Este)** constructed in highly ornate Chenes style with Chaac masks and serpents.

The Church (La Iglesia)   Next to the annex is one of the oldest buildings at Chichén, absurdly named the Church. Masks of Chaac decorate two upper stories. Look closely and you'll see other pagan symbols among the crowd of Chaacs: an armadillo, a crab, a snail, and a tortoise. These represent the Maya gods called bacah, whose job it was to hold up the sky.

Temple of Obscure Writing (Akab Dzib)   Beloved of travel writers, this temple lies east of the Edifice of the Nuns. Above a door in one of the rooms are some Maya glyphs, which gave the temple its name, since the writings have yet to be deciphered. In other rooms, traces of red handprints are still visible. Reconstructed and expanded over the centuries, Akab Dzib may well be the oldest building at Chichén.

Old Chichén (Chichén Viejo)   For a look at more of Chichén's oldest buildings, constructed well before the time of Toltec influence, follow signs from the Edifice of the Nuns southwest into the bush to Old Chichén, about half a mile away. Be prepared for this trek with long trousers, insect repellent, and a local guide. The attractions here are the **Temple of the First Inscriptions** (Templo de los Inscripciones Iniciales), with the oldest inscriptions discovered at Chichén, and the restored **Temple of the Lintels** (Templo de los Dinteles), a fine Puuc building.

WHERE TO STAY

The expensive hotels in Chichén are all set in beautiful surroundings displaying the local flora's finery. All have 800 numbers for reservations, which I recommend using. Some of these hotels do a lot of business with tour operators—they can be empty one day and full the next.

EXPENSIVE

Hacienda Chichén. Zona Arqueológica, 97751 Chichén-Itzá, Yuc. ☎ and fax 985/1-0045. (Reservations: Casa del Balam, calle 60 no. 488, 97000 Mérida, Yuc. ☎ **800/624-8451** in the U.S., or 99/24-8844; fax 99/24-5011. www.wotw.com/casadelbalam.) 21 units. A/C. $93 double. AE, DC, DISC, MC, V. Free guarded parking.

This is the smallest and most private of the hotels at the ruins. It was a hacienda that in 1923 served as the headquarters for the Carnegie Institute's excavations. Several bungalows were built to house the staff; these are now the guest rooms. Each is simply furnished and decorated. They are separated from each other by a short distance, and each has a porch from which you can enjoy the beautiful grounds. The main building belonged to the hacienda. It houses the terrace restaurant and the lobby, and has a pool beside it.

✪ **Hotel Mayaland.** Zona Arqueológica, 97751 Chichén-Itzá, Yuc. ☎ 985/1-0127. (Reservations: Mayaland Resorts, av. Colón 502, 97000 Mérida, Yuc.; ☎ **800/ 235-4079** in the U.S., or 99/25-2122; fax 99/25-7022.) 95 units. A/C TV. High season $133 double, $192 bungalow. Low season 10% off. AE, MC, V. Free guarded parking.

Glancing out the lobby doorway, you can't lose sight of the ruins; before you sits El Caracol (the observatory). Rooms in the main building are connected by a wide, tiled veranda, tiled bathrooms (with tubs), and colonial-style furnishings. Maya-inspired bungalows with beautifully carved furniture are tucked into the wooded grounds. The grounds are gorgeous, with huge trees and lush foliage—the hotel has had 75 years to get them in shape. There are three pools, a restaurant, a grill, and a buffet. Mayaland has a shuttle service between the hotel and Mérida for about $35 each way.

The Hotel Mayaland in the past has maintained rental-car offers that make the hotel a bargain. The official policy seems to be under revision, however, so you may want to ask about their offers.

Hotel Villa Arqueológica. Zona Arqueológica, 97751 Chichén-Itzá, Yuc. ☎ **800/258-2633** in the U.S., 985/1-0034, or 985/6-2830. 40 units. A/C. High season $110 double. Low season $70 double. AE, MC, V.

A lovely hotel built around a pool partially shaded by two large flamboyan trees, and the background is formed by bougainvillea. The rooms are not large but are very comfortable. Each comes with a double and an oversized single bed. There are tennis courts, and the hotel's restaurant features international and Yucatecan food.

MODERATE

Pirámide Inn. Km 118 Carretera Mérida–Valladolid, 97751 Pisté, Yuc. ☎ **985/1-0115.** Fax 985/10114. 44 units. A/C. $27–$40 double. No credit cards.

Less than a mile from the ruins at the edge of Pisté, this hospitable inn has large motel-like rooms equipped with two double beds or one king-size bed. You might want to check your mattress for its sag factor before accepting the room. Hot water comes on between 5 and 9am and 5 and 9pm. Water is purified in the tap for drinking. There is a pool in the midst of landscaped gardens, which include the remains of a pyramid wall. Try to get a room in the back. If you're coming from Valladolid, it's on the left, and from Mérida look for it on the right.

Stardust Inn. Calle 15A no. 34A, Carretera Mérida–Valladolid, 97751 Pisté, Yuc. ☎ and fax 985/1-0122. (Reservations: calle 81A no. 513, 97000 Mérida, Yuc.; ☎ **99/84-0072.**) 57 units. A/C TV. $50 double. AE, MC, V. Free parking.

The two-story Stardust Inn is built around a pool and a shaded courtyard. Each of the comfortable rooms has a tile floor, a shower, nice towels, and one or two double beds or three single beds; check the condition of your mattress before selecting a room. During high season, there's a video bar/disco on the first floor; it's open during other times of the year if there are groups. If tranquillity is one of your priorities, ask if the disco is going to kick into gear before you rent a room. The very nice air-conditioned restaurant adjacent to the lobby and facing the highway serves all three meals and is open from 7:30am to 9:30pm.

INEXPENSIVE

Hotel Dolores Alba. Km 122 Carretera Mérida–Valladolid, Yuc. No phone. (Reservations: Hotel Dolores Alba, calle 63 no. 464, 97000 Mérida, Yuc. ☎ **99/28-5650;** fax 99/28-3163; e-mail: asanchez@Yucatan.com.mx.) 30 units. A/C. $22–$27 double. No credit cards. Free parking.

This place is of the motel variety, perfect if you come by car. It is a bargain for what you get: two pools (one of them unlike any I have ever seen); palapas and hammocks around the place for the benefit of the guests; and large and comfortable rooms. The restaurant serves good meals at moderate prices. Free transportation is provided to the ruins and the Caves of Balankanche during visiting hours, though you will have to take a taxi to get back. The hotel is on the highway 1½ miles east of the ruins (toward Valladolid).

Posada Novelo. Carretera Mérida–Valladolid, 97751 Pisté, Yuc. ☎ and fax **985/1-0122.** 11 units. $12 double. MC, V. Free parking in front.

Operated by the Stardust Inn next door, this hotel is in effect the budget wing of the main hotel. Rooms are attached in a row and linked by a covered walkway; all have one or two beds and are sparsely furnished but clean. Hot water is a rarity.

WHERE TO DINE

Reasonably priced meals are available at the restaurant in the visitors' center at the ruins and at hotels in Pisté. Hotel restaurants near the ruins jump quite a bit in price. In Pisté, however, many places cater to large groups, which descend on them en masse for lunch after 1pm.

Cafetería Ruinas. In the Chichén-Itzá visitors' center. No phone. Breakfast $4; sandwiches $4–$5; main courses $5–$8. No credit cards. Daily 9am–5pm. MEXICAN/ITALIAN.

Though it has the monopoly on food at the ruins, this cafeteria actually does a good job with such basic meals as enchiladas, spaghetti, and baked chicken. Eggs are cooked to order, as are burgers, and the coffee is very good. Sit outside at the tables farthest from the crowd and relax.

La Fiesta. Carretera Mérida–Valladolid, Pisté. No phone. Main courses $4–$6; comida corrida $6.50. No credit cards. Daily 7am–9pm (comida corrida served 12:30–5pm). REGIONAL/MEXICAN.

With Maya motifs on the wall and colorful decorations, this is one of Pisté's long-established restaurants catering especially to tour groups. Though relatively expensive, the food is very good. You'll be quite satisfied unless you arrive when a tour group is being served, in which case service to individual diners may suffer. Going toward the ruins, La Fiesta is on the west end of town.

Puebla Maya. Carretera Mérida–Valladolid, Pisté. No phone. Fixed-price lunch buffet $7. No credit cards. Daily 1–5pm. MEXICAN.

Opposite the Pirámide Inn, the Puebla Maya looks just like its name, a Maya town with small white huts flanking a large open-walled palapa-topped center. Inside, however, you cross an artificial lagoon, planters drip with greenery, and live musicians play to the hundreds of tourists filling the tables. Service through the huge buffet is quick, so if you've been huffing around the ruins all morning, you have time to eat and relax before boarding the bus to wherever you're going. You can even swim in a lovely landscaped pool.

Restaurant Bar "Poxil." Calle 15 s/n, Carretera Mérida–Valladolid, Pisté. ☎ **985/1-0123.**
Breakfast $3–$4; main courses $3–$5. No credit cards. Daily 7am–8pm. MEXICAN/
REGIONAL.

A *poxil* is a Maya fruit somewhat akin to a guanábana. Although this place doesn't
serve them, what is on the menu is good, though not gourmet, and the price is
right. You will find the Poxil near the west entrance to town on the south side of
the street.

A SIDE TRIP TO THE GRUTAS (CAVES) DE BALANKANCHE

The Grutas de Balankanche are 3½ miles from Chichén-Itzá on the road to Valladolid and Cancún. Taxis will make the trip and wait, but they are also usually on
hand when the tours let out. The entire excursion takes about half an hour, but the
walk inside is hot and humid. The natural caves here became wartime hideaways.
You can still see traces of carving and incense burning, as well as an underground
stream that served as the sanctuary's water supply. Outside, take time to meander
through the botanical gardens, where most of the plants and trees are labeled with
their common and scientific names.

The caves are open daily. Admission is $3. Use of a video camera costs an addi-
tional $4. Children under 6 are not admitted. Guided tours in English are at 11am
and 1 and 3pm, and in Spanish, at 9am, noon, and 2 and 4pm. Tours go only if
there is a minimum of six people and take up to 30 people at a time. Double-check
these hours at the main entrance to the Chichén ruins.

5 Valladolid

25 miles E of Chichén-Itzá; 100 miles SW of Cancún

Valladolid (pronounced *bye*-ah-doh-*leed*) is a small, pleasant colonial city halfway
between Mérida and Cancún. The people here are friendly and informal, and,
except for the heat, life is easy. The city's economy is based on commerce and small-
scale manufacture. Valladolid boasts a large cenote in the center of town and
another one 3 miles down the road to Chichén. A restoration project has reconstructed several rows of colonial housing in the neighborhood surrounding the convent of San Bernardino de Siena. Side trips to Holbox and Ekbalam (see below) can
be mounted from Valladolid, and you should consider staying here rather than at
one of the more expensive hotels at Chichén.

ESSENTIALS

GETTING THERE & DEPARTING   By Car   From either Mérida or Cancún,
you have two choices for getting to Valladolid: the toll road (cuota) or Highway
180. The **cuota** passes a few miles north of the city, and the exit is at the crossing of **Highway 295** to Tizimín. **Highway 180** takes significantly longer because it
passes through a number of tiny villages and over their not-so-tiny speed bumps.
Both 180 and 295 lead directly to the main square. Leaving is just as easy: from the
main square, calle 41 turns into 180 east to Cancún; calle 39 heads to 180 west to
Chichén-Itzá and Mérida. To take the cuota to either Mérida or Cancún, take calle
40. (See "City Layout," below.)

By Bus   Expresso de Oriente has eight first-class buses per day to/from Mérida,
nine buses to/from Cancún, three to/from Tulum, and three to/from Playa del
Carmen. To secure a seat you can buy a ticket a day in advance. In addition, first-
class buses make a stop in Valladolid while passing through (*de paso*) on the way to
Cancún. To get to Chichén-Itzá you must take a second-class bus, which leaves
every hour and sometimes on the half-hour.

Centuries of Conflict: Spanish & Maya in the Yucatán

Though Spanish conquerors landed in the region as early as 1511, the systematic pacification of Yucatán began only in in 1526—5 years after the completion of the conquest of the highlands in 1521. The Maya were understandably skeptical of the Spaniards, so the Yucatán project took 2 decades. It was finally achieved by three men, all with the same name: Francisco de Montejo the Elder (also called El Adelantado, the pioneer), who started the process; his son, Francisco Montejo the Younger (known as El Mozo, the lad); and a cousin. Montejo the Elder sailed from Spain in 1527 with 400 soldiers and landed at Cozumel, but was forced to relaunch his campaign from the western coast, where he could more easily receive supplies from New Spain (Mexico).

From Mexico, he conquered what is now the state of Tabasco (1530), pushing northward to the Yucatán. But, after 4 difficult years (1531–35), he was forced to return to Mexico—penniless and exhausted. In 1540, Montejo the Younger and his cousin (another Francisco de Montejo) took over the cause, successfully establishing a town at Campeche and another at Mérida (1542); by 1546, virtually all of the peninsula was under their control.

A few weeks after the founding of Mérida, the greatest of the various Maya leaders, Ah Kukum Xiú, head of the Xiú people, offered himself as El Mozo's vassal and was baptized, giving himself the name Francisco de Montejo Xiú. With the help of the Elder's troops, Montejo the Younger and his cousin then accomplished their objective: the defeat of the Cocoms. By allying his people with the Spaniards, Xiú triumphed over the Cocoms but surrendered the freedom of the Yucatecan Maya. In later centuries, warfare, disease, slavery, and emigration all led to the decline of the peninsula's population. Fray Diego de Landa, second bishop of Yucatán, banished much of the history of the Maya culture when he ordered the mass destruction of the priceless Maya códices, or "painted books," at Maní in 1562; only three survived, and scholars continue to struggle with the complex Maya alphabet.

The Yucatán seethed under the heavy yoke of Spanish colonial administration until the War of Independence (begun in 1810) liberated Mexico and the Yucatán in 1821. In that same year, the Spanish governor of the Yucatán resigned, and the Yucatán, too, declared its independence. Though the Yucatán decided to rejoin with independent Mexico 2 years later, this period of sovereignty is testimony to the Yucatecan spirit of separatism. That spirit rose again in 1846 when the Yucatán seceded a second time from Mexico.

ORIENTATION   Visitor Information   There is a small tourism office in the Palacio Municipal where you can get a map but little else.

City Layout   Valladolid has the standard layout for towns in the Yucatán: Streets running north-south are even numbers; those running east-west are odd numbers. The main plaza is bordered by calle 39 on the north, 41 on the south, 40 on the east, and 42 on the west. The plaza is named Parque Francisco Cantón Rosado, but everyone simply calls it **El Centro.** Valladolid has two bus stations at the corners of calles 39 and 46, and 37 and 54. For all practical purposes, they are interchangeable; departing buses pass by both stations. Taxis are easy to come by.

After the War of Independence, sugarcane and henequen cultivation were introduced on a large scale, organized around vast landed estates called haciendas—
each employing hundreds of Maya as virtual slaves. During the Yucatecan war of
secession, weapons were issued to the Maya to defend independent Yucatán
against attack from Mexico or the United States. Subsequently the Maya turned
these same weapons on their local oppressors, setting off the **War of the Castes**
in 1847.

The native Maya ruthlessly attacked and sacked Valladolid and strengthened
their forces with guns and ammunition bought from British merchants in Belize
(British Honduras). By June 1848, they held virtually all the Yucatán except
Mérida and Campeche—and Mérida's governor had already decided to abandon
the city.

Ancient traditions then triggered one of the strangest occurrences in Yucatecan
history. It was time to plant the corn; native Maya fighters dropped their weapons
and returned to tend the fields. Meanwhile, the new central government of
Mexico sent reinforcements in exchange for the Yucatán's resubmission to Mexican authority. Government troops took the offensive, driving many of the Maya
to the wilds of Quintana Roo, in the southeastern reaches of the peninsula.

Massed in southern Quintana Roo, the Maya, seeking inspiration for their
rebellion, invented the cult of the Talking Crosses, fabricated in 1850 by a Maya
ventriloquist and a mestizo "priest," who borrowed from legends of "talking idols"
that flourished for centuries throughout the Yucatán—notably Cozumel. A
"talking cross" first appeared at Chan Santa Cruz (today's Felipe Carrillo Puerto),
and soon its brethren inflamed the Maya.

The Yucatecan authorities seemed content to let the rebels and their talking
crosses rule the southern Caribbean coast, launching only minor skirmishes
until the late 1800s. The rebel government received arms from the British in
Belize, and in return allowed the British to cut lumber in rebel territory. At the
turn of the century, Mexican troops armed with modern rifles penetrated the
rebel territory, soon putting an end to this brave, mystical episode in Yucatecan
history.

The town of Chan Santa Cruz was renamed in honor of a Yucatecan governor,
Felipe Carrillo Puerto, and the Yucatán was finally a full and integral part of
Mexico—although the eastern reaches were barely populated and became a "no-
man's land."

EXPLORING VALLADOLID

Before it became Valladolid, the city was a Maya settlement called Zací (zah-*kee*),
which means "white hawk." There are two cenotes in the area, one of which is called
Cenote Zací—located at the intersection of calles 39 and 36, in a small park in the
middle of town. The walls and part of the roof of the cenote have been opened up,
and a trail leads down close to the water. Caves, stalactites, and hanging vines contribute to a wild, prehistoric atmosphere. The park features a large palapa restaurant
that is popular with local residents, plus three traditional Maya dwellings that house
a small photograph collection and some historical materials on Valladolid. Admission is 50¢.

To the southwest of El Centro is the Franciscan monastery of **San Bernardino de Siena** (1552). Most of the compound was built in the early 1600s; a large underground river is believed to pass under the convent and surrounding neighborhood, which is called Barrio Sisal. "Sisal" is in this case a corruption of the Mayan phrase *sis-ha,* meaning "cold water." The barrio has undergone extensive restoration and is a delight to behold.

Valladolid's main square is the social center of town and a thriving market for the prettiest Yucatecan dresses to be found anywhere. On its south side is the principal church, **La Parroquia de San Servacio.** Vallesoletanos, as the locals call themselves, believe that almost all cathedrals in Mexico point east, and they cherish a local legend to explain why theirs points north—but don't believe a word of it. On the east side of the plaza is the municipal building known modestly as *El Ayuntamiento.* Be sure to appreciate the four dramatic paintings outlining the history of the peninsula. In particular, note the first panel, featuring a horrified Maya priest as he foresees the arrival of Spanish galleons. On Sunday nights, from beneath the stone arches of the ayuntamiento, the municipal band plays *jaranas* and other traditional music of the region.

SHOPPING

The **Mercado de Artesanías de Valladolid** at the corner of calles 39 and 44 gives you a good idea of the local merchandise. Perhaps the main handicraft of the town is embroidered Maya dresses, which can be purchased here or from women around the main square. The latter also sell, of all things, Barbie-doll–size Maya dresses! Just ask, "¿Vestidos para Barbie?" and out they come. The area around Valladolid is cattle country; the local leather goods are exceptional, and some of the best sandals and *huaraches* and leather goods are sold over the main plaza, above the municipal bazaar. An Indian named Juan Mac makes *alpargatas,* the traditional everyday footwear of the Maya, in his factory on calle 39, two doors south of the plaza; look for a doorway painted yellow. Most of his output is for locals, but he's happy to knock some out for travelers.

Valladolid also produces a highly prized **honey** made from the tzi-tzi-ché flower. You can find it and other goods at the **town market** on calle 32 between calles 35 and 37. The best time to see the market is Sunday morning.

WHERE TO STAY

Hotels (and restaurants) here are less expensive than the competition in Chichén. Occupancy rates are very high, so you should make reservations.

Hotel El Mesón del Marqués. Calle 39 no. 203, 97780 Valladolid, Yuc. ☎ **985/6-3042** or 985/6-2073. Fax 985/6-2280. 73 units. A/C TV TEL. $35 double. AE. Free secured parking.

The Mesón del Marqués is a very comfortable and gracious hotel. The first courtyard surrounds a fountain and is draped in hanging plants and bougainvillea. This, the original house, mostly holds a good restaurant (see "Where to Dine," below). In back is another courtyard with plenty of greenery and a pool. There is always hot water, and most of the rooms are sheltered from city noise. It's on the north side of El Centro, opposite the church.

Hotel María de la Luz. Calle 42 no. 193, 97780 Valladolid, Yuc. ☎ and fax **985/6-2071,** or 985/6-2071. 41 units. A/C TV. $20 double. MC, V. Free secured parking.

The two stories at the María de la Luz are built around an inner swimming pool. The rooms have been refurbished with new tile floors and bathrooms and new mattresses; some have balconies overlooking the square. The wide interior space holds a restaurant that is quite comfortable and airy for most of the day—a popular place for breakfast. The hotel is on the west side of the main square.

WHERE TO DINE

Valladolid is not a center for haute cuisine, but you should try some of the regional specialties. The lowest restaurant prices are found in the **Bazar Municipal,** a little arcade of shops beside the Hotel El Mesón del Marqués right on the main square.

Hostería del Marqués. Calle 39 no. 203. ☎ **985/6-2073.** Breakfast $3–$5; main courses 3.50–$7. AE. Daily 7am–11:30pm. MEXICAN/YUCATECAN.

This is part of the Hotel El Mesón del Marqués, facing the main square. The patio is calm and cool for most of the day. The menu is extensive and features local specialties. If you are hungry, try the Yucatecan sampler. Any of the enchiladas are good. The guacamole was a hit on my last visit.

SIDE TRIPS FROM VALLADOLID
CENOTE DZITNUP

The Cenote Dzitnup (also known as Cenote Xkeken), 2½ miles west of Valladolid off Highway 180, is worth a side trip, especially if you have time for a dip. Descend a short flight of rather perilous stone steps, and at the bottom, inside a beautiful cavern, is a natural pool of water so clear and blue it seems plucked from a dream. If you decide to take a swim, be sure you don't have creams or other chemicals on your skin, as they damage the habitat for the small fish and other organisms living there. Also, no alcohol, food, or smoking is allowed after you enter the cavern.

Admission is $1. The cenote is open daily from 8am to 5pm.

EKBALAM: RECENTLY EXCAVATED MAYA RUINS

About 11 miles north of Valladolid, off the highway to Río Lagartos, is the spectacular site at Ekbalam, which means "star jaguar" in Mayan. Recently opened and largely unknown to tourists, the Ekbalam ruins are years away from complete renovation, but a must-see for travelers who have access to a rental car. Take calle 40 north out of Valladolid, to Highway 295; go 11 miles to the sign marking the Ekbalam turnoff. Follow a narrow, winding road through a small village, and watch the jungle for mounds that indicate the presence of undiscovered ruins leading to the main site. Ekbalam is 8 miles from the highway; the entrance fee is $1, plus $4 for each video camera. The site is open from 8am to 5pm every day; on our last visit, the custodians obligingly admitted us at 6pm to clamber on the main pyramid.

Built between 100 B.C. and A.D. 1200, the smaller buildings are architecturally unique—especially the large and perfectly restored **Caracol.** The principal buildings in the main group have been reconstructed beautifully, but the huge and imposing main pyramid will take years to complete. Flanked by two smaller pyramids, the central temple is 517 feet long and 200 feet wide, and though only a little more than 100 feet high, feels easily as tall as the biggest structures in Chichén and Uxmal. You can see the restoration work in progress: stones are carefully separated, numbered and arranged, then reassembled by archaeologists from INAH, the national institute for anthropology. The caretaker/guide led us up the rocky, forested path to the summit, where we watched a full moon rise to illuminate the jungle for a radius of 35 miles. In the middle distance, unrestored ruins loom to the north and the southwest, and you can spot the tallest structures at **Cobá,** 30 miles to the southeast. Also plainly visible are the **raised causeways** of the Maya—the sacbeob that appear as raised lines in the forest vegetation. More than any of the better-known sites, Ekbalam at dusk excites a sense of mystery and awe at the scale of Maya civilization, and the utter ruin to which it came.

Río Lagartos Nature Reserve: Nesting Flamingos

Some 50 miles north of Valladolid (25 miles north of Tizimín) on Highway 295 is Río Lagartos, a 118,000-acre refuge established in 1979 to protect the largest nesting population of flamingos in North America. Found in the park's dunes, mangrove swamps, and tropical forests are jaguars, ocelots, sea turtles, and at least 212 bird species (141 of which are permanent residents).

With flamingos, the earlier you get out to see them, the better. There was a hotel in Río Lagartos, but it was never any good and now is closed. One option is to stay the night in Tizimín, which is about 30 minutes away. The best place to stay there is **Hotel 49,** on calle 49 373-A (☎ **986/3-2136**) by the main square. The owner can give you good advice about going to the nature preserve. There is not much to do in Tizimín unless you are there in the first 2 weeks of January, when it holds the largest fair in the Yucatán. The prime fiesta day is January 6: the Epiphany, known popularly as *Día de los Reyes*. The fiesta is celebrated with lots of music, carnival rides, etc.

SEEING THE RÍO LAGARTOS REFUGE Río Lagartos is a small fishing village of around 3,000 people who make their living from the sea and from the occasional tourist who shows up to see the flamingos. Colorfully painted homes face the Malecón (the oceanfront street), and brightly painted boats dock along the same half-moon–shaped port.

If you arrive by car, you have the option of driving to the salt plant at Los Colorados and out over the flats to the shore of the lagoon, where you can get fairly close to a large colony. Otherwise, go straight to the dock area in Río Lagartos, where you can hire a boat to the large flamingo colony for $75, which can be split among up to 6 people; the trip takes 4 to 6 hours. Or you can get a shorter trip to a closer colony by for $20. Ask around for Filiberto Pat Zem, a reliable boatman who takes the time to give a good tour.

Although thousands of flamingos nest near here from April to August, it is prohibited by law to visit their nesting grounds. Flamingos need mud with particular ingredients (including a high salt content) in order to multiply, and this area's mud does the trick. Flamingos use their special bills to suck up the mud, and they have the unique ability to screen the contents they need from it. What you see on the boat trip is a mixture of flamingos, frigates, pelicans, herons in several colors, and ducks. Don't allow the boatman to frighten the birds into flight for your photographs; it causes the birds to eventually leave the habitat permanently.

Isla Holbox

A remote island off the farthest eastern point of the Yucatán Peninsula, Holbox (pronounced whole-*bosh*) is a half-deserted fishing village, a modest wildlife refuge, and a desert-island getaway for travelers seeking solitude. From Valladolid, take Highway 180 east for 90 kilometers towards Cancún; turn north after Nuevo Xcan at the tiny crossroads of El Ideal. Drive nearly 100 kilometers north (on a poorly maintained state highway) to the tiny port of Chiquila, where you can leave your car in a secured estacionamento; walk 200 yards to the pier and haggle over the $15 boat ride 2 miles to the island. There is a ferry, but it runs only three times per day.

In the late 1840s, Holbox was refuge for European landowners fleeing Indian mobs during the Caste Wars. Nowadays, the village of Holbox is empty when the fishing fleet is out, but only half-populated at the best of times. Disbark and proceed directly to **Villas Delfines,** a small but elegant palapa cluster on the beach, 15 minutes east of the docks by foot, on the Gulf side of the island. Each palapa can accommodate three people and comes with ceiling fans, mosquito netting, and a comfortable porch and hammock. Owned by Cancún resort executives, the Villas are exquisitely designed for simple living, and the kitchen is staffed by a very able cook—don't bother with the restaurants in town. Manager German Masotta and his wife maintain the compound in perfect order, and guests do little but eat, drink, and swim off the endless white-sand beach facing north towards Cuba. The Gulf here is clean and shallow, but it's not the clear turquoise waters of the Caribbean, however. Take some reading materials, or borrow from the paperback library of German and Spanish best-sellers—there's no TV, no nightlife, and (if you remembered your mosquito repellent) no hassle. Word-of-mouth keeps the palapas occupied, so call ahead for reservations at ☎ **98/84-8606,** or fax at 98/84-6342.

7

Tabasco & Chiapas

Even though these two states aren't part of the Yucatán, we've included them because it allows us to present Mexico's **Maya region** in its entirety. Many travelers who go to the Yucatán to see Chichén-Itzá and Uxmal also take a side trip down to Chiapas to see the famous ruins of Palenque, and some go even farther, all the way to San Cristóbal to visit the Highland Maya.

Chiapas and Tabasco differ from the Yucatán in a number of ways. They have higher rainfall levels and none of the limestone formations that make for underground rivers and cenotes. Consequently, you find here two of the largest rivers in Mexico: the Grijalva and the Usumacinta. The jungle, covering most of Tabasco and the eastern lowlands of Chiapas, becomes more lush and varied. Central Chiapas features the cool highlands with scattered cloud forests wherever the land has been left untouched. Getting there from Palenque is not hard, and it's wonderful to feel the cool mountain air after trekking around in the heat and humidity of the lowlands.

Tabasco is a small state along the Gulf Coast. It is rich in oil, and the capital, Villahermosa, has all the marks of a boomtown. It was in this coastal region that the Olmec, the mother culture of Mesoamerica, rose to prominence. In Villahermosa, at the **Parque Museo de la Venta,** you can see the artifacts that this culture left to posterity, including some of its famous, gigantic monolithic heads.

In **Chiapas,** the two areas that hold the most interest are the eastern lowland jungles and the central highlands. In the former lie the famous ruins of **Palenque,** a city of the classic age of Maya civilization. These ruins look unspeakably old, and the surrounding jungle seems poised to reclaim them should ever their caretakers falter in their duties. Deeper into the interior, for those willing to make the trek, are the sites of Yaxchilán and Bonampak. The central highlands are just as dramatic, but easier to enjoy. Of particular interest are the colonial city of **San Cristóbal de las Casas** and surrounding Indian villages. The Indians here cling so tenaciously to their beliefs and traditions that this area at one time was more frequented by anthropologists than tourists. Knowing anthropologists, I suspect this was also due in some measure to the beauty and agreeable climate of San Cristóbal.

Lately there has been some political violence in this area—a massacre in Acteal, near San Cristóbal, and some killings in the

Ocosingo area, which lies between Palenque and San Cristóbal. No foreigners were attacked in these events, and no restrictions were placed on travel to Palenque or the San Cristóbal region. I toured the area a month after the events took place, and saw little disruption of the day-to-day affairs of the local people. The State Department has not issued a travel advisory for the region, but before you go, get the most current information you can by checking out the state park Web site.

EXPLORING TABASCO & CHIAPAS

Airline and bus service to this area have improved a lot in the last few years. There is convenient air service from the Yucatán to Villahermosa, Tuxtla Gutiérrez, San Cristóbal, and Palenque. Coming from the Yucatán by land, you would most likely go through Campeche, which is about 5 hours from Palenque and about the same for Villahermosa. From Palenque it is about 5 hours to San Cristóbal; from Villahermosa it's a little more.

Palenque can be seen in a day. A couple of worthwhile side trips would add a day or two, and if you plan on going to Bonampak and Yaxchilán, add 2 full days. San Cristóbal and the nearby villages have so much to offer that I would consider 4 days to be a minimum; 1 week would be more realistic.

1 Villahermosa

89 miles NW of Palenque; 293 miles SW of Campeche; 100 miles N of San Cristóbal de las Casas

Villahermosa (pop. 265,000), the capital of the state of Tabasco, is right at the center of Mexico's oil boom—but it's off-center from just about everything else. Were it not for oil, the city's proximity to the ruins of Palenque, and several good museums, visitors would have little reason to come here. Nevertheless, oil wealth has transformed this provincial town into a more attractive and obviously prosperous modern city, making it a comfortable crossroads in your Mexican journeys.

Prosperity has recently brought the city a number of developments, including a beautiful park surrounding the Parque Museo de la Venta; a high-class business and hotel development called Tabasco 2000; the CICOM development, with theaters and the **Museo Regional de Antropología Carlos Pellicer Camara;** and the pedestrians-only shopping area along avenida Benito Juárez. You really shouldn't miss the **Parque Museo de la Venta,** which contains the Olmec remains found at La Venta northwest of Villahermosa.

ESSENTIALS
GETTING THERE & DEPARTING

BY PLANE   Getting to Villahermosa on the major Mexican airlines requires going through Mexico City. **Mexicana** (☎ **800/531-7921** or 93/16-3132; 93/56-0101 at the airport) and **Aeromexico** (☎ **800/237-6639** or 93/12-1528) both have three flights a day to/from Mexico City, and all connections go through there. **Aviación de Chiapas (Aviacsa)** (☎ **93/16-5700,** or 93/56-0132 at the airport) flies twice a day to Mexico City, twice a week to Cancún, and every day to Mérida. **AeroLitoral,** another regional airline and a subsidiary of Aeromexico (☎ **800/237-6639** or 93/12-6991), goes through Mexico with a connection on to Veracruz, Tampico, Monterrey, and Houston. **Aerocaribe** (☎ **800/531-7921** or 93/16-5046), a subsidiary of Mexicana, has a direct flight to Veracruz and a puddle-jumper that goes Oaxaca–Tuxtla–Villahermosa–Mérida–Cancún–Havana.

Road Conditions & Warnings

The drive between Villahermosa and Chetumal (about 350 miles) can seem interminable if the road is in poor condition. Vast parts of it are quite lonely; the U.S. State Department includes this road on its warning list due to car and bus hijackings. If you take it, one possible stopover between the two would be at Xpujil, 62 miles west of Chetumal. (See "Side Trips from Bacalar: The Río Bec Ruin Route" in chapter 5.) Another potential stopover is Francisco Escárcega, but only in an emergency. Once here, you're not too far from wherever you're going.

BY CAR   Paved **Highway 195** connects the Tabascan capital of Villahermosa with Tuxtla Gutiérrez, the capital of the state of Chiapas. Between these cities lie Palenque and San Cristóbal de las Casas. The road to Palenque is a good one, and the drive should take about 2 hours. Between Villahermosa and San Cristóbal de las Casas, the road, although paved, sometimes has stretches with many potholes. Often a portion of the roadway caves in, and traffic slows to one lane; these conditions occur more frequently during the rainy season between May and October. The trip to San Cristóbal takes a minimum of 5 hours from Villahermosa. The paved, mountainous (and very curvy) road between San Cristóbal and Tuxtla is in good condition, and the trip takes about 1½ hours.

BY BUS   The first-class **ADO** station is at Mina and Merino, 3 blocks off Highway 180. Buses for most destinations leave from here, and the station houses many lines. Most ticket booths offer computerized ticketing, and you can look at the computer screen and select your seat. Eight first-class ADO buses leave for Palenque (3 hours) between 6am and 7:45pm. Deluxe service to Palenque (2 hours) leaves at 8am and 1:30pm. Additional first-class buses go to Mexico City and most major Gulf Coast cities. **Autotransportes Cristóbal Colón** has seven daily buses to Tuxtla Gutiérrez (passing through Palenque and San Cristóbal de las Casas), Tapachula, Oaxaca, and Mexico City. **UNO** runs luxury buses with 25 seats, smoking and no-smoking sections, self-service refreshments, video movies, and air-conditioning. They go to Mexico City, Veracruz, Puebla, and Mérida. You can reserve seats up to 2 days in advance.

ORIENTATION

ARRIVING   Driving in from Villahermosa's **airport,** which is 6½ miles east of town, you'll cross a bridge over the Río Grijalva, then turn left to reach downtown. Both multipassenger minibuses and private taxis are available for transportation into the city, with the minibus costing the least. However, don't linger in the terminal and expect a minibus to still be at the curb when you're ready. Minibuses leave when they fill up, and only taxis will be available.

From the **bus station,** local buses marked "Mercad–C. Camionera" or simply "Centro" leave frequently for the center of town. Taxis are readily available in front of the station.

Parking downtown can be difficult, but there are several parking lots near the hotels I recommend below. Use one that's guarded around the clock.

VISITOR INFORMATION   The best source of information is at the **State Tourism Office** in the Tabasco 2000 complex, Paseo Tabasco 1504, SEFICOT Building, Centro Administrativo del Gobierno (☎ **93/16-2890**). Inconveniently located opposite the Liverpool department store and an enclosed shopping center on the second floor of the building, it's open Monday through Friday from 8am to

4pm. There are two other branches—the **airport office** is staffed daily from 10am to 5pm, and **La Venta Park** has an office open Tuesday through Sunday from 10am to 5pm. The staff can supply rates and telephone numbers for the hotels, as well as useful telephone numbers for bus companies and airlines.

CITY LAYOUT   The hotels and restaurants I recommend are located off the main streets: **Madero, Pino Suárez,** the **Malecón,** and **Grijalva/Ruíz Cortinez.** Highway 180 skirts the city, so a turn onto Madero or Pino Suárez will take you into the center of town.

Your point of reference in town can be **Plaza Juárez,** the main square, bounded by the streets Zaragoza, Madero, Sánchez, and Carranza. The plaza is just off the center of the downtown district, at the north end of the pedestrian zone, with the Río Grijalva to its east and Highway 186 to its north. Within this area is the **pedestrian zone,** with roads closed to traffic for 5 blocks. This zone is often called **Centro,** or **Zona Luz.** At the south end of the pedestrian zone is the **Plaza de Armas** bounded by 27 de Febrero, Guerrero, Maquiliz, and Independencia, and with the Palacio de Gobierno at its north end. Villahermosa's main thoroughfare is **avenida Madero,** running south from Highway 186 past the Plaza Juárez to the river, where it intersects with the riverside avenue, the **Malecón.** I have used the river, Plaza Juárez, Plaza de Armas, and the popular Restaurant Galerías Madan as points of reference.

GETTING AROUND   All the **city buses** converge on avenida Pino Suárez at the market and are clearly labeled for Tabasco 2000, Parque La Venta, and Centro.

Taxis from the center of town to main sites such as the Parque La Venta are inexpensive. If you're getting around **by car,** you'll be glad to know that Villahermosa's streets are well marked, with arrows clearly designating the direction of traffic.

FAST FACTS: American Express is represented by Turismo Nieves, bulevar Simón Sarlat 202 (☎ **93/14-1888**). The telephone **area code** is **93.**

EXPLORING VILLAHERMOSA

Major sights in Villahermosa include the Parque Museo de la Venta, the Museo Regional de Antropología Carlos Pellicer Camara, the History of Tabasco Museum, and the Museum of Popular Culture (see below). You can hit the high points in a day.

If you need to shop for any necessities or luxuries, head for the indoor shopping mall at Tabasco 2000 or the shops lining avenida Madero.

The most popular side trip from Villahermosa is to the archaeological site of Palenque, covered later in this chapter.

Parque Museo de la Venta. Av. Ruíz Cortínez. ☎ **93/14-1652.** Museum $2; still camera free (no flash). Archaeological Park $1; no video. Daily 8am–5pm. Take Paseo Tabasco northeast to Highway 180 and turn right; it's less than a mile down on your right next to the Exposition Park.

This recently refurbished park incorporates not only the fascinating outdoor La Venta Museum, but also the **regional zoo,** and the **Museo Olmeca de la Venta,** an exceptionally well-done explanation of the Olmec civilization.

La Venta was one of three major Olmec cities during the Preclassic period (2,000 B.C.–A.D. 300). The mammoth heads you see in the park were found when the ruins of La Venta were discovered in 1938. Today all that remains of the once-impressive city are some grass-covered mounds—once earthen pyramids—84 miles west of Villahermosa. All the gigantic heads and other important sculptures have been moved from the site to this interesting museum/park. Allow at least 2 hours to wander through the jungle-like sanctuary and to look at the 3,000-year-old sculpture and listen to the birds that inhabit the grounds. *Important note:* Mosquitoes can be thick during certain times of the year, so bring insect repellent.

On a walk through the park, you'll see the indoor museum that explains the Olmec throughout time; Olmec relics, sculptures, and mosaics; a mock-up of the original La Venta; and, of course, three colossal Olmec heads. Carved around 1000 B.C., these heads are 6½ feet high and weigh around 40 tons. The faces seem to be half-adult, half-infantile, with the fleshy, undulating lips characteristic of Olmec art. The basalt rock was transported from the nearest source, over 70 miles from La Venta, which is all the more impressive when you realize the sculptors had no wheels to move it. The multi-ton rock was thought to have been brought by raft from the quarry to the site. At least 17 heads have been found: four at La Venta, 10 at San Lorenzo, and three at Tres Zapotes—all Olmec cities on Mexico's east coast.

On your stroll through the park, notice the other fine stone sculptures and artistic achievements of the Olmecs, who are considered to have created the first civilization in Mexico and the first art style in Mesoamerica with their monumental works (chiseled without the use of metal). Their exquisite figurines in jade and serpentine, which can be seen in the Museo Regional de Antropología (see below), far exceeded any other craft of this period.

✪ **Museo Regional de Antropología Carlos Pellicer Camara.** CICOM Center, av. Carlos Pellicer 511. ☎ **93/12-6344.** Admission $1.50. Daily 9am–6pm; gift shop Tues–Sun 10am–4pm.

This museum, on the west bank of the river a mile south of the town center, is well organized and architecturally bold and attractive. The pre-Hispanic artifacts on display include not only Tabascan finds (Totonac, Zapotec, and Olmec) but also those of other Mexican and Central American cultures.

The first floor contains the auditorium, bookstore, and gift shop; most of what interests visitors is on the upper floors, reached by an elevator or the stairs. The second floor is devoted to the Olmec, while the third floor features artifacts relating to central Mexico, including the Tlatilco and Teotihuacán cultures; the Huasteca culture of Veracruz, San Luis Potosí, and Tampico states; and the west-coast cultures of Nayarit state. Photographs and diagrams provide vivid images, but the explanatory signs are mostly in Spanish. Look especially for the figurines that were found in this area and for the colorful *Codex* (an early book of pictographs).

Museo de Historia de Tabasco (Casa de los Azulejos). At the corner of 27 de Febrero and av. Juárez. No phone. Admission 75¢. Daily 10am–4pm.

Take half an hour and head to the pedestrian-only zone to see this museum, which presents the history of Tabasco from pre-Columbian times to the present through documents, artifacts, and pictures. Every room is decorated with tiles in the Spanish and Italian baroque style, and the building's blue-and-white–tiled exterior, with wrought-iron balconies, is worth a snapshot. Most explanations are in Spanish. There's a nice gift shop off the lobby featuring books and products of the state of Tabasco.

Museo de Cultura Popular. Calle Zaragoza 810, at Juárez. ☎ **93/12-1117.** Free admission. Daily 10am–4pm; gift shop daily 10am–4pm.

This museum is 3 blocks north and 4½ blocks west of the Museo de Historia (see above). As you enter, on the right there's a small gift shop with baskets, carved gourds, embroidered regional clothing, and chocolate from Tabasco. Displays in the next room show the state's regional clothing and dance costumes. In the back is a

Villahermosa Area

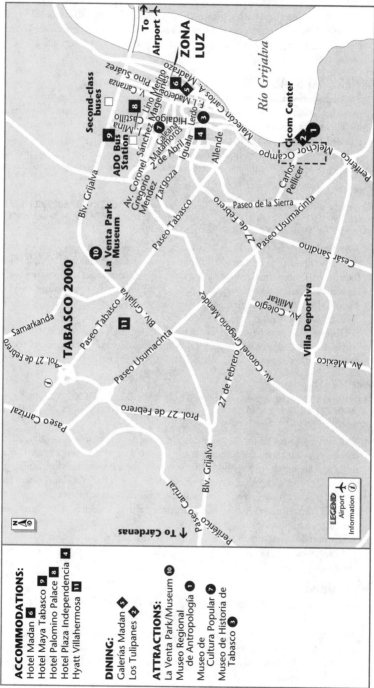

ACCOMMODATIONS:
Hotel Madan 6
Hotel Maya Tabasco 9
Hotel Palomino Palace 8
Hotel Plaza Independencia 4
Hyatt Villahermosa 11

DINING:
Galerías Madan 5
Los Tulipanes 2

ATTRACTIONS:
La Venta Park/Museum 10
Museo Regional de Antropología 1
Museo de Cultura Popular 7
Museo de Historia de Tabasco 3

2-0097

Chontal hut, complete with typical furnishings and a recorded conversation of two female villagers talking about the high cost of living. Student guides are often on hand for a free explanation. Another room shows ceremonial pottery and household utensils.

WHERE TO STAY

The area around the intersections of avenidas Juárez and Lerdo, sometimes referred to as the "Zona Luz," is now one of the best places to stay; the streets are pedestrian malls closed to traffic. One drawback to this plan is parking, though there are guarded lots on the outskirts of the mall.

Room rates in Villahermosa are distressingly high, especially considering what you get. The price headings used below are for doubles during high season.

EXPENSIVE

✪ **Hyatt Villahermosa.** Av. Juárez 106, 86000 Villahermosa, Tab. ☎ **800/233-1234** in the U.S., or 93/15-1234. Fax 93/15-5808. 209 units. A/C MINIBAR TV TEL. $107 double; $142 Regency Club room. AE, DC, MC, V. Free guarded parking.

A quick taxi ride from the Parque La Venta, the Hyatt is a mainstay among travelers to Villahermosa. The beautifully furnished rooms are quiet and comfortable. Floors 6 through 10 hold the Regency Club, where guests receive special amenities such as separate check-in, daily newspaper, continental breakfast, and evening cocktails. There's also a business center, and guests can rent cellular phones. The Hyatt is at Tabasco and bulevar Grijalva.

Dining: Two restaurants and two bars fill dining needs from refined to cafe style.

Amenities: Laundry and room service, travel agency, car rental; pool, two tennis courts, boutiques, beauty shop, pharmacy, business center.

MODERATE

Hotel Maya Tabasco. Av. Ruíz Cortínez 907 (Apdo. Postal 131), 86000 Villahermosa, Tab. ☎ **800/221-6509** in the U.S., or 93/14-4466. Fax 93/12-1097. 156 units. A/C TV TEL. $59 double. AE, DC, MC, V. Free parking.

You can't go wrong in this comfortable and busy hotel; consider it a value, since it cost twice as much to stay here before the devaluation and the services are that of a more upscale hotel. It's not the Hyatt, however, but it's darn close for comfort and service. The large, carpeted rooms come with a choice of single, double, and king-size beds. Some rooms have individually controlled air-conditioning, and some are centrally controlled. It's located on the main highway, convenient to the bus station, museums, and downtown.

Dining: Two restaurants, one formal and one informal, cover all meals.

Amenities: Laundry and room service, travel agency, car rental, pool, pharmacy/gift shop.

INEXPENSIVE

Hotel Madan. Madero 408, 86000 Villahermosa, Tab. ☎ **93/12-1650.** Fax 93/14-3373. 20 units. A/C TV TEL. $33 double. AE, CB, MC, V. Free secure parking.

The two-story Madan is another convenient downtown hotel within walking distance of the pedestrians-only zone and central-city museums. The pleasant rooms are clean and carpeted. On the second floor, you'll find a comfortable sitting room and cold-water dispenser. It's between Reforma and Lerdo.

Hotel Palomino Palace. Av. Mina 222, 86000 Villahermosa, Tab. ☎ **93/12-8431.** 45 units. $22 double. No credit cards. Free parking on the street.

Directly across from the first-class bus station, the Palomino is surprisingly clean and quiet. The rooms are small, with a couple of shelves for clothes, no closets, and blue-tiled bathrooms with hot showers. Those overlooking avenida Mina are the noisiest; there are a few rooms away from the street that should be your first choice. The restaurant off the lobby is open daily from 6am to midnight.

✪ **Hotel Plaza Independencia.** Independencia 123, 86000 Villahermosa, Tab. ☎ **93/12-7541** or 93/12-1299. Fax 93/14-4724. 90 units. A/C TV TEL. $39 double. AE, MC, V. Free parking.

Of the many hotels in this price range, the Plaza Independencia is one of the best. The rooms, which are on six floors served by an elevator, contain avocado drapes and rugs and nice bamboo furnishings, including small desks. Some rooms have balconies, and from the top floor you can see the river. It's the only budget hotel with a pool and enclosed parking. There's an off-lobby restaurant and a bar. To find the hotel from the Plaza de Armas, face in the direction of the Malecón and walk to the right on Guerrero a half block to the corner of Macuiliz. Turn right and walk a block to Independencia and turn left; the hotel is a half block ahead on the right.

WHERE TO DINE

Just like other Mexican cities, Villahermosa is beginning to receive U.S.-franchise restaurants, but those listed below serve Mexican specialities.

Galerías Madan. Madero 408. ☎ **93/12-1650.** Breakfast $2.25–$3.50; comida corrida $3.50; main courses $3–$5. AE, CB, DC, MC, V. Daily 7am–11:30pm (comida corrida served 1–4pm). MEXICAN.

Situated in a lobby of shops, this calm, soft pink, air-conditioned restaurant serves a comida corrida of soup, rice, a main course, vegetables, coffee, and dessert. The empañadas de carne (meat pies) are superior, and the tamales are just plain good. Large windows look onto the street, and the room has the feel of a hotel coffee shop where downtown shoppers and business types gather. It's between Lerdo de Tejada and Reforma.

✪ **Los Tulipanes.** CICOM Center, Periférico Carlos Pellicer Camara 511. ☎ **93/12-9209** or 93/12-9217. Main courses $7–$20. AE, MC, V. Daily 1–9pm. SEAFOOD/STEAKS.

Supremely popular with the local upper class, Los Tulipanes offers pricey but good food and excellent service. The staff seems to serve a full house with ease, and on busy days, a guitar trio strolls and serenades. Since the restaurant is located near the Río Grijalva and the Pellicer Museum of Anthropology, you can combine a visit to the museum with lunch here. They may bring you a plate of tostones de plátano—a monster-size tortilla made of banana instead of corn. In addition to seafood and steaks, there are such Mexican specialties as chiles rellenos, tacos, and rejelagarto empanadas.

A SIDE TRIP TO CHOCOLATE PLANTATIONS & THE RUINS OF COMALCALCO

Fifty miles from Villahermosa is Comalcalco, the only pyramid site in Mexico made of kilned stone. Your route will take you through Tabasco's cacao (chocolate)-growing country, where you can visit plantations and factories to see the cacao from the pod on the tree to the finished chocolate bars.

You'll need a car to enjoy the cacao touring, but Comalcalco itself can be reached by bus from Villahermosa. ADO has first-class buses twice daily. From the town of Comalcalco, take a taxi or a VW minivan to the ruins, which are 2 miles farther.

Travel agencies in Villahermosa offer a Comalcalco day trip as well. Generally it leaves at 8am and returns around 5pm.

By car, the fastest route from Villahermosa is on Highway 190 west to Cárdenas, then north on Highway 187. Along the road to Cárdenas are numerous banana plantations and roadside stands loaded with the yellow fruit, one of the primary cash crops of the region. As you come into Cárdenas, look for the Alteza chocolate factory of the cooperative **Industriador de Cacao de Tabasco (INCATAB).** There's a sales shop in front where you can buy boxes of chocolate in all its variations. The big boxes of chocolate they sell are actually filled with small, wrapped, two-bite bars—which make great gifts and snacks.

Cárdenas is the center of cacao processing, but the fruit itself is grown in plantations in a wide area west of Villahermosa as far south as Teapa and north to the coast. After you turn right at Cárdenas onto Highway 187, you'll begin passing trees laden with the heavy cacao pod, full of small beans.

Twelve miles before Comalcalco, in the village of Cunduacan, stop and ask for directions to the **Asociación Agrícola de Productores de Cacao.** It's on the main street, but the sign isn't visible. Mornings are best for a tour during November through April when there's an abundance of cacao. Here, the cacao beans are received from the growers, and processing begins. First the beans are fermented in huge tubs for a little over a week, and you see the beans in various stages of bubbling fermentation. Then they are mechanically dried for 16 hours. A fresh white cacao bean is slightly larger and fatter than a lima bean, but after roasting it's brown and bitter and smaller than a black-eyed pea. The roasted beans are sacked and sent to the INCATAB chocolate cooperative in Cárdenas.

Along this route are many mom-and-pop cacao plantations, where families grow and process their own cacao and sell it at local markets and roadside stands rather than to the cooperative. One of these is **Rancho La Pasadita,** 4½ miles before Comalcalco on the right. Look carefully for the sign (it's a bit obscured), but the sign on the pink-and-blue house says CHOCOLATE CASERO LA PASADITA. Here Aura Arellano has 19 acres of cacao trees that she planted in the 1950s. She will gladly take you out back where the trees grow, and if it's bean season (November through April) you'll more than likely see workers hacking open the football-shaped cantaloupe-size pods and dumping the contents in big wicker baskets. She ferments her beans the traditional way, in a hollowed-out, canoe-size wooden container. She dries and toasts the beans on a small *comal* (clay pan) over an open fire until they are hard like a nut, after which she grinds them to a powder, mixes it with sugar to cook, and makes it into logs for hot chocolate. These she sells in her living-room storefront. You see this type of chocolate for sale in shops in Villahermosa.

Comalcalco, 25 miles from Cárdenas, is a busy agricultural center with an interesting market where you can buy wicker baskets, like those used to ferment cacao and *pichanchas* (a gourd with multiple holes in it), used to extract flavor from fresh cacao beans for a refreshing drink.

The **ruins of Comalcalco** are about 2 miles on the same highway past the town; watch for signs to the turnoff on the right. Park in the lot and pay admission to the visitors' center by the museum. The museum, with many pre-Hispanic artifacts, is small but interesting and worth the 20 minutes or so it takes to see it. Unfortunately, all the descriptions are in Spanish, but there's a history of the people who lived here, the Putún/Chongal Maya, a rough people who were traders, spoke fractured Mayan, and were believed to be those who founded or greatly influenced Chichén-Itzá.

The neat, grass-covered site spreads out grandly as you enter, with pyramidal mounds left, right, and straight ahead. Comalcalco means "house of the comals" in Nahuatl. A comal is a round clay pan used for roasting and making tortillas. All around the grounds you'll see shards of kilned brick that were used to sheath the sides of the pyramidal structures. These bricks were made with clay mixed with sand and ground oyster shell. Owing to the fragile nature of these ruins, there are many NO SUBIR signs warning visitors not to climb particular structures. Others have paths and arrows pointing to the top. From the **palace** there's a fabulous view of the whole site. On the **Acropolis,** under a protective covering, are remains of a few stucco and plaster masks in surprisingly good condition, although there are few of them. Seeing the ruins takes an hour or so. Admission is $2, and the site is open daily from 8am to 5pm. The afternoon light is great for photographs.

2 Palenque

89 miles SE of Villahermosa; 143 miles NE of San Cristóbal de las Casas

The ruins of Palenque look out over the jungle from a tall ridge, which projects from the base of steep mountains also swathed in jungle. It is a dramatic sight colored by the mysterious and ancient feel of the ruins themselves. The temples here are in the classic style with tall, high-pitched roofs crowned with elaborate combs. Inside many are representations in stone and plaster of the rulers and their gods, which give evidence of a cosmology that is and perhaps will remain impenetrable to our understanding. This is one of the grand archaeological sites of Mexico.

Five miles from the ruins is the town of Palenque. There you can find lodging and food, as well as make travel arrangements. Transportation between the town and ruins is cheap and convenient.

ESSENTIALS
GETTING THERE & DEPARTING

BY PLANE   The new airport has service to various destinations via **Aerocaribe** (☎ 934/5-0618): Cancún (five flights per week); Mérida (two nonstop flights per week); San Cristóbal (four nonstop flights per week); Tuxtla (five flights per week—two nonstop). There is one flight per week to Oaxaca with a stop in Tuxtla, and two flights per week requiring a change of planes. Mexico City (five flights per week) requires changing planes. Aerocaribe is a subsidiary of **Mexicana** (☎ 800/531-7921).

BY CAR   The 143-mile trip from San Cristóbal to Palenque takes 5 to 6 hours and passes through lush jungle and mountain scenery. Take it easy, though, since potholes and other hindrances occur. Highway 186 from Villahermosa is in good condition, and the trip from there should take about 2 hours. Expect military roadblocks and cursory inspection of your travel credentials and perhaps your vehicle.

BY BUS   The two first-class bus stations are about a block apart from each other. Both are on Palenque's main street between the main square and the turn-off for the ruins. The smaller company, **Transportes Rodolfo Figueroa,** offers good first-class bus service to/from San Cristóbal and Tuxtla (four per day—5 hours to San Cristóbal, 6½ to Tuxtla). Cristóbal Colón offers service to those destinations as well as to Campeche (six per day, 5 hours), Villahermosa (nine per day, 2 hours), and Mérida (two per day, 9 hours).

ORIENTATION

VISITOR INFORMATION The **State Tourism Office** (☎ and fax **934/ 5-0356**) is a block before the main square, where avenida Juárez intersects Abasolo. The office is open Monday through Saturday from 8:30am to 9pm.

CITY LAYOUT At one end of avenida Juárez, the main street, is the **main plaza,** at the other is the impossible-to-miss **Maya statue.** To the right of the statue is the entrance to the Cañada, to the left is the road to the ruins, straight ahead past the statue is the airport and the highway to Villahermosa. The distance between the main square and the monument is a half mile.

La Cañada, a restaurant and hotel zone, is a small area of tucked into the rain forest. Here, you'll find shaded, unpaved streets, a few small hotels and restaurants and stands of artists who carve and paint. Aside from the main plaza area, this is the best location for travelers without cars, since the town is within a few blocks and the buses that run to the ruins pass by La Cañada.

GETTING AROUND The cheapest way to get back and forth from the ruins is on the white **VW buses,** which depart from the terminal at avenidas Juárez and Allende every 10 minutes from 6am to 6pm. The buses pass La Cañada and hotels along the road to the ruins, but they may not stop if they're full. Roads are not good, making these buses the best method for getting to the ruins.

FAST FACTS The telephone area code is **934.** As for the **climate,** Palenque's high humidity is downright oppressive in the summer, especially after rain showers. During the winter, the damp air can be chilly in the evenings. Rain gear is important any time of year.

EXPLORING PALENQUE

The real reason for being here is the ruins; although they can be toured in a morning, many people savor Palenque for days. There are no must-see sights in town. The La Cañada area west of town (see "City Layout," above) is a pleasant spot for a leisurely lunch and for browsing through Maya reproductions made by local artists.

PARQUE NACIONAL PALENQUE

The archaeological site of Palenque underwent several changes in 1994, which culminated in the opening of a new **museum/visitor center** on the highway to the ruins. The complex includes a large parking lot, a refreshment stand serving snacks and drinks, and several shops. The museum, although not large, is worth the time it takes to see it; it's open Tuesday through Sunday from 10am to 5pm. It contains well-chosen and artistically displayed exhibits, including the jade contents of recently excavated tombs. (The museum was robbed in 1996, but most of the jade pieces have been recovered.) Explanatory texts, in both Spanish and English, explain the life and times of the magnificent city of Palenque. New pieces are constantly being added as they are uncovered in ongoing excavations.

The **main entrance,** about a mile beyond the museum, is at the top of a hill at the end of the paved highway. There, you'll find a large parking lot, a refreshment stand, a ticket booth, and several shops. Among the vendors selling souvenirs by the parking lot are Lacandón Indians wearing white tunics and hawking bows and arrows.

Admission to the ruins is $2; free on Sunday. There's a $4 charge for each video camera used. Parking at the main entrance and at the visitor center is free. The site and visitor center shops are open daily from 8am to 4:45pm; King Pacal's crypt is open daily from 10am to 4pm.

Palenque Archaeological Site

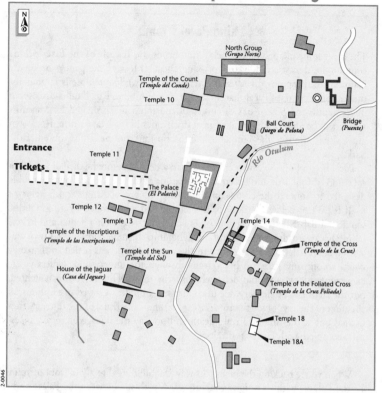

TOURING THE RUINS Pottery found during the excavations shows that people lived in this area as early as 300 B.C. During the Classic period (A.D. 300–900), the ancient Maya city of Palenque was a ceremonial center for the high priests; the civilization peaked at around A.D. 600 to 700.

When John Stephens visited the site in the 1840s, the cleared ruins you see today were buried under centuries of accumulated earth and a thick canopy of jungle. The dense jungle surrounding the cleared portion still covers yet unexplored temples, which are easily discernible in the forest even to the untrained eye. But be careful not to drift too far from the main paths. Recently there have been two incidents where a single tourist went into the rain forest to inspect unreconstructed temples and was assaulted.

Of all the ruins in Mexico open to the public, this is the most haunting because of its majesty and sense of the past. Scholars have unearthed names of the rulers and their family histories, putting visitors on a first-name basis with these ancient people etched in stone. Read about it in *A Forest of Kings,* by Linda Schele and David Friedel.

As you enter the ruins from the entrance, the building on your right is the **Temple of the Inscriptions,** named for the great stone hieroglyphic panels found inside. Just to your right as you face the Temple of the Inscriptions is **Temple 13,** which is receiving considerable attention from archaeologists. Recently, the burial of another richly adorned personage was discovered here, accompanied in death by an adult female and an adolescent. These remains are still being studied, but the treasures are on display in the museum.

King Pacal's Tomb

The great stone hieroglyphic panels found inside the **Temple of the Inscriptions** contain the dynastic family tree of King Pacal. (Most of the panels are in the National Anthropological Museum in Mexico City.) The temple is famous for the tomb, or crypt, of Pacal that the archaeologist Alberto Ruz Lhuller discovered in its depths in 1952. Ruz's discovery of the tomb is considered by Mayanist scholars to be among a handful of great discoveries in the Maya world. Ruz's own grave site is opposite the Temple of the Inscriptions, on the left as you enter the park.

Pacal began building the temple less than a decade before he died at age 80 in A.D. 683. It took Ruz and his crew four seasons of digging to clear out the rubble designed to conceal the crypt containing the remains of King Pacal. The crypt itself is 80 feet below the floor of the temple and was covered by a monolithic sepulchral slab 12½ feet long and 7 feet wide, engraved with a depiction of Pacal falling backwards from the land of the living into the underworld. Four men and a woman were left at the entrance to the crypt when it was sealed so that they could accompany Pacal on his journey through the underworld. Unless you're claustrophobic, you should definitely visit the tomb. The way down is lighted, but the steps can be slippery due to condensed humidity. Carved inscriptions on the sides of the crypt (which visitors can't see) show the ritual of the funerary rites carried out at the time of Pacal's death and portray the lineage of Pacal's ancestors, complete with family portraits.

When you're back on the main pathway, the building directly in front of you will be the **Palace,** with its unique watchtower. A pathway between the Palace and the Temple of the Inscriptions leads to the **Temple of the Sun, the Temple of the Foliated Cross, the Temple of the Cross,** and **Temple 14.** This group of temples, now cleared and in various stages of reconstruction, was built by Pacal's son, Chan-Bahlum, who is usually shown on inscriptions as having six toes. Chan-Bahlum's plaster mask was found in Temple 14 next to the Temple of the Sun. Archaeologists have recently begun probing the depths of the Temple of the Sun in search of **Chan-Bahlum's tomb.** Little remains of this temple's exterior carving. Inside, however, behind a fence, a carving of Chan-Bahlum shows him ascending the throne in A.D. 690. The panels, which are still in place, depict Chan-Bahlum's version of his historic link to the throne.

The North Group, to the left of the Palace, is also undergoing restoration. Included in this area are the **Ball Court** and **the Temple of the Count,** so named because Count Waldeck camped there in the 19th century. The explorer John Stephens camped in the Palace when it was completely tree- and vine-covered, spending sleepless nights fighting off mosquitoes. At least three tombs, complete with offerings for the underworld journey, have been found here. The lineage of at least 12 kings has been deciphered from inscriptions left at this marvelous site.

Just past the North Group is a small building (once a museum) now used for storing the artifacts found during the restorations. It is closed to the public. To the right of the building, a stone bridge crosses the river, leading to a pathway down the hillside to the new museum. The path is lined with rocks and has steps in the steepest areas, leading past the **Cascada Motiepa,** a beautiful waterfall that creates a series of pools perfect for cooling weary feet. Benches are placed along the way as

Palenque Accommodations & Dining

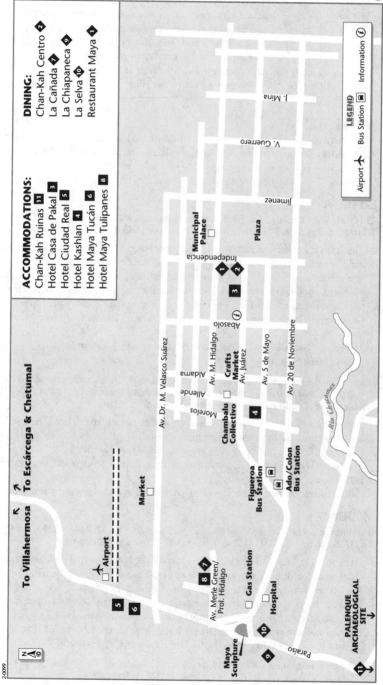

ACCOMMODATIONS:
Chan-Kah Ruinas **11**
Hotel Casa de Pakal **3**
Hotel Ciudad Real **5**
Hotel Kashlan **4**
Hotel Maya Tucán **6**
Hotel Maya Tulipanes **8**

DINING:
Chan-Kah Centro **2**
La Cañada **7**
La Chiapaneca **9**
La Selva **10**
Restaurant Maya **1**

LEGEND
Airport ✈ Bus Station ◼ Information ⓘ

To Villahermosa
To Escárcega & Chetumal

Airport

Market

Av. Dr. M. Velasco Suárez

Municipal Palace

Independencia

Plaza

Abasolo

Aldama

Allende

Morelos

Av. M. Hidalgo

Crafts Market

Av. Juárez

Av. 5 de Mayo

Av. 20 de Noviembre

Chambalu Collectivo

Figueroa Bus Station

Ado/Colon Bus Station

Av. Merle Green/
Prol. Hidalgo

Gas Station

Hospital

Maya Sculpture

Paraíso

PALENQUE ARCHAEOLOGICAL SITE

Río Chacamax

J. Mina

V. Guerrero

Jiménez

N

2.0099

rest areas, and some small temples have been reconstructed near the base of the trail. In the early morning and evening, you may hear monkeys crashing through the thick foliage by the path; if you keep noise to a minimum, you may spot wild parrots as well. Walking downhill (by far the best way to go), it will take you about 20 minutes to reach the main highway. The path ends at the paved road across from the museum. The colectivos going back to the village will stop here if you wave them down.

WHERE TO STAY

The fanciest hotel in town (the Hotel Misión Park Inn Palenque) gets too many complaints for me to recommend it. And with the recent addition of some upscale hotels, it faces a lot of competition. Transportation to and from the ruins is easy from just about any hotel and should not be of concern when choosing one.

EXPENSIVE

✪ **Chan-Kah Ruinas.** Km 30 Carretera Palenque, 29960 Palenque, Chi. ☎ **934/ 5-1100.** Fax 934/5-0820. 72 units. A/C. $75 double. AE, MC, V. Free parking.

This hotel is a collection of comfortable, roomy bungalows that offer privacy, quiet, and the surroundings of a tropical forest. Some are air-conditioned; some are not. The grounds are beautifully laid out around a stream, and there is a large, inviting pool with rock floor. The hotel is on the road to the ruins midway between the ruins and the town. Christmas prices may be higher than those quoted here, and you may be quoted a higher price if you reserve a room in advance from the United States.

Dining/Diversions: Outdoor restaurant/bar serving Mexican food.
Amenities: Swimming pool.

Hotel Ciudad Real. Carretera a Pakal-Na, 29960 Palenque, Chi. (Reservations made in San Cristóbal.) ☎ **967/8-0187.** E-mail: 103144.2762@compuserve.com. 72 units. A/C TV TEL. $80 double. AE, DC, DISC, MC, V. Free secured parking.

This is your best bet for creature comforts and modern convenience. The hotel is on the highway to the airport. The rooms are large, well lit, and comfortably furnished. Facilities include pool, bar, restaurant, and travel agency.

Dining/Diversions: A restaurant serves international food; a bar features live marimba music at night.
Amenities: Swimming pool, wading pool, travel agency, handcrafts store.

MODERATE

Hotel Maya Tucan. Carretera Palenque, 29960 Palenque, Chi. ☎ **934/5-0290.** Fax 934/ 5-0337. 60 units. A/C TV TEL. $53 double. AE, MC, V. Free secured parking.

Get a room in back and you will have a view of the hotel's natural pond. All rooms come with double beds. They are adequate in size and cheerfully decorated. The air-conditioner is quiet and gets the job done. Facilities include pool, restaurant, bar, and sometimes a discotheque—when large tour groups are present (which might bear asking about before checking in). The grounds are well kept in a tropical fashion, and scarlet macaws kept by the hotel fly about the parking lot. The Maya Toucan is a stone's throw from the Ciudad Real on the highway to the airport.

Hotel Maya Tulipanes. Calle Merle Green 6, 29960 Palenque, Chi. ☎ **934/5-0201.** Fax 934/5-1004. 50 units. A/C TV TEL. $49 double. AE, MC, V. Free parking.

This hotel tries hard to remind you why you have come to Palenque—Maya statues, carvings, and paintings fill the hallways and public areas in this rambling, overgrown, but comfortable 2-story hotel. And because the hotel is in the Cañada, it has a definite tropical-forest feel; the dark shade is a cool respite from the sun's glare. Rooms vary from section to section, so ask to see rooms in different parts of the hotel. A new addition to the hotel is a small pool.

INEXPENSIVE

Hotel Casa de Pakal. Av. Juárez 10, 29960 Palenque, Chi. ☎ **934/5-0443.** 15 rms. A/C. $22 double. AE, MC, V.

This bright, relatively new four-story hotel far might be the best bargain in town if you don't have a car. The air-conditioning is strong and quiet. The rooms are a little small but far brighter and cleaner than those at nearby establishments, and they come with one double and one single bed covered with chenille spreads. A good restaurant is on the premises. The hotel is a half block west of the main plaza.

Hotel Kashlan. 5 de Mayo 105, 29960 Palenque, Chi. ☎ **934/5-0297.** Fax 934/5-0309. 59 units. A/C. $20–$31 double. No credit cards.

This is the closest hotel to the bus station and is a dependable establishment. The clean rooms have interior windows opening onto the hall, marble-square floors, nice bedspreads, tile bathrooms, small vanities, and luggage racks. Show owner Ada Luz Navarro your Frommer's book and you'll receive a discount. Higher prices are for rooms with air-conditioning (there are 29, and some of the new ones are quite comfortable); ceiling fans (in 30 rooms) are powerful. The hotel restaurant features vegetarian food. Trips around the region, including to Agua Azul and Misol Ha, can also be arranged at the hotel.

WHERE TO DINE

Avenida Juárez is lined with many small restaurants, none of which is exceptional. There are a couple in the main plaza, some on the road to the ruins, and a couple in the Cañada that I do like.

MODERATE

✪ **La Chiapaneca.** Carretera Palenque Ruinas. ☎ **934/5-0363.** Main courses $7–$9. AE, MC, V. Daily 8am–12pm. MEXICAN.

Palenque's traditional best restaurant continues to serve top-notch regional cuisine in a pleasant tropical setting. Though it has a thatched roof, the dining room is large and refined. The pollo Palenque (chicken with potatoes in a tomato-and-onion sauce) is a soothing choice; save room for the flan. Mexican wines are served by the bottle. La Chiapaneca is about a 20-minute walk from the Maya statue toward the ruins.

La Selva. Km. 0.5 Carretera Palenque Ruinas. ☎ **934/5-0363.** Main courses $4–$17. AE, MC, V. Daily 8am–12pm. MEXICAN/INTERNATIONAL.

La Selva (the jungle) offers fine dining in a large, outdoor space under a beautiful thatched roof and beside well-tended gardens. The menu includes seafood, fresh-water fish, steaks, and enchiladas. The most expensive thing on the menu, and something you find very rarely, is Pigua—a freshwater lobster that is caught in the large rivers of southeast Mexico. These can get quite large—the size of small regular lobsters. I especially liked the fish stuffed with shrimp or the mole enchiladas.

INEXPENSIVE

Chan-Kah Centro. Juárez 2. ☎ **934/5-0318.** Breakfast $2.25–$3; Comida corrida $3–$4; main courses $4–$7. AE, MC, V. Daily 7am–11pm. Mexican.

This attractive hotel restaurant is the most peaceful place to eat in town. The waiters are extremely attentive, and the food is fairly well prepared (avoid the tough beef, though). The second-story bar overlooks the main plaza—you can have your meal served there. The restaurant is on the west side of the main plaza at the corner of Independencia and Juárez.

La Cañada. Prolongación av. Hidalgo 12. ☎ **934/5-0102.** Main courses $5–$9. No credit cards. Daily 7am–10pm. MEXICAN.

This palapa restaurant tucked into the jungle is one of the best in town, though it never seems crowded. Though the dining room has a dirt floor, the place is spotless, the service attentive, and the food good, if not exceptional. Try one of the local specialties such as pollo mexicano or bean soup. This restaurant is in the Hotel La Cañada.

✪ **Restaurant Maya.** Av. Independencia s/n. ☎ **934/5-0042.** Breakfast $3–$4; main courses $4–$5. No credit cards. Daily 7am–11pm. MEXICAN/STEAKS.

The most popular place in town among tourists and locals, Restaurant Maya is opposite the northwest corner of the main plaza near the post office. Breezy and open, it's managed by a solicitous family. At breakfast, there are free refills of very good coffee. Try the tamales or any of the other local dishes or traditional Mexican fare.

ROAD TRIPS FROM PALENQUE
SPECTACULAR WATERFALLS AT AGUA AZUL & CASCADA DE MISOL HA

The most popular excursion from Palenque is a day trip to the Misol Ha waterfall and Agua Azul. **Misol Ha** is about 12 miles from Palenque off the road to Ocosingo. Visitors swim in the waters below the falls and scramble up slippery paths to smaller falls beside the large one, which drops about 90 feet before spraying its mist on the waters below. There's a small restaurant run by the ejido cooperative that owns the site. Entrance costs around $1.25. Approximately 24 miles beyond Misol Ha on the same road are the **Agua Azul waterfalls,** a truly spectacular series of beautiful cascades tumbling into a wide river. Seeing both is a full day trip. Visitors can picnic and relax (bring something to sprawl on), swim, or clamber over the slippery cascades and go upstream for a look at the jungle encroaching the water. Agua Azul is prettiest after 3 or 4 consecutive dry days; heavy rains can make the water very murky. Check with guides or other travelers about the water quality before you decide to go. Cost to enter is around $3. Trips can be arranged through **Viajes Shivalva Tours, Viajes Toniná** (see "Bonampak & Yaxchilán: Ruins & Rugged Adventure," below), or the **Hotel Kashlan.** Another way to go is to take a **special colectivo** from the same company that runs colectivos to the ruins. You can find them on Juárez by the main plaza. They make the trip to Agua Azul and the Cascada de Misol Ha every day, with two round trips beginning at 10am; the last van departs Agua Azul for Palenque at 6:30pm. Be sure to check this with the drivers. They may wait until six or eight people want to go, or decide to make only one trip.

BONAMPAK & YAXCHILÁN: RUINS & RUGGED ADVENTURE

Intrepid travelers may wish to consider the 2-day excursion to the Maya ruins of Bonampak and Yaxchilán. The **ruins of Bonampak,** southeast of Palenque on the Guatemalan border, were discovered in 1946. The **mural** discovered on the interior walls of one of the buildings is the greatest battle painting of pre-Hispanic Mexico. Reproductions of the vivid murals found here are on view in the Regional Archaeology Museum in Villahermosa.

You can fly or drive to Bonampak. Several tour companies offer a 2-day (minimum) tour by four-wheel-drive vehicle to within 4½ miles of Bonampak. You must walk the rest of the way to the ruins. After camping overnight, you continue by river to the extensive ruins of the great Maya city, Yaxchilán, famous for its highly ornamented buildings. Bring rain gear, boots, a flashlight, and bug repellent. All tours include meals but vary in price ($80 to $120 per person); some take far too many people for comfort (the 7-hour road trip can be unbearable).

The two most reputable tour operators in Palenque are Viajes Shivalva and Viajes Toniná. **Viajes Shivalva** is at calle Merle Green 1 (Apdo. Postal 237), Palenque, Chi. 29960 (☎ **934/5-0411;** fax 934/5-0392). Office hours are Monday through Friday from 7am to 3pm. A branch office is now open a block from the zócalo (main plaza) at the corner of Juárez and Abasolo (across the hall from the State Tourism Office). It's open Monday through Saturday from 9am to 9pm (☎ **934/ 5-0822**). **Viajes Toniná** is at calle Juárez 105 (☎ **934/5-0384**).

Information about **ATC Tours and Travel** can be obtained at their office in San Cristóbal de las Casas. This agency has a large number of clients (and thus the best chance of making a group) and offers a large number of tours. Among its offerings is a 1-day trip to the ruins of Tikal in Guatemala for five people; another tour takes in Yaxchilán, Bonampak, and Tikal with a minimum of four people. Though rustic, they have the only permanent overnight accommodations at Yaxchilán at their Posada del Río Usumacinta. Their headquarters are in San Cristóbal (see "San Cristóbal de las Casas," below). See also "Active Vacations in the Yucatán" in chapter 3 for U.S. companies offering this trip.

3 San Cristóbal de las Casas

143 miles SW of Palenque; 50 miles E of Tuxtla Gutiérrez; 46 miles NW of Comitán; 104 miles NW of Cuauhtémoc; 282 miles E of Oaxaca

San Cristóbal (population 90,000) is a colonial town of plastered stone or adobe walls and red-tile roofs. It lies in a lovely valley, nearly 7,000 feet high. Part of the town's name is derived from the 16th-century bishop Fray Bartolomé de las Casas, who sought to protect native peoples from exploitation. The area is home to a large population of Indians who speak Mayan languages such as Tzotzil or Tzeltal. San Cristóbal is the major market center for these Indians, who trek down from the surrounding mountains. Some groups, such as the Lacandóns (who number only about 450) seldom come into town; they live so far off in the forests of eastern Chiapas that it takes 6 days on horseback to get to their territory.

Probably the most visible among the local indigenous groups are the **Chamula.** The men wear baggy thigh-length trousers and white or black serapes, while the women wear blue rebozos, gathered white blouses with embroidered trim, and black wool wraparound skirts.

Another local Indian group is the **Zinacantecan,** whose male population dresses in light-pink overshirts with colorful trim and tassels and sometimes short pants. Hat ribbons (now a rare sight) are tied on married men, while ribbons dangle loosely from the hats of bachelors and community leaders. The Zinacantecan women wear beautiful, brightly colored woven shawls along with black wool skirts. You may also see **Tenejapa** men clad in knee-length black tunics and flat straw hats and Tenejapa women dressed in beautiful reddish and rust-colored *huipils.* Women of all groups are barefooted, while men wear handmade sandals or cowboy boots.

There are several Indian villages within reach of San Cristóbal by road: Chamula, with its weavers and highly unorthodox church; Zinacantán, whose residents practice a unique religion; Tenejapa, **San Andrés,** and **Magdalena,** known for brocaded textiles; **Amatenango del Valle,** a town of potters; and **Aguacatenango,** known for embroidery. Most of these "villages" consist of little more than a church and the municipal government building, with homes scattered for miles around and a general gathering only for church and market days (usually Sunday).

Evangelical Protestant missionaries recently have converted large numbers of indigenous peoples, and in some villages new converts find themselves expelled from their homelands; in Chamula, for example, as many as 30,000 people have been expelled. Many of these people, called *expulsados* (expelled ones), have taken up residence in new villages on the outskirts of San Cristóbal de las Casas. They still wear their traditional dress. Other villages, such as Tenejapa, allow the Protestant church to exist and villagers to attend it without prejudice.

Although the influx of tourists is increasing and the influence of outsiders (including Mexicans) is inevitably chipping away at the culture, the Indians aren't really interested in acting or looking like the foreigners in their midst. They may steal glances at tourists or even stare curiously, but mainly they pay little attention to outsiders.

You'll hear the word *ladino* here; it refers to non-Indian Mexicans or people who have taken up modern ways, changed their dress, dropped their Indian traditions and language, and decided to live in town. It may be used derogatorily or descriptively, depending on who is using the term and how.

Other local lingo you should know about includes *Jovel,* San Cristóbal's original name, used often by businesses; and *coleto,* meaning someone or something from San Cristóbal. You'll see signs for tamales coletos, coleto bread, and coleto breakfast.

ESSENTIALS
GETTING THERE & DEPARTING

BY PLANE   San Cristóbal's airport offers service through one major airline: **Aerocaribe** (☎ 961/2-0020), a subsidiary of **Mexicana** (☎ 800/531-7921). There is nonstop service to/from Tuxtla (four flights per week) and Palenque (four flights per week). To/from Mérida (twice a week) is one-stop service. All other destinations require changing planes: Cancún (four flights per week), Mexico City (four flights per week), Oaxaca (four flights per week), Huatulco (three flights per week), Veracruz (three flights per week), and Acapulco (three flights per week).

Charter-flight arrangements or flight changes on any airline in another city can be made through **ATC Tours and Travel,** across from El Fogón de Jovel Restaurant in San Cristóbal (☎ 967/8-2550; fax 967/8-3145).

BY CAR   From Tuxtla, a 1½-hour trip, the road winds through beautiful mountain country. The road between Palenque and San Cristóbal de las Casas is adventurous and provides jungle scenery, but portions of it may be heavily potholed, washed out, or have dangerous dips; the trip takes about 5 hours.

BY TAXI   Taxis from Tuxtla Gutiérrez to San Cristóbal leave from both the airport and the Cristóbal Colón bus station.

BY BUS   The two bus stations in town are directly across the Pan American Highway from each other. The smaller one belongs to **Transportes Rodolfo Figueroa (TRF),** which provides first-class service to/from Tuxtla (every 40 minutes) and Palenque (four buses per day with a stop in Ocosingo—cheaper than the competition). For other destinations go to the large station run by **ADO** and its affiliates Cristóbal Colón and Maya de Oro. This company offers service to/from

Zapatista Uprising & Lingering Tensions

In January 1994, Indians from this area rebelled against the ladino-led towns and Mexican government over health care, education, land distribution, and representative government. Their organization, the **Zapatista Liberation Army (Ejercito Zapatista de Liberacion Nacional, or EZLN),** and its leader, Subcomandante Marcos, have become world famous. Since the revolt, discussions between government officials and the leadership of the EZLN have been on-again-off-again. Progress has been made, but the principal issues remain unresolved, and tension still exists in the area. In December 1997 and January 1998 there were more killings, but they may have been more the result of local political division rather than the tension between Zapatistas and the national government. I was in San Cristóbal shortly afterward, and there was no evidence of tension in the town or the valley. Life was normal. The only visible signs I found of the confrontation were the initials EZLN painted on a few walls, and little Subcomandante Marcos dolls, replete with black ski masks, offered for sale by street vendors (a very hot-selling item, by the way). Locals gave no evidence of concern. Tourists were present in large numbers. Only the newspapers made an issue of the confrontation. Much to my surprise, there were no military roadblocks on the highway connecting Palenque, Ocosingo, and San Cristóbal; troops did make stops on the road from San Cristóbal to Oaxaca, but they were checking for illegal immigrants from Central America. Before traveling to Chiapas, check your news sources and see if the State Department has issued any advisories: www.state.gov.

Tuxtla (12 buses per day), Palenque (almost every hour), and several other destinations: Mérida (two buses per day), Villahermosa (two buses per day), Oaxaca (two buses per day), and Puerto Escondido (two buses per day).

ORIENTATION

ARRIVING   To get to the main plaza if you're arriving by car from Oaxaca/Tuxtla, turn left on avenida Insurgentes (there's a traffic light); if you're coming from Palenque/Ocosingo, turn right. From the bus station, the main plaza is 9 blocks north up avenida Insurgentes (a 10-minute walk slightly uphill). Cabs are cheap and plentiful.

VISITOR INFORMATION   The **Municipal Tourism Office** (☎ 967/8-0660, ext. 126; fax 967/8-0135), on the main square in the town hall, across the street from the cathedral, is well organized and has a friendly, helpful staff. The office keeps convenient hours: Monday through Saturday from 9am to 8pm and Sunday from 9am to 2pm. Check the bulletin board here for apartments, shared rides, cultural events, and local tours. Or try the **State Tourism Office** across the main plaza, at av. Hidalgo 2 (☎ 967/8-6570); it's open Monday through Friday 9am to 9pm, Saturday 9am to 8:30pm, and Sunday 9am to 2pm. Both offices are helpful, but the state office is open an hour later and usually isn't as busy.

CITY LAYOUT   San Cristóbal is laid out on a grid; the main north-south axis is **Insurgentes/Utrilla** and the east-west axis is **Mazariegos/Madero.** All streets change names when they cross either of these streets. **Real de Guadalupe** seems to have become a main drag for tourism-related businesses. The market is 9 blocks north along Utrilla. From the market, minibuses (colectivos) trundle to outlying villages.

San Cristóbal de las Casas

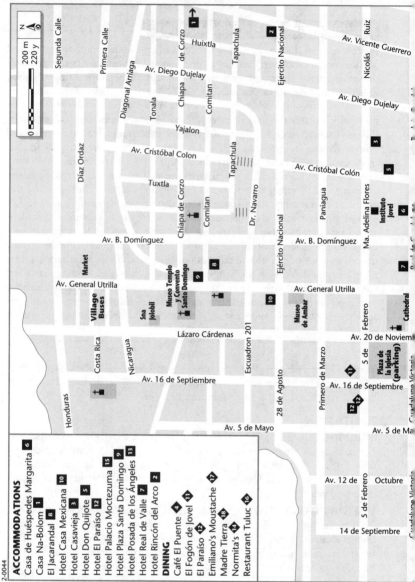

ACCOMMODATIONS
Casa de Huéspedes Margarita **6**
Casa Na-Bolom **1**
El Jacarandal **8**
Hotel Casa Mexicana **10**
Hotel Casavieja **3**
Hotel Don Quijote **5**
Hotel El Paraíso **12**
Hotel Palacio Moctezuma **15**
Hotel Plaza Santa Domingo **9**
Hotel Posada de los Ángeles **13**
Hotel Real de Valle **7**
Hotel Rincón del Arco **2**

DINING
Café El Puente **4**
El Fogón de Jovel **11**
El Paraíso **2**
Emiliano's Moustache **17**
Madre Tierra **18**
Normita's **14**
Restaurant Tuluc **16**

Take note that this town has at least three streets named "Domínguez" and two streets named "Flores." There's Hermanos Domínguez, Belisário Domínguez, and Pantaleón Domínguez, and María Adelina Flores and Dr. José Flores.

GETTING AROUND   Most of the sights and shopping in San Cristóbal are within walking distance of the plaza.

Urbano buses—minibuses—take residents to and from town and the outlying neighborhoods. All buses pass by the market and central plaza on their way through town. Utrilla and avenida 16 de Septiembre are the two main arteries; all buses use the market area as the last stop. Any bus on Utrilla will take you to the market.

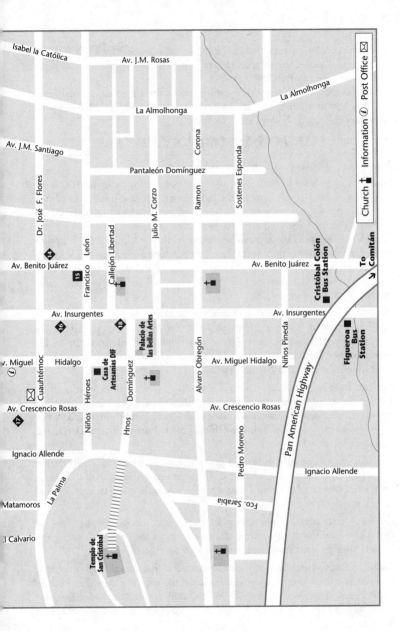

Isabel la Católica
Av. J.M. Rosas
La Almolhonga
La Almolhonga
Av. J.M. Santiago
Corona
Sostenes Esponda
Pantaleón Domínguez
Julio M. Corzo
Ramon
Dr. José F. Flores
Callejón Libertad
León
Francisco
Av. Benito Juárez
15
Av. Benito Juárez
Cristóbal Colón Bus Station
To Comitán
Av. Insurgentes
16
18
Av. Insurgentes
Niños Pineda
Palacio de las Bellas Artes
Alvaro Obregón
Figueroa Bus Station
v. Miguel
Hidalgo
Cuauhtémoc
Casa de Artesanías DIF
Domínguez
Av. Miguel Hidalgo
Héroes
Av. Crescencio Rosas
Niños
Hnos
Av. Crescencio Rosas
Pedro Moreno
17
Pan American Highway
Ignacio Allende
Ignacio Allende
La Palma
Matamoros
Fco. Sarabia
l Calvario
Templo de San Cristóbal

Church ✝ Information ⓘ Post Office ⊠

Colectivos to outlying villages depart from the public market at avenida Utrilla. Buses late in the day are usually very crowded. Always check to see when the last or next-to-last bus returns from wherever you're going, then take the one before that—those last buses sometimes don't materialize, and you might be stranded. I speak from experience!

Rental cars come in handy for trips to the outlying villages and may be worth the expense when shared by a group, but keep in mind that insurance is invalid on unpaved roads. There's a **Budget** rental-car office here at av. Mazariegos 36 (☎ 967/8-3100). You'll save money by arranging the rental from your home country; otherwise, a day's rental with insurance will cost $62 for a VW Beetle with manual transmission, the cheapest car available. Office hours are Monday through Sunday from 8am to 1pm and 5 to 8pm.

Bicycles are another option for getting around the city; a day's rental is about $12, and bike tours are offered at **Los Pinguinos,** av. 5 de Mayo 10-B (no phone), open daily 9:15am to 2:30pm and 4 to 7pm.

FAST FACTS: San Cristóbal de las Casas

Area Code   The telephone area code is 967.

Books   *Living Maya* by Walter Morris, with photography by Jeffrey Fox, is the best book to read to understand the culture, art, and traditions around San Cristóbal de las Casas, as well as the unsolved social, economic, and political problems that gave rise to the 1994 Chiapas Indian uprising. *The People of the Bat: Mayan Tales and Dreams from Zinacantán,* by Robert M. Laughlin, is a priceless collection of beliefs from that village near San Cristóbal. Another good book with a completely different view of today's Maya is *The Heart of the Sky* by Peter Canby, who traveled among the Maya to chronicle their struggles (written before the Zapatista uprising).

Bookstore   For a wide selection of new and used books and reading material in English, go to **La Pared,** av. Hidalgo 2 (☎ **967/8-6367**), next to the state tourism office. The owner, Dana Gay, is very helpful and informed. Or try **Librería Soluna,** Real de Guadalupe 13B and Insurgentes 27. These stores have a good number of books in English as well.

Bulletin Boards   Since San Cristóbal is a cultural crossroads for travelers from all over the world, several places maintain bulletin boards with information on Spanish classes, local specialty tours, rooms or houses to rent, rides needed, etc. These include boards at the **Tourism Office, Café el Puente, Madre Tierra,** and **Casa Na-Bolom.**

Climate   San Cristóbal can be cold day or night year-round, especially during the winter. Most hotels are not heated, although some have fireplaces. There is always a possibility of rain, but I would particularly avoid going to San Cristóbal from late August to late October.

Currency Exchange   There are at least five casas de cambio on Real de Guadalupe near the main square and a couple under the colonnade facing the square. Most are open until 8pm, and some are open Sunday.

E-mail   The Cyberc@fe is in the little concourse that cuts through the block that is just east of the main square. Look for the entrance on either Real de Guadalupe or Francisco Madero (☎ **967/8-7488**). It is the largest Internet cafe I have seen in Mexico, with several well-connected machines and a few other toys besides.

Homestays   **Café el Puente** (see "Where to Dine," below), besides being a gathering place, restaurant, and telephone center, can also arrange homestays.

Parking   If your hotel does not have parking, use the underground public lot (estacionamiento) located in front of the cathedral, just off the main square on 16 de Septiembre. Entry is from calle 5 de Febrero.

Post Office   The **post office** (correo) is at Crescencio Rosas and Cuauhtémoc, a block south and west of the main square. It's open Monday through Friday from 8am to 7pm and Saturday from 9am to 1pm.

Photography Warning

Photographers should be very cautious about when, where, and at whom or what they point their cameras. In San Cristóbal, taking a photograph of even a chile pepper can be a risky undertaking; local people just do not like having people take pictures. Especially in the San Cristóbal market, people who think they or their possessions are being photographed may angrily pelt photographers with whatever object is at hand—rocks or rotten fruit. Be respectful and ask first. You might even try offering a small amount of money in exchange for taking a picture. Young handcraft vendors will sometimes offer to be photographed for money.

In villages outside of San Cristóbal, there are strict rules about photography. To ensure proper respect by outsiders, villages around San Cristóbal, especially Chamula and Zinacantán, require visitors to go to the municipal building upon arrival and sign an agreement (written in Spanish) not to take photographs. The penalty for disobeying these regulations is stiff: confiscation of your camera and perhaps even a lengthy stay in jail. And they mean it!

Spanish Classes The **Centro Bilingue,** at the Centro Cultural El Puente, Real de Guadalupe 55, 29250 San Cristóbal de las Casas, Chi. (☎ **800/303-4983** in the U.S., or ☎ and fax 967/8-3723), offers classes in Spanish. The **Instituto Jovel,** María Adelina Flores 21 (Apdo. Postal 62), 29250 San Cristóbal de las Casas, Chi. (☎ and fax **967/8-4069**), gets high marks for its Spanish courses. It also offers courses in weaving and cooking. Both schools can arrange homestays for their students.

Telephone **Centro el Puente** at the Café el Puente, Real de Guadalupe 55 (☎ and fax **967/8-1911**), offers telephone and fax service at reasonable prices. Besides sending faxes, they'll receive faxes and hold them for you. The telephone service is open Monday through Saturday from 9am to 2pm and 5 to 9pm.

EXPLORING SAN CRISTÓBAL

San Cristóbal, with its beautiful scenery, clean air, and mountain hikes, draws many visitors. However, the town's biggest attraction is its colorful, centuries-old indigenous culture. The Chiapanecan Maya, attired in their beautifully crafted native garb, surround tourists in San Cristóbal, but most travelers take at least one trip to the outlying villages to get a close-up of Maya life.

ATTRACTIONS IN TOWN

Catedral. 20 de Noviembre at Guadalupe Victoria. No phone. Free admission. Daily 7am–6pm.

San Cristóbal's main cathedral was built in the 1500s and boasts fine timber work and a very fancy pulpit.

Museo de Ambar. Plaza Silvan, Utrilla 10. ☎ **967/8-3507.** Free admission. Daily 9:30am–7pm. From the plaza, walk 2½ blocks north on Utrilla (going toward the market); the museum will be on your left.

Seen from the street, this place looks like just another store, but pass through the small shop area and you'll find the long, narrow museum a fascinating place to browse. It's the only museum in Mexico devoted to amber, a fossilized resin thousands of years old mined in Chiapas near Simojovel. Owner José Luis Coría Torres has assembled more than 250 sculpted amber pieces as well as a rare collection of

---

Special Events in & near San Cristóbal

In nearby Chamula, **Carnaval,** the big annual festival that takes place days before Lent, is a fascinating mingling of the Christian pre-Lenten ceremonies and the ancient Maya celebration of the five "lost days" at the end of the 360-day Maya agricultural cycle. Around noon on Shrove Tuesday, groups of village elders run across patches of burning grass as a purification rite. Macho residents then run through the streets with a bull. During Carnaval, roads are closed in town, and buses drop visitors at the outskirts.

Nearby villages (except Zinacantán) also have celebrations during this time, although they're perhaps not as dramatic. Visiting these villages, especially on the Sunday before Lent, will round out your impression of Carnaval in all its regional varieties. In Tenejapa, the celebrants are still active during the Thursday market after Ash Wednesday.

During Easter and the week after, when the annual **Feria de Primavera** (Spring Festival) is held, San Cristóbal is ablaze with lights and excitement and gets hordes of visitors. Activities include carnival rides, food stalls, handcraft shops, parades, and band concerts. Hotel rooms are scarce and more expensive.

Another spectacle is staged July 22 to 25, the dates of the annual **Fiesta of San Cristóbal,** honoring the town's patron saint. The steps up to San Cristóbal church are lit with torches at night. Pilgrimages to the church begin several days earlier, and on the night of the 24th, there's an all-night vigil.

For the **Día de Guadalupe,** on December 12, honoring Mexico's patron saint, the streets are gaily decorated, and food stalls line the streets leading to the church honoring her high on a hill.

---

amber with insects trapped inside and amber fused with fossils. Amber jewelry and other objects are also for sale.

Museo Templo y Convento Santo Domingo. Av. 20 de Noviembre. ☎ **967/8-1609.** Church free; Museum $2. Museum open Tues–Sun 10am–5pm.

Inside the front door of the carved-stone plateresque facade, there's a beautiful gilded wooden altarpiece built in 1560, walls with saints, and gilt-framed paintings. Attached to the church is the former Convent of Santo Domingo, which houses a small museum about San Cristóbal and Chiapas. The museum, housed on three floors, has changing exhibits and often shows cultural films. It's 5 blocks north of the zócalo.

✪ **Casa Na-Bolom.** Av. Vicente Guerrero 3, 29200 San Cristóbal de las Casas, Chi. ☎ **967/8-1418.** Fax 967/8-5586. $3 group tour and film *La Reina de la Selva,* an excellent 50-minute film on the Bloms, the Lacandóns, and Na-Bolom (in Spanish) is available Tues–Sun 11:30am, and another (in English) at 4:30pm. The extensive library devoted to Maya studies is open Mon–Thurs 9am–3pm, Fri 9–11am. The Artesanía Lacandón gift shop is open Tues–Sun 10am–2pm and 4–7pm. Leave the square on Real de Guadalupe, walk 4 blocks to av. Vicente Guerrero, and turn left; Na-Bolom is 5½ blocks up Guerrero.

If you're interested in the anthropology of this region, you'll want to visit this house-museum. Stay here if you can. The house, built as a seminary in 1891, became the headquarters of anthropologists Frans and Trudy Blom in 1951 and the gathering place of outsiders interested in studying the region. Frans Blom led many early archaeological studies in Mexico, and Trudy was noted for her photographs of the Lacandón Indians and her efforts to save them and their forest homeland. A room at Na-Bolom contains a selection of her Lacandón photographs, and postcards of the photographs are on sale in the gift shop. A tour of the home includes the displays of pre-Hispanic artifacts collected by Frans Blom; the cozy library with its numerous volumes about the region and the Maya; and the gardens Trudy Blom started for the ongoing reforestation of the Lacandón jungle. Trudy Blom died in 1993, but Na-Bolom continues to operate as a nonprofit public trust.

The 12 guest rooms, named for surrounding villages, are decorated with local objects and textiles. All rooms have fireplaces and private bathrooms. Prices for rooms (including breakfast) are $35 single and $45 double.

Even if you're not a guest here you can come for a meal, usually a delicious assortment of vegetarian and other dishes. Just be sure to make a reservation at least 2½ hours in advance, and be on time. The colorful dining room has one large table, and the eclectic mix of travelers sometimes makes for interesting conversation. Breakfast costs $4, lunch and dinner $5 each. Following breakfast at 8 to 10am, tours to San Juan Chamula and Zinacantán are offered by a guide not affiliated with the house. (See "The Nearby Maya Villages & Countryside," below.)

Palacio de las Bellas Artes. Av. Hidalgo, 4 blocks south of the plaza. No phone.

Be sure to check out this building if you are interested in the arts. It periodically hosts dance events, art shows, and other performances. The schedule of events is usually posted on the door if the Bellas Artes is not open. There's a public library next door.

Templo de San Cristóbal. Exit the zócalo on av. Hidalgo and turn right onto the third street (Hermanos Domínguez); at the end of the street are the temple steps.

For the best view of San Cristóbal, climb the seemingly endless steps to this church and mirador (lookout point). A visit here requires stamina. By the way, there are 22 more churches in town, some of which also demand strenuous climbs.

HORSEBACK RIDING

The **Casa de Huéspedes Margarita** and **Hotel Real del Valle** (see "Where to Stay," below) can arrange horseback rides for around $15 for a day, including a guide. Reserve your steed at least a day in advance. A horse-riding excursion might go to San Juan Chamula, to nearby caves, or just up into the hills.

THE NEARBY MAYA VILLAGES & COUNTRYSIDE

The Indian communities around San Cristóbal are fascinating worlds unto themselves. If you are unfamiliar with these indigenous cultures, you will understand and appreciate more of what you see by visiting them with a guide, at least for a first foray out into the villages. Guides are acquainted with members of the communities and are viewed with less suspicion than newcomers. These communities have their own laws and customs—and visitors' ignorance is no excuse. Should something happen, the state and federal authorities will not intervene except in case of a serious crime. There are three guides who go to the neighboring villages.

Pepe leaves from **Casa Na-Bolom** (see "Attractions in Town," above) for daily trips to San Juan Chamula and Zinacantén at 10am if there is a minimum of five people. Minivan transportation and a knowledgeable guide are included in the $10 per person price. The tour returns to San Cristóbal between 2 and 3pm.

Another tour is led by a very opinionated mestiza woman, **Mercedes Hernández Gómez.** Mercedes, a largely self-trained ethnographer, is extremely well informed about the history and folkways of the villages. She explains (in English) the religious significance of what you see in the churches, where shamans try to cure Indian patients of various maladies. She also facilitates tourists' firsthand contact with Indians. Her group goes by minivan to the village or villages she has selected; normally tours return to the plaza at about 2:30pm. You can meet her near the kiosk in the main plaza at 9am (she will be carrying an umbrella). The tour costs $10 per person.

Two additional guides, **Alex and Raul,** can be found in front of the cathedral at 9am. They give tours of the Indian villages (also for $10 per person) in both English and Spanish.

For excursions farther afield, see "Road Trips from San Cristóbal" at the end of this section.

CHAMULA & ZINACANTÁN   A side trip to the village of San Juan Chamula will really get you into the spirit of life around San Cristóbal. Sunday, when the market is in full swing, is the best day to go for shopping; but other days, when you'll be unimpeded by anxious children selling their crafts, are better for seeing the village and church. Colectivos to San Juan Chamula leave the municipal market in San Cristóbal about every half hour. Don't expect anyone in these vans to speak English or Spanish, and the driver may be around 11 or 12 years old and barely able to see over the steering wheel.

The village, 5 miles northeast of San Cristóbal, is the **Chamula cultural and ceremonial center.** Activity centers on the huge church, the plaza, and the municipal building. Each year, a new group of citizens is chosen to live in the municipal center as caretakers of the saints, settlers of disputes, and enforcers of village rules. As in other nearby villages, on Sunday local leaders wear their leadership costumes with beautifully woven straw hats loaded with colorful ribbons befitting their high position. They solemnly sit together in a long line somewhere around the central square. Chamula is typical of other villages in that men are often away working in the "hot lands" harvesting coffee or cacao, while women stay home to tend the sheep, the children, the cornfields, and the fires. It's almost always the women's and children's work to gather sticks for fires, and you see them along roadsides bent under the weight.

Don't leave Chamula without seeing the **church interior.** As you step from bright sunlight into the candlelit interior, it will take a few minutes for your eyes to adjust. The tile floor is covered in pine needles scattered amid a meandering sea of lighted candles. Saints line the walls, and before them people are often kneeling and praying aloud while passing around bottles of Pepsi Cola. Shamans are often on hand, passing eggs over sick people or using live or dead chickens in a curing ritual. The statues of saints are similar to those you might see in any Mexican Catholic church, but they take on another meaning to the Chamulas that has no similarity to the traditional Catholic saints other than in name. Visitors can walk carefully through the church to see the saints or stand quietly in the background and observe.

Carnaval, which takes place just before Lent, is the big annual festival. The Chamulas are not a very wealthy people, as their economy is based on agriculture, but the women are the region's best wool weavers, producing finished pieces for themselves and for other villages.

In Zinacantán, a wealthier village than Chamula, you must sign a rigid form promising *not to take any photographs* before you are allowed to see the two side-by-side **sanctuaries.** Once permission is granted and you have paid a small fee, an escort will usually show you the church, or you may be allowed to see it on your own. Floors may be covered in pine needles here, too, and the rooms are brightly sunlit. The experience is an altogether different one from that of Chamula.

AMATENANGO DEL VALLE   About an hour's ride south of San Cristóbal is Amatenango, a town known mostly for its **women potters.** You'll see their work in San Cristóbal—small animals, jars, and large water jugs—but in the village, you can visit the potters in their homes. Just walk down the dirt streets. Villagers will lean over the walls of family compounds and invite you in to select from their inventory. You may even see them firing the pieces under piles of wood in the open courtyard or painting them with color derived from rusty iron water. The women wear beautiful red-and-yellow *huipils,* but if you want to take a photograph, you'll have to pay.

   To get here, take a colectivo from the market in San Cristóbal, but before it lets you off, be sure to ask about the return-trip schedule.

AGUACATENANGO   Located 10 miles south of Amatenango, this village is known for its **embroidery.** If you've visited San Cristóbal shops before arriving here, you'll recognize the white-on-white or black-on-black floral patterns on dresses and blouses for sale. The locals' own regional blouses, however, are quite different.

TENEJAPA   The **weavers** of Tenejapa make some of the most beautiful and expensive work you'll see in the region. The best time to visit is on market day (Sunday and Thursday, though Sunday is best). The weavers of Tenejapa taught the weavers of San Andrés and Magdalena—which accounts for the similarity in their designs and colors. To get to Tenejapa, try either to find a colectivo in the very last row by the market or hire a taxi. On Tenejapa's main street, several stores sell locally woven regional clothing, and you can bargain for the price.

THE HUITEPEC CLOUD FOREST   Pronatura, a private nonprofit ecological organization, offers environmentally sensitive tours of the cloud forest. The forest is a haven for **migratory birds,** and more than 100 bird species and 600 plant species have been discovered here. Guided tours are Tuesday to Sunday, 9am to 12pm at a cost of $18 per group (up to eight people). Make reservations a day in advance. Their office is at av. Benito Juárez 11-B (☎ **967/8-5000**). To reach the reserve on your own, drive on the road to Chamula; the turnoff is at km 3.5. The reserve is open Tuesday through Sunday from 9am to 4pm.

SHOPPING

Many Indian villages near San Cristóbal are noted for their weaving, embroidery, brocade work, leather, and pottery, making the area one of the best in the country for shopping. The craftspeople make and sell beautiful woolen shawls, indigo-dyed skirts, colorful native shirts, and magnificently woven *huipils,* all of which often come in vivid geometric patterns. Working in leather, they are artisans of the highest caliber, making sandals and men's handbags. There's a proliferation of tie-dyed *jaspe* from Guatemala, which comes in bolts and is made into clothing, as well as other textiles from that country. There are numerous shops up and down the streets leading to the market. Calle Real de Guadalupe has more shops than any other street.

CRAFTS

Casa de Artesanías DIF. Niños Héroes at Hidalgo. ☎ **967/8-1180.**

Crafts are sold in a fine showroom in one of the city's old houses. Here you'll find such quality products as lined woolen vests and jackets, pillow covers, amber jewelry, and more. In back is a fine little museum showing costumes worn by villagers who live near San Cristóbal. Open Tuesday through Saturday from 9am to 2pm and 5 to 8pm.

Central Market. Av. Utrilla. No phone.

The market buildings and the surrounding streets offer just about anything you need. The market in San Cristóbal is open every morning except Sunday (when each village has its own local market), and you'll probably enjoy observing the sellers as much as the things they sell. See the "Photography Warning" in "Fast Facts," above, regarding photography here. The mercado is north of the Santo Domingo church, about 9 blocks from the zócalo.

El Encuentro. Calle Real de Guadalupe 63-A. ☎ 967/8-3698.

You should find some of your best bargains here—at a minimum you'll think the price is fair. The shop carries many regional ritual items, such as new and used men's ceremonial hats, false saints, and iron rooftop adornments, plus many *huipils* and other textiles. It's open Monday through Saturday from 9am to 8pm and is found between Dujelay and Guerrero.

La Alborada, Centro Desarrollo Comunitario DIF. Barrio María Auxiliadora. No phone.

At this government-sponsored school, young men and women from surrounding villages come to learn how to hook Persian-style rugs, weave fabric on foot looms, sew, make furniture, construct a house, cook, make leather shoes and bags, forge iron, and grow vegetables and trees for reforestation. Probably the most interesting crafts for the general tourist are the rug-making and weaving. Artisans from Temoaya in Mexico State learned rug-making from Persians, who came to teach this skill in the 1970s. The Temoaya artisans in turn traveled to San Cristóbal to teach the craft to area students, who have since taught others. The beautiful rug designs are taken from brocaded and woven designs used to decorate regional costumes. Visitors should stop at the entrance and ask for an escort. You can visit all the various areas and see students at work or simply go straight to the weavers. There's a small sales outlet at the entrance selling newly loomed fabric by the meter, leather bags, rugs, and baskets made at another school in the highlands. La Alborada is in a far southern suburb of the city off the highway to Comitán, to the right. To get here take the "María Auxiliadora" urbano bus from the market. Ask the driver to let you off at La Alborada. The same bus makes the return trip, passing through the town center and ending its route at the market.

La Galería. Hidalgo 3. ☎ 967/8-1547.

This lovely gallery beneath a cafe has expositions by well-known national and international painters. Also for sale are the paintings and greeting cards by Kiki, the owner, a German artist who has found her niche in San Cristóbal. There are some Oaxacan rugs and pottery, plus unusual silver jewelry. Open daily from 10am to 9pm.

TEXTILE SHOPS

Kun Kun SC. Real de Mexicanos 21. ☎ 967/8-1417.

The name means "little by little." This cooperative society to aid local native artisans sells mostly ceramic tiles, weavings, and pottery. The weavings are made of locally produced wool that has been spun, dyed, and woven by members. Kun Kun holds workshops for artisans on such things as working with floor looms, which you can watch when visiting the store. The tiles are wonderful. Also, if you're interested, ask about classes in using a backstrap loom.

Plaza de Santo Domingo. Av. Utrilla.

The plazas around this church and the nearby Templo de Caridad are filled with women in native garb selling their wares. Here you'll find women from Chamula weaving belts or embroidering, surrounded by piles of loomed woolen textiles from their village. More and more Guatemalan shawls, belts, and bags are included in their inventory. There are also some excellent buys in Chiapanecan-made wool vests, jackets, rugs, and shawls similar to those in Sna Jolobil (see below), if you take the time to look and bargain. Vendors arrive between 9 and 10am and begin to leave around 3pm.

Sna Jolobil. Calzada Lázaro Cárdenas 42 (Plaza Santo Domingo). ☎ **967/8-2646.**

Meaning "weaver's house" in the Mayan language, this place is located in the former convent (monastery) of Santo Domingo, next to the Templo de Santo Domingo between Navarro and Nicaragua. This cooperative store is operated by groups of Tzotzil and Tzeltal craftspeople and has about 3,000 members who contribute products, help in running the store, and share in the moderate profits. Their works are simply beautiful; prices are set and high—as is the quality. Be sure to take a look. Open Monday through Saturday from 9am to 2pm and 4 to 6pm; credit cards are accepted.

Tzontehuitz. Real de Guadalupe 74. ☎ and fax **967/8-3158.**

About 3½ blocks from the plaza, this shop is one of the best on calle Real de Guadalupe, near the corner of Diego Dujelay. Owner Janet Giacobone specializes in her own textile designs and weavings. Some of her work is loomed in Guatemala, but you can also watch weavers using foot looms in the courtyard. Hours are Monday through Saturday from 9am to 2pm and 4 to 7pm.

Unión Regional de Artesanías de los Altos (also known as J'pas Joloviletic). Av. Utrilla 43. ☎ **967/8-2848.**

Another cooperative of weavers, this one is smaller than Sna Jolobil (see above) and not as sophisticated in its approach to potential shoppers. It sells blouses, textiles, pillow covers, vests, sashes, napkins, baskets, and purses. It's near the market and worth looking around. Open Monday through Saturday from 9am to 2pm and 4 to 7pm, and Sunday from 9am to 1pm.

WHERE TO STAY

Keep in mind that among the most interesting places to stay in San Cristóbal is the ex-seminary turned hotel-museum; see **Casa Na-Bolom** in "Attractions in Town," above, for details.

For really low-cost accommodations, there are basic but acceptable *hospedajes* and *posadas,* which charge about $6 for a single and $8 to $12 for a double. Usually these places are unadvertised; if you're interested in a very cheap place to stay, ask around in a restaurant or cafe, and you're sure to find one, or go to the tourist office, which often displays notices of new hospedajes on the metal flip rack in the office. Some of the best economical offerings are on calle Real de Guadalupe, east of the main square.

VERY EXPENSIVE

✪ **El Jacarandal.** Comitán 7, 29200 San Cristóbal de las Casas, Chi. ☎ and fax **967/8-1065.** 4 units. $160 per person for double occupancy; includes all meals, drinks, and activities. No credit cards.

El Jacarandal is the home of Nancy and Percy Wood—who choose to entertain guests and, in so doing, elevate the practice to a form of high art. This is not merely a lodging. You can stay here for a week without ever having to look for outside entertainment. The owners keep a stable of horses for the use of their guests and like to go for morning rides. They also enjoy showing their guests the Indian villages, the Huitepec cloud forest, and the Maya ruins that are not far from the city, or simply letting the guests lounge around a bit or do some exploring on their own. Meals are not to be missed. Fidelia the cook is most able, and on many occasions local anthropologists, environmentalists, or prominent citizens drop in for a bite and a chat. The house and grounds themselves are lovely; sometimes it's hard to tear yourself away. From the patio where breakfast is taken, the garden and trees present a lovely foreground of green to the background of red-tile roofs and church cupolas, and behind everything else, the mountains. The rooms come with one or two beds. Accommodations are gracious and engaging, as is everything in the house.

MODERATE

✪ **Hotel Casa Mexicana.** 28 de Agosto 1, 29200 San Cristóbal de las Casas, Chi. ☎ **967/8-1348.** Fax 967/8-2627. E-mail: Hcasamex@mail.internet.com.mx. 52 units. TV TEL. $57 double. AE, MC, V. Free secure parking.

This lovely hotel—created from a large mansion, with a grand exterior—is a conveniently located deluxe addition to the San Cristóbal scene. The entryway reveals a lovely courtyard and fountain. The carpeted rooms have excellent reading lights, electric heaters for those chilly nights, and either one or two double beds with handsome carved headboards. Guests are welcome to use the sauna, and inexpensive massages can be arranged. The hotel handles a lot of large tour groups; it can be quiet and peaceful one day and full and bustling the next. It is 4 blocks north of the main plaza at the corner of Utrilla and Agosto/Eje Nacional.

Hotel Casavieja. Ma. Adelina Flores 27, 29200 San Cristóbal de las Casas, Chi. ☎ and fax **967/8-5223** or 967/8-0385. 40 units. TV TEL. $55 double. AE, MC, V. Free parking.

The Casavieja is one of the choice hotels in San Cristóbal. Originally built in 1740, restoration and new construction have faithfully replicated the original design and detail complete with wood-beam ceilings. The size and beautiful furnishings of the carpeted rooms, plus the very welcome heaters, create an ideal cozy nest. The hotel's stylish restaurant, Doña Rita, faces the interior courtyard with tables on the patio or inside and offers reasonable prices, but service is slow. Fifteen rooms across the street house the tour groups, which in the past have created lots of noise in this otherwise tranquil hotel. The hotel is 3½ blocks northeast of the plaza between Cristóbal Colón and Diego Dujelay.

✪ **Hotel Rincón del Arco.** Ejército Nacional 66, 29200 San Cristóbal de las Casas, Chi. ☎ **967/8-1313.** Fax 967/8-1568. 36 units. TV TEL. $42 double. MC, V. Free parking.

This well-run hotel has comfortable rooms at a good price. The original section of this former colonial-era home is built around a small interior patio and dates from 1650. Rooms in this part are spacious with tall ceilings and carpet over hardwood floors. The adjacent new section faces a large grassy yard with a view of the mountains. These rooms are nicely furnished and come with beds covered in thick handsome bedspreads made in the family factory. Some are furnished in antiques, others in colonial style. Some have small balconies; all have fireplaces. In fact, if this hotel were a bit closer to the plaza, the rooms would be much more expensive. Consider it a value. Owner José Antonio Hernández is eager to make your stay a good one. There's a restaurant just behind the lobby. The hotel offers special discounted prices to students, but make arrangements in advance and be able to show university identification. The hotel is 8 blocks northeast of the main plaza at the corners of Ejército Nacional and V. Guerrero.

INEXPENSIVE

Casa de Huéspedes Margarita. Real de Guadalupe 34, 29200 San Cristóbal de las Casas, Chi. ☎ and fax **967/8-0957.** 24 units (none with bathroom). $7.50 single, $10 double. AE, MC, V.

This inexpensive place offers rooms arranged around a courtyard where the young backpackers congregate. The rooms have sagging mattresses and bare light bulbs hanging from the ceiling; the shared bathrooms are only fair. Margarita's also has horse rentals and offers tours to the nearby ruins and to the Sumidero Canyon near Tuxtla Gutiérrez. You'll find this lodging 1½ blocks east of the plaza between avenida B. Domínguez and Colón.

Hotel Don Quijote. Colón 7, 29200 San Cristóbal de las Casas, Chi. ☎ **967/8-0920** and fax 967/8-0346. 24 units. TV. $25 double. MC, V. Free secure parking 1 block away.

The small rooms here are crowded with furniture, and closets are small, but the rooms are well lit, carpeted, and coordinated with warm, beautiful textiles hand woven in the family factory. All have two double beds with lamps over them, private tiled bathrooms, and plenty of hot water. It's 2½ blocks east of the plaza, near the corner of Colón.

✪ **Hotel El Paraíso.** Av. 5 de Febrero 19, San Cristóbal de las Casas, 29200 Chi. ☎ **967/8-0085.** 13 units. TEL. $35 double. AE, MC, V.

This is a safe haven from busloads of tour groups. Rooms, which have patchwork bed covers and reading lights, are lovely but small; some even have a ladder to a loft holding a second bed. The entire hotel is decorated in terra-cotta and blue with beautiful wooden columns and beams supporting the roof. The restaurant may be the best in town.

Hotel Palacio de Moctezuma. Juárez 16, 29200 San Cristóbal de las Casas, Chi. ☎ **967/8-0352** or 967/8-1142. Fax 967/8-1536. 42 units. TV TEL. $24 double. No credit cards. Free limited parking.

Near the plaza, this three-story hotel is filled with bougainvillea and geraniums. Fresh-cut flowers tucked around tile fountains are a hallmark of this hotel. The rooms have coordinated drapes and bedspreads, red carpeting, and modern tiled showers. Alas, they are very cold in winter. Two suites have a TV and refrigerator. Overstuffed couches face a large fireplace in the lobby bar, and the cozy restaurant looks out on the interior courtyard. On the third floor is a solarium with comfortable tables and chairs and great city views. The hotel is 3½ blocks southeast of the main plaza at the corner of Juárez and León.

Hotel Plaza Santo Domingo. Utrilla 35, 29200 San Cristóbal de las Casas, Chi. ☎ **967/8-1927.** Fax 967/8-6514. 30 units. TV TEL. $20 double. MC, V. Limited parking.

This hotel, established in 1992, is ideally situated—close to the Santo Domingo Church, near the bustling market area. Rooms are nicely furnished and carpeted. Each comes with a small closet and small desk below the TV, which is set high on the wall. Bathrooms are trimmed in blue-and-white tile, and the sink area is conveniently placed outside the shower area. A large and pleasant indoor dining room is off the lobby, along with a smaller patio dining area and a large bar. This is one of the few places near Santo Domingo and the market where you can get a good meal and use clean restrooms.

Hotel Posada de los Angeles. Calle Francisco Madero 17, 29200 San Cristóbal de las Casas, Chi. ☎ **967/8-1173** or 967/8-4371. Fax 967/8-2581. 20 units. TV TEL. $32 double. AE, MC, V.

Vaulted ceilings and skylights make this three-story hotel seem much larger and brighter than many others in the city. Rooms have either two single or two double beds, and the bathrooms are large, modern, and immaculately clean; windows open onto a pretty courtyard with a fountain. The rooftop sundeck is a great siesta spot.

Hotel Real de Valle. Real de Guadalupe 14, 29200 San Cristóbal de las Casas, Chi. ☎ **967/8-0680.** Fax 967/8-3955. 36 units. $20 double. No credit cards.

The 24 new rooms in the back three-story section have new bathrooms, big closets, and a brown-and-cream decor. In addition to a rooftop solarium, you'll find a small cafeteria and an upstairs dining room with a big double fireplace.

WHERE TO DINE

San Cristóbal is not known for its cuisine, but you can eat well at several restaurants. **El Fogon de Jovel,** below, is the place to try typical Chiapanecan fare. Also, if you are interested you might come across some local dishes, including tamales, *butifarra* (a type of sausage), and *pox* (pronounced "posh," it's a distilled sugar-and-corn drink similar to aguardiente). For baked goods, try the **Panadería Mercantil** at Mazariegos 17 (☎ 967/8-0307). It's open Monday through Saturday from 8am to 9:30pm, and Sunday from 9am to 9pm.

MODERATE

El Fogón de Jovel. 16 de Septiembre 11. ☎ **967/8-1153.** Main courses $4–$8. No credit cards. Daily 12:30–10pm. CHIAPANECAN.

The waiters here wear local costumes, and walls are hung with Guatemalan and Chiapanecan prints and folk art. Each dish and regional drink is explained on the menu, which is available in English. A basket of warm handmade tortillas with six filling condiments arrives before the meal. Among the specialties are corn soup, mole chiapaneco, pork or chicken adobado in a delicious chile sauce, and pepian, a dish of savory chile-and-tomato sauce served over chicken. For a unique dessert try the changleta, which is half of a sweetened, baked chayote—so delicious you may want two. Cooking classes for small groups can be arranged, but make reservations well in advance. The restaurant is only a block northwest of the plaza at the corner of Guadalupe Victoria/Real de Guadalupe and 16 de Septiembre.

✪ **El Paraíso.** Av. 5 de Febrero 19 (in the Hotel El Paraíso). ☎ **967/8-0085.** Breakfast $2.25–$3.25; main courses $4–$12. AE, MC, V. INTERNATIONAL.

This is my favorite restaurant in San Cristóbal; just about anything is good here except for the Swiss rarebit. The cuts of meat are especially tender, the margaritas especially dangerous (one is all it takes). Specialties include the Swiss cheese fondue for two, the Eden salad, and the brochette. This small, quiet restaurant is where locals go for a splurge. It's 2 blocks from the main plaza.

✪ **Madre Tierra.** Insurgentes 19. ☎ **967/8-4297.** Main courses $2–$6; comida corrida $6. No credit cards. Restaurant, daily 8am–9:45pm (comida corrida served after 12); bakery, Mon–Sat 9am–8pm, Sun 9am–noon. INTERNATIONAL/VEGETARIAN.

For vegetarians and nonvegetarians alike, Madre Tierra is a good place for a cappuccino and pastry or an entire meal. The comida corrida is very filling, or try the chicken curry, lasagna, and fresh salads. The bakery specializes in whole-wheat breads, pastries, pizza by the slice, quiche, grains, granola, and dried fruit. The restaurant serves the bakery's goods and other delicious fare in an old mansion with wood-plank floors, long windows looking onto the street, and tables covered in colorful Guatemalan jaspe. Madre Tierra is 3½ blocks south of the plaza.

INEXPENSIVE

Café el Puente. Real de Guadalupe 55. No phone. Breakfast $1.75–$2.50; soups and salads $1–$2; pastries 75¢–$2. No credit cards. Mon–Sat 7am–11pm. MEXICAN/AMERICAN.

Ex-Californian Bill English has turned an old mansion into a cafe/cultural center where tourists and locals can converse, take Spanish classes, arrange a homestay, leave a message on the bulletin board, and send and receive faxes. How's that for a one-stop place? The cafe takes up the main part of the building, and a weaver's shop and travel agency are to the side. Movies are presented nightly in an interior patio and meeting room. It's the kind of place you return to often: for fresh waffles and coffee in the morning, for an inexpensive lunch or dinner of brown rice and vegetables. The long bulletin board is well worth checking out if you're looking for a ride, a place to stay, or information on out-of-the-way destinations. It's 2½ blocks east of the plaza between Dujelay and Cristóbal Colón.

Emiliano's Moustache. Crescencio Rosas 7. ☎ **967/8-7246.** Comida corrida $2.50; taco plates $4–$6; main courses $3–$6. No credit cards. Daily 8am–12am. MEXICAN/TACOS.

Like any right-thinking tourist, I initially avoided this place on account of its unpromising name and some cartoonlike charro figures by the door. But a conversation with some local folk overruled my prejudice and tickled my sense of irony. Sure enough, when I went in, the place was crowded with *coletos* enjoying the restaurant's highly popular comida corrida and delicious tacos, and there was not a foreigner in sight. The daily menu is posted by the door for inspection; if it isn't appealing, you can choose from a menu of taco plates (a mixture of fillings cooked together and served with tortillas and a variety of hot sauces). Any Mexican will be quick to confess that Mexico is a nation of *taqueros:* A good taco is much appreciated. Here, you can pick from the menu of taco plates, which are quite filling, or ask for an order of traditional tacos such as tacos al pastor.

Normita's. Av. Juárez 6 at Dr. Jose Flores. No phone. Breakfast $2–$2.50; comida corrida $3.25; pozole $2; tacos $1. No credit cards. Daily 7am–11pm (comida corrida served 1:30–7pm). MEXICAN.

Normita's is famous for its pozole, a hearty chicken and hominy soup to which you add a variety of things. It also offers cheap, dependable, short-order Mexican mainstays. It's an informal "people's" restaurant; the open kitchen takes up one corner of the room, and tables are scattered in front of a large paper mural of a fall forest scene from some faraway place. It's 2 blocks southeast of the plaza.

Restaurant Tuluc. Insurgentes 5. ☎ **967/8-2090.** Breakfast $1.50–$2.50; main courses $3–$4; comida corrida $3. No credit cards. Daily 7am–10pm (comida corrida served 1–5pm). MEXICAN/INTERNATIONAL.

A real bargain with its popular comida corrida, Tuluc also has that rarity of rarities in Mexico: a nonsmoking section. The house specialty is the filete Tuluc, a beef filet wrapped around spinach and cheese served with fried potatoes and green beans. The Chiapaneco breakfast is a filling quartet of juice, toast, two Chiapanecan tamales, and your choice of tea, coffee, cappuccino, or hot chocolate. Tuluc is 1½ blocks south of the plaza between Cuauhtémoc and Francisco León.

COFFEEHOUSES

Since Chiapas-grown coffee is highly regarded, it's natural to find a proliferation of coffeehouses here. Most are concealed in the nooks and crannies of San Cristóbal's side streets. Try **Café La Selva,** Crescencio Rosas 9 (☎ **967/8-7244**) for coffee served in all its varieties and brewed from organic beans (and well known for its baked goods), open daily 9am to 11pm. Or for the more traditional-style cafe where locals meet to talk over the day's news, try **Café San Cristóbal,** Cuauhtémoc 1 (☎ **967/8-3861**), open Monday through Saturday from 9am to 10pm and Sunday from 9am to 9pm.

SAN CRISTÓBAL AFTER DARK

San Cristóbal is blessed with a wide variety of nightlife species, both resident and migrating. There is a lot of live music, which is surprisingly good and varied. The bars/restaurants are cheap—none charges a cover; only one charges a minimum tab. And they are easy to get to: You can hit all the places mentioned below without setting foot in a cab. Weekends are best, but any night is good.

El Cocodrilo. Plaza 31 de Marzo. ☎ **967/8-0871.** Live music daily 9–11pm.

El Cocodrilo, in the Hotel Santa Clara on the main plaza, is a good place to start the evening off. The band begins to play at 9. The musicians do a lot of cover tunes of the Beatles and Santana, but they put their own stamp on the music. A typical thing they might do is play a rock 'n' roll standard to a reggae beat and mix in some funk riffs. The live music shuts down at 11.

La Margarita. Real de Guadalupe 34. No phone. Live music daily 9:30pm–12am.

Starting at 9:30 you can catch flamenco at this popular restaurant bar a block and a half from the plaza. The band consists of two guitarists, congas, and bass. It plays flamenco-style music with a lot of flair, if not all the passion of real flamenco. As the night progresses, they might get into some Latin jazz. You can't go wrong here unless you are in the mood to dance. The live music ends at 11:30 to 12.

Las Velas. Madero 14. ☎ **967/8-7584.** $2.50 minimum tab. Live music daily 11pm–1am.

Bands here play with a rougher edge than the one at El Cocodrilo. Some get into Latin beats and "rock en Español," which is increasingly gaining a foothold all over the world. The place is designed in a way that guarantees it to be crowded. The cost of admission if you are male is to be frisked for weapons, but this is more for setting the ambience than actual security. All the locals I spoke with said nothing has ever happened there or at any other of the bars that would warrant such a practice. Las Velas appeals to a younger crowd than most of these places.

Latino's. Mazarriegos 19. ☎ **967/8-2083.** Live music Mon–Sat 10pm–2am.

A large dance floor and a really impressive nine-piece house band playing salsa and merengue are an invitation to dance. This was the best band I heard in San Cristóbal. The place fills up on weekends with people of all ages, and everybody dances.

Madre Tierra. Insurgentes 19 (above the restaurant). ☎ **967/8-4297.** Daily 10:30–late.

This would be the place to close out an evening. Here both the crowd and the band are looser than at other places. One comes here more for the society and the bohemian setting than the music. The band specializes in blues, reggae, rock—just about anything that has a slow, steady bass line, and a solid downbeat. The place is unpretentious, the music is loud, and the mostly young crowd friendly. It closes when the last person leaves—sometimes around 6 in the morning.

ROAD TRIPS FROM SAN CRISTÓBAL

Several travel agencies in town offer excursions to nearby villages (see "The Nearby Maya Villages & Countryside," above) and those farther away. Strangely, except

To Misol–Ha & Palenque ↖

Tila

Tumbalá

Agua Azul

← To Pichucalco & Villahermosa

195

Huitiupán

Simojovel

El Bosque

Jitotol

Bochil

Chalchihuitán

Magdalenas

San Andrés Larráinzar

San Pedro Chenalhó
Mitontic

Soyaló

Ixtapa

Tenejapa

San Juan Chamula

Zinacantán

Huitepec

△ Tzóntehuitz

← To Chiapa de Corzo & Tuxtla Gutiérrez

San Cristóbal de las Casas

El Arcotete

Ecatepec

Grutas de San Cristóbal

190

Villa de Chiapilla

Teopisca

Amatenango del Valle

→ To Comitán

↓ To Las Rosas & Venustiano Carranza

Yajalón

Chilón

Bachajón

Temo

Pantelhó

Cancuc

Ocosingo

Toniná

Abasolo

Oxchuc

Altamirano

Huixtán

Chanal

0   12.5 mi.
    20 km
N

2-0045

where noted otherwise, the cost of the trip includes a driver but does not necessarily include either a bilingual guide or guided information of any kind. You pay extra for those services, so if you want to be informed while taking a tour, be sure to ask if the tour is merely transportation or if it includes a knowledgeable guide as well.

RUINS OF TONINÁ

The Maya ruins of Toniná ("house of rocks") are 2 hours from San Cristóbal and 8½ miles east of Ocosingo. Dating from the classic period, the terraced site covers an area of at least 9 square miles. Extensive excavations are under way here during the dry season.

As early as A.D. 350, Toniná emerged as a separate dynastic center of the Maya and has the distinction of having the last recorded date of the long count yet found (A.D. 909) on a small stone monument. The date signifies the end of the Classic period. Another stone, dated A.D. 711, discovered here depicts the captured King Kan-Xul of Palenque (the younger brother of Chan-Bahlum and the son of King Pacal); the portrait shows him with his arm tied by a rope but still wearing his royal headdress. Recently a huge stucco panel was unearthed picturing the Lord of Death holding Kan-Xul's head, confirming long-held suspicions that the king died at Toniná.

At the moment there are no signs to guide visitors through the site, so you're on your own. The caretaker can also show you around (in Spanish), after which a tip is appreciated. Ask at the **Casa de Huéspedes Margarita** in San Cristóbal (see "Where to Stay," above) about guided trips to Toniná (four-person minimum). The trip includes the services of a bilingual driver, a tour of the site, lunch, and a swim in the river. From November through February, you'll see thousands of swallows swarming near the ruins.

You can go on your own by bus to Ocosingo and from there take a taxi to the ruins, but have the taxi wait for your return. The ruins are open daily from 8am to 5pm; admission is $2.

PALENQUE, BONAMPAK & YAXCHILÁN

Many visitors to San Cristóbal want to visit the ruins of Palenque near Villahermosa and the Bonampak and Yaxchilán ruins on Mexico's border with Guatemala. A trip to Palenque can be accomplished in a long day-trip from San Cristóbal, but I don't recommend it because Palenque really should be savored. Bonampak and Yaxchilán are easier to see from Palenque.

For arranging these trips from San Cristóbal, I highly recommend **ATC Tours and Travel,** located across from El Fogón restaurant, calle 5 de Febrero 15 at the corner of 16 de Septiembre (☎ **967/8-2550;** fax 967/8-3145). The agency has bilingual guides and good vehicles. See the Palenque section, above, for details on Bonampak and camping overnight at Yaxchilán; see "Active Vacations in the Yucatán" in chapter 3 for other ATC regional tours focusing on birds and orchids, textiles, hiking, and camping.

If you're considering a day trip to the archaeological site of Palenque using ATC (mentioned above) or a similar travel agency, here's how your tour will be arranged. You start at 7 or 8am and within 3 hours reach the Agua Azul waterfalls, where there's a 1½-hour stop to swim. From there it's another 1½-hour drive to Palenque. You'll have about 2 hours to see the site. If your group agrees, you can skip the swim and have more time at Palenque. It'll be a minimum 16-hour day and cost about $80 per person with a minimum of four people traveling.

CHINCULTIC RUINS, COMITÁN & MONTEBELLO NATIONAL PARK

Almost 100 miles southeast of San Cristábal, near the border with Guatemala, is the Chincultic archaeological site and Montebello National Park, with **16 multi-colored lakes** and exuberant pine-forest vegetation. Forty-six miles from San Cristóbal is Comitán, a pretty hillside town of 40,000 inhabitants known for its flower cultivation and a sugarcane-based liquor called *comitecho.* It's also the last big town along the Pan–American Highway before the Guatemalan border.

The Chincultic ruins, a late classic site, have barely been excavated, but the main **acropolis,** set high up against a cliff, is magnificent to see from below and worth the walk up for the view. After passing through the gate, you'll see the trail ahead; it passes ruins on both sides. Steep stairs leading up the mountain to the acropolis are flanked by more unexcavated tree-covered ruins. From there, you can gaze upon distant Montebello Lakes and miles of cornfields and forest. The paved road to the lakes passes six lakes, all different colors and sizes, ringed by cool pine forests; most have parking lots and lookouts. The paved road ends at a small restaurant. The lakes are best seen on a sunny day, when their famous brilliant colors are optimal.

Most travel agencies in San Cristóbal offer a daylong trip that includes the lakes, the ruins, lunch in Comitán, and a stop in the pottery-making village of Amatenango del Valle. If you're driving, follow Highway 190 south from San Cristóbal through the pretty village of Teopisca and then through Comitán; turn left at La Trintaria, where there's a sign to the lakes. After the Trintaria turnoff and before you reach the lakes, there's a sign pointing left down a narrow dirt road to the Chincultic ruins.

4 Tuxtla Gutiérrez

51 miles W of San Cristóbal; 173 miles S of Villahermosa; 151 miles NW of Ciudad Cuauhtémoc on the Guatemalan border

Tuxtla Gutiérrez (alt. 1,838 ft.; pop. 300,000) is the boomtown capital of the wild, mountainous state of Chiapas. Coffee is the basis of the region's economy, accompanied recently by oil discoveries. Tuxtla is a business town; there are some attractive parts, but nothing to keep you here more than a day or two. For tourists, it's mainly a way station en route to San Cristóbal, Oaxaca, or Villahermosa. The main attraction in town is the zoo; 10 minutes east of Tuxtla is the pleasant small town of Chiapa de Corzo, which is the point of departure for a tour of the Sumidero Canyon.

ESSENTIALS
GETTING THERE & DEPARTING

BY PLANE   **Aviación de Chiapas** (known as **Aviacsa, ☎ 961/2-6880** or 961/2-8081) can get you to several cities in Mexico, but all flights go through Mexico City—even flights to Cancún, Chetumal, Mérida, Guatemala City, Villahermosa, and Oaxaca. **Aerocaribe,** a subsidiary of Mexicana (**☎ 961/2-0020** or 961/2-5402) has five flights a day to/from Mexico City, with connections to all major cities. Another route connecting Tuxtla to other cities starts in Oaxaca and continues to Tuxtla, Villahermosa, Mérida, Cancún, and Havana; it returns in the same order; you can make connections in Oaxaca for Huatulco and other beach resorts; there is no nonstop service to Mérida or Cancún. There are nonstop flights to Palenque, San Cristóbal (only 1 hour away by car), Tapachula (on the Guatemalan border), and Veracruz.

Due to its peculiar weather, Tuxtla has two airports: **Terán** and **Llano San Juan.** The airlines use one for 6 months of the year (October to April) and the other for the other 6 months—although there is occasional juggling back and forth. Be sure to double-check which airport you're departing from, and allow enough time to get there. The Terán airport is 5 miles from town; the Llano San Juan airport is 18. There is taxi and minivan service from both airports.

BY CAR   From Oaxaca you enter Tuxtla by Highway 190. From Villahermosa, or Palenque and San Cristóbal, you'll enter at the opposite end of town on the same highway coming from the east. In both cases, you'll arrive at the large main square at the center of town, La Plaza Cívica. (See "City Layout," below.)

From Tuxtla to Villahermosa, take Highway 190 east past the town of Chiapa de Corzo; soon you'll see a sign for Highway 195 north to Villahermosa. To San Cristóbal and Palenque, take Highway 190 east. The road from Tuxtla to San Cristóbal and Palenque is beautiful but tortuous. It's in good repair to San Cristóbal, but there may be bad spots between San Cristóbal and Palenque. The trip from Tuxtla to Villahermosa takes 8 hours by car; the scenery is beautiful.

BY BUS   The first-class bus station (**☎ 961/2-2624**) is at the corner of streets 2 Norte and 2 Poniente (see "City Layout, below"). All bus lines serving this station and the deluxe section across the street (**Uno, Maya de Oro, Cristóbal Colón, Servicios Altos**) belong to the same parent company, **ADO**. At the main station they sell tickets to all buses. All buses are air-conditioned and have bathrooms. There are two levels of first class; the first-class *económico* has less legroom. Then there's deluxe, which features a few extras: slightly better seats, better movies, and free coffee and soda. There are buses every half hour to San Cristóbal, eight buses a day to Villahermosa, three or four buses a day to Oaxaca, and five to Palenque. There's usually no need to buy a ticket ahead of time, except during holidays.

ORIENTATION

ARRIVING   The Llano San Juan airport is off Highway 190 west of town, about 40 minutes away; the Terán airport is off of the same highway going east of town, about 15 minutes away. Minivans colectivos are much cheaper if you can find one; they leave as soon as they are full. The **ADO/Cristóbal Colón** bus terminal is downtown.

VISITOR INFORMATION   The **Tourist Office** (☎ 961/2-5509 or 961/2-4535) is in the Secretaría de Fomento Económico building (previously called the Plaza de las Instituciones) on avenida Central/bulevar Domínguez, near the Hotel Bonampak Tuxtla. It's on the first floor of the plaza and is open Monday through Friday from 8am to 9pm. Most questions can be answered at the information booth in front of the office. There are also information booths at the **international airport** (staffed when flights are due) and at the **zoo** (open Tuesday through Sunday from 9am to 3pm and 6 to 9pm).

CITY LAYOUT   Tuxtla is laid out on a grid. The city's main street, **avenida Central,** is the east-west axis and is the artery through town for Highway 190. In the west it becomes **bulevar Belisario Domínguez,** and in the east it becomes **bulevar Angel Albino Corzo. Calle Central** is the north-south axis. The rest of the streets have names that include one number and two directions. This tells you how to get to the street. For example, to find the street 5 Norte (north) Poniente (west) you would walk 5 blocks north of the center of town, and turn west (which is left). To find 3 Oriente Sur, you would walk 3 blocks east from the main square and turn south. When people indicate intersections, they can shorten the names, because it's redundant. The bus station is at the corner of 2 Norte and 2 Poniente.

GETTING AROUND   **Buses** to all parts of the city converge upon the Plaza Cívica along calle Central. **Taxi** fares are higher here than in other regions.

FAST FACTS: The local **American Express** representative is Viajes Marabasco, Plaza Bonampak, Loc. 4, Col. Moctezuma, near the tourist office (☎ 961/2-6998; fax 961/2-4053). Office hours are Monday through Friday 9am to 1:30pm and 3:30 to 6:30pm. The **telephone area code** is **961.**

TUXTLA'S MUSEUM & ZOO

Most travelers simply pass through Tuxtla on their way to San Cristóbal or Oaxaca. The excellent zoo and the Sumidero Canyon are the top sights, though you might also visit the Parque Madero and its anthropology museum.

Calzada de los Hombres Illustres. 11 Nte. Oriente at 5 Oriente Nte. Park and botanical garden free. Museum $2; free on Sunday. Museum Tues–Sun 9am–4pm; botanical garden daily 8:30am–5pm; children's area Tues–Sun 8am–8pm. The park is 15 blocks northwest of the main plaza; catch a colectivo along avenida Central or walk about 15 minutes east along 5 Oriente Nte.

Tuxtla's cultural highlights are clustered in this area, once referred to as the Parque Madero. The park also holds the **Regional Museum of Anthropology,** a botanical garden, a children's area, and the city theater. The museum features exhibits on the lifestyles of the people of Chiapas and some artifacts from the state's archaeological sites. In one short stop you can learn about Chiapas's past civilizations, its flora, and its present-day accomplishments. It also has a FONART (government crafts) shop and cafeteria.

Miguel Álvarez del Toro Zoo (ZOOMAT). Bulevar Samuel León Brinois, southeast of downtown. Free admission; donations solicited. Tues–Sun 9am–5:30pm. The zoo is about 5 miles southeast of downtown; buses for the zoo can be found along av. Central and at the Calzada.

Located in the forest called El Zapotal, ZOOMAT is one of the best zoos in Mexico. The collection of animals and birds indigenous to this area gives the visitor a tangible sense of what the wilds of Chiapas are like. Jaguars, howler monkeys, owls, and many more exotic animals are kept in roomy cages that replicate their home terrain, and the whole zoo is so deeply buried in vegetation that you can almost pretend you're in a natural habitat. Unlike at other zoos I've visited, the animals are almost always on view; many will come to the fence if you make a kissing noise.

SHOPPING

The government-operated **Casa de las Artesanías,** blv. Domínguez 2035 (☎ **961/ 2-2275),** is both a shop and gallery. The two stories of rooms feature a fine, extensive collection of crafts grouped by region and type from throughout the state of Chiapas. It's open Monday through Saturday from 10am to 8pm.

WHERE TO STAY

As Tuxtla booms, the center of the hotel industry has moved out of town, west to Highway 190. As you come in from the airport, you'll notice the new motel-style hotels, such as the Hotel Flamboyan, Palace Inn, Hotel Laganja, and La Hacienda. All of these are more expensive than those listed below, which are in the heart of town.

✪ **Hotel Bonampak Tuxtla.** Blv. Domínguez 180, 29030 Tuxtla Gutiérrez, Chi. ☎ **961/3-2050.** 70 units. A/C TV TEL. $50 double. AE, MC, V. Free secured parking.

This large, sprawling hotel has a swimming pool, tennis court, travel agency, boutique, coffee shop, and nice restaurant. The rooms facing the street are noisy, even with the air-conditioning on, but the interior rooms are blissfully quiet. The hotel's coffee shop, one of the best in town, is often packed with locals and tourists. The extensive menu includes an economical comida corrida. It's on the outskirts of downtown, where avenida 14 de Septiembre becomes bulevar Domínguez.

Hotel Esponda. 1 Poniente Nte. 142, 29030 Tuxtla Gutiérrez, Chi. ☎ **961/2-0080.** Fax 961/2-9771. 50 units. TV TEL. $20 double. AE, MC, V. Free parking.

In a city where inexpensive rooms are hard to come by, the Esponda is an excellent choice. Its rooms are in a nondescript 5-story building with an elevator. The brown, green, and yellow decor is a bit unsettling, but the rooms are perfectly satisfactory— each has one, two, or three double beds; showers (without doors or curtains); big closets; and powerful ceiling fans. The hotel is conveniently located 1 block from the Plaza Cívica, near the Cristóbal Colón bus station.

Gran Hotel Humberto. Av. Central 180, 29030 Tuxtla Gutiérrez, Chi. ☎ **961/2-2080.** Fax 961/2-9771. 112 units. A/C TV TEL. $37 double. AE, MC, V. Free parking.

This older 10-story, inner-city hotel is your best budget bet in booming Tuxtla. It's clean and comfortable enough, with well-kept furnishings dating from the 1950s. However, it isn't always an oasis of peace and quiet, especially on weekends when church bells compete with the ninth-floor nightclub. The location is ideal—it's in the center of town half a block from Plaza Cívica restaurants and the Mexicana airline office and 1½ blocks from the Cristóbal Colón bus station.

WHERE TO DINE

Tuxtla's main plaza, the **Plaza Cívica** (avenida Central at 1 Poniente), is actually two plazas separated by avenida Central. Rimming the edges are numerous restaurants, many of which serve customers outdoors under umbrella-shaded tables. The restaurants change names with frequency, so I won't recommend one over another. Just stroll the area and pick one that looks interesting, clean, and reasonably priced.

Las Pichanchas. Av. Central Ote. 837. ☎ **961/2-5351.** Tamales $1–$2 each; main courses $4–$7. AE, DC, MC, V. Daily noon–midnight (live marimba music 2:30–5:30pm and 8:30–11:30pm; patio dinner show Tues–Sun at 9pm). Closed New Year's Day and the 2 days following Easter. MEXICAN.

No trip to Tuxtla Gutiérrez is complete without a meal at this colorfully decorated restaurant devoted to the regional food and drink of Chiapas. Inverted pichanchas (pots full of holes used to make nixtamal masa dough) are hung on posts as lanterns. For a sampler plate, try the platón de carnes frías (cold meat platter that includes different local sausages, ham, cheese, and tortillas) or the platón de botana regional (a variety of hot tidbits). The cold meat platter and the especially tasty butifarra (sausage) both feed two or three people nicely. Since Chiapan tamales are tastier and larger than those you may have eaten elsewhere, you must try at least one. From the Hotel Humberto in the center of town, walk 6 to 8 blocks south; you'll find the restaurant on the left.

ROAD TRIPS FROM TUXTLA GUTIÉRREZ
CHIAPA DE CORZO & THE SUMIDERO CANYON

The small town of **Chiapa de Corzo** is a 30-minute, 8-mile ride by bus from the main square (buses leave every 15 minutes in the morning, every 30 minutes in the afternoon), or a 10- to 15-minute ride by colectivo—they leave every 10 minutes from their stand at the corner of 3 Oriente and 3 Sur. Those going on to San Cristóbal or over the mountains to the Yucatán will pass through this town on their way.

Chiapa de Corzo has a small **museum** on the main square dedicated to the city's lacquer industry; an interesting church; a colonial fountain; and a small **pyramid,** somewhat restored and visible from the road. In the museum, you can often see women learning the regional craft of lacquer painting, and sometimes mask makers give carving demonstrations and lessons.

From this town you can embark on a spectacular trip to the **canyon of El Sumidero.** Boat rides through the canyon leave from the docks in Chiapa de Corzo when there are enough people (six to eight). Cost per person is about $7. You can tour the canyon on your own by taking a bus or taxi to Chiapa de Corzo and negotiating a ride along the riverbed; the cost should be around $40 for five people for a 2-hour ride. But the best way to see the canyon is by boat.

Appendix

A Telephones & Mail

USING THE TELEPHONES

Generally within a city, you will be dialing a five- or six-digit number. **To call long distance (abbreviated "lada") within Mexico,** you'll need to dial the national long-distance code **01** prior to dialing a two- or three-digit area code. In total, Mexico's telephone numbers are eight digits in length. Mexico's area codes (*claves*) are usually listed in the front of telephone directories. Area codes are listed before all phone numbers in this book.

International long-distance calls to the United States or Canada are accessed by dialing **001,** then the area code and seven-digit number. For other international dialing codes, dial the operator, at **04.**

For additional details on making calls in Mexico and to Mexico, see chapter 3, "Planning a Trip to the Yucatán."

POSTAL GLOSSARY

Airmail Correo Aéreo
Customs Aduana
General Delivery Lista de Correos
Insurance (insured mail) Seguros
Mailbox Buzón
Money Order Giro Postale
Parcel Paquete
Post Office Oficina de Correos
Post Office Box (abbreviation) Apdo. Postal
Postal Service Correos
Registered Mail Registrado
Rubber Stamp Sello
Special Delivery, Express Entrega Inmediata
Stamp Estampilla or Timbre

B Basic Vocabulary

Most Mexicans are very patient with foreigners who try to speak their language; it helps a lot to know a few basic phrases.

I've included a list of certain simple phrases for expressing basic needs, followed by some common menu items.

ENGLISH–SPANISH PHRASES

English	Spanish	Pronunciation
Good day	**Buenos días**	*bway*-nohss-*dee*-ahss
How are you?	**¿Cómo está usted?**	*koh*-moh ess-*tah* oo-*sted*?
Very well	**Muy bien**	mwee byen
Thank you	**Gracias**	*grah*-see-ahss
You're welcome	**De nada**	day *nah*-dah
Goodbye	**Adiós**	ah-*dyohss*
Please	**Por favor**	pohr fah-*vohr*
Yes	**Sí**	see
No	**No**	noh
Excuse me	**Perdóneme**	pehr-*doh*-ney-may
Give me	**Déme**	*day*-may
Where is . . . ?	**¿Dónde está . . . ?**	*dohn*-day ess-*tah*?
the station	**la estación**	lah ess-tah-*seown*
a hotel	**un hotel**	oon oh-*tel*
a gas station	**una gasolinera**	oon-uh gah-so-lee-*nay*-rah
a restaurant	**un restaurante**	oon res-tow-*rahn*-tay
the toilet	**el baño**	el *bahn*-yoh
a good doctor	**un buen médico**	oon bwayn *may*-thee-co
the road to	**el camino a/hacia**	el cah-*mee*-noh ah/*ah*-see-ah
To the right	**A la derecha**	ah lah day-*reh*-chuh
To the left	**A la izquierda**	ah lah ees-ky-*ehr*-thah
Straight ahead	**Derecho**	day-*reh*-cho
I would like	**Quisiera**	key-see-*ehr*-ah
I want	**Quiero**	*kyehr*-oh
to eat	**comer**	ko-*mayr*
a room	**una habitación**	oon-nuh ha-bee tah-*seown*
Do you have?	**¿Tiene usted?**	tyah-nay oos-*ted*?
a book	**un libro**	oon *lee*-bro
a dictionary	**un diccionario**	oon deek-seown-*ar*-eo
How much is it?	**¿Cuánto cuesta?**	*kwahn*-to *kwess*-tah?
When?	**¿Cuándo?**	*kwahn*-doh?
What?	**¿Qué ?**	kay?
There is (Is there . . . ?)	**(¿)Hay (. . . ?)**	eye?
What is there?	**¿Qué hay?**	kay eye?
Yesterday	**Ayer**	ah-*yer*
Today	**Hoy**	oy
Tomorrow	**Mañana**	mahn-*yawn*-ah
Good	**Bueno**	*bway*-no
Bad	**Malo**	*mah*-lo
Better (best)	**(Lo) Mejor**	(loh) meh-*hor*
More	**Más**	mahs
Less	**Menos**	*may*-noss
No smoking	**Se prohíbe fumar**	say pro-*hee*-bay foo-*mahr*
Postcard	**Tarjeta postal**	tar-hay-ta pohs-*tahl*
Insect repellent	**Rapellante contra insectos**	rah-pey-*yahn*-te *cohn*-trah een-*sehk*-tos

MORE USEFUL PHRASES

English	Spanish	Pronunciation
Do you speak English?	¿Habla usted inglés?	ah-blah oo-*sted* een-*glays*?
Is there anyone here who speaks English?	¿Hay alguien aquí Qué hable inglés?	eye *ahl*-ghee-en ah-key *ah*-blay een-*glays*?
I speak a little Spanish.	Hablo un poco de español.	*ah*-blow oon *poh*-koh day ess-pah-*nyol*
I don't understand Spanish very well.	No (lo) entiendo muy bien el español.	noh (loh) ehn-tee-*ehn*-do myee bee-ayn el ess-pah-*nyol*
The meal is good.	Me gusta la comida.	may *goo*-sta lah koh-*mee*-dah
What time is it?	¿Qué hora es?	kay *oar*-ah ess?
May I see your menu?	¿Puedo ver el menú (la carta)?	*puay*-tho veyr el may-*noo* (lah *car*-tah)?
The check please.	La cuenta por favor.	lah *quayn*-tah pohr fa-*vorh*
What do I owe you?	¿Cuánto lo debo?	*Kwahn*-toh loh *day*-boh?
What did you say?	¿Mande? (colloquial expression for American "Eh?")	*Mahn*-day?
More formal:	¿Cómo?	*Koh*-moh?
I want (to see) a room	Quiero (ver) un cuarto (una habitación)...	Key-*yehr*-oh vehr oon *kwar*-toh
for two persons with (without) bath.	para dos personas con (sin) baño.	pahr-ah doss pehr-*sohn*-as kohn (seen) *bah*-nyoh
We are staying here only	Nos quedamos aquí solamente...	nohs kay-*dahm*-ohss ah-*key* sohl-ah-*mayn*-tay
one night.	una noche.	oon-ah *noh*-chay
one week.	una semana.	oon-ah say-*mahn*-ah
We are leaving tomorrow.	Partimos (Salimos) Mañana.	Pahr-*tee*-mohss (sah-*lee*-mohss) mahn-*yan*-ah)
Do you accept traveler's checks?	¿Acepta usted cheques de viajero?	Ah-*sayp*-tah oo-*sted* *chay*-kays day bee-ah-*hehr*-oh?
Is there a laundromat near here?	¿Hay una lavandería cerca de aquí?	Eye oon-ah lah-*vahn*-day-*ree*-ah *sehr*-ka day ah-*key*?
Please send these clothes to the laundry.	Hágame el favor de mandar esta ropa a la lavandería.	*Ah*-ga-may el fah-*vhor* day mahn-*dahr* *ays*-tah *rho*-pah a lah lah-*vahn*-day-*ree*-ah

NUMBERS

1	**uno** (ooh-noh)	17	**diecisiete** (de-*ess*-ee-*syeh*-tay)
2	**dos** (dohs)	18	**dieciocho** (dee-*ess*-ee-*oh*-choh)
3	**tres** (trayss)	19	**diecinueve** (dee-*ess*-ee-*nway*-bay)
4	**cuatro** (*kwah*-troh)		
5	**cinco** (*seen*-koh)	20	**veinte** (*bayn*-tay)
6	**seis** (sayss)	30	**treinta** (*trayn*-tah)
7	**siete** (*syeh*-tay)	40	**cuarenta** (kwah-*ren*-tah)
8	**ocho** (*oh*-choh)	50	**cincuenta** (seen-*kwen*-tah)
9	**nueve** (*nway*-bay)	60	**sesenta** (say-*sen*-tah)
10	**diez** (dee-ess)	70	**setenta** (say-*ten*-tah)
11	**once** (*ohn*-say)	80	**ochenta** (oh-*chen*-tah)
12	**doce** (*doh*-say)	90	**noventa** (noh-*ben*-tah)
13	**trece** (*tray*-say)	100	**cien** (see-en)
14	**catorce** (kah-*tor*-say)	200	**doscientos** (*dos*-se-en-tos)
15	**quince** (*keen*-say)	500	**quinientos** (*keen*-ee-ehn-tos)
16	**dieciseis** (de-*ess*-ee-sayss)	1000	**mil** (meal)

TRANSPORTATION TERMS

English	Spanish	Pronunciation
Airport	**Aeropuerto**	Ah-*ay*-row-por-tow
Flight	**Vuelo**	Boo-*ay*-low
Rental Car	**Arrendadora de Autos**	Ah-rain-da-*dow*-rah day autos
Bus	**Autobús**	ow-toh-*boos*
Bus or truck	**Camión**	ka-me-*ohn*
Lane	**Carril**	kah-*rreal*
Nonstop	**Directo**	dee-*reck*-toh
Baggage (claim area)	**Equipajes**	eh-key-*pah*-hays
Intercity	**Foraneo**	fohr-ah-*nay*-oh
Luggage storage area	**Guarda equipaje**	gwar-daheh-key-*pah*-hay
Arrival gates	**Llegadas**	yay-*gah*-dahs
Originates at this station	**Local**	loh-*kahl*
Originates elsewhere; stops if seats available	**De Paso**	day-*pah*-soh
First class	**Primera**	pree-*mehr*-oh
Second class	**Segunda**	say-*goon*-dah
Nonstop	**Sin Escala**	seen ess-*kah*-lah
Baggage claim area	**Recibo de Equipajes**	ray-*see*-boh day eh-key-*pah*-ys
Waiting room	**Sala de Espera**	*Saw*-lah day ess-*pehr*-ah
Toilets	**Sanitarios**	Sahn-ee-tahr-*ee*-oss
Ticket window	**Taquilla**	tah-*key*-lah

C Menu Glossary

Achiote   Small, red seed of the annatto tree.

Achiote preparada   A prepared paste found in Yucatán markets made of ground achiote, wheat and corn flour, cumin, cinnamon, salt, onion, garlic, and oregano. Mixed with juice of a sour orange or vinegar and put on broiled or charcoaled fish (tikin chick) and chicken.

Agua fresca   Fruit-flavored water, usually watermelon, canteloupe, chia seed with lemon, hibiscus flour, or ground melon seed mixture.

Antojito A Mexican snack, usually masa-based with a variety of toppings such as sausage, cheese, beans, onions; also refers to tostadas, sopes, and garnachas.

Atole A thick, lightly sweet, warm drink made with finely ground rice or corn and usually flavored with vanilla.

Birria Lamb or goat meat cooked in a tomato broth, spiced with garlic, chiles, cumin, ginger, oregano, cloves, cinnamon, and thyme and garnished with onions, cilantro, and fresh lime juice to taste; a specialty of Jalisco state.

Botana A light snack—an antojito.

Buñuelos Round, thin, deep-fried crispy fritters dipped in sugar.

Cabrito Grilled kid; a northern Mexican delicacy.

Carnitas Pork that's been deep-cooked (not fried) in lard, then steamed and served with corn tortillas for tacos.

Ceviche Fresh raw seafood marinated in fresh lime juice and garnished with chopped tomatoes, onions, chiles, and sometimes cilantro and served with crispy, fried whole-corn tortillas.

Chayote Vegetable pear or merleton, a type of spiny squash boiled and served as an accompaniment to meat dishes.

Chiles rellenos Poblano peppers usually stuffed with cheese, rolled in a batter, and baked; other stuffings include ground beef spiced with raisins.

Churro Tube-shaped, breadlike fritter, dipped in sugar and sometimes filled with cajeta or chocolate.

Cochinita pibil Pork wrapped in banana leaves, pit-baked, and served with a pibil sauce of achiote, sour orange, and spices; common in Yucatán.

Corunda A triangular tamal wrapped in a corn leaf; a Michoacan specialty.

Enchilada Tortilla dipped in a sauce and usually filled with chicken or white cheese and sometimes topped with tomato sauce and sour cream (enchiladas Suizas—Swiss enchiladas), or covered in a green sauce (enchiladas verdes), or topped with onions, sour cream, and guacamole (enchiladas Potosiños).

Epazote Leaf of the wormseed plant, used in black beans and with cheese in quesadillas.

Escabeche A lightly pickled sauce used in Yucatecan chicken stew.

Frijoles charros Beans flavored with beer; a northern Mexican specialty.

Frijoles refritos Pinto beans mashed and cooked with lard.

Garnachas A thickish small circle of fried masa with pinched sides, topped with pork or chicken, onions, and avocado or sometimes chopped potatoes, and tomatoes, typical as a botana in Veracruz and Yucatán.

Gorditas Thickish fried-corn tortillas, slit and stuffed with choice of cheese, beans, beef, chicken, with or without lettuce, tomato, and onion garnish.

Gusanos de maguey Maguey worms, considered a delicacy, and delicious when charbroiled to a crisp and served with corn tortillas for tacos.

Horchata Refreshing drink made of ground rice or melon seeds and ground almonds, and lightly sweetened.

Huevos Mexicanos Eggs with onions, hot peppers, and tomatoes.

Huevos Motulenos Eggs atop a tortilla, garnished with beans, peas, ham, sausage, and grated cheese; a Yucatecan specialty.

Huevos rancheros Fried egg on top of a fried corn tortilla covered in a tomato sauce.

Huitlacoche Sometimes spelled "cuitlacoche," mushroom-flavored black fungus that appears on corn in the rainy season; considered a delicacy.

Machaca Shredded dried beef scrambled with eggs or as salad topping; a specialty of Northern Mexico.

Manchamantel   Translated means "tablecloth stainer," a stew of chicken or pork with chiles, tomatoes, pineapple, bananas, and jicama. Sometimes listed as "mancha manteles."

Masa   Ground corn soaked in lime, used as a basis for tamales, corn tortillas, and soups.

Mixiote   Lamb baked in a chile sauce or chicken with carrots and potatoes, used as basis for tamales, corn tortillas, and soups.

Pan de Muerto   Sweet or plain bread made around the Days of the Dead (Nov. 1–2), in the form of mummies, dolls, or round with bone designs.

Pan dulce   Lightly sweetened bread in many configurations, usually served at breakfast or bought at any bakery.

Papadzules   Tortillas stuffed with hard-boiled eggs and seeds (cucumber or sunflower) in a tomato sauce.

Pavo relleno negro   Stuffed turkey Yucatán-style, filled with chopped pork and beef, cooked in a rich, dark sauce.

Pibil   Pit-baked pork or chicken in a sauce of tomato, onion, mild red pepper, cilantro, and vinegar.

Pipian   Sauce made with ground pumpkin seeds, nuts, and mild peppers.

Poc chuc   Slices of pork with onion marinated in a tangy sour orange sauce and charcoal broiled; a Yucatecan specialty.

Pollo Calpulalpan   Chicken cooked in pulque; a specialty of Tlaxcala.

Pozole   A soup made with hominy and pork or chicken, in a tomato-based broth Jalisco-style, or a white broth Nayarit-style, or green chile sauce Guerrero-style, and topped with a choice of chopped white onion, lettuce or cabbage, radishes, oregano, red pepper, and cilantro.

Pulque   Drink made of fermented sap of the maguey plant; best in the state of Hidalgo and around Mexico City.

Quesadilla   Flour tortillas stuffed with melted white cheese and lightly fried.

Queso relleno   "Stuffed cheese" is a mild, yellow cheese stuffed with minced meat and spices; a Yucatecan specialty.

Rompope   Delicious Mexican eggnog, invented in Puebla, made with eggs, vanilla, sugar, and rum.

Salsa verde   A cooked sauce using the green tomatillo and pureed with mildly hot peppers, onions, garlic, and cilantro; on tables countrywide.

Sopa de calabaza   Soup made of chopped squash or pumpkin blossoms.

Sopa de lima   A tangy soup made with chicken broth and accented with fresh lime; popular in Yucatán.

Sopa seca   Not a soup at all, but a seasoned rice which when translated means "dry soup."

Sopa Tarascan   A rib-sticking pinto-bean–based soup, flavored with onions, garlic, tomatoes, chiles, and chicken broth and garnished with sour cream, white cheese, avocado chunks, and fried tortilla strips; a specialty of Michoacán state.

Sopa Tlalpeña   A hearty soup made with chunks of chicken, chopped carrots, zucchini, corn, onions, garlic, and cilantro.

Sopa Tlaxcalteca   A hearty tomato-based soup filled with cooked nopal cactus, cheese, cream, and avocado with crispy tortilla strips floating on top.

Sopa tortilla   A traditional chicken broth–based soup, seasoned with chiles, tomatoes, onion, and garlic, bobbing with crisp fried strips of corn tortillas.

Sope   Pronounced *soh*-pay, a botana similar to a garnacha, except spread with refried beans and topped with crumbled cheese and onions.

Tacos al pasto   Thin slices of flavored pork roasted on a revolving cylinder dripping with onion slices and juice of fresh pineapple slices.

Tamal   Incorrectly called tamale (tamal singular, tamales plural); meat or sweet filling rolled with fresh masa, then wrapped in a corn husk or banana leaf and steamed; many varieties and sizes throughout the country.

Tepache   Drink made of fermented pineapple peelings and brown sugar.

Tikin xic   Also seen on menus as "tikin chick"; charbroiled fish brushed with achiote sauce.

Tinga   A stew made with pork tenderloin, sausage, onions, garlic, tomatoes, chiles, and potatoes; popular on menus in Puebla and Hidalgo states.

Torta   A sandwich, usually on bolillo bread, usually with sliced avocado, onions, and tomatoes, with a choice of meat and often cheese.

Torta Ahogado   A specialty of Lake Chapala is made with a scooped-out roll, filled with beans and beef strips and seasoned with a tomato or chile sauce.

Tostadas   Crispy fried corn tortillas topped with meat, onions, lettuce, tomatoes, cheese, avocados, and sometimes sour cream.

Venado   Venison (deer) served perhaps as pipian de venado, steamed in banana leaves and served with a sauce of ground squash seeds.

Xtabentun (pronounced shtah-ben-*toon*)   A Yucatán liquor made of fermented honey and flavored with anise. It comes *seco* (dry) or *crema* (sweet).

Zacahuil   Pork leg tamal, packed in thick masa, wrapped in banana leaves, and pit baked, sometimes pot-made with tomato and masa; specialty of mid- to upper Veracruz.

Index

See also separate Accommodations and Restaurant indexes, below.
Page numbers in italics refer to maps.

GENERAL INDEX

FROMMER'S® COMPLETE TRAVEL GUIDES
(Comprehensive guides with selections in all price ranges—from deluxe to budget)

Alaska
Amsterdam
Arizona
Atlanta
Australia
Austria
Bahamas
Barcelona, Madrid & Seville
Belgium, Holland &
    Luxembourg
Bermuda
Boston
Budapest & the Best of
    Hungary
California
Canada
Cancún, Cozumel & the
    Yucatán
Cape Cod, Nantucket &
    Martha's Vineyard
Caribbean
Caribbean Cruises &
    Ports of Call
Caribbean Ports of Call
Carolinas & Georgia
Chicago
China
Colorado
Costa Rica
Denver, Boulder &
    Colorado Springs
England
Europe
Florida

France
Germany
Greece
Hawaii
Hong Kong
Honolulu, Waikiki & Oahu
Ireland
Israel
Italy
Jamaica & Barbados
Japan
Las Vegas
London
Los Angeles
Maryland & Delaware
Maui
Mexico
Miami & the Keys
Montana & Wyoming
Montréal & Québec City
Munich & the Bavarian Alps
Nashville & Memphis
Nepal
New England
New Mexico
New Orleans
New York City
Nova Scotia, New
    Brunswick &
    Prince Edward Island
Oregon
Paris
Philadelphia & the Amish
    Country

Portugal
Prague & the Best of the
    Czech Republic
Provence & the Riviera
Puerto Rico
Rome
San Antonio & Austin
San Diego
San Francisco
Santa Fe, Taos &
    Albuquerque
Scandinavia
Scotland
Seattle & Portland
Singapore & Malaysia
South Pacific
Spain
Switzerland
Thailand
Tokyo
Toronto
Tuscany & Umbria
USA
Utah
Vancouver & Victoria
Vermont, New Hampshire &
    Maine
Vienna & the Danube Valley
Virgin Islands
Virginia
Walt Disney World &
    Orlando
Washington, D.C.
Washington State

FROMMER'S® DOLLAR-A-DAY GUIDES
(The ultimate guides to comfortable low-cost travel)

Australia from $50 a Day
California from $60 a Day
Caribbean from $60 a Day
England from $60 a Day
Europe from $50 a Day
Florida from $60 a Day
Greece from $50 a Day
Hawaii from $60 a Day
Ireland from $50 a Day

Israel from $45 a Day
Italy from $50 a Day
London from $70 a Day
New York from $75 a Day
New Zealand from $50 a Day
Paris from $70 a Day
San Francisco from $60 a Day
Washington, D.C., from
    $60 a Day

FROMMER'S® MEMORABLE WALKS

Chicago
London

New York
Paris

San Francisco

FROMMER'S® PORTABLE GUIDES

, Ixtapa/	Dublin	Puerto Vallarta, Manzanillo
:enejo	Las Vegas	& Guadalajara
	London	San Francisco
a Wine	Maine Coast	Sydney
ry	New Orleans	Tampa Bay & St. Petersburg
n & Savannah	New York City	Venice
	Paris	Washington, D.C.

FROMMER'S® NATIONAL PARK GUIDES

nyon	Yosemite & Sequoia/
Parks of the American West	Kings Canyon
ne & Grand Teton	Zion & Bryce Canyon

THE COMPLETE IDIOT'S TRAVEL GUIDES
(The ultimate user-friendly trip planners)

ations	Las Vegas	New York City
our Trip to Europe	Mexico's Beach Resorts	San Francisco
	New Orleans	Walt Disney World

SPECIAL-INTEREST TITLES

War Trust's Official Guide to	Outside Magazine's Adventure Guide
il War Discovery Trail	to the Pacific Northwest
s Caribbean Hideaways	Outside Magazine's Guide to Family Vacations
& Present	Places Rated Almanac
City with Kids	Retirement Places Rated
Times Weekends	Washington, D.C., with Kids
agazine's Adventure Guide	Wonderful Weekends from Boston
England	Wonderful Weekends from New York City
agazine's Adventure Guide	Wonderful Weekends from San Francisco
hern California	Wonderful Weekends from Los Angeles

THE UNOFFICIAL GUIDES®
(Get the unbiased truth from these candid, value-conscious guides)

	Florida with Kids	Miami & the Keys	Skiing in the West
Aissouri	The Great Smoky	Mini-Mickey	Walt Disney World
	& Blue Ridge	New Orleans	Walt Disney World
	Mountains	New York City	Companion
	Las Vegas	San Francisco	Washington, D.C.

FROMMER'S® IRREVERENT GUIDES
(Wickedly honest guides for sophisticated travelers)

London	New Orleans	San Francisco
Manhattan	Paris	Walt Disney World
		Washington, D.C.

FROMMER'S® DRIVING TOURS

Florida	Ireland	Scotland
France	Italy	Spain
Germany	New England	Western Europe

WHEREVER YOU TRAVEL, HELP IS NEVER FAR AWAY.

From planning your trip to

providing travel assistance along

the way, American Express®

Travel Service Offices are

always there to help.

American Express Travel Service
Offices are found in central locations
throughout Cancun, Cozumel and Yucata

Travel

http://www.americanexpress.com/travel